في ذكرى

مارك لينز

Gingko-St Andrews Series

Series Editor
Ali Ansari

Iran and Global Decolonisation

Politics and Resistance after Empire

Edited by
Firoozeh Kashani-Sabet and Robert Steele

GINGKO

First published in 2023 by
GINGKO
4 Molasses Row
London SW11 3UX

A CIP catalogue record for this book is available from the British Library.

Hardback: ISBN 978-1-914983-08-5
ebook: ISBN 978-1-914983-09-2

Typeset in Times by MacGuru Ltd
Printed in the United Kingdom by Clays Ltd, Elcograf S.p.A.

www.gingko.org.uk

Contents

Transliteration

The transliteration follows the system employed by the journal *Iranian Studies*, which adopts ayn (‘) and hamza (’). However, for simplification we have opted not to use the long a (ā) and common names such as Abbas and Ali have been spelled without the ayn.

Acknowledgements

This volume is the result of a workshop organised by the Department of History at the University of Pennsylvania and the Department of Near Eastern Languages and Cultures at the University of California, Los Angeles, on 20 and 21 May 2021. We recognise the gracious support of both departments to ensuring the success of the workshop. The conversations that arose from the workshop were enriched by the many scholars who took part as discussants and chairs, and those who provided detailed feedback on chapters. These include: Maryam Ahmadi, Roham Alvandi, Cheikh Anta Babou, Lee Cassanelli, Stephanie Cronin, Rasmus Christian Elling, Ann Farnsworth-Alvear, Kevan Harris, Shabnam Holliday, Afshin Matin-Asgari, Ciruce Movahedi-Lankarani, Zahra Moravvej, Golnar Nikpour, Marie Ostby, Siavush Randjbar-Daemi, Golbarg Rekabtalaei, Sara Saljoughi, Cyrus Schayegh, Lior Sternfeld, Sevil Suleymani, and Maaike Warnaar. We thank all of them for their valuable contributions.

We are grateful to Gingko for taking on this project and to Ali Ansari for including the volume in his St Andrews Series.

Introduction: Iran and Global Decolonisation

Firoozeh Kashani-Sabet and Robert Steele

In 1961, the French philosopher and anticolonial activist, Jean-Paul Sartre, penned an introduction to *The Wretched of the Earth*, the penetrating book by Caribbean psychiatrist, Frantz Fanon. A scathing indictment of colonialism, oppression, and violence, Sartre's essay seemed to condone violence in its support of armed anticolonial struggles. Upon its publication, in an essay titled *On Violence*, the philosopher Hannah Arendt criticised Sartre for this apparent endorsement of violence. As a prominent intellectual and quintessential representative of a European society coming to terms with its crimes as a colonial power, Sartre expressed complete solidarity with Fanon. He observed poignantly: 'Our victims know us by their scars and their chains, and it is this that makes their evidence irrefutable.'[1] Sartre made a mockery of European humanism, which pretentiously invoked culture and humanity while at the same time enabling inhumanity, cruelty, and oppression. Sartre went so far as writing that 'no gentleness can efface the marks of violence; only violence itself can destroy them'. Sartre seemingly validated the rebel's violence as 'emancipatory' – a necessary stage in the process of self-discovery and liberation.[2] More to the point, Fanon

---

1 Jean-Paul Sartre, 'Preface', *Wretched of the Earth*, translated by Constance Farrington, 1963, 13.
2 Sartre, 'Preface', 21.

determined that 'decolonization is always a violent phenomenon' – violent because it necessitated the 'replacement' of one oppositional group or '"species" of men by another' and because violence marred their initial encounter.[3]

In turn, Arendt read Sartre's preface, and Fanon's work, as signalling the rejection of nonviolent resistance movements by 'new militants' and the rise of New Left ideologies. Arendt dismissed what she perceived as the shrill shallowness of violent student groups. Her indictment, however, revealed deeply problematic views of 'Black Power' adherents, who had experienced centuries of systemic racism.[4] The debates about radical politics, colonial resistance, and violence infiltrated Persian intellectual circles, too, as Iran grappled with the legacies of imperialism and occupation. Iranian thinkers encountered Fanon through the writings of a young and idealistic writer – Ali Shariati – widely considered one of the key ideologues of the Islamic Revolution of 1979 and through the other Persian translators of his works.[5] While living in Paris (1959–1964), Shariati had read news of the Algerian Revolution and sympathised deeply with the Algerian people's struggle. He devoured Third Worldist literature, which profoundly influenced his worldview and later writings, and communicated with Fanon, whom he later referred to as 'my genius friend, one of the most beautiful heroic figures in these cowardly times'.[6]

---

3 Fanon, *Wretched of the Earth*, 35.
4 Hannah Arendt, *On Violence*, 1969, 18–19.
5 Seyed Javad Miri, 'Frantz Fanon in Ali Shariati's Reading: Is it Possible to Interpret Fanon in a Shariatian Form?', *Frantz Fanon and Emancipatory Social Theory*, 2019, 184–216. Also, Arash Davari, 'A Return to Which Self?: 'Ali Shari'ati and Frantz Fanon on the Political Ethics of Insurrectionary Violence', *Comparative Studies of South Asia, Africa and the Middle East* 34/1, May 2014, 86–105; Farzaneh Farahzad, 'Voice and Visibility: Fanon in the Persian Context', *Translating Frantz Fanon Across Continents and Languages*, ed. Kathryn Batchelor and Sue-Ann Harding, 2017. For a recent investigation of Shariati and Fanon, see Eskandar Sadeghi-Borujerdi, 'Who Translated Fanon's The Wretched of the Earth into Persian?', *Jadaliyya*, 13 August 2020. Available online: https://www.jadaliyya. com/Details/41564/ Who-Translated-Fanon%E2%80%99s-The-Wretched-of-the-Earth-into-Persian.
6 'Letter to Ali Shariati', *Frantz Fanon: Alienation and Freedom*, ed. Jean Khalifa and Robert J.C. Young, 2018, 668. For a discussion on Third Worldist thought in the philosophy of Shariati and Jalal Al-e Ahmad, see Farhad Khosrokhavar, 'Third

For its part, the Pahlavi state strove to adopt some of the language of decolonisation. However, the shah's alliance with the United States during an era of global anti-Americanism[7] – as well as his creation of a secret police (SAVAK) – tarnished Iran's gestures to the developing world. The shah showed affinity for regional leaders and rebels, whether in the Middle East or elsewhere, so long as they eschewed communist ideologies and armed struggles informed by radical socialist thought. The Soviet Union (and its previous incarnation, the Russian Empire) had played a chequered and pernicious role in Iran, but so had the West. While the shah ignored – and in some cases supported – the excesses of the United States in world politics, Iran's radical left whitewashed the authoritarian and sometimes violent, hierarchical impulses of many radical leftist and communist groups.

Iran's reclamation of decolonisation was therefore less straightforward. At the conclusion of the Second World War, Iran, like other countries occupied or overseen by foreign governments, experienced tumult. From Syria to Senegal, local communities hoped to break loose from the chains of imperial bondage that had tied them politically to global Western powers.[8] Iran was no different. Its experience of occupation during the Second World War, despite having declared its neutrality, highlighted yet again the country's inability to run its affairs independently. After the war, Iran pointedly addressed the question of power and control by voting to nationalise its oil industry. Though the oil consortium agreement of 1954 was an inadequate compromise, it helped to bring in much-needed revenue to the country. As Iran slowly acquired economic independence, it began to flex its political muscles and assert a more independent foreign policy.[9]

This volume gathers together different narratives compiled chronologically to show the evolution of Iran's experiences and perspectives of

---

Worldist Iranian Intellectuals: Shariati and Ale-Ahmad', *Mapping the Role of Intellectuals in Iranian Modern and Contemporary History*, ed. Ramin Jahanbegloo, 2020, 64–93.

7 Peter J. Katzenstein, and Robert O. Keohane eds, *Anti-Americanisms in World Politics*, 2011.

8 On the anticolonial struggle for self-determination, see Adom Getachew's vital contribution, *Worldmaking after Empire: The Rise and Fall of Self-Determination*, 2019.

9 See Rouhollah K. Ramazani, *Iran's Foreign Policy, 1941–1973: A Study of Foreign Policy in Modernizing Nations*, 1975.

decolonisation, as well as its political and intellectual engagement with the decolonised world. It contributes to an emerging trend in the historiography that considers Iran's transnational and global connections in the late twentieth century. The purpose of the book is thus to write Iran into the history of decolonisation. However, doing so must also acknowledge the existence of two simultaneous and parallel, but ultimately clashing, positions on decolonisation in Iran. On the one hand, the Pahlavi state and the shah used the language of decolonisation to advance Iran's diplomacy in global conflicts without forcing it to clash openly with Western imperial powers (for example, the United States and France). On the other hand, Iranian dissidents and regime critics used the language of decolonisation to oppose the shah's diplomacy (for example, toward the United States and Oman) and to mobilise against his regime, which they considered illegitimate after the Anglo-American sponsored coup of 1953 removed Prime Minister Mohammad Mosaddeq from power.

Cyrus Schayegh and Yoav Di-Capua have offered useful theoretical insights on decolonisation movements outside of Iran. As they note, decolonisation 'was not simply the negotiation and management of the transfer of state power ("changing the flag"), central to classic histories of empire', but 'a complex multiphase process'.[10] Moreover, it did not just concern those nations that had achieved independence, nor merely the countries of the Global South, but 'it was one of a handful of macrohistorical processes shaping the modern world as a whole'.[11] Decolonisation was a process that did not end with independence, as these former colonial territories retained a degree of economic and political dependence on the European powers who had ruled over them. In her work, Firoozeh Kashani-Sabet has taken these arguments further by contending that decolonisation constituted 'a humanitarian necessity'.[12]

Like the rest of the world, Iran was shaped by and responded to these global processes. In the introduction to his *The Age of Aryamehr*, Roham

---

10 Cyrus Schayegh and Yoav Di-Capua, 'Why Decolonization?' *International Journal of Middle East Studies* 52/1, 2020, 137.

11 Schayegh and Di-Capua, 'Why Decolonization?', 138.

12 Firoozeh Kashani-Sabet, 'The Anti-Aryan Moment: Decolonization, Diplomacy, and Race in Late Pahlavi Iran', *International Journal of Middle East Studies* 53/4, 2021, 691–702.

Alvandi discusses how the two global processes of the Cold War and decolonisation profoundly affected how Pahlavi Iran envisioned its place in the world. Although the shah was firmly on the side of the United States in the Cold War, Alvandi argues that 'the Pahlavi state sought to project an image of a resurgent Iran as an autonomous actor within the Western bloc'.[13] In the context of the changing world order that decolonisation presented, the shah attempted to 'serve as a bridge between East and West, North and South'.[14] Alvandi's innovative volume offers a fresh look at Iran's multi-directional diplomacy and makes a compelling case for Iran's influence and dominant role in global politics.[15]

Historically, much of the scholarship on Iran's foreign interactions during the late Pahlavi period has focused on the United States and the Soviet Union, while its relations with the rest of the world, in particular the Global South, received comparatively little attention. In recent years, the situation has changed, and there is an emerging body of scholarship that analyses Iran's global interactions during the Pahlavi period, introducing themes and sources that allow us better to understand Iran's relationships with both imperial and non-imperial powers.[16]

---

13 Roham Alvandi, 'Iran in the Age of Aryamehr', *The Age of Aryamehr: Late Pahlavi Iran and its Global Entanglements*, ed. Roham Alvandi, 2018, 17.
14 Alvandi, 'Iran in the Age of Aryamehr'.
15 Other works have trodden similar ground, such as Shahram Chubin and Sepehr Zabih, *The Foreign Relations of Iran: A Developing State in a Zone of Great Power Conflict*, 1974; Nikki R. Keddie and Rudi Matthee eds., *Iran and the Surrounding World: Interactions in Culture and Cultural Politics*, 2002; Shireen Hunter, *Iran's Foreign Policy In the Post-Soviet Era: Resisting the New International Order*, 2010; and Houchang Chehabi, Peyman Jafari and Maral Jefroudi eds., *Iran in the Middle East: Transnational Encounters and Social History*, 2015. Alvandi's work is novel for its focus on the late Pahlavi period.
16 Alvandi ed., *The Age of Aryamehr*, 2018; Firoozeh Kashani-Sabet, 'Colorblind or Blinded by Color? Race, Ethnicity, and Identity in Iran', *Sites of Pluralism: Community Politics in the Middle East*, ed. Firat Oruc, 2019, 153–180; Houchang Chehabi, 'South Africa and Iran in the Apartheid Era', *Journal of Southern African Studies* 42/4, 2016, 687–709; William Figueroa, 'China and the Iranian Revolution: New Perspectives on Sino-Iranian Relations, 1965–1979', *Asian Affairs*, 2022; Firoozeh Kashani-Sabet, *Heroes to Hostages: America and Iran, 1800–1988*, 2023; Robert Steele, 'The Keur Farah Pahlavi Project and Iranian-Senegalese Relations in the 1970s', *Iranian Studies* 54/1–2, 2021, 169–192; Robert Steele, 'Two Kings of Kings: Iran-Ethiopia Relations Under Mohammad Reza Pahlavi and Haile Selassie',

Building on this body of literature, this volume's authors address three broad themes in their contributions. First, they consider that although Iran was not formally colonised, it was subject to various forms of imperialism in the modern period. Second, authors engage with the complicated position of the Pahlavi state in the international system at the time. Iran found itself at the centre of the Cold War, but at the same time tried to negotiate its diplomacy with some subtlety and independence of thought. In other words, the late Pahlavi state forged a parallel Third World path, which diverged from the discourse of leftist intellectuals even as it shared certain aspects of their ideologies. In the 1950s, 1960s and 1970s, Iran significantly expanded its networks in the Global South and tried to find allies among several newly constituted countries. How, therefore, did Iran's unique position in the world affect and define its treatment of decolonisation? Third, authors try to draw distinctions between state-to-state relations and decolonising discourses and non-state actors who also forged intellectual connections with actors from the Global South. By exploring these questions, this volume contributes to literature on decolonisation, late Pahlavi social, cultural, and political history, and pre-revolutionary intellectual history, particularly works that address the politics of resistance, global solidarity, and race. In doing so, it also reconsiders the intellectual foundations of the 1979 Islamic Revolution.

Iran's Experiences with Imperialism and Colonisation

Iran had for some two hundred years suffered at the hands of imperial powers, which violated Iran's sovereignty and imposed on Iran economically, politically, and militarily. Iran's territorial vulnerability resurfaced when the Ottomans waged border wars against Safavids in Iraq.[17] The imperial competition over Persian territory continued in 1723, when, taking advantage of the turmoil in Iran following the invasion of the Ghilzai Afghans and their capture of the capital of the Safavid Empire,

---

The International History Review 43/6, 2021, 1375–1392; and Maaike Warnaar, *Onze vriend op de pauwentroon: Nederland en de laatste sjah van Iran*, 2023.
17 Firoozeh Kashani-Sabet, 'Fragile Frontiers: The Diminishing Domains of Qajar Iran', *International Journal of Middle East Studies* 29/2, May 1997, 207.

Isfahan, and in an attempt to check Ottoman expansion in the Caucasus, the Russian Empire under Tsar Peter the Great occupied the northern region of Gilan on the Caspian coast.[18] This land was returned in 1732 with the Treaty of Rasht, but by the end of the century, the Russian Empire once again threatened Iran's borders. The eighteenth century had been devastating for Iran. The early decades were marked by Safavid decline and territorial losses, and the eighty years following the fall of Isfahan in 1722 were marred by endless war, internal conflict, displacement, and economic decay. At a time when the populations of the developing European nations grew rapidly, the population of Iran saw significant decline. According to some estimates, the population of Iran fell from nine million at the beginning of the century to six million at its end.[19] By comparison, the population of Britain increased from around five million in 1700 to nearly nine million by 1800.

The early decades of Qajar rule at the beginning of the nineteenth century brought an end to the civil war that had blighted the previous one, but the weakness of the Iranian state left it vulnerable to the ambitions of its imperial neighbours; Russia, which threatened the Caucasus, and Britain, which came to see Iran as a barrier, protecting the jewel in the crown of its empire, India, from Russian expansion. The Qajars fought two devastating wars against the Russian Empire in 1804–1813 and 1826–1828, which led to the signing of the Treaty of Golestan (1813) and the Treaty of Turkmanchay (1828). As a result of these treaties, the Qajar Empire relinquished much of its territories in the Caucasus, lost a naval presence in the Caspian, accepted unfavourable tariffs on trade, and granted Russian merchants unprecedented privileges in Persia. The signing of the Treaty of Turkmanchay provoked riots in Tehran, during which a mob, stirred up by radical mullahs, stormed the Russian embassy and murdered nearly all the Russians there, including the Russian minister plenipotentiary, Alexander Griboyedov. Later, under the terms of the Treaty of Paris,

---

18 N.A. Satavov, 'The Circum-Caspian Areas within the Eurasian International Relationships at the Time of Peter the Great and Nadir-Shah Afshar', *Iran and the Caucasus* 5, 2001, 94–95; Michael Axworthy, *Sword of Persia: Nader Shah from Tribal Warrior to Conquering Tyrant*, 2006, 63–64.
19 Michael Axworthy, 'Introduction', *Crisis, Collapse, Militarism and Civil War: The History and Historiography of 18th Century Iran*, ed. Michael Axworthy, 2018, 2.

signed in 1857 after the British invasion of Iran in response to Naser al-Din Shah's capture of Herat in 1856, Persia relinquished its claims to Herat and granted further diplomatic and commercial privileges to the British.[20] As a response to its weakening position vis-à-vis the great powers, Iran signed agreements with third nations, such as the United States in 1856, to try to 'minimise the negative impact of Russian and British domination by bringing outside powers into the balance, so that Iran could manoeuvre among them'.[21] However, in reality, the granting of capitulatory rights to foreign nations further eroded Iran's independence.[22]

The diminishing of Iran's sovereignty was achieved by the British and Russian Empires not merely by occupying territories, many of which had been considered part of the Persianate world for centuries, in Central Asia, the Caucasus, the Persian Gulf and in Sistan and Baluchistan, but also by exerting control over Iran's economy, its industries, its military, and its politics. Not content with the advantages gained through the Treaty of Paris, the British sought more concessions over the following decades, which further reflected the extraordinary power imbalance that had developed between Iran and Britain. Iranians' awareness of and disgust at this exploitation were evident in the reaction to the concession granted to Paul Julius Reuter in 1872, which would provide him exclusive control of the country's roads, telegraph, factories and mills, public works, and natural resources. George Nathaniel Curzon later wrote that the deal represented 'the most complete and extraordinary surrender of the entire industrial resources of a kingdom into foreign hands that has ever been dreamed of, much less accomplished in history'.[23]

The reaction to this concession, not only in Iran, but in Europe's capital cities, where governments were aware that the deal would diminish any competition in Persia and essentially turn the country into a British tributary state, led to its annulment. Shortly thereafter, the British Major G.F. Talbot

20 Kashani-Sabet, 'Fragile Frontiers', 209–213 and 217–221.
21 Michael Zirinsky, 'Riza Shah's Abrogation of Capitulations, 1927–1928', *The Making of Modern Iran*, ed. Stephanie Cronin, 2003, 82.
22 For further discussion see Ali Gheissari, 'Unequal Treaties and the Question of Sovereignty in Qajar and Early Pahlavi Iran', *Durham Middle East Papers* 106, 2023.
23 Curzon, *Persia and the Persian Question*, vol. 1, 1892, 480.

purchased a fifty-year monopoly of Iran's tobacco industry for a nominal sum paid to the royal treasury. As a result, tobacco farmers were forced to sell tobacco at a fixed price, merchants at the bazaar were excluded from another industry at the expense of foreigners, and resentment among the Islamic authorities grew due to the further presence of foreigners in Iran. Protests erupted across the country, led by a leading mujtahid, Hajj Mirza Hasan Shirazi, who issued a fatwa calling for a complete national boycott of tobacco. Another leader of the movement was Jamal al-Din Afghani, a fierce anti-imperialist and pan-Islamist, who believed that Islam needed to reform in order to reflect changes in the modern world.[24] From London, the diplomat and patriotic intellectual Mirza Malkam Khan urged his allies to oppose the concession. That these figures of such disparate political hues were brought together to oppose this concession demonstrates the strong anti-imperial strain running through Iranian society at this time, impelled by Iran's recent encounters with British and Russian imperialism.

Many more of these lopsided treaties that subjected Iran to economic and political inequalities were implemented without popular revolt, including the concession granted to the British businessman William Knox D'Arcy in 1901, which gave him full rights to seek, extract, and ultimately sell Iranian oil. The surrendering of precious resources to foreign powers, who, not content with seizing Iranian territory, were now exploiting Iran's land and resources at will, had a profound impact on Iranians' idea of imperialism. One cannot understand the oil nationalisation movement of the early 1950s without understanding the trauma that this audacious plunder had on the Iranian national psyche.[25]

At the same time as the British and Russians eroded Iran's sovereignty, Iranians were ruled by a series of despotic kings, who wielded complete control over politics, and whose extravagant lifestyles stood in sharp contrast to the poverty experienced by the masses. During the late nineteenth century, protests against despotism, imperialism, and ultimately political disenfranchisement increased in frequency and intensity, leading

---

24 For a biography of Afghani, see Nikki Keddie, *Sayyid Jamal ad-Dīn 'al-Afghanī': A Political Biography*, 1972.
25 Firoozeh Kashani-Sabet, *Frontier Fictions: Shaping the Iranian Nation, 1804–1946*, 1999, 79.

ultimately to the Constitutional Revolution of 1906–1911. The Constitutional Revolution, with its embrace of humanism and humanitarianism (*adamiyat va insaniyat*), placed checks for the first time on the sovereign and attempted to define the parameters of his powers.[26]

Imperial aggression ultimately crushed the constitutional dream. In 1907, the Anglo-Russian Convention was agreed, which divided Iran into spheres of influence; Russia held the northern regions bordering its empire, the British gained the south-east regions of Sistan and Baluchistan bordering India, and a neutral zone was established in between. The British, having supported the constitutionalists by granting them *bast* (sanctuary) at the British legation, were now seen as having betrayed them by leaving them at the mercy of Mohammad Ali Shah and the Russian-sponsored Cossacks. In signing the Anglo-Russian Convention of 1907, both the British and Russians had pledged to 'respect the integrity and independence of Persia'. However, just four years later, in 1911, Russia launched a full invasion of Iran, occupied Tabriz and Qazvin, and bombarded the Imam Reza Shrine in Mashhad, where many were taking sanctuary.[27] To protect their interests, the British occupied the trade routes between Bushehr, Shiraz, and Kerman. As well as controlling Iran through military force, the British and Russians also blocked infrastructural development in Iran, such as railways, for fear that it would benefit the other side.[28] In this way, the colonial powers conspired to ensure that Iran was kept in a perpetual state of weakness.

During the First World War, in spite of Iran's declared neutrality, its territorial integrity was again desecrated, as it was occupied by not only Russian and British forces, but Turkish and German, too. The First World War was devastating for Iran. It had suffered a severe famine in 1917 and

---

26 Firoozeh Kashani-Sabet, 'Hallmarks of Humanism: Hygiene and Love of Homeland in Qajar Iran', *The American Historical Review* 105/4, 2000, 1171–1203.
27 Rudi Matthee, 'Infidel Aggression: The Russian Assault on the Holy Shrine of Imam Reza, Mashhad, 1912', *Russians in Iran: Diplomacy and Power in the Qajar Era and Beyond*, ed. Rudi Matthee and Elena Andreeva, 2018, 136–170.
28 D.W. Spring, 'The Trans-Persian Railway Project and Anglo-Russian Relations, 1909–14', *The Slavonic and East European Review* 54/1, 1976, 70–71; Mikiya Koyagi, *Iran in Motion: Mobility, Space, and the Trans-Iranian Railway*, 2021, 28–29.

1918 as a result of the interruption of trade and agricultural production. This was followed by the cholera and typhus epidemics, and the global influenza pandemic in 1918–1919. According to some estimates, between 1917 and 1921, as many as two million Iranians died, including one quarter of the rural population. Nonetheless, the abrogation of the Anglo-Russian Treaty of 1907 and the new Bolshevik regime's pledge to withdraw its troops from Iranian territory reawakened Iran's irredentist ambitions, and instilled in its nationalist politicians a renewed confidence.[29] Indeed, the Iranian delegation that unsuccessfully sought to gain access to the Paris Peace Conference, enjoyed, in the words of Ali Ansari, 'a self confidence that belied the political realities of the day', as it aimed to obtain not only reparations for war damages, but also the restoration of much its former territory.[30]

As it happened, this optimism was misplaced. The British blocked the Iranian delegation's admission to the conference and Iran ended up with the so-called Anglo-Persian Agreement, signed by Iran's prime minister Vosuq al-Dowleh, foreign minister Firuz Mirza, and finance minister Akbar Mirza Sarem al-Dowleh. Under the terms of this agreement, Britain pledged to 'respect the independence and integrity of Persia', but it would have provided the British with extraordinary and unprecedented control over vast swathes of Iran's resources, infrastructure, military, and finances. Had the agreement been ratified by the Majles, Iran 'would have been little better than a mandate', observed the historian Laurence Elwell-Sutton.[31] If the war brought death and destruction, the Anglo-Persian Agreement intensified the hatred of British imperialism and initiated a political paralysis that would last until the 1921 coup and the emergence of Reza Khan.[32]

There is a long-established popular narrative which argues that Reza

---

29 Firoozeh Kashani-Sabet, *Frontier Fictions*, 150.
30 Ali Ansari, *Modern Iran since 1797: Reform and Revolution*, 2019, 114; and Kashani-Sabet, *Frontier Fictions*, 150–152. On Iran's delegation in Paris, see Oliver Bast, 'Putting the Record Straight: Vosuq al-Dowleh's Foreign Policy in 1918/19', *Men of Order: Authoritarian Modernization under Atatürk and Reza Shah*, ed. Touraj Atabaki and Erik J. Zürcher, 2004, 266–270.
31 Laurence Elwell-Sutton, *Modern Iran*, 1941, 67.
32 Ervand Abrahamian, *Iran Between Two Revolutions*, 1982, 117. On politics in Iran from 1919 to 1921, see Cyrus Ghani, *Iran and the Rise of Reza Shah: From Qajar Collapse to Pahlavi Power*, 2000.

Pahlavi was little more than a British stooge,[33] but his reign was predicated on a determination 'in the shortest possible time to eliminate foreign influence in Persia and to make her once more a country capable of standing on her own feet and respected by the world'.[34] One of the events that most clearly demonstrates this desire was the abrogation of capitulatory rights, announced in May 1927.[35] On 9 May 1928, the day the capitulatory rights officially ended, the newspaper *Ettela'at* called for a national celebration (*jashn-e melli*). The article was headlined 'Abolition of the capitulations of the judicial independence of Iran', and read: 'On this day, the most outstanding historical step has been taken for Iran's independence.'[36] The repeated use of the word independence here is striking. Iran had not been colonised, but it had surrendered many of its rights and resources to foreigners, so was not independent either. Thus, the ending of capitulations in 1928 was seen as an important step towards regaining national sovereignty and wresting control from foreign powers. Nearly fifty years later, the event was still recognised as monumental in Iran's modern history. On 24 April 1976, during the year-long celebrations marking the fiftieth anniversary of the Pahlavi dynasty, Shah Mohammad Reza Pahlavi and Empress Farah attended a ceremony at the Ministry of Foreign Affairs to celebrate the anniversary of the end of capitulations.[37] The event was also marked by the release of a book published by the Ministry of Foreign Affairs, titled *The Capitulation System and Its Abolishment in Iran.*[38]

Despite Reza Shah's efforts to strengthen Iran's military so that it would be able to stand up to a foreign attack, in 1941 Iran's sovereignty was again flagrantly disregarded by imperial powers. Reza Shah had declared neutrality in the Second World War, yet, in August 1941, to protect the oil fields in the Caucasus from a Nazi assault and to ensure that supply routes to Russia remained open, Russia and Britain invaded. Earlier, the Allies had demanded that Reza Shah expel from Iranian territory all Germans working and residing there. Reza Shah's refusal to kowtow to the imperial

---

33 A narrative outlined and challenged by Sadeq Zibakalam in his *Reza Shah*, 2019.
34 Laurence Elwell-Sutton, *Persian Oil*, 1954, 60.
35 See Zirinsky, 'Riza Shah's Abrogation of Capitulations, 1927–1928'.
36 *Ettela'at*, 19 Ordibehesht 1307/9 May 1928, 1–2.
37 *Gahnameh-ye Panjah Saleh-ye Shahanshahi-ye Pahlavi*, vol. 5, 1985, 2411.
38 *Nezam-e Kapitulasiyun va Elgha-ye an dar Iran*, 1355.

powers was seen as evidence of his Nazi sympathies and this provided a convenient excuse to invade. On 25 August, 40,000 Soviet troops crossed into Iranian territory from the north, with 1,000 tanks. The British invaded from Basra with 20,000 ground troops, along with RAF squadrons and warships, first securing the oil fields and then pushing northwards.[39] Overwhelmed by the size and power of the invading force, the Iranian army disintegrated, and three weeks later, with the Allied forces close to reaching the capital, Reza Shah abdicated, fled to Isfahan, and from there to a life in exile. He died in Johannesburg in 1944, far away from his beloved Iran, a broken man.[40]

In recent years, efforts have been made to correct the Eurocentric nature of Second World War historiography and to explore the impact the war had on countries outside of Europe, including Iran.[41] The impact the war had on Iran was great, and the mark it left on its population profound and lasting. Reza Shah had been unpopular, but the audacity of Britain and Russia in invading and occupying a country that had declared neutrality in the war united Iranians in a sense of 'disbelief and revulsion'.[42] To add to this humiliation, the rial was set at an unreasonable rate against the British pound, with the result that Iran would have to pay for the pleasure of the British occupation. The Pahlavi-era diplomat Fereydoun Hoveyda recalled that bars frequented by foreign troops had signs at the entrance that read 'Iranians and dogs forbidden'.[43] The foreign occupation also had a huge impact on the worldview of Mohammad Reza Pahlavi, who had ascended the throne during this turbulent period. Speaking to the emperor of Ethiopia, Haile Selassie, on his state visit to Iran in 1964, the shah spoke

---

39 Ashley Jackson, *Persian Gulf Command: A History of the Second World War in Iran and Iraq*, 2018, 151.
40 On Reza Shah's final years in exile, see Shaul Bakhash's recent work, *The Fall of Reza Shah: The Abdication, Exile, and Death of Modern Iran's Founder*, 2021.
41 See, for example, Jackson, *Persian Gulf Command*; Adrian O'Sullivan, *Nazi Secret Warfare in Occupied Persia (Iran): The Failure of the German Intelligence Services, 1939–45*, 2014; Adrian O'Sullivan, *Espionage and Counterintelligence in Occupied Persia (Iran): The Success of the Allied Secret Services, 1941–45*, 2015; Sajjad Ra'i Gallujeh et al., *Asnadi az Eshghal-e Iran dar Jang-e Jahani-ye Dovvom*, 1389.
42 Fariborz Mokhtari, *In the Lion's Shadow: The Iranian Schindler and His Homeland in the Second World War*, 2012.
43 Fereydoun Hoveyda, *The Fall of the Shah*, 1980, 70.

of their shared experiences of imperial aggression, for the emperor had been forced into exile in 1935 following the invasion of Ethiopia by Italian forces. The shah recalled that as a student in Switzerland he read about the Italian invasion of Ethiopia:

> Shortly afterwards, the country of me and my father suffered a similar fate [and] I once again remembered the events that had befallen you. We also fought to preserve the freedom of our nation because our country was occupied by foreigners.[44]

In a later interview, the shah again spoke about the humiliation of foreign occupation, for when in 1943, Stalin, Roosevelt, and Churchill held a congress in Tehran, he was not given advanced notice of the meeting and was largely ignored by his guests.[45] Of Churchill, the shah was particularly scathing: 'He didn't even bother to come and call on me at my residence, although I was King of the host country.'[46]

In the first chapter of this volume, addressing the skewed historiography, which often only considers Iran important insofar as events there contributed to the strategic aims of the Allies, Firoozeh Kashani-Sabet explores the Iranian experience of the war. Iran was not formally colonised by the invading forces, but for the duration of the five-year occupation, it might well have been. Using a wide range of previously untapped Persian printed and archival documents, Kashani-Sabet demonstrates that the loss of life the occupation brought, the mismanagement of the economy, and the appropriation of Iran's resources by the occupying forces amounted to the diminishment of Iran's sovereignty and planted the seeds of resentment and revolt. Another way the authority of the invaders was exerted was through the administration of justice. In her contribution to the volume, Pardis Minuchehr builds on this social analysis, to examine the little-studied subject of the Iranian prisoners of the Allied occupation. By using a range of archival material from Iran and the United Kingdom, Minuchehr weaves together historical portraits of the Iranian internees of war. She

---

44 *Ettela'at*, 26 Shahrivar 1343/17 September 1964, 17.
45 Abbas Milani, *The Shah*, 2011, 101.
46 R.K. Karanjia, *The Mind of a Monarch*, 1977, 69.

argues that in many instances the arbitrary arrest and mistreatment of the internees created a deep trauma for key members of Iran's political elite who suffered quietly from the occupation. These experiences would shape their mindset and actions in the decades after the war.

The removal of Reza Shah in 1941 marked the re-emergence of the type of political expression that had been suppressed under his rule. Scores of political parties and newspapers were set up, and politicians who had been banished by the Reza Pahlavi autocracy once again returned to the political stage. Among them was Mohammad Mosaddeq, who set up the National Front (Jebhe-ye Melli) in 1949 in order to protect the constitution, ensure that elections were free and fair, to keep a check on the creeping authoritarianism of Mohammad Reza Pahlavi, and eventually, to champion the cause of oil nationalisation. In the third chapter of the volume, Mattin Biglari offers fresh insights on the ways in which the oil struggle galvanized Iranian labourers and their global community of supporters. The fight for improved work conditions and upward mobility gained momentum not only among oilmen, but among Iranian women as well, and the decolonisation of the oil industry became part of the global struggle for social justice and economic equity. As Biglari shows, Iran's oil nationalisation movement received support from oilmen in Mexico and from labourers in other industries. In this way, Iran's fight for economic freedom became a rallying cry for similar injustices in the Middle East and elsewhere.

Decolonisation

In the decades after the Second World War, dozens of countries in Africa and Asia achieved independence from colonial rule, mirroring similar processes that had taken place earlier in the Americas. This period of rapid decolonisation fundamentally changed the dynamics of global politics. Between 1946 and 1970, membership of the United Nations increased from 35 to 127 nations, and the organisation became a forum in which these newly independent states could argue for the continuation of decolonisation and the recognition of national rights. The Iranian government watched these developments closely. As each new country declared independence, the Iranian government was quick to send messages of recognition and congratulations, though in doing so was careful not to damage relations with its European allies. For example, Iran decided to postpone the recognition of the independent republic of Mauritania pending the resolution of the dispute between France and Morocco over the issue.[47] Thomas Bédrède's chapter in this volume examines Iran's involvement in another decolonisation movement in North Africa, the Algerian War of Independence. As Bédrède demonstrates, Iran navigated this delicate situation carefully. Iran could not openly support France in the conflict, as this stance would isolate it in much of the Middle East. Nonetheless, many Iranian intellectuals, as well as members of the Pahlavi elite, gravitated toward French education. The Pahlavi state tried to respect France's position by negotiating in skilful diplomacy as it recognised that many Persian intellectuals and students openly supported the Algerian revolutionaries.

As the shah consolidated his rule in the years following the removal of Mosaddeq in 1953, and as a result of the changing world order brought about by decolonisation, he was able to think more clearly about the role Iran could play on the global stage. Iran sent goodwill delegations to Libya, Tunisia, and Morocco in 1957, with another travelling to Ethiopia, Kenya, Uganda, Tanganyika (Tanzania), Ghana, Nigeria, and Ivory Coast in 1964. As a result of Iran's efforts, it developed relationships across the Global South, from Brazil and Argentina,[48] to Indonesia, Malaysia, Ethiopia, and South Africa. In his contribution to this volume, Fernando Camacho Padilla explores the expansion of Iran's global ties during the late 1950s and early 1960s, through its relationship with the Dominican Republic. At a time when Iran's interactions with countries in the Caribbean were almost non-existent, Iran developed an intriguing and unlikely relationship with the regime of Rafael Trujillo. As Camacho Padilla demonstrates, the relationship flourished due to the familial links between the Dominican Republic's ambassador in Tehran Leland Rosemberg and the shah, which gave the ambassador extensive access to the Pahlavi court. As a result, trade relations between the two countries expanded, and Rosemberg

---

47 'Maroc-Iran-Sudan: Diplomatie et Problème Mauritanien', n.d., Centre des Archives Diplomatiques de Nantes, 184PO/1/417.

48 Fernando Camacho Padilla, 'Las relaciones entre Latinoamérica e Irán durante la última década de la dinastía Pahleví', *Anuario de Historia de América Latina* 56, 2019, 66–96.

provided the shah with an ally that could help him to monitor Cuban activity in the Middle East.

Decolonisation presented both challenges and opportunities for the Pahlavi state. Iran was represented at the Bandung Conference in 1955, for example, but as Bédrède demonstrates in his chapter, was something of a reluctant participant.[49] In the context of Afro-Asian solidarity, Iran was again an interloper. The shah, therefore, joined and even led those movements that best suited his political agenda. For example, he and King Hassan II of Morocco were partners in calling for the creation of an Islamic solidarity movement, which would serve as an alternative bloc to counter the radicalism of Nasser.[50] This call for Islamic unity was expressed clearly by the shah during his visit to Morocco in 1966, but the first conference was not held until 1969, in response to the arson attack on the Al-Aqsa Mosque in Jerusalem, which had 'sent a wave of indignation through the Muslim world'.[51]

The shah held a prominent position during the first conference, held in Rabat, and was the first to address the delegates after King Hassan's opening remarks. The shah said:

> We are gathered here to get to know each other more and better, to
> love one another more, to coordinate our actions, and to discuss all the
> issues that contribute to the advancement of the great and lofty goals

---

49 On the historical background to Bandung, see Lorenz M. Lüthi, *Cold Wars: Asia, The Middle East, Europe*, 2020, 266–278. For a study of Bandung and its legacy, see Christopher Lee's edited volume, *Making a World After Empire: The Bandung Moment and Its Political Afterlives*, 2019.

50 Ardeshir Zahedi, *Khaterat-e Ardeshir Zahedi*, vol. 3, 2020, 215. The shah and Hassan were not the only ones calling for Islamic solidarity. For example, from 6 to 12 March 1965, Indonesia convened in Bandung an Afro-Asian Islamic Conference, which not only denounced Anglo-American imperialism, but also resolved to improve the status of Muslim women. British Embassy, Djakarta, 17 March 1965, 'Declaration of the Africa – Asia Islamic Conference', and 'The Position and the Role of Muslim Women', FO 371/18038.

51 Gilles Kepel, *Jihad: The Political Trail of Islam*, translated by Anthony F. Roberts, 2002, 74; Shameem Akhtar, 'The Rabat Summit Conference', *Pakistan Horizon* 22/4, 1969, 336. For a Persian account, see 'Konferans-e 'Ali-ye Saran-e Keshvarha-ye Islami dar Rabat Mazhar-e Ettehad va Yek Jahati 'Alam-e Islam', *Nashriyeh-e Hilal* 95, Azar 1347, 6–11.

of Islam. I think that all the delegates will share in the excitement that the convening of this great conference has created, because the convening of this conference is, in fact, the greatest event that has taken place in the history of Muslim countries. This should be pursued with passion and perseverance, and this community should not be our first and last community. Such conferences should continue in order to increase understanding and increase feelings of brotherhood among Muslims and exchange views.[52]

Yet in his speech, the shah did not directly reference the attack on Al-Aqsa, nor did he criticise Israel. To him, the conference was a challenge to Nasserism and a call to his allies to unite against revolutionary movements. In short, he employed the language of Bandung, but he did not embrace its spirit.[53]

Saudi Arabia and Pakistan also played key roles in trying to mobilise the Islamic *ummah* through such congresses. At the Rabat Summit, King Faysal had broached the idea of an 'Islamic pact' to the shah,[54] and in 1970 Saudi Arabia convened the Conference of Islamic Foreign Ministers and tried to lead efforts to unite an often-divided global Islamic community. Saudi Arabia proposed the creation of a Secretariat to assert its leadership on Islamic issues.[55] Ultimately, when the Second Congress was held in Lahore in 1974, the shah refused to attend, due to the presence of the Libyan president Muammar Qadaffi, who had sought to take a leading role in the Arab world following the death of Egypt's Nasser in 1970.[56] Such events should, therefore, be seen in the context of not only solidarity, but also competition and rivalry in the politics of the Global South.

---

52 *Ettela'at*, 1 Mehr 1348/23 September 1969, 4.
53 Following Ervand Abrahamian, Arash Davari argues that the shah disingenuously adopted Third Worldist positions to achieve his political goals. See Arash Davari, 'On Inexactitude in Decolonization', *Comparative Studies of South Asia, Africa and the Middle East* 40/3, 2020, 631.
54 Akhtar, 'The Rabat Summit Conference', 337.
55 December 1970, British Embassy, Jeddah, Foreign and Commonwealth Office (FCO) 8/1734, British National Archives, Kew.
56 On Libya and Iran at this time see Hasan 'Ali Yari 'Ravabet-e Siyasi-ye Iran va Libi dar Dowreh-ye Pahlavi-ye Dovvom (Ruyaravi-e Shah va Qazafi)', *Nameh-ye Tarikh Pazhuhan* 24, 1389, 130–151.

The next two chapters examine the intricate and entwined nature of events in the Global South in the era of decolonisation and the Cold War.[57] In the literature, the shah is often presented as a weak leader on the global stage, who easily succumbed to US pressure and who was essentially a tool of the United States. A growing body of literature has challenged this characterisation in recent years.[58] In his chapter, Arash Azizi examines both the Iranian contribution to one of the major events in America's post-Second World War history, the Vietnam War, and the impact that the war had on the opposition to the shah in the 1960s and 1970s. America's involvement in the Vietnam War polarised public opinion against it. At a time when the United States was facing civil rights crises at home, its hugely unpopular war in Southeast Asia further eroded belief in its international altruism. In this prickly conflict, as in others that pitted an imperial power against a small and comparatively defenceless nation, Iran pursued its diplomacy gingerly. America's heavy bombing campaigns unleashed a maelstrom of negativity, which, though one-sided, nonetheless exposed a humanitarian crisis. Iran tried not to abandon its ally, the United States, but simultaneously ministered assistance to the Vietnamese.

The withdrawal of the British from the Persian Gulf in 1971 allowed the shah to assert Iranian hegemony of the Persian Gulf and subsequently attempt to establish a leading position in the entire Indian Ocean region. In this context, the shah became greatly concerned about the growing Soviet presence in the Horn of Africa. In his chapter, Robert Steele examines how Iran's fears of Africa turning Red drove the shah to support Somalia in the Ogaden War of 1977–1978. This remarkable episode in late Pahlavi foreign relations demonstrates Iran's ambitions as a leader of the Global South, but also the shah's limitations, for the shah was prevented by the United States from supplying US-made weapons to Siad Barre.

It was not just through economic investment and supplying arms that the shah sought to demonstrate Iran's strength on the global stage. In the 1960s and 1970s, Iran championed many causes within international

---

57 For further discussion, see the introduction to Leslie James and Elisabeth Leake's edited volume, *Decolonization and the Cold War: Negotiating Independence*, 2015.

58 For example, Roham Alvandi, *Nixon, Kissinger, and the Shah*, 2014; and Michael Axworthy, *Revolutionary Iran*, 2013.

organisations, such as the United Nations. One of the most notable causes advocated was combatting illiteracy. To demonstrate support for this endeavour, in September 1965, Iran hosted the UNESCO World Congress of Ministers of Education on the Eradication of Illiteracy. In his speech to the congress, the shah urged the world to mobilise all 'available human and material resources for the purpose of waging a final battle against ignorance'. 'This crusade', he continued, 'is one of the noblest and heaviest tasks that man has ever ventured upon for his own true emancipation, and for world peace.'[59] Shortly after, the shah pledged the equivalent of one day's budget of the Iranian armed forces to the UNESCO campaign and urged other nations to make similar pledges.[60] Two years later, in October 1967, the Committee for the International Fight Against Illiteracy (*Komiteh-ye Peykar-e Jahani ba Bisavadi*) was set up, headed by the shah himself.[61]

At around the same time, in April and May 1968, Iran hosted the International Conference on Human Rights in Tehran. The United Nations commemorated the twentieth anniversary of the Declaration of Human Rights and declared 1968 the year of human rights. The first gathering of its kind, the Human Rights Conference in Tehran brought together a range of state and non-governmental actors. The conference paid special attention to prominent themes such as racial discrimination, gender inequalities, hunger, and illiteracy, among others. While critics have dismissed the conference as largely a staged event, in her chapter, Kashani-Sabet calls for a reassessment of the conference by proposing qualitative yardsticks in assessing its impact. Coming on the heels of the Russell Tribunal, the conference offered a different framework for understanding the significance of human rights in international settings.

---

59 'Shah's speech to the Campaign to end Illiteracy', September 1965, Shoja'
al-Din Shafa Archives, Bibliothèque Universitaire des Langues et Civilisations,
Paris.
60 'Shah's Donation to UNESCO to Fight Illiteracy', *Karachi Morning News*, 4
May 1966.
61 Farian Sabahi, *The Literacy Corps in Pahlavi Iran (1963–1979): Political Social
and Literary Implications*, 2002, 157.

Anti-Imperial Protests and Social Movements

Although the shah presented himself as a champion of human rights, many of his subjects came to view him as a cruel autocrat, who ruled with an iron fist and denied them freedom of liberty and expression. Various opposition groups were set up during the 1960s and 1970s, inspired by different ideologies, but all of which to varying degrees saw their struggle for freedom as part of a global anti-imperial moment.[62] Relatedly, in their important recent volume, *Global 1979: Geographies and Histories of the Iranian Revolution*, Arang Keshavarzian and Ali Mirsepassi explore 'the making of the Iranian Revolution not as a byproduct of globalization, nor merely a local or national phenomenon, but as an expression of the wide interconnectedness shaping a radically unequal and disjointed, yet inextricable interrelated world of simultaneities.'[63] Building on this, the final four chapters in this volume investigate aspects of the global interconnectedness of the 1960s and 1970s, to demonstrate how discourses of anti-imperialism from Europe to China and South America, found expression also among Iran's revolutionaries.

As Leonard Willy Michael demonstrates in his chapter, various leftist opposition groups abroad, particularly those in Europe, embraced the language of colonialism in their critiques of the Pahlavi regime. To these activists, the analytical engagement with decolonisation was an opportunity to clarify their own positions, confirm their theories, and attack the approaches of political rivals. The shah was presented by these groups as akin to the pro-Western leaders of the newly independent countries of the Global South, who were stifling true anti-colonial independent movements. By engaging with these developments, Michael's chapter not only contributes to the historiography of the Iranian Left, but also sheds a light on the impact of global decolonisation on the transnational community of politically active Iranians in Europe.

The year 1971 was important in the context of Iran's foreign relations. In October, the shah announced his arrival on the global stage with his grand celebrations at Persepolis and the British withdrawal from the Persian Gulf in December allowed him to consolidate power in the region and think

---

62 Firoozeh Kashani-Sabet, 'The Anti-Aryan Moment'.
63 Arang Keshavarzian and Ali Mirsepassi eds., *Global 1979: Geographies and Histories of the Iranian Revolution*, 2021.

more clearly about how Iran could influence political affairs far beyond the Middle East.[64] This was also the year that Pahlavi Iran accelerated its rapprochement with communist China. Iran sent two delegations to China in April 1971, one led by Princess Ashraf and the other by Princess Fatemeh and Leila Hoveyda, which led to the formal establishment of political ties in August.[65] As a sign of these developing friendly ties, China sent a representative to the celebrations at Persepolis two months later,[66] and in 1972, Empress Farah and Prime Minister Hoveyda paid an official visit to China.

While political ties were being forged between the shah and the Maoist regime, elements of the Iranian opposition were inspired by Mao's example to rise up against the Pahlavi autocracy. In his chapter, William Figueroa demonstrates that although frequently dismissed by scholars as insignificant at best and partly responsible for the failure of the Left at worst, Maoism contributed to the spread of open opposition to the shah among Iranian students and was part of a larger discourse of armed struggle among both activists and militants. Iranian student activists read, criticised, endorsed, and rejected Maoist literature as part of their own attempts to understand the nature of imperialism and Iran's own position in the international world, and as part of their political, personal, and ideological struggles against rivals and enemies. These students attempted to forge intellectual connections with China and Cuba and participated in an international discourse of anti-colonial solidarity. Juxtaposing moments of state-to-state connections with interactions between non-state actors also sheds new light on the process of Sino-Iranian rapprochement and highlights the impact of the unofficial on expressions of official policy.

While clear physical engagement resulted in the transfer of knowledge between opposition groups in Europe, China, and Iran, there is evidence that knowledge was transferred through intellectual engagement, too. In his chapter, Javier Gil Guerrero explores the similarities between Latin American Liberation Theology and theories developed by some of Iran's Islamic intellectuals during the 1960s and 70s. These intellectuals looked

---

64 Robert Steele, 'Pahlavi Iran on the Global Stage: The Shah's 1971 Persepolis Celebrations', *The Age of Aryamehr*, ed. Roham Alvandi, 2018, 110–146.
65 'Joint Communique on Establishment of Diplomatic Relations between China and Iran', *Peking Review* 14/34, 20 August 1971, 4.
66 Steele, 'Pahlavi Iran on the Global Stage', 136–137.

beyond the physical plunder of Iran's resources at the hands of Western imperialists to consider the harm that cultural imperialism had on Iran's spiritual and cultural worth. In the case of Shariati, combatting this reality required ideological rearmament of the country with the development of an ideology that mixed Shia Islam with Marxism. With this new interpretation, Iranian intellectuals sought to put Iran within the global struggle against colonialism and develop a theory of resistance that, albeit anchored on a concern with cultural authenticity, could appeal and inspire movements beyond those in the country or the region. This resulted in an intense dialogue between the different traditions of Shia Islam with the new leftist ideologies and schools of thought arising in Europe.

There is a rich and growing body of literature on Iran's militant revolutionaries, as well as their physical and ideological links to revolutionary movements around the world.[67] One of the most prominent organisations was the Fada'iyan-e Khalq, whose activism was inspired by both Islamist and socialist ideals. In his contribution to the volume, Carson Kahoe explores how the Fada'iyan perceived the global imperial struggle through their periodical *Kar*, published between 1979 and 1982, and how they viewed this fight as part of a larger global struggle.

Each of the contributors to this volume have examined different aspects of decolonisation within a global framework. The chapters and the subjects they cover have integrated the Iranian perspective of imperialism and decolonisation by reading this history as part of a pervasive global process that involved Iran in complicated ways, both directly and indirectly. We hope that the volume will form an important and timely contribution to scholarly discussions already taking place, add new perspectives, and inspire further work on Iran's global interactions and race relations in the late Pahlavi period and beyond.

---

67 See, for example, Peyman Vahabzadeh, *A Guerrilla Odyssey: Modernization, Secularism, Democracy, and Fadai Period of National Liberation in Iran, 1971–1979*, 2010; Rasmus Christian Elling, '"In a Forest of Humans": The Urban Cartographies of Theory and Action in 1970s Iranian Revolutionary Socialism', *Global 1979: Geographies and Histories of the Iranian Revolution*, ed. Arang Keshavarzian and Ali Mirsepassi, 2021, 141–177; and Ali Rahnema, *Call to Arms: Iran's Marxist Revolutionaries: Formation and Evolution of the Fada'is, 1964–1976*, 2021.

Bibliography

Abrahamian, E. *Iran Between Two Revolutions*, Princeton, 1982.

Akhtar, S. 'The Rabat Summit Conference', *Pakistan Horizon* 22/4, 1969, 336–340.

Alvandi, R. *Nixon, Kissinger and the Shah*, Oxford, 2014.

Alvandi, Roham ed. *The Age of Aryamehr: Late Pahlavi Iran and its Global Entanglements*, London, 2018.

Ansari, A.M. *Modern Iran since 1797: Reform and Revolution*, London, 2019.

Arendt, H. *On Violence*, San Diego, 1969.

Axworthy, M. *Sword of Persia: Nader Shah from Tribal Warrior to Conquering Tyrant*, London, 2006.

Axworthy, M. *Revolutionary Iran: A History of the Islamic Republic*, London, 2013.

Axworthy, M. ed. *Crisis, Collapse, Militarism and Civil War: The History and Historiography of 18th Century Iran*, Oxford, 2018.

Bakhash, S. *The Fall of Reza Shah: The Abdication, Exile, and Death of Modern Iran's Founder*, London, 2021.

Bast, Oliver. 'Putting the Record Straight: Vosuq al-Dowleh's Foreign Policy in 1918/19', *Men of Order: Authoritarian Modernization under Atatürk and Reza Shah*, ed. Touraj Atabaki and Erik J. Zürcher, London, 2004, 260–281.

Camacho Padilla, F. 'Las relaciones entre Latinoamérica e Irán durante la última década de la dinastía Pahleví', *Anuario de Historia de América Latina* 56, 2019, 66–96.

Chehabi, Houchang, Peyman Jafari and Maral Jefroudi eds., *Iran in the Middle East: Transnational Encounters and Social History*, London, 2015.

Chehabi, H.E. 'South Africa and Iran in the Apartheid Era', *Journal of Southern African Studies* 42/4, 2016, 687–709.

Chubin, S., and S. Zabih. *The Foreign Relations of Iran: A Developing State in a Zone of Great Power Conflict*, Berkeley, 1974.

Curzon, G.N. *Persia and the Persian Question*, London, 1892.

Davari, A. 'A Return to Which Self?: ʿAli Shariʿati and Frantz Fanon on the Political Ethics of Insurrectionary Violence', *Comparative Studies of South Asia, Africa and the Middle East* 34/1, May 2014, 86–105.

Davari, A. 'On Inexactitude in Decolonization', *Comparative Studies of South Asia, Africa and the Middle East* 40/3, 2020, 627–635.

Elling, Rasmus Christian. '"In a Forest of Humans": The Urban Cartographies of Theory and Action in 1970s Iranian Revolutionary Socialism', *Global 1979: Geographies and Histories of the Iranian Revolution*, ed. Arang Keshavarzian and Ali Mirsepassi, Cambridge, 2021, 141–177.

Elwell-Sutton, L.P. *Modern Iran*, London, 1941.

Elwell-Sutton, L.P. *Persian Oil: A Study in Power Politics*, London, 1954.

Fanon, F. *Wretched of the Earth*, translated by Constance Farrington, New York, 1963.

Farahzad, Farzaneh. 'Voice and Visibility: Fanon in the Persian Context', *Translating Frantz Fanon Across Continents and Languages*, ed. Kathryn Batchelor and Sue-Ann Harding, New York, 2017.

Figueroa, W. 'China and the Iranian Revolution: New Perspectives on Sino-Iranian Relations, 1965–1979', *Asian Affairs*, 2022.

Gahnameh-ye Panjah Saleh-ye Shahanshahi-ye Pahlavi, 5 vols, Paris, 1985.

Getachew, A. *Worldmaking after Empire: The Rise and Fall of Self-Determination*, Princeton, 2019.

Ghani C. *Iran and the Rise of Reza Shah: From Qajar Collapse to Pahlavi Power*, London, 2000.

Gheissari, A. 'Unequal Treaties and the Question of Sovereignty in Qajar and Early Pahlavi Iran', *Durham Middle East Papers* 106, 2023.

Golujeh, Sajjad Ra'i et al. ed. *Asnadi az Eshghal-e Iran dar Jang-e Jahan-e Dovvom*, Tehran, 1389.

Hoveyda, F. *The Fall of the Shah*, New York, 1980.

Hunter, S. *Iran's Foreign Policy In the Post-Soviet Era: Resisting the New International Order*, Santa Barbara, 2010.

James, Leslie and Elisabeth Leake eds. *Decolonization and the Cold War: Negotiating Independence*, Oxford, 2015.

Jackson A. *Persian Gulf Command: A History of the Second World War in Iran and Iraq*, New Haven, 2018.

Karanjia, R.K. *The Mind of a Monarch*, London, 1977.

Kashani-Sabet, F. 'Fragile Frontiers: The Diminishing Domains of Qajar Iran', *International Journal of Middle East Studies* 29/2, May 1997, 205–234.

Kashani-Sabet, F. *Frontier Fictions: Shaping the Iranian Nation, 1804–1946*, Princeton, 1999.

Kashani-Sabet, F. 'Hallmarks of Humanism', Hygiene and Love of Homeland in Qajar Iran', *The American Historical Review* 105/4, 2000, 1171–1203.

Kashani-Sabet, Firoozeh. 'Colorblind or Blinded by Color? Race, Ethnicity, and Identity in Iran', *Sites of Pluralism: Community Politics in the Middle East*, ed. Firat Oruç, Oxford, 2019, 153–180.

Kashani-Sabet, F. 'The Anti-Aryan Moment: Decolonization, Diplomacy, and Race in Late Pahlavi Iran', *International Journal of Middle East Studies* 53/4, 2021, 691–702.

Kashani-Sabet, F. *Heroes to Hostages: America and Iran, 1800–1988*, Cambridge, 2023.

Katzenstein, Peter J., and Robert O. Keohane eds. *Anti-Americanisms in World Politics*, Ithaca, 2011.

Keddie, N. *Sayyid Jamal ad-Dīn 'al-Afghanī': A Political Biography*, Berkeley, 1972.

Keddie, Nikki R. and Rudi Matthee eds. *Iran and the Surrounding World: Interactions in Culture and Cultural Politics*, Seattle, 2002.

Kepel, G. *Jihad: The Political Trail of Islam*, translated by Anthony F. Roberts, Cambridge, USA, 2002.

Keshavarzian, Arang and Ali Mirsepassi eds. *Global 1979: Geographies and Histories of the Iranian Revolution*, Cambridge, 2021.

Khalifa, J. and R.J.C. Young. *Frantz Fanon: Alienation and Freedom*, translated by Steven Corcoran, London, 2018.

Khosrokhavar, Farhad. 'Third Worldist Iranian Intellectuals: Shariati and Ale-Ahmad', *Mapping the Role of Intellectuals in Iranian Modern and Contemporary History*, ed. Ramin Jahanbegloo, London, 2020, 64–93.

'Konferans-e 'Ali-ye Saran-e Keshvarha-ye Islami dar Rabat Mazhar-e Ettehad va Yek Jahati 'Alam-e Islam', *Nashriyeh-e Hilal* 95, Azar 1347, 6–11.

Koyagi M. *Iran in Motion: Mobility, Space, and the Trans-Iranian Railway*, Stanford, CA, 2021.

Lee, C.J. *Making a World After Empire: The Bandung Moment and Its Political Afterlives*, Athens, USA, 2019.

Lüthi, L.M. *Cold Wars: Asia, The Middle East, Europe*, Cambridge, 2020.

Matthee, R. 'Infidel Aggression: The Russian Assault on the Holy Shrine of Imam Reza, Mashhad, 1912', *Russians in Iran: Diplomacy and Power in the Qajar Era and Beyond*, ed. Rudi Matthee and Elena Andreeva, London, 2018, 136–170.

Milani, A. *The Shah*, New York, 2011.

Ministry of Foreign Affairs, *Nezam-e Kapitulasiyun va Elgha-ye an dar Iran*, Tehran, 1355/1976.

Miri, S.J. 'Frantz Fanon in Ali Shariati's Reading: Is it Possible to Interpret Fanon in a Shariatian Form?', *Frantz Fanon and Emancipatory Social Theory*, Leiden, 2019, 184–216.

Mokhtari, F. *In the Lion's Shadow: The Iranian Schindler and His Homeland in the Second World War*, 2012.

O'Sullivan, A. *Nazi Secret Warfare in Occupied Persia (Iran): The Failure of the German Intelligence Services, 1939–45*, London, 2014.

O'Sullivan, A. *Espionage and Counterintelligence in Occupied Persia (Iran): The Success of the Allied Secret Services, 1941–45*, London, 2015.

Rahnema, A. *Call to Arms: Iran's Marxist Revolutionaries: Formation and Evolution of the Fada'is, 1964–1976*, London, 2021.

Ramazani, R.K. *Iran's Foreign Policy, 1941–1973: A Study of Foreign Policy in Modernizing Nations*, Charlottesville, 1975.

Sabahi, F. *The Literacy Corps in Pahlavi Iran (1963–1979): Political Social and Literary Implications*, Lugano, 2002.

Sadeghi-Boroujerdi, E. 'Who Translated Fanon's The Wretched of the Earth into Persian?', *Jadaliyya*, 13 August 2020. Available online: https://www.jadaliyya.com/Details/41564/Who-Translated-Fanon%E2%80%99s-The-Wretched-of-the-Earth-into-Persian

Sartre, Jean-Paul. 'Preface', Frantz Fanon, *Wretched of the Earth*, translated by Constance Farrington, New York, 1963, 7–26.

Satavov, N.A. 'The Circum-Caspian Areas within the Eurasian International Relationships at the Time of Peter the Great and Nadir-Shah Afshar', *Iran and the Caucasus* 5, 2001, 93–100.

Schayegh, C. and Y. Di-Capua. 'Why Decolonization?' *International Journal of Middle East Studies* 52/1, 2020, 137–145.

Spring, D.W. 'The Trans-Persian Railway Project and Anglo-Russian Relations, 1909–14', *The Slavonic and East European Review* 54/1, 1976, 60–82.

Steele, Robert. 'Pahlavi Iran on the Global Stage: The Shah's 1971 Persepolis Celebrations', *The Age of Aryamehr*, ed. Roham Alvandi, London, 2018, 110–146.

Steele, R. 'The Keur Farah Pahlavi Project and Iranian-Senegalese Relations in the 1970s', *Iranian Studies* 54/1–2, 2021, 169–192.

Steele, R. 'Two Kings of Kings: Iran-Ethiopia Relations Under Mohammad Reza Pahlavi and Haile Selassie', *The International History Review* 43/6, 2021, 1375–1392.

Vahabzadeh, P. *A Guerrilla Odyssey: Modernization, Secularism, Democracy, and Fadai Period of National Liberation in Iran, 1971–1979*, Syracuse, USA, 2010.

Warnaar, M. *Onze vriend op de pauwentroon: Nederland en de laatste sjah van Iran*, Zutphen, 2023.

Yari, H.A. 'Ravabet-e Siyasi-ye Iran va Libi dar Dowreh-ye Pahlavi-ye Dovvom (Ruyarui-ye Shah va Qazafi)', *Nameh-ye Tarikh-e Pazhuhan* 24, 1389, 130–151.

Zahedi, A. *Khaterat-e Ardeshir Zahedi*, vol. 3, Bethesda, 2020.

Zibakalam, S. *Reza Shah*, 2019.

Zirinsky, Michael. 'Riza Shah's Abrogation of Capitulations, 1927–1928', *The Making of Modern Iran*, ed. Stephanie Cronin, London, 2003, 81–98.

1

The 'Bridge of Victory': The Allied Occupation of Iran and its Consequences

Firoozeh Kashani-Sabet

On 15 March 1939 the crown prince of Iran, Mohammad Reza Pahlavi, married his teenage Egyptian fiancée, Fawzia Bint Fuad.[1] To the outside world, the union appeared auspicious: the couple produced a daughter, Princess Shahnaz Pahlavi, in October 1940, and less than a year later, the prince ascended the Iranian throne. But this blissful portrait of harmony would not last. The Allied invasion of Iran robbed the country of autonomous rule and depleted its resources. Iran was regarded as the 'bridge of victory' (in Persian: *pol-e piruzi*), a phrase that came to describe its role as the critical link enabling the delivery of supplies to the Soviet Union and therefore the success of the Allies. Though the country's contribution to the global war effort often appears merely as a footnote in the Western historiography of the Second World War, Iran recalls its involvement very differently. In less than three decades, Europeans had twice taken over the country. Its territory and transportation infrastructure provided a safe conduit for war materiel during a dire phase of the war. In 1945, when it was time for the Allied troops to leave, the Soviet Union decided against

---

1 'Egyptian Princess Weds Iranian Heir', *The New York Times*, 16 March 1939, 23.

departing Iran. Instead, it fuelled separatist movements that undermined the country's stability.[2]

How did the hardships of occupation influence Iranians in an era of decolonisation? For one, it incited a decade of domestic turmoil that came to a head during the oil crisis. The privations of war, compounded by the humiliation of military impotence, toughened the resolve of Iranians in demanding the country's independence. Yet the political vigour that emerged shortly after the war also exposed old fractures that would test Iranian society and its interactions with America and other global powers. The war revealed persistent sources of turbulence for Iran, in which the United States became embroiled in unprecedented ways: foreign intervention; the politics of ethnicity; and socio-economic disparities.

In 1941, the United States provided support for the war through the Lend-Lease Act, which allowed it to assist countries vital to its defence. By late 1943 the appearance of nearly 30,000 US troops as part of the newly constituted Persian Gulf Command involved Americans prominently in Iranian affairs, from managing daily interactions to implementing US global strategy.[3] For a brief interlude it seemed that the occupying powers and Iran actually concurred on something life-affirming and important – namely, harbouring the Polish refugees who had made the difficult trek to the unknown land of Iran. American diplomats, and even President Roosevelt himself, recognised poverty and economic underdevelopment as social challenges facing the region.[4] The hope that the principles of the Atlantic Charter might be applied to the Middle East persisted. The Atlantic Charter – a declaration that Great Britain and the United States had issued in 1941 (only days before the invasion of Iran) – strove to promote open trade, arms control, and national self-determination.[5] Smarting under wartime occupation, Iran reluctantly relinquished

---

2 Gary R. Hess, 'The Iranian Crisis of 1945–46 and the Cold War', *Political Science Quarterly* 89/1, March 1974, 117–146.

3 Ashley Jackson, *Persian Gulf Command: A History of the Second World War in Iran and Iraq*, 2018, Chapter 1 for significance of oil for Britain during this time.

4 Nathan Godfried, 'Economic Development and Regionalism: United States Foreign Relations in the Middle East, 1942–5', *Journal of Contemporary History* 22/3, July 1987, 482–485.

5 Elizabeth Borgwardt, *A New Deal for the World: America's Vision for Human*

much of its national autonomy. In January 1942 Iran signed the Tripartite Treaty with the occupying powers, which affirmed Iran's cooperation with the Allies but also provided some nominal reassurances of Iran's territorial integrity.[6]

At first, the contrasts in style between Anglo–Soviet and American interventions in Iran stood out starkly. While Britain and the Soviet Union tried to realise their age-old desire to carve out spheres of influence in the midst of war, they could not achieve complete freedom of action. The United States had arrived on the scene, and the Anglo–Soviet forces remained in dire need of American war materiel. As the United States watched Iran collapse on multiple fronts, it tried to alleviate some of the domestic causes of unrest. The perceptive reflections of the US ambassador to Iran, Louis Goethe Dreyfus, who occupied this post from 1939 to 1944, account for this sympathetic perspective. Dreyfus cautioned that Americans could not adopt 'a "holier than thou" or "aren't we wonderful" kind of propaganda' – a mindset that had turned the British in Iran into antagonists. Dreyfus cast serious doubt on 'the disdainful and uninformed assumption that "native" peoples are incompetent'.[7] Although Dreyfus optimistically volunteered Iran as the 'ideal proving ground for the Atlantic Charter', the overarching Allied war objectives left this promise unfulfilled.[8]

The Allied involvement in Iran had enormous domestic implications overlooked by Cold War historians. The radicalism of post-war Iranian politics, with its caustic anti-Western (and anti-foreign) sentiments, took root during the demeaning years of occupation. My analysis draws on the historiography of Anglo–American relations in Iran, some of which treats Iran as one of many 'cases' in the Middle East or Mediterranean caught in the Cold War.[9] At the same, I move away from the Anglo–American

---

Rights, 2005, 3–5.

6 A. H. Hamzavi, 'Iran and the Tehran Conference', *International Affairs* 20/2, April 1944, 192. Also, James A. Bill, *The Eagle and the Lion: The Tragedy of American–Iranian Relations*, 1988, 18.

7 Dreyfus, Tehran, 3 May 1943, no. 543, 'Comments on an Editorial in the Providence Journal Quoted in the Radio Bulletin No. 104 Regarding the Rail Supply Route Through Persia'.

8 Louis G. Dreyfus to Secretary of State, No. 511, Tehran, 7 April 1943, 7.

9 For example, William Roger Louis, *Imperialism at Bay, 1941–1945: The United States and the Decolonization of the British Empire*, 1977; Ritchie Ovendale,

model, which considers these events principally as they affected the United States, Great Britain, and the West. Key studies include the analysis of Bruce Kuniholm, who plainly recognised that 'pursuit of national interests by the Great Powers was the basic issue during World War II'.[10] Mark Lytle's work focuses on the expansion of US–Iranian relations during the war years and criticises the diplomatic reasoning that turned Iran into a Cold War pawn.[11] Ashley Jackson's voluminous and important study of the Persian Gulf Command discusses key war objectives and notes Iran's social hardships during the occupation. However, Jackson sometimes elides the situations of Iraq and Iran during the war but concedes nonetheless that 'the allies were directly responsible for wheat shortages'.[12] Simply making this statement does not shed sufficient light on the ways in which Iranians wrote about and tried to survive these privations. By contrast, this chapter projects the voices of suffering Iranians who were often powerless to counter Allied decision-making.

The expression 'Anglo–American', used to assess Iran's international relations, is both apt and awkward.[13] Such a phrase implies alliance and unified objectives. However, it also eschews the contrasts in British and American decision-making in Iran, which at times surfaced starkly during the occupation. Building on a new body of research, this chapter argues that Iran was not just a case study in the Cold War. It was a country whose inhabitants endured foreign occupation and a global conflict not of its creation. Britain and the Soviet Union failed to offer Iran any reparations, and Britain, in particular, continued its punitive campaign of depriving Iran of its rightful share of oil in Abadan. In addition, it failed to acknowledge Iran's claims in the southern regions of the Persian Gulf, which Britain summarily declared an Arabian coast devoid of any meaningful Persian presence.[14]

Anglo–American Relations in the Twentieth Century, 1998; and Terry H. Anderson, *The United States, Great Britain, and the Cold War, 1944–1947*, 1981.

10 Bruce Robellet Kuniholm, *The Origins of the Cold War in the Near East: Great Power Conflict and Diplomacy in Iran, Turkey, and Greece*, 1980, 130.

11 Mark H. Lytle, *The Origins of the Iranian–American Alliance, 1941–1953*, 1987.

12 Jackson, *Persian Gulf Command*, 236.

13 Simon Davis, 'The Persian Gulf in the 1940s and the Question of an Anglo–American Middle East', *History* 95/1, January 2010, 64–88.

14 Firoozeh Kashani-Sabet, 'Pandering in the Persian Gulf: Arabia, Iran and Anglo–American Relations, 1900–1971', *American–Iranian Dialogues: From*

I rely on a host of previously unused (or underused) Iranian sources that document the Iranian perspective of the occupation and question some of the British claims concerning the extent of Nazi German influence in the country at the outbreak of the Second World War. Finally, I document Iranian reactions to the atomic bombing of Japan and the emergence of US supremacy at the end of the Second World War. Iranian sources demonstrate the depth and range of troubles that Iran faced as an occupied nation, making it difficult for the country to manage social crises such as typhus and famine. As this close analysis of Iranian experiences shows, the occupation robbed Iran of its sovereignty and the ability to maintain basic functions of governance. Available works on the war do not provide sufficient evidence of Iran's political paralysis and its sacrifices through a detailed reading of the existing but unexplored Persian literature on the subject. Iran's post-war politics became shaped around the humiliating experiences of imperialism and occupation. These events proved painful for the Great Powers, too, as the course of Iran's post-revolutionary history has shown. A generation of young adults grew up in this environment and remembered the degradation of Iranian society during the Second World War.

The Occupation Begins

The Anglo–Soviet invasion, codenamed Operation Countenance by Britain, began on 25 August 1941 and lasted until 17 September. The day after its completion, Reza Shah abdicated and sailed to Mauritius, and later Johannesburg, South Africa, where his life ended in exile. Reza Shah's stay in Mauritius was unhappy, not only because he was exiled and could only communicate in Persian, but also because he disliked the climate and evidently 'the preponderance of coloured population'.[15] Britain did not want Reza Shah exiled somewhere close to Iran as it feared that the fallen monarch might plan his return to the country. It had been rumoured that his son, Mohammad Reza Shah, was considering nominating his father as

---

Constitution to White Revolution, C. 1890s–1960s, ed. Matthew Shannon, 2021, Chapter 4.

15 Qatar Digital Library (hereafter QDL), From Mauritius Sir B. Clifford to Secretary of State for the Colonies, 12 November 1941.

a candidate in the upcoming elections.[16] In addition, the rapid downfall of the shah has been attributed in part to the animosity that Sir Reader Bullard, British minister to Iran and later ambassador, felt towards him.[17] Bullard had gained extensive experience in the Middle East as a colonial official in Iraq and Arabia prior to his posting to Iran.[18] While Bullard's negative impression of Reza Shah dealt the king a serious blow, Bullard's views must not be taken at face value.[19] More than a month after his departure, the ex-shah was still trying to convince British authorities that he had not acted against their interests or in favour of Germany.[20]

The prompt surrender of Iran's Caspian Sea fleet indicated the desperation of Iran's forces, which had tried to maintain neutrality. According to an Iranian source attibuted to two naval officers, Daryabod Faraj Allah Rasa'i, who had trained in Italy during the interwar years, and Naval Commander Ja'far Fozuni, Rear Admiral Gholam Ali Bayandor had impressed upon his officers the importance of Iran's impartiality, particularly as a small number of Italian and German ships had taken refuge in Iran. He noted further that until the early morning hours of 25 August 1941, Iranians had only experienced the global conflict from afar, but the invasion destroyed people's sense of calm. In Arvand Rud (Shatt al-Arab), Iranian warships, which had previously sailed peacefully alongside British warships suddenly found themselves under attack by them on the day of invasion.[21] The abandoned arms of the demoralised army were then 'recovered by the Lurs, Kurds, Kashkais and other tribesmen' – a situation that fuelled tribal and ethnically-driven aspirations for autonomy.

In a spectacular show of propaganda warfare, announcements by Allied forces warned Iranians about the German danger in the country and their

---

16 QDL, IOR/L/PS/12/3518, Coll 28/107 'Persia (Iran) Movements of the ex-Shah.'
17 Shaul Bakhash, 'Britain and the Abdication of Reza Shah', *Middle Eastern Studies* 52/2, 318–334.
18 Ann K. S. Lambton, 'Obituary: Sir Reader William Bullard', *Bulletin of the School of Oriental and African Studies, University of London* 40/1, 1977, 130–134.
19 Kashani-Sabet, *Heroes to Hostages*, Chapter 7.
20 QDL, IOR/L/PS/12/3518, Coll 28/107 'Persia (Iran) Movements of the ex-Shah.' From Mauritius Sir B. Clifford to Secretary of State for the Colonies, 24 October 1941.
21 National Library and Archives of Iran (hereafter NLAI), 264/30251, 'Ru Nevesht-e Asnad-e Marbut beh Vaqayeh-e 1320'.

ایرانیان !

هزارها آلمانی در خاك شما هستند اینها به تدبیر بمقدمات مهمی در صناعت حاثر کنه اند و فقط منتظر یك كلمه از هیتلر هستند که منابع اصلی مالیه شمارا قار و مار سازند سفارت آلمان برای اینها تشکیلات جامعی ترتیب داده و هرکدامشان بمامورین مخصوص معین اند شما میدانید به تحریکات آلمانها چه فتنه و آشوبی در عراق تولید شد قطعاً اینها هیچ تردیدی نخواهند داشت در ایران هم همین کار را بکنند ـ

عین همین وضعیت در بسیاری از ممالك کوچك اروپا دیدۀ مشهد پیش از غلبه آلمانها برانها ـ

آقایانی که در ایران اختیاراتی دارند از تحذیرات مکرر ماراجع دخطر ماندن آلمانها در خاك شما اجاهل کرده اند و این مخاطره تنها برای شما نیست برای انگلیس و روس هم همین حال را دارد ما مصمم برفتن آلمانها هستیم و اگر ایرانها آنها را بیرون نیکنند انگلیس و روس اینکار را خواهند کرد قوای ما مقاومت قابذیر است ـ

ایرانیان ! ما با شما نه نزاعی داریم و نه هم سوء قصدی نسبت بمملكت شما و هستی و زندگی شما ما فقط میخواهیم آلمانهای ملعون را بیرون برانیم چرا اینها غرضی جز اینکه کشور شما هم یك میدان ستیز و خونریزی واقع گردد و منظورك شود ندارند اگر شما حالا با ما مساعدت کنید ما بشما مساعدت خواهیم کرد چه حالا چه در آینده ـ

nefarious intentions. As a leaflet alerted: 'Iranians! There are thousands of Germans in your territory …. They are waiting for a single word from Hitler to take over your financial institutions …. A similar situation has occurred in smaller European countries.' The flyer, addressed directly to the local population, provided predictable assurances that the occupying powers had 'no conflict' with the Iranian people, but simply wanted to oust the 'cursed Germans' (*Almanihayeh-e mal'un*). [22] Local residents saw the carnage and strove to help. According to officer Rasa'i, who was serving in the Persian Gulf naval force, in the extreme heat of the summer a woman dressed in rags shared the water she was carrying in a jug.[23] The invasion was neither simple nor peaceful. The effort to persuade Iranians that the invasion was intended to expel the Germans did not succeed. Promptly after the invasion, London reiterated its line that the attack was directed against Germans, and not Iranians.[24]

Discontent with the shah's rule had emanated from various quarters representing the Iranian political spectrum, including the religious classes, political activists, elites, landowners, and intellectuals. The approach of Soviet troops toward Tehran only hastened Reza Shah's decision to abdicate on 16 September 1941. Although there was little consensus over who should succeed the deposed king, the shah's eldest child acceded to the throne in accordance with the Iranian constitution.

The war years exposed the glaringly unequal relationship between Iran and the nations that had occupied it, but Britain would have a hard time abandoning its privileged status. Immediately following the invasion, in nearby Bahrain, Britain kept a watchful eye over dhows coming from Iran in case Axis nationals looking to escape had boarded the vessels.[25] A night patrol was promptly set up that detained a boat to Qatar from Iran with ten Iranians lacking passports on board en route to Bahrain. British authorities considered making an example of the captain enabling these passages.[26] Additional

22 NLAI, 264/30251, 'Ru Nevesht-e Asnad-e Marbut beh Vaqayeh-e 1320'.
23 NLAI, 264/30251, 'Ru Nevesht-e Asnad-e Marbut beh Vaqayeh-e 1320'.
24 'British and Russian Troops Enter Iran: Nazis Forestalled Infiltration Danger Compels Action Timely Invasion Under Command of General Wavell Germans Take Flight', *South China Morning Post,* 26 August, 1941.
25 QDL, IOR/R/15/2/722, 'File 28/30 War. Hostilities in Iran', 2 September 1941.
26 QDL, IOR/R/15/2/722, 'File 28/30 War. Hostilities in Iran', 2 September 1941.

reports warned that over a hundred Germans had escaped from Tehran and were moving south.[27] Yet interestingly, the ex-shah also had to leave Iran by travelling south to Bandar Abbas, an arduous trip that took several days.[28]

Britain planned 'to secure oil fields', as well as to maintain open lines of communication in the Persian Gulf. To achieve its military goals, it implemented measures to protect Iran from Axis attacks and infiltration.[29] Elvadore R. Noderer, a press correspondent for the *Daily Tribune*, reported from Tehran not long after the start of hostilities. Noderer had arrived in Tehran during a blackout. He had travelled from Ankara by traversing the mountainous terrain that eventually led him to the capital. At first, he hiked through the defenceless city of Miyaneh southeast of Tabriz less than an hour after the Soviet army had dropped 30 bombs on it. This attack had resulted in over a dozen deaths and around twice that number of injuries. Unsure about what was happening, crowds rushed to the streets, some carrying 'bomb fragments'.[30] In Tehran people discussed the onslaught in 'hushed voices', while hotel workers used candles in bowls to light up their surroundings. Earlier in the day, in anticipation of the chaos, the capital had prepared for 'any eventuality'. Banks conducted 'brisk business', while long queues formed outside of kerosene shops and bakeries.[31] News then arrived that the Soviet troops had bombed three northern cities, Qazian, Pahlavi (Anzali), and most seriously, Qazvin. Air strikes later targeted Zanjan, known for its fruit growing, where the rail station was apparently 'demolished'. Karaj and Mashhad faced aerial attacks as well.[32] In the south, British forces had bombed Ahvaz and damaged Iranian ships in the ports of Bandar Shahpur and Khorramshahr.[33]

---

27 QDL, IOR/R/15/2/722, 'File 28/30 War. Hostilities in Iran', 26 September 1941.
28 QDL, IOR/L/PS/12/3518, Coll 28/107 'Persia (Iran) Movements of the ex-Shah', The Residency, Bushehr, 17 October 1941. Also, Shaul Bakhash, *The Fall of Reza Shah: The Abdication, Exile, and Death of Modern Iran's Founder*, 2021, 61–66.
29 Anita L.P. Burdett, ed. *Iran: Political Developments, 1941–1946, British Documentary Sources: Iran under Allied Occupation*, vol. 1, 1941, 401.
30 E. R. Noderer, 'An Eyewitness Picture of Iran During Invasion: Tribune Writer Tells Graphic Story', *Chicago Daily Tribune*, 30 August 1941, 1.
31 Noderer, 'An Eyewitness Picture of Iran During Invasion', 1.
32 Noderer, 'An Eyewitness Picture of Iran During Invasion', 1.
33 'Iranian Move Reported: Iran Seeks Peace as Cabinet Quits March into Iran Meets Little Resistance', *The New York Times*, 28 August 1941, 1.

In the capital, residents feared similar attacks and were warned to take precautions. Tehran did not have air-raid shelters, but people were given instructions about warning signals and the telephone numbers of first-aid centres. Food shortages and hoarding became evident from the outset, and public transportation was limited. Many foreign diplomats and their communities sought refuge in the compounds of their respective legations, but some Americans chose not to remain there. Others used tents containing beds, blankets, and some food. Noderer noted that Tehran residents had anticipated the arrival of forces from Soviet Russia, but once calm was restored, many congregated on street corners to listen to the news being read aloud.[34] Nearly two weeks later, other war correspondents arrived on the scene and reported on the frequent presence of Russian soldiers in northern Iranian cities. Russell Hill, a reporter with the *New York Herald Tribune*, wrote that at the dining room of Qazvin's main hotel, he joined Soviet soldiers in a vodka toast calling for the defeat of Nazi Germany. From the commissar, Hill learned about the extensive fighting in Tabriz and the futility of Iranian resistance to Russian tanks.[35]

Iran surrendered its military positions, and therefore its sovereignty, not only in the Persian Gulf, but throughout the country, as war materiel was transported across its territory to the Soviet Union. By October 1941, long-time Iranian diplomat Seyyed Hasan Taqizadeh had returned once again to England to serve as the Iranian ambassador there, despite 'his German wife and his recent absence from his country'.[36] Iran's new king, Mohammad Reza Shah Pahlavi, opened the Thirteenth Majles during this period of intense upheaval. In his inaugural speech, the young monarch acknowledged the country's reluctant embroilment in the war and urged the cooperation of the deputies and cabinet members in securing the country's independence.[37] Prime Minister Foroughi, in assessing the Anglo–Soviet invasion, recognised that the Second World War, in its scope, resembled

---

34 E. R. Noderer, 'An Eyewitness Picture of Iran During Invasion', 1 & 4.

35 Russell Hill, 'Reporter Finds Strong Force of Russians in Iran: Tanks, Planes, Cavalry and Infantry Co-Operated in Invasion with British', *New York Herald Tribune*, 7 September 1941, 1.

36 Buckingham Palace, 10 October 1941, Burdett ed. *Iran: Political Developments*, 483.

37 *Mozakerat-e Majles*, 13th Session, 22 Aban 1320/13 November 1941, preface.

no other conflicts previously waged, which in his view had been typically limited to outstanding territorial issues. The rapid defeat of Iran's modest armed forces put the government on the defensive as the young shah confronted his monumental responsibilities.

The Homeland Responds to Occupation

Press censorship made it difficult for candid reporting to take place on the international situation. Some Iranian journalists eventually opted for satire or chose to explore cultural themes. One weekly magazine, *Ettela'at Haftegi*, connected to the daily newspaper, provided briefings about the war front and filled in the week's news with reviews of films, fashion, and sports. A long article introduced the movie, *Wizard of Oz*, first released in 1939, to Iranian audiences. Regular features included short sections on recreational games like bridge and chess, women's beauty, childcare, and essays on different world capitals. The emphasis on seemingly trivial subjects in the Iranian weekly press suggested that Iranians strove to maintain a semblance of normality in the midst of extraordinary domestic changes and international crises.

On the anniversary of the invasion, an Iranian periodical recalled the bravery of the military personnel who had lost their lives as a result of the Allied attack. The newspaper, *Aftab-e Taban* ('The Shining Sun') printed pictures of several dead soldiers and suggested that the Third of Shahrivar (25 August) become a day of remembrance, not only for Iran but for the world. On that day, Iran 'lost its bravest and most devoted soldiers', and the paper recalled the sacrifices of its fighters in protecting the country's independence. It requested that a location be commemorated as the 'Tomb of the Unknown Soldier' (*qabr-e sarbaz-e gomnam*) as a reminder of the valour of Iran's military figures who gave their lives in defence of the country's independence.[38] By contrast, Western sources covering Iran during the war years typically did not provide such personal details and interventions in discussing the invasion.

None of this diminished the daily toll of deprivation brought on by the invasion. Immediately following the attack, Tehran's residents were faced

---

38 *Aftab-e Taban*, No. 20, 8 Shahrivar 1321/30 August 1942, 1–2.

Aftab-e Taban, No. 20, 8 Shahrivar 1321/30 August 1942, 1–2.

with food shortages, and reports of hoarding emerged.[39] Throughout 1942, Britain, which controlled much of Iran's transportation and supply routes, failed to furnish the promised amounts of wheat to Iran, contributing to a devastating bread shortage and general food insecurity. On 8 December 1942, rioters protested outside the Majles (parliament) building about the scarcity of bread and set Prime Minister Ahmad Qavam's home on fire. Ambulances, though in short supply, arrived to minister to the injured. Hospital records put the number of dead at eight people and the injured at forty-four.[40] The Tehran authorities redoubled their efforts to restore calm by reassuring merchants and others that rabble-rousers would not be able to harm 'the livelihood, lives, or tranquillity' (mal va jan va asayesh) of residents.[41] British reports blamed the shortage on 'hoarders and speculators', while Iran held the occupying forces responsible. Lack of information and coordination between the Soviet and British authorities on the delivery of wheat to Tehran only exacerbated the problems.[42] While the rioting subsided within days, the food situation remained a thorny problem throughout the war. Azerbaijan, which also grappled with ethnic unrest fuelled by the Soviet Union, faced serious food shortages. British authorities acknowledged that 'the condition of the people in the poorer quarters of the town is really bad. Deaths from starvation are not uncommon and malnutrition is increasing the death-rate from disease.'[43] The lack of responsibility and oversight for these food shortages only hurt Iranian residents, many of whom became silent victims of the Allied occupation.[44]

Iran was unable to address these pressing issues effectively, which exacerbated regional and ethnic divisions. American diplomat Louis Dreyfus

---

39 Dreyfus to the Department of State, 26 August 1941, FRUS, 1941, The British Commonwealth; The Near East and Africa, vol. 3, doc. 404.

40 NLAI, Vezarat-e Farhang, Edareh'e Koll-e Daneshgadeh-e Pezeshki va Bemarestanha, 21 Azar 1321/12 December 1942.

41 NLAI, Sepahbod Amir Ahmadi, Farmandeh-e Padgan-e Markez va Farmandar-e Nezamiyeh-e Tehran, 'E 'lamiyeh-e Farmandariye Nezami'.

42 A.L.P. Burdett, ed., Iran: Political Developments: 1941–1946, 3: 549–554.

43 Burrell, R.M., and Robert L. Jarman, Iran: Political Diaries, 1881–1965, 1997, 12–26.

44 Bertel E. Kuniholm to Louis G. Dreyfus, Jr., Tabriz, File No. 800/861.31, 1 February 1943, 1.

observed that the Iranian army was largely powerless and unable to control tribal conflagrations, which had burst open during the occupation.[45] As a result, Dreyfus urged Iran to take a different approach to managing its tribes. Reza Shah had failed to implement a compassionate policy that would involve tribal communities in state initiatives. The tribes had complained about the seizure of their lands and forced settlement.[46] The power struggle with tribes had undermined the legitimacy and rule of Reza Shah, whose policies had done little to endear him to those constituencies. The tribal confederations, however, were not entirely blameless, as their destabilising policies over political power sometimes undermined attempts at forging unity or effecting change through existing legal and political relationships (whatever their shortcomings).[47]

The United States dispatched military and financial missions to Iran over the following year. John N. Greely arrived in 1942 but was soon superseded in this role by Major General Clarence Ridley, who was limited in his efforts to revamp the army.[48] Colonel H. Norman Schwarzkopf, former commander of the New Jersey State Police (and father of the US general who commanded coalition forces in the Persian Gulf War of 1990–1991), took on the task of reforming the gendarmerie. America had alerted its advisors that some Iranians might be disinclined to cooperate.[49] Many Ira-

---

45 Louis Dreyfus to Secretary of State, No. 616: 'Iranian Government Forces Suffer Severe Defeat at Hands of Kashkai and Boir Ahmadi Tribesmen at Samirun', Tehran, Iran, 16 July 1943, 3. Accessed via History Vault: Folder – 003105-009-0121: 'Iran political affairs: conditions in Azerbaijan, relations with the Allies, internal security and tribes, Tehran riots, Kurdish affairs, conditions in Khuzestan.'
46 Louis Dreyfus to Secretary of State, No. 616, 16 July 1943, 3.
47 In 1921, Reza Shah took over a country riven by the First World War. In an effort to centralise the country and to impose order by a central government, he embarked on an authoritarian top-down reform programme that did not brook power-sharing. However, he had a formidable task before him as the central government had broken down just before the war. Although many tribal leaders were influential in securing constitutional rule in Iran, some also were unwilling to abdicate some of their authority to the new institutions of governance that they had helped to create. Tribal organization, like the state itself, suffered from an authoritarian mindset and model of entrenched tradition of hierarchical leadership. For more on this idea, see my forthcoming monograph, *Tales of Trespassing: Borderland Histories of Iran, Iraq, and the Persian Gulf.*
48 FRUS, (1943), vol. 4, 510.
49 FRUS, (1943), vol. 4, 514.

nians understandably resented the Allied intrusion into their lives even as they hoped the advisors would alleviate some of the country's hardships. Iranians expressed grave concern over inflation and the escalating costs of living. A year into the occupation, the dwindling food supplies angered Iranians, who blamed their difficulties on the occupying powers. Majles deputies deliberated these issues, which Britain conceded represented the opinions of the general populace.[50]

Iran saw the imposition of Allied censorship during the war. Some believed that wartime censorship contributed to the country's instability. In 1943, diplomatic reports confirmed continuing Allied censorship of the Iranian press. Concern remained over the possibility that the newspapers might go their own way as they had censured the government 'for suppression of papers'.[51] Iranian journalists eventually managed to express their frustration over the war despite the censorship. Information control, however, existed in other ways. The occupying powers engaged in various forms of 'war publicity' in Iran. In 1942, an American study argued that although Iran was 'racially' diverse, the basic interests of the different social and tribal groups were similar enough to enable American propaganda efforts to focus on showing the country as a 'trusted' power with 'no ambitions' for the control of Iran.[52] As the population of Iran at the time remained largely rural or concentrated in small towns, it was advised that the 'propaganda to be disseminated' should 'be of a simple nature' to conform to 'the workings of the oriental mind'.[53] America focused on trying to strengthen its ties with the Iranian populace and convincing Iranians of an Allied victory. US officials engaged in publicity efforts, including film propaganda. They contended that the pro-German posture among some Iranians had to do with their 'popular dislike of the

50 QDL, IOR/L/PS/12/556, Bullard to Foreign Office, October 22, 1942.
51 'Report of the British Legation Staff Meeting, January 14, 1942', accessed via History Vault. Although the document uses the date 1942, I believe that is a typographical error as the document follows in chronological order the minutes of the British Legation meetings in January 1943.
52 'Publicity in Iran', Memorandum Prepared for Mr. Frank Mauran, Office of Co-ordinator of Information, Washington', 2 February 1942. Attachment No. 196, 'Enclosing a Report Prepared by Secretary Fritzlan Containing Suggestions as to War Publicity in Iran', 3 February 1942.
53 'Publicity in Iran', 2.

British and Russians', and that Germany might win the war. To turn Iranians against Germany, American personnel suggested that details about the German concentration camps be shared with Iranians as this 'would appeal in a very real way to the people'.[54] Moreover, they stressed that Iranians, being prone to flattery, 'should be flattered', and their contributions to art, poetry, and architecture highlighted.[55] They determined that an effective way of spreading such propaganda was the use of 35-millimeter films for showing in public theatres and using Persian-language commentary, which avoided Afghan and Indian Persian dialects that Iranians apparently found 'distasteful'.[56] In the final months of 1942, films projected in Iran included a reissue of *Mutiny on the Bounty*; *Fantasia*; and most significantly, *The Great Dictator* – Charlie Chaplin's masterful parody of Hitler produced in 1940.[57] Cinema Iran Company showed many American films, including *The Great Dictator*, while other theatres like Cinema Maiak also screened American movies.[58] To reach areas that lacked cinemas, American personnel recommended that 'trucks equipped with 16-millimeter sound projectors' be employed. The use of coloured posters and the Tehran Radio Station served as other ways to promote US propaganda.[59]

Unlike the British, the US did not regard the press as the most effective way of spreading their message given the high rate of illiteracy in Iran and the limited circulation of newspapers in Tehran.[60] Eventually, photos displaying US war efforts appeared in tea houses and Tehran cafés and some provinces. However, outside of Iranian military personnel, few showed any interest in these images.[61] In the north, Soviet Russia was disseminating propaganda in the regions of Guilan, Mazandaran, Azerbaijan, Gorgan, and Khorasan, and its activities were viewed as consisting 'chiefly

---

54 'Publicity in Iran', 3.
55 'Publicity in Iran', 2–3.
56 'Publicity in Iran', 3.
57 [Cordell] Hull, Telegram to US Legation, Tehran, 12 January 1943, enclosure.
58 Ibid.
59 'Publicity in Iran', 4.
60 Ibid., 4.
61 Louis G. Dreyfus, 'Report on American Publicity in Iran', No. 362, 21 October 1942.

in fostering separatist movements'. The Soviets relied on 'free cinemas' to spread their message.[62]

After the invasion Iranians had diminished access to German and Axis propaganda, although some still could tune into Axis broadcasts in private homes. US informants found it difficult to determine the extent of Japanese and Italian propaganda given the 'absence of facilities for monitoring' in Iran.[63] Nevertheless, some Iranians expressed a 'feeling of comradeship' for Germans, in part because of their 'repugnance for the British'. Moreover, the effectiveness of propaganda films had its limits. According to an American missionary, the audience in a cinema in a poor part of town 'cheered wildly for Hitler and at decidedly the wrong places when a British war film was shown'.[64] For its part, the US relied on paper propaganda as well, including pamphlets and flyers, published in Persian or French, to advertise American films or war activities. In addition, one thousand copies of an illustrated pamphlet on the life of President Franklin Delano Roosevelt, written in Persian and French, were promptly distributed.[65]

To control the news, the government of Ahmad Qavam had suppressed eight Iranian newspapers by September 1942. The occupying powers remained intent on managing the spread of information about the war. Iranian public opinion appeared more favourable considering Japan's 'retreat' in China and Germany's setbacks in Egypt.[66] Wartime circumstances produced chaos in other ways. A year after the invasion, an errant German aircraft had seemingly lost its way and had dropped propaganda leaflets written in Turkish over Pahlavi (Anzali). It was thought that the leaflets had been intended for Soviet-occupied Azerbaijan. However,

62 'Publicity in Iran', 2.

63 William S. Farrell to Louis G. Dreyfus, 1 September 1942, in reference to the Bi-Monthly Service Report of the Near East Department of the British Broadcasting Corporation, 18 June 1942.

64 Louis G. Dreyfus, Tehran, 13 May 1942, No. 264, 'Enclosing a Notice Published by Iranian Police Concerning Iranian Treaty Obligations Toward British and Soviets'.

65 Louis G. Dreyfus, Tehran, 23 April 1943, No. 530, 'Informational Activities in Iran'.

66 A. D. Fritzlan, 'Memorandum on the Meeting on Press and Propaganda Held at the British Legation on September 9, 1942'.

Allied officials determined that 'the dropping of leaflets' over Pahlavi (Anzali) had 'produced no reaction'.[67]

During the occupation, the Soviet and British authorities expanded their cultural influence in their respective spheres in Iran. In the north, Russian movies, including one on Pushkin, were shown and the Russian language was commonly heard on the streets. The British, while finding it hard 'to overcome the accumulated prejudices and suspicions of the last 50 years', organised teas at which the atmosphere was thick with propaganda. They also tried to show sometimes outdated and ineffective war films. The radio remained an important source of news for Iranians, who tuned into broadcasts from Ankara that offered news from both the Allied and German fronts.[68]

The ties between America and Iran grew in both positive and negative ways. Foreign engineers, soldiers, physicians, and pilots populated various corners of the country, using its territory with virtual freedom to facilitate the war effort. Iranians mingled casually with the growing number of foreign troops and accustomed themselves to these jarring realities. The Trans–Iranian Railway, completed in 1938, became the conduit through which supplies reached Russia. The Persian Gulf Command evolved from previous military units deployed in the region during the war. Detachments to Iran arrived in late 1942, and Major-General Donald Connolly assumed control of the operation, which continued until 1944 when the command wrapped up much of its work. The Allied invasion of Iran opened up the country to thousands of American servicemen, many of whom had little desire or inclination to serve there. Joel Sayre, who was a member of the Command, documented the sour mood of the troops.[69]

The Majles approved a military mission intended to revamp the Iranian gendarmerie in October 1943. Headed by Colonel H. Norman Schwarzkopf, the mission's objective was to advise the Interior Ministry on the reorganisation.[70]

---

67 A. D. Fritzlan, 'Memorandum on Press and Propaganda Meeting At British Legation', 16 September 1942.
68 'Soviet Propaganda in Iran'; 'Axis Propaganda in Iran'; 'British Propaganda in Iran': Enclosed with files from December 1942.
69 Joel Sayre, *Persian Gulf Command: Some Marvels on the Road to Kazvin*, 1945, 3–4.
70 US Legation in Tehran, Telegram, No. 1033, 22 October 1943, from Dreyfus.

In recognition of his work, Colonel Schwarzkopf had previously been the superintendent of the New Jersey State Police, and for his labours he eventually received the Iranian Medal of Merit.[71] Schwarzkopf would later use elements of this force to subdue rebels during the ensuing Azerbaijan crisis as Iran struggled to counter Soviet interference in the province.[72]

By this stage, Iran had declared war on Germany and aligned its official position with that of the Allied forces. America, which had not been initially involved in the occupation of Iran, played a vital role in working to alleviate some of the wartime stresses imposed upon Iranians, including food shortages, epidemic outbreaks, and the like. But this proved, yet again, a complicated relationship given the negative feelings that were brewing against the occupation. Tehran became the centre of global negotiations as it welcomed the triumvirate of Winston Churchill, Franklin Delano Roosevelt, and Joseph Stalin. The Tehran Conference, convened from 28 November until 1 December 1943, gave the Allied powers the opportunity to consolidate war plans and to make strategic decisions about the next phase of the conflict. Adding to the intrigue, the Soviet foreign minister Vyacheslav Molotov shared the news that Germany had apparently hatched a plot to assassinate one or more members of the Big Three.[73] In the end, the meeting went ahead successfully, and the Allied powers issued a declaration to respect Iran's territorial integrity. The conference gripped the imagination of the Iranian public as well, and a Persian-language biography of Winston Churchill went on sale.[74]

Arthur C. Millspaugh: A Quandary

An American financial adviser, Dr. Arthur Chester Millspaugh, returned to Iran to tackle the country's economic woes. Millspaugh had previously served in Iran from 1922 to 1927, when he had helped to reorganise the

---

71 'Iran Decorates Schwarzkopf', *The New York Times,* 27 October 1945.

72 'Col. Schwarzkopf Protecting Iran Capital Against Rebels', *Los Angeles Times,* 24 November 1945.

73 Paul. D. Mayle, *Eureka Summit: Agreement in Principle and the Big Three at Tehran, 1943,* 1987, 57.

74 See an advertisement for the Churchill biography by Mohammad Khalil Javaheri in *Ettela'at,* 15 Farvardin 1323/4 April 1944.

treasury. During his second mission, from 1942 to 1945, to improve Iran's finances he implemented a progressive income tax programme that faced opposition.[75] When he first assumed his office, the Bank faced financial challenges. Diamonds and silver were sold on the market, while plans were drawn up to introduce the sale of gold, particularly from South Africa.[76] The US Legation also proposed a postponement of lend-lease payments. In his report, however, Millspaugh unambiguously acknowledged that the 'war is, of course, the fundamental cause of Iran's troubles'.[77] Despite putting in place changes that were intended to alleviate the lack of food, he achieved little success.

Feeling the economic pinch, low-ranking government employees petitioned the Majles to address the country's woes.

> Our children do not get proper food, they are weak and pale because they do not get butter and milk. We cannot feed them with 200 grams bread, they crying out day and night for food, and for fruit we have to show them the picture of it. What is this tragic and disastrous life that we and our children are having, and what is the fault of these children? Why no one cares for us? The 5% children's allowance is not even sufficient for one sickness case of a child.[78]

Their salaries fell far short of what they could afford in rent and food to support their families with the bare necessities, not luxury items such as automobiles and radios. Employees throughout the country faced similar hardships. In Hamadan, 'owing to poverty and destitution', government

---

75 Millspaugh to Dreyfus, 'Enclosure with Despatch No. 540, dated April 29, 1943, from the American Legation Tehran', 25 April 1943. Also, Dreyfus to Department of State,'Enclosing Copy of Letter Addressed by Dr. Millspaugh to Prime Minister Outlining Iranian Financial Situation and Urging Passage of Certain Legislation', No. 602, 4 July 1943.
76 Millspaugh to Dreyfus, 'Enclosure No. 1 with Desptach No. 583 dated June 12, 1943 for the American Legation, Tehran, Iran', 8 June 1943.
77 Report of the Administrator General of the Finances of Iran for the Month of Esfand 1321/20 February–21 March 1943.
78 Enclosure with Despatch No. 594 dated 30 June 1943, from the American Legation, Tehran, Iran.

employees stopped work. Reports from Kerman, Rasht, and Semnan confirmed similar deprivations.[79]

Millspaugh's decisions remained enormously unpopular, and the satirical press did not shy away from expressing its dissatisfaction with his policies. One cartoon showed the frustrated reaction of merchants in the bazaar upon learning of Millspaugh's appointment and his economic plans. Another cartoon targeted the astronomical increase in the cost of living, which Millspaugh had not done enough to reduce. It depicted an Iranian figure struggling to hold down Millspaugh, who had promised a decline in inflationary cost, from soaring into the air propelled by the skyrocketing prices.[80] The critical newspaper, *Iran-e Ma*, summed up the economic hardships in this way: 'Living is more expensive; it is more difficult to meet our needs; and complaints are increasing from residents in the capital and its outskirts about the ineffective distribution of goods'.[81]

Millspaugh's drastic economic experimentation in Iran was derided as the 'Adventure of a yankee [sic] in Iran'. Millspaugh was cast in the role of Don Quixote, while his sidekick, Sancho Panza, was likened to *'pahlavan panbeh'* – a humorous figure in Iranian puppetry who displays bravado as a strong leader but who is in reality a coward. Notwithstanding the mixed metaphors, the Millspaugh mission met with cynicism and did little to make America a popular occupying force in Iran, where citizens cared more about relieving their economic hardship. One image forcefully brought home this basic message. It depicted the 'permanently hungry', gazing enviously through the window of a restaurant at the food on display. The caption sardonically read: 'So! It appears that new dishes, which we had never before seen in our lives, have been cooked!'[82] The

---

79 Millspaugh to Dreyfus, 18 June 1943, 'Memorandum Sent to Minister of Finance by Minster of Justice', 12 Khordad 1322/3 June 1943.

80 *Baba Shamal*, 8 Ordibehesht 1322/29 April 1943.

81 *Iran-e Ma*, 'Siyasat-e eqtesadi-ye Millspaugh', 2nd Year, No. (138)/282, 10 Azar 1323/1 December 1944, 1–2. The American Legation was well aware of the negative press the Millspaugh mission was receiving. In a despatch, they had translated a copy of an article that appeared in *Mard-e Emruz* on 8 April 1944. Enclosure No. 2 with Despatch No. 915 of 18 April 1944. Accessed via History Vault: Folder #: 003105-015-0162. Found in: Confidential U.S. Diplomatic Post Records, Middle East, 1942–1944: Iran.

82 *Baba Shamal*, First Year, No. 11, 2 Tir 1322/24 June 1943, 1.

Iran-e Ma, 'Siyasat-e eqtesadi-ye Millspaugh', 2nd Year, No.
(138)/282, 10 Azar 1323/1 December 1944, 1–2.

public's cynicism over promises of food aid resonated powerfully in this
image.

Mismanagement of funds and food supplies fanned people's impa-
tience with the occupying powers and their collaborating government. In
a gesture of goodwill, Mrs. Dreyfus, the wife of the American Minister
in Iran, toured the poor areas of the capital during those trying months,
distributing food parcels to the needy. She also founded an institute and
haven to help those afflicted with typhoid and typhus.[83]

---

83 Mrs. Dreyfus would be remembered lovingly by the Iranian elite as several

Public Health Scares and Social Conditions

With the breakdown of social order came disease. In 1942, Iran faced a worsening typhus outbreak, which became hard to track and manage. Absence of uniform reporting methods and fact-gathering techniques led to reliable doctors offering vastly varying estimates of the scale of contagion. Over the course of a single week, Qum and Kashan reported 'no epidemic', while Kermanshah and Rezaiyeh acknowledged severe outbreaks.[84] Iran urgently sought to obtain from the United States doses of typhus vaccines. Although Iran had requested a million vaccines, supplies remained scarce. The US Typhus Commission visited Iran and recommended that vaccinations be made available to medical and public health officials on request. The commission did not, however, propose inoculating the general civilian population, despite the perceived risk of epidemic outbreak in Iran.[85]

Louse-born typhus grew prevalent in populations that suffered from poverty and low hygiene. To reduce lice (*shepesh*), and by extension to curb the diffusion of typhus, the Tehran municipality created the Association for the Prevention of Typhus (*anjoman-e jelogiri az bimariye typhus*) and provided free bathing facilities to enable more frequent washing and selfcare habits. The municipality also issued advertisements to educate communities about the need to bathe at least once a week and to maintain clean homes.[86] The Association delivered a circular in which it described the 'frightening nightmare' (*kabus-e vahshatnak*) that typhus had wreaked upon Iranians, and especially the families of the bereaved. It feared that the winter months would worsen the epidemic. While acknowledging the government's responsibility in managing the typhus outbreak, the Association emphasised the public's simultaneous role in controlling the spread

---

articles in the journal of the Iran–American society demonstrate. For example, see, Forough Hekmat, 'Bongah-e Dreyfus', *Majalleh-e Iran va Imrika*, 1st year, No. 11, Azar 1325/December 1946. Mrs. Dreyfus's effort to feed and clothe the needy, including the children, are mentioned here.

84 Colonel Robert H. Givens, Jr., Weekly Intelligence Bulletin, 9 April 1943.

85 Middle East Supply Centre, Memorandum to Mr. Marshall MacDuffie, Jr., Director of Material, 'Typhus Fever and Typhus Fever Vaccine in Iran', 30 June 1943.

86 NLAI, 240/43992, 'Ersal-e Agahihayeh Shahrbani beh Vezarat-e Darayi', 22 Aban 1322/14 November 1943.

of the disease by upholding a hygienic lifestyle. Workers employed in the Department of Health were enjoined to educate Iranians about the dangers of the disease and its transmission through public health campaigns that included posting placards in cinemas and publishing informative articles in newspapers. The Department also strived to provide homecare for the infirm, when possible, and ambulance services to transport patients requiring hospitalisation.[87] Owners of inns and coffeehouses were further instructed to report sick travelers to health authorities; to prevent their intermingling with other visitors; and to keep the belongings of travellers who had died of the disease while in their custody in separate quarters. Health officials recognized, however, that poverty and food insecurity (*kam ghazayi va faqr*) only exacerbated these dire conditions that made the typhus epidemic difficult to control.[88]

Around the same time, Iran opened its borders to several thousand Polish refugees forcibly deported from Soviet-occupied regions.[89] The customs and passport divisions of Pahlavi (Anzali) reported that over 14,000 displaced persons had arrived in the country.[90] Yusef Abad Garden in Tehran became one of several designated locations for Polish immigrants.[91] Others ended up in makeshift camps, while some Polish women were accommodated in the homes of Iranian citizens. Concern grew that some of the refugee women might marry the homeowners and have children, making it difficult to ascribe nationality. It was recommended that a commission be created to determine nationality in such instances and to monitor the refugees.[92] Several hundred Polish immigrants suffered from

---

87 NLAI, 293/32444, Vezarat-e Keshvar, Edareh-e Koll-e Behdari, Bakhshnameh (Circular), 1322/1943.
88 NLAI, 293/32444, Vezarat-e Keshvar, Edareh-e Koll-e Behdari, Bakhshnameh (Circular), 1322/1943. This file also contains the statute of the Association for the Prevention of Typhus.
89 Lior Sternfeld, '"Poland Is Not Lost While We Still Live": The Making of Polish Iran, 1941–45', *Jewish Social Studies* 23/3, Spring–Summer 2018, 101–127; Kashani-Sabet, *Heroes to Hostages*, Chapter 7.
90 NLAI, 240/10348, 'Vorud-e Mohajerin-e Lahestani', 14 Shahrivar 1321/5 September 1942.
91 NLAI, 293/3639, Vezarat-e Keshvar, Edareh-e siyasi, 'Vaz'iyat-e Lahestaniha'.
92 NLAI, 293/3639, Vezarat-e Keshvar, Edareh-e Koll-e Shahrbani, 25 Shahrivar 1321/16 September 1942.

illnesses, including typhus, and a number of them were transferred to the few available hospitals.[93]

The American Red Cross worked hard to distribute supplies and minister care to Polish refugees, especially vulnerable women and children who faced outbreaks of cholera, smallpox, typhus, typhoid, and meningitis. The circumstances of sick children remained 'pitiful', with the infirm 'lying on cotton mattresses on the floors of the improvised rooms'.[94] Several of the children who arrived were 'motherless' and 'terribly undernourished', in need of clothes, blankets, medicines, and other necessities. The Pasteur Institute in Iran had plans to manufacture vaccines for typhus and other infectious diseases.[95]

American military physicians became involved in other facets of Iranian public health crises. Dr. Bennett F. Avery, US director of public health, offered his insights to the Iranian minister of health. Avery advised Iranian health officials to focus on preventive medicine to reduce the incidents of infectious diseases (malaria, typhoid, hookworm, dysentery, tuberculosis, typhus, and venereal disease) and to decrease the rates of infant mortality. Moreover, Iran faced a shortage of skilled medical and public health personnel, which Avery suggested could be alleviated with the opening and expansion of educational facilities. Improvements in nutrition and quarantine control ranked high among other recommended measures to contain the spread of epidemics.[96]

The war proved challenging for the occupiers as well. Russian soldiers suffered from low morale. For entertainment and to lift their spirits, theatrical troupes and artists arrived from Baku, Yerevan, and Turkestan. Russian officers apparently complained that 'there are no women', and those who walked in the streets were 'all veiled'.[97] After an increase in the number of venereal

---

93 NLAI, 293/3639, Vezarat-e Keshvar, Statistics collected 6 Ordibehesht 1321/26 April 1942.
94 Louis G. Dreyfus, No. 239, 'Excerpts from Communications Addressed by American Red Cross Representative in Tehran to Director Red Cross Middle East Concerning Polish Refugee Problem', 2 April 1942.
95 Maurice Barber to Ralph Bain, Director of American Red Cross, Middle East, 20 April 1942.
96 Dr. Bennett F. Avery to Iranian Minister of Health, 12 May 1944.
97 Bertel E. Kuniholm to Louis G. Dreyfus, Tabriz, Iran, 7 July 1942, 6.

disease cases, the 'Red Army began a systematic clean up of brothels around town'.[98] Among the lower classes, women re-veiled in 'a complete reversion to the period preceding Shah Reza'.[99] The desire of the 'ulama 'to get back the power they once wielded' was attributed to this change. The 'Moslem Mollahs', described as 'agents provocateurs of the Germans', appeared also to fuel anti-sectarian conflict.[100] Iranians had legitimate reasons for complaint against the occupying authorities who were 'seizing property such as household equipment, furniture, vehicles, and even bank funds, apparently carried out under military orders'.[101] Iranians with insufficient funds or influence had little choice but to succumb to such pressures.

In Tabriz, Iran's second largest city during the war, grim conditions persisted. Sheets of flatbread remained the staple diet of its inhabitants. The shortage of flour combined with daily rations often left the poor hungry. On his arrival in the city, American Consul Richard Ford was struck by 'the number of screaming infants'. Inquiring into the matter, he concluded that 'these cries were merely hungry cries emanating from homes where the day's bread supply had not stretched quite all the way around the family circle'.[102] Young children in Tabriz, often forced to work in rug factories, posed other social challenges, as Iran lacked effective child labour legislation preventing abuses: 'For most Tabriz rugs are woven by children, generally little girls ... although many boys of similar ages are also employed'.[103] Many younger children lacked clothes, and the attire of the 'destitute group' amounted to rags or 'masterpieces of patches'.[104] The absence of basic necessities exposed the deprivations that countless Iranians had endured.

---

98 Kuniholm to Dreyfus, 7 July 1942, 5.
99 Bertel E. Kuniholm to Louis G. Dreyfus, Tabriz, Iran, 12 June 1942.
100 Kuniholm to Dreyfus, 12 June 1942, 1–2.
101 Samuel G. Ebling, American Consul, File No. 800, 'First Impressions of Political Situation in Azerbaijan', 3 May 1943.
102 Richard Ford, American Consul, File No. 800, 'Memorandum Concerning the Social and Political Economy of Azerbaijan', Completed 1 October 1943, Tabriz, Iran, 2 October 1943, 14.
103 Ford, 'Memorandum Concerning the Social and Political Economy of Azerbaijan', 15.
104 Ford, 'Memorandum Concerning the Social and Political Economy of Azerbaijan', 13–14.

Baba Shamal, First Year, No. 11, 2 Tir 1322/24 June 1943, 1.

Wartime exposed the class divisions in Iranian society and the impact of imperial intervention in Iran. The occupation meant that Iran's 'independence' was not a reality, but a diplomatic euphemism designed to soften the impact of the Western powers' colonial stranglehold. Iran's survival was necessary for the success of the war effort, but survival did not enable freedom of action or independence. The country's experiences in the global conflict would translate into support for decolonisation movements after the end of the Second World War.

An End in Sight

War-weary and rundown, Iran reflected on Europe's Armageddon as news trickled in about the impending defeat of Germany. An Iranian cartoon mocked the political shortsightedness that had facilitated Hitler's rise to power in the Third Reich. Its caption read: 'Whoever brought a donkey to power can bring it down.'[105] This image lambasts the misguided political forces that had empowered Hitler in the first place. Technological secrets of the war slowly surfaced in Iran as well. One source reported the discovery of radar technology that had enabled Allied aircraft to fly in inclement weather to reach their targets.[106]

The nuclear attacks on Japan in August 1945 left their imprint on Iran, as they did on the entire world. The destruction of Hiroshima, described as no longer habitable after the atomic bombing, prompted the wry newspaper subheading: 'Will they turn the ocean water into vapour as well?'[107] Another newspaper expressed public anxiety by heralding the nuclear age with a parody of Persian miniature paintings. With its depiction of the physical destruction of human features, this illustration – entitled 'From the Miniatures of Iran's Nuclear Century' – mocked the supposed technological advances that had produced nuclear weapons, returning humanity

---

105 *Ashofteh*, 1 Shahrivar 1324/23 August 1945.
106 *Iran-e Ma*, 20 Esfand 1323/11 March 1945.
107 *Iran-e Ma*, 18 Mordad 1324/9 August 1945. Also, 17 Mordad 1945/8 August 1945 on Truman's announcement about his directive to use the atomic bomb against Japan. *Iran-e Ma* also noted that when it had previously talked about the possibility of a nuclear bomb and its range of destruction, its reports had been greeted with scepticism in some quarters.

Ashofteh, 1 Shahrivar 1324/23 August 1945.

Baba Shamal, 25 Mordad 1324/16 August 1945.

to an earlier age of barbarity. This cartoon also lampooned the political chaos in Iran at the time.[108]

Another newspaper reported on the destruction caused by the atomic bombs, pointing out that at least Americans had attempted to reduce civilian deaths in targeting Nagasaki, a shipping and industrial complex. Yet it also noted that initial reports gauged the destruction caused by this second bomb to be comparable to that of the first.[109] Several issues of *Mard-e Emruz*, edited by Mohammad Mas'ud, discussed war-related matters, including the impact of the atomic bomb. One cartoon pictured the Statue of Liberty holding a new, presumably atomic, torch and indicating that the light and heat generated from an atomic bomb is purportedly comparable to that of the sun. The caption read: 'Henceforth, earth will circumambulate (*tavaf* [in a reference to the Muslim hajj]) the Statue of Liberty.'[110] The new dominant position of the United States even threatened and rivalled the power of Islam.

The clear message of the cartoon was that the destructive power of the bomb had unleashed a new and unknown international order which placed the United States in a dangerous position. Above all, Iran awaited the departure of foreign armies and the end of the occupation. This desire was reflected in an image that depicted the three heads of state whose countries had invaded Iran engaged in conversation before a map of Iran with an 'exit door' (*darb-e khoruj*) behind it. [111]

*

In 1946, after a struggle that became one of the first points of tension in the Cold War, the Soviet Union left Iran. The end of the global conflict signalled a new world order – the rise of an international rivalry between the former allies, the United States and the Soviet Union.[112] The young

---

108 *Baba Shamal*, 25 Mordad 1324/16 August 1945.
109 *Iran-e Ma*, 19 Mordad 1324/10 August 1945.
110 *Mard-e Emruz*, No. 44, Single Issue (tak shomareh), Mordad 1324/August 1945. Nedayeh *Azadi* included an article on Dr. Einstein and his related discoveries.
111 *Ashofteh* 15th Year, No. 8, 27 Ordibehesht 1324/17 May 1945.
112 Stephen L. McFarland, 'A Peripheral View of the Origins of the Cold War: The Crises in Iran, 1941–47', *Diplomatic History* 4/4, Fall 1980, 333–351. McFarland

Mard-e Emruz, No. 44, Single Issue (tak shomareh), Mordad 1324/August 1945.

Ashofteh 15th Year, No. 8, 27 Ordibehesht 1324/17 May 1945.

shah cultivated close ties with the USA, which he fervently came to believe would facilitate his rule. But even at this early stage, some Iranians expressed mixed feelings about America.

The cultural institution known as the Iran–America Society signalled a new phase in US–Iranian relations by inaugurating its journal in 1946 – a literary endeavour written simultaneously in Persian and English. This collaboration had its roots in the interwar period, and the attempt to forge cultural ties between the two countries. Its contributors composed pieces that strove to dampen the cynicism that Iranians felt toward the occupying powers, including the United States, who had, in their eyes, worsened the country's economic crisis, exacerbated poverty, and caused the devaluation of its currency. War-weariness and suspicion ran deep. Iran had endured many setbacks during the war, ranging from the mismanagement of its economy and the exploitation of its resources by foreign powers to the territorial threats that openly endangered its unity. The individuals who regularly contributed to this journal imagined an amicable and productive partnership that would deliver mutual benefits to both societies. Missing from these accounts were the poignant testimonies of young Iranians who would recall these bleak days with anger and eventually fulminate against the imperial powers that inflicted these adversities upon the country.

Bibliography

Ashofteh.

Bakhash, S. *The Fall of Reza Shah: The Abdication, Exile, and Death of Modern Iran's Founder*, London, 2021.

Bill, J.A. *The Eagle and the Lion: The Tragedy of American–Iranian Relations*, New Haven, 1998.

---

supports the 'third-power *movazaneh* strategy' that regarded America as the necessary third force needed to offset the power of the occupiers, Britain and the Soviet Union. Also, Bruce Kuniholm, *The Origins of the Cold War in the near East: Great Power Conflict and Diplomacy in Iran, Turkey, and Greece*, 1980. For more on the Azerbaijan crisis, see the following works: Louise Fawcett, *Iran and the Cold War: The Azerbaijan Crisis of 1946*, 1992; and Touraj Atabaki, *Azerbaijan: Ethnicity and Autonomy in Twentieth-Century Iran*, 1993.

Borgwardt, E. *A New Deal for the World: America's Vision for Human Rights*, Cambridge, 2005.

Bullard, R. and E. C. Hodgkin. *Letters from Tehran: A British Ambassador in World War II Persia*, 1991.

Burdett, A.L.P. ed. *Iran: Political Developments, 1941–1946: British Documentary Sources: Iran under Allied Occupation*, London, 2008.

Burrell, R.M. and R.L. Jarman. *Iran: Political Diaries, 1881–1965*, Cambridge, 1997.

Central Office of Information, *Paiforce: The Official Story of the Persia and Iraq Command, 1941–1946*, 1948.

Davis, S. 'The Persian Gulf in the 1940s and the Question of an Anglo–American Middle East', *History* 95/1, 2010, 64–88.

'Egyptian Princess Weds Iranian Heir', *The New York Times*, 16 March 1939, 23.

Godfried, N. 'Economic Development and Regionalism: United States Foreign Relations in the Middle East, 1942–5', *Journal of Contemporary History* 22/3, 1978, 481–500.

Hamzavi, A. H. 'Iran and the Tehran Conference', *International Affairs* 20/2, April 1944, 192–203.

Hess, G.R. 'The Iranian Crisis of 1945–46 and the Cold War', *Political Science Quarterly* 89/1, March 1974, 117–146.

Jackson, A. *Persian Gulf Command: A History of the Second World War in Iran and Iraq*, New Haven, 2018.

Jenkins, J. 'Iran in the Nazi New Order, 1933–1941', *Iranian Studies*, 49/5, 2016, 727–751.

Kozhanov, N.A. 'The Pretexts and Reasons for the Allied Invasion of Iran in 1941', *Iranian Studies* 45/4, July 2012, 479–497.

Kuniholm, B.R. *The Origins of the Cold War in the Near East: Great Power Conflict and Diplomacy in Iran, Turkey, and Greece*, Princeton, 1980.

Ladjevardi, H. *Labor Unions and Autocracy in Iran*, Syracuse, USA, 1985.

Lytle, M.H. *The Origins of the Iranian–American Alliance, 1941–1953*, New York, 1987.

Majalleh–e Iran va Imrika.

Majd, M.G. *August 1941: The Anglo–Russian Occupation of Iran and Change of Shahs*, Lanham, 2012.

O'Sullivan, A. *Nazi Secret Warfare in Occupied Persia (Iran): The Failure of the German Intelligence Services, 1939–45*, London, 2014.

Mard-e Emruz.

Mayle, P.D. *Eureka Summit: Agreement in Principle and the Big Three at Tehran, 1943*, Newark, 1987.

McFarland, S.L. 'A Peripheral View of the Origins of the Cold War: The Crises in Iran, 1941–47', *Diplomatic History* 4/4, Fall 1980, 333–351.

Sayre, J. *Persian Gulf Command: Some Marvels on the Road to Kazvin*, New York, 1945.

Sternfeld, L. '"Poland Is Not Lost While We Still Live": The Making of Polish Iran, 1941–45.' *Jewish Social Studies*, vol. 23, no. 3, Spring–Summer 2018, 101–127.

Yazdi, M.K.M. *Arzesh-e Masa'i-ye Iran dar Jang*, 1945.

2

Trauma and Decolonisation: The Sultanabad (Arak) Camp, German Espionage, and the Allied Occupation of Iran during the Second World War

Pardis Minuchehr

'In wartime, truth is so precious that she should always be attended by a bodyguard of lies' (Winston Churchill)

In September 1943, Ahmad Matin-Daftari, a former prime minister of Iran, boarded a train at Tehran's central station to report for captivity in the British internment camp at Sultanabad (Arak) – allegedly as a Fifth Column conspirator. In his memoirs, *Khaterat-e Yek Nakhost Vazir* ('The Memoirs of a Prime Minister'), the former prime minister (also the son-in-law and nephew of a future prime minister, Mohammad Mosaddeq), described what he called the 'injustice' and 'madness' of being held captive during the Second World War, in the company of over two hundred other Iranians.[1] Transformed by this unexpected reversal of fate, Matin-Daftari,

---

1 Ahmad Matin-Daftari, *Khaterat-e Yek Nakhost Vazir*, 1992, 218. These quotations are part of Matin-Daftari's farewell speech from Arak, which is also recounted in Nurollah Larudi's *Asiran*, 1953, 281–283. From Sultanabad (Arak), Matin-Daftari travelled to Rasht to be interrogated further by the Soviet troops.

who was a legal expert himself, denounced his and his fellow inmates' mistreatment by the invading British forces and decried the 'useless pressure and suffering', they endured 'in sheer contradiction to all principles of international law and human rights'. He said in a farewell speech at the camp, quite poignantly, that 'he found something positive in the pain that this internment had caused'. He averred that 'against the expectations of the invading foreigners, one extraordinary result was reaped', namely 'the joining together of a group of splendid and knowledgeable elements of this country [Iran]'. The internment camp, Matin-Daftari declared, was a locus where 'accident and fate introduced him to a group of patriotic, goal-oriented, and motivated individuals who were at the same time erudite, authentic, and nation-loving', an exceptional condition that would not otherwise have been possible 'outside of these [captivity] circumstances'. In this vein, he referred to an exceptional emotional and intellectual bond the captives had formed in Allied captivity, an incarceration that proved fateful for the future of a tumultuous Iran. Such stories of occupation, its associated feelings of anger, resentment, and defeat, which have been overlooked in the historiography of modern Iran, became of paramount importance for the revolution that transformed the country less than forty years later. In other words, a series of disregarded incidents during the invasion set the stage for a revolution which had global consequences.

The invasion and occupation of Iran shook the country to its core.[2] In the summer of 1941, soldiers occupied Iranian cities and villages, and many who resisted this occupation were rounded up to be taken to makeshift prisons – among them over two hundred highly educated individuals in prominent positions. These people were detained at the behest of the Allied forces, with the expressed intention of stifling dissent against colonial rule. In 1953, Nurollah Larudi published *Asiran* ('Captives'),[3] a comprehensive account of the captivity of hundreds of political figures during the war. Larudi himself was one of these captives, arrested apparently because of the discovery of a photograph of him in Qashqai clothes holding a rifle and surrounded by other potentially subversive elements. The long subtitle of Larudi's *Asiran* is: 'The atrocities of the gangster forces of the

---

2 See Firoozeh Kashani-Sabet's contribution to this volume (Chapter 1).

3 Nurollah Larudi, *Asiran*, 281–282.

British in Iran, including the biography of two years of captivity of 180 Iranian nationalists and notables and celebrated personalities and officers and heads and some of the foreign citizens in the Allied political confinement during the Second World War'. The book explores the reasons why many of the captives were taken prisoner, presenting this captivity as the greatest injustice they encountered during the war. *Asiran* includes descriptions of the personalities and professions of many of the Sultanabad (Arak) detainees along with their political allegiance, as well as relevant information regarding what happened to them in colonial captivity. While there are other published and unpublished narratives of captivity by the Allied forces, none is as comprehensive as Larudi's eyewitness account.[4] More importantly, Larudi supplies fascinating details of the British forces' planning, and the place they held the captives in a makeshift internment camp, guarded by Indian soldiers, two hours south of Tehran in Sultanabad (Arak). He also highlights the harshness of their treatment, where captives were interrogated as common criminals, without any regard for their elite social status within Iranian society.[5] Based on a range of primary sources – including autobiographical accounts, declassified documents of the British forces, and recently opened Iranian archives held in the Iranian National and Majles libraries – this study examines the dynamic between the captives of Sultanabad (Arak) and their role in Iran's decolonisation process.

In addition to the former prime minister, Ahmad Matin-Daftari (1897–1971), several generals, judges, lawyers, railway officers, technocrats, and businessmen were held in the internment camp. Among the captives, we find names of prominent members of the judiciary such as Ali Hey'at and Ali Akbar Musavizadeh; attorneys such as Ebrahim Sepehr, Sheykh 'Abdol-Majid Minuchehr Shirazi, Hoseyn Ali Naqibzadeh Mashayekh and Mahmud Moshaver; railroad administrators such as Ja'far Sharif-Emami

---

4 These include Mahmud Shervin and Hamid Karamipur, *Khaterat-e Doktor Mahmud Shervin*, 2005; Mahmud Shervin, *Dowlat-e Mosta'jal: Doctor Mohammad Mosaddeq, Ayatollah Kashani*, 1995; Ahmad Ali Sepehr, *Khaterat-e Siyasi-ye Movarrekh al-Dawleh Sepehr*, 1995; Habibollah Naubakht, *Dar Bazdashtgah-e Ajaneb. Khaterat va Asnad. Majmu'eh-ye az Khaterah-ye Navisandegan-e Nokhbe va Aks-ha va Asnad-e Mo'tabar*. Tehran, 1369 [1990]; and Anushiravan Khalatbari, *Mahbusin-e Motaffeqin dar Iran 1322–1324*, 1385 [2006].
5 Larudi, *Asiran*, 251–303.

(a future prime minister),[6] Nasseh Nateq, Fazlollah Mirhadi, Hanafi Ramazani, Hoseyn Banu-Azizi, Esma'il Ashraf, Manuchehr Farzin, and the civil engineer Abbas Mazda; feared generals such as Farajollah Aqevli, 'Abolhasan Purzand, Mohammad Sadeq Kupal, Colonel Sadeq Feruhar, Yahya Vera, Hasan Baqa'i, Nader Batmanghelich, Mahmoud Jahanbeglu and Fazlollah Zahedi (another future prime minister); and journalists such as Khosrow Eqbal (editor of *Nabard*, Tehran),[7] Jahangir Tafazzoli (editor of *Iran-e Ma*, Tehran),[8] Hoseyn-Qoli Katebi (editor of *Faryad*, Tabriz), Abbas Hakim Ma'ani (editor of satirical *Mahshar*, Tehran) and Bagher Hejazi (editor of *Vazifeh*, Tehran).[9] Sayyid 'Abol-Qassem Kashani was the only member of the clergy detained and Habibollah Naubakht, the only incumbent deputy of the thirteenth Majles.

Individuals were brought in for questioning either based on allegations of their covert contacts with German agents in Iran, or for their outspoken rhetoric against the Allied countries, but with very little in the way of concrete evidence against them. Even the American envoy Louis G. Dreyfus criticised the arrests made by the Allied forces, stating in a telegram on 18 April 1942 that 'Evidence of guilt is sketchy, vague and circumstantial'.[10] Several deputies, including deputy Tehranchi, refuted the official British narrative about their guilt, and in an impassioned stance during the Majles public session retorted that 'arrested people could not be guilty'.[11] At the

---

6 Jafar Sharif-Emami in an interview with Habib Ladjevardi, New York, NY, 12 May 1983, Iranian Oral History Collection, Harvard University, transcript 3, 3.
7 Khosrow Eqbal has discussed his captivity in Harvard's Oral History Project. See, Khosro Eghbal (sic) in an interview with Zia Sedghi, Washington, 25 June 1985, Iranian Oral History Collection, Harvard University, transcript 1.
8 Ya'qub Tavakkoli ed., *Khaterat-e Jahangir Tafazzoli*, 1376 [1997].
9 Iranian National Library Archives (Henceforth NLAI) 10948-1910, Interior Ministry Files, Confidential letter, 10 Shahrivar 1322/2 September 1943, 3. Other pages in this file also include names of detainees that the *Shahrbani* was required to round up and hand over to the British forces.
10 Cited in Mohammad Gholi Majd, *Iran Under Allied Occupation in World War II: The Bridge to Victory & A Land of Famine*, 2016, 52.
11 Coll 28/44 'Persia. Internal. Fars affairs & Shiraz situation' [124r] (247/843), British Library: India Office Records and Private Papers, IOR/L/PS/12/3447, in Qatar Digital Library, https://www.qdl.qa/archive/81055/ vdc_100044969594.0x000032.

same time, the Iranian press stated forcefully in article after article that the captives were innocent.

It is necessary to note that the colonial occupation was followed by a series of traumatic events that have since defined Iran's modern history. Amir Abbas Hoveyda, who was the longest serving prime minister in Iran's history (1965–1977) and was executed after the revolution, asserted in a television interview that the occupation marked a 'dark era' for Iran.[12] For him, Iran's history of war punctuated the traumatic events of the colonial occupation of August/September 1941, an occupation that brought with it an urgency to respond. This response took the form of various decolonisation efforts, a decolonisation that here refers to the direct and urgent response to rid Iran of occupying forces.

It is not an understatement to say that the colonial occupation had long-lasting consequences in terms of the political and social well-being of Iran. Furthermore, this occupation confirmed the weakness of the Iranian military, the instability of its institutions, and the vulnerability of its people. During this period, mass starvation, plague, and a typhoid pandemic complicated the conditions on the ground for everyone. Believing the situation to be untenable for the Iranian government, Mohammad Ali Forughi, the first and last prime minster of Reza Shah's reign (1925–1941), devised a radical solution for Reza Shah to tender his resignation in a handwritten note only a few days after the occupation. In this reluctantly composed note, Reza Shah named his twenty-one-year-old son, Mohammad Reza, as the successor to his throne on 16 September 1941.[13] Generally considered to be one of the most rational, level-headed, knowledgeable, and credible ministers, who had been instrumental in bringing Reza shah to the throne, the ailing Forughi now manoeuvred to depose Reza Shah and to act, once again, as the kingmaker, this time for his son.[14]

The change of a monarch in Iran was seen as favourable by the British,

---

12 Interview with Amir Abbas Hoveyda, 1974: https://www.youtube.com/watch?v=PH5uCsRXkIw. Also see Amir Ghorbani ed., *Khaterat-e Amir Abbas Hoveyda*, www.Tarikhirani.ir, 1394.
13 The US Minister in Iran (Dreyfus) to the Secretary of State, 19 September 1941, Foreign Relations of the United States Diplomatic Papers, 1941, The British Commonwealth; The Near East and Africa, vol. III, doc. 454.
14 Ervand Abrahamian, *A History of Modern Iran*, 2019, 101.

but the Allies needed to force, and put pressure upon, the sometimes-defiant Iranian government to cooperate with them in arresting some of the most prominent Iranian notables. At the same time, the Allies strenuously sought to preserve their public image by mandating restrictions on the Iranian press, to ensure that journalists were unable to question the occupiers and hold them to account. In more than one instance, Sir Reader Bullard, the British ambassador, asked the Iranian prime minister to suppress the publication of anti-British rhetoric in certain newspapers.[15]

The occupation had thus created a tumultuous and chaotic political climate. Captives experienced this trauma together in tents housing four detainees each in the Sultanabad camp, guarded by the 6th Indian Division.[16] The higher-ranking captives were provided with private quarters and were allowed to have a servant – Ahmad Matin-Daftari, for example, was granted permission to hire an Armenian male servant to accompany him into detention. He also joked that the authorities might provide the detainees with the services of an Armenian mullah to help them with the religious Shia mourning ceremonies.[17]

Various groups viewed the political transformation taking place after the departure of Reza Shah differently. The Tudeh party was founded during the occupation, whereas others were deeply anxious about the uncertainty it caused. Meanwhile, the captives in the Allied camps found themselves victims of an unwanted war fought thousands of kilometres away. The Iranian captives shared a penchant for political independence, an anti-colonial stance, and an impassioned love for their homeland. People who had enjoyed a high social status up to then were suddenly rounded up and treated like violators of the law, with many of them kept in the dark about why they had been detained. Detention orders were handed down to the Iranian government by both British and Soviet officials without giving any

---

15 *Asnadi az Matbu'at-e Iran, 1320–1340*, 1378, 1–23. Several of these documents concern the British ambassador's request to intervene with the press and censor anti-British material.

16 The headquarters of the 6th Indian Division was established at Sultanabad (Arak), by 15 October 1941. See Coll 28/97 (1) 'Persia. Diaries. Tehran Intelligence Summaries.' [324 r] (647/807) Ref: IOR/L/PS/12/3503.

17 Matin-Daftari, *Khaterat*, 218.

tangible reasons for the arrest warrants; a situation that flew in the face of the established laws of the country.

The Colonial Occupation and the Fall of Reza Shah

In August 1941 (a period referred to as *Shahrivar [13]20*), Soviet forces attacked Iran from the north while the British occupied the southern coast of Iran. The Soviet and the British forces joined battle with the much weaker Iranian navy and artillery and it took the invaders no time to sweep aside the Iranian military with the most advanced firepower of the day. From the northern border, the Soviets entered from six points, concentrating their forces in Mashhad, Tabriz, and Rasht, and taking over law enforcement in those areas. To this day, the population of those cities remember Soviet troops walking down their streets, eating ice cream, shopping in stores, and imposing curfews at night. The British attacked and quickly occupied the Persian Gulf ports, inflicting few casualties, and brought with them the Indian 6th Division.

Unbeknownst to the rest of the world, and especially to Iranians, the terms of this blitzkrieg invasion had been formulated by Winston Churchill and Franklin D. Roosevelt in a far-away location, on the turbulent waters of the Atlantic Ocean.[18] The Atlantic Charter included a thorough and meticulous plan to establish a safe, expedient, and essential route to transport arms, ammunitions, and food supplies from the Persian Gulf to the beleaguered Soviet Union. In 1941, Moscow lived under constant threat of being overrun by the rapidly-advancing German army. Fear of the collapse of the Soviets in the face of Operation Barbarossa and the advance of German forces into the Middle East region through the 'Gateway to Caucasia', a long-held Hitlerian dream – or more like fantasy – alarmed the Allies. Given the frightening scenario of Hitler crossing the Caucasus into Iran, however implausible and unrealistic this may have been, drastic

---

18 On Iran and the Atlantic Charter, see Christopher D. O'Sullivan, *FDR and the End of Empire. The World of the Roosevelts*, 2012, 69–87. There are several good scholarly accounts of the invasion of Iran. See, for example, Richard Anthony Stewart, *Sunrise at Abadan: the British and Soviet Invasion of Iran, 1941*, 1988; Mohammad Gholi Majd, *Great Britain and Reza Shah*, 2001; and Ashley Jackson, *Persian Gulf Command: A History of the Second World War in Iran and Iraq*, 2018.

measures had to be taken to prevent the fall of Moscow to Germany, lest Hitler become unstoppable.[19]

To triumph in the war, the 'bridge to victory', the metaphor applied to the route between the Persian Gulf and the Soviet Union, needed to be secured. However, the ingenious plan had left out one major unpredictable element, namely the concession of the Iranian government, and with that the permission of Reza Shah's state to use its land as a wartime 'Persian Corridor'. After failing to gain Reza Shah's consent, the Allies decided to seize control of the 'Persian Corridor' by force. Reza Shah's government viewed the occupation as a clear violation of international law on a par with any other. However, the fear of losing more casualties than those already incurred at the beginning of the invasion left the Iranians with no choice but to bow to the will of the more powerful forces.[20] Accordingly, the Iranian government ordered its army to stand down and to offer no resistance, thus opening the way for an unhindered Allied invasion and with it the suppression of the population by the occupiers.

Two extensive and remarkable studies on counterintelligence in Iran during the war have uncovered the rationale, as well as the anxiety and paranoia, behind the arrests of those taken to Sultanabad (Arak). In *Nazi Secret Warfare in Occupied Persia (Iran)*[21] and *Espionage and Counterintelligence in Occupied Persia (Iran)*,[22] Adrian O'Sullivan presents many accounts of the British activities in Iran. O'Sullivan's books thus offer an essential basis for understanding the Allied mindset in the Middle East during the Second World War. While he concentrates on German operatives and operations, his research provides an invaluable insight into how the Allied forces defined their operations in Iran, regardless of what

---

19 Jennifer Jenkins, 'Iran in the Nazi New Order, 1933–1941', *Iranian Studies* 49/5, 2016, 727–751.

20 Safa' al-din Tabara'iyan ed., *Iran dar Eshqal-e Mottafeqin: Majmu'eh Asnad va Madarek 1318–1324,* 1371. This volume includes a series of national Iranian documents starting from prior to the occupation until afterwards.

21 Adrian O'Sullivan, *Nazi Secret Warfare in Occupied Persia (Iran): The Failure of the German Intelligence Services, 1939–45,* 2014.

22 Adrian O'Sullivan, *Espionage and Counterintelligence in Occupied Persia (Iran): The Success of the Allied Secret Services, 1941–45,* 2015. Also, see Suleyman Seydi, 'Intelligence and Counter-Intelligence Activities in Iran during the Second World War', *Middle Eastern Studies* 46/5, 2010, 733–752.

consequences they may have had for the local population. The war mission superseded any other Allied concern at the time.

Trauma and the Tripartite Agreement

The war descended upon Iran despite the country's declared neutrality. Iranians promptly confronted the trauma of the foreign occupation and opposed it urgently, especially at a time when ruling institutions fell into disarray due to the sudden, unexpected departure of the iron-fisted monarch, the ascent to the throne of an inexperienced ruler, and the incarceration of many prominent leaders. The country's calls for decolonisation were urgent and prompted immediate responses to the trauma of Shahrivar 20 (August 1941).

One of the formal responses to the invasion, namely the drafting of the Tripartite Agreement between Iran, Great Britain, and the Soviet Union, proved to be an arduous, intractable, and controversial task.[23] The negotiations over the treaty took many months before all parties agreed upon its public unveiling. On the day Mohammad Ali Forughi presented the agreement in the Majles on 25 January 1942, an incident took place 'of great political importance' according to the American minister Dreyfus.[24] On this day, a furore broke out in the Majles after a protester threw a rock at the prime minister, who was standing at the podium, only just missing him. Within seconds the attacker jumped onto the podium and physically attacked the old man with his fists and feet before others came to Forughi's aid and restrained the assailant. After the incident, the prime minister was led out of the chambers to collect himself. He returned after thirty minutes and, speaking from the same podium, wistfully said of the assault: 'of course it is regretful, but not surprising'.[25] He continued by expressing a

---

23 Coll 28/109 'Persia. Anglo–Soviet–Persian Treaty of Alliance, 1942.' [2r] (3/442), British Library: India Office Records and Private Papers, IOR/L/PS/12/3520, Qatar Digital Library. https://www.qdl.qa/archive/81055/vdc_100061616228.0x000004.
24 Mohammad Gholi Majd, *Iran Under Allied Occupation in World War II: The Bridge to Victory & A Land of Famine*, 2016, 32.
25 Mashruh-e Mozakerat-e Majles-e Melli, Doreh 13, 5 Bahman 1320/25 January 1942. Majles Library.

generous understanding for those who 'misunderstood' the contents of the treaty and acted 'mistakenly'. But he emphasised that those views should not prevent rational people from taking the right decision, and acting to implement the treaty for 'the good of the country'.[26]

Under the terms of the treaty, the Allied forces undertook to regard their presence in Iran as necessary only for the duration of the war and in no way as a military occupation, even though many in the country considered the situation to be precisely that. In the treaty, the Allies also pledged 'to respect' the country's 'territorial integrity' and 'political leadership', and promised to leave Iran six months after the end of the war – a pledge that was ultimately left unfulfilled. Allied forces promised to alleviate the economic challenges arising from Iran's enforced participation in the war. In return, Iran agreed to secure rewards and privileges for the Allied forces to use its roads and railroads to transport military artillery and other necessary supplies.

The Tripartite Agreement – concluded on 29 January 1942 – sought to ensure that the occupation would not be prolonged, ostensibly to prevent Iran from losing control of its independence and access to its resources for a long period. In short, it offered a vague assurance that occupation would not result in colonisation. This agreement also made Iran an ally of the Allied forces, despite its decidedly neutral stance at the beginning of the war. The Iranian Majles had requested the addition of a clause emphasising that the Allied forces should not be allowed to coerce Iran into war, nor be allowed to request the participation of Iranian troops in the war. As predicted, on 9 September 1943, Iran declared war against Nazi Germany. This was done despite the stipulations in the Tripartite Agreement that allowed Iran to maintain its neutral position. Unwittingly, the treaty had dragged Iran into the war, and forced it to abandon its former neutrality.

Parliamentarians had also requested that several revisions be made to the Tripartite Agreement. These suggestions included requests to add clauses about expenses incurred by the Allied forces in Iran, which would mandate the occupiers to pay these costs so that Iranians would not shoulder them. Furthermore, the Majles concluded that the treaty had certain

---

26 Mashruh-e Mozakerat-e Majles-e Melli, Doreh 13, 5 Bahman 1320 /25 January 1942.

benefits for Iran, which they hoped would continue even after the end of the war. In spite of these amendments, the revised treaty still faced opposition in the Majles. As a seasoned and respected politician, Foroughi had managed to gain the support of most of Iran's parliamentarians. Even so, a small number expressed their mistrust of the treaty, foremost among them Habibollah Naubakht, the deputy from Fasa, who protested vociferously against the ratification of the Tripartite Agreement. He argued in erudite, flowery language against the agreement, and his speech was later published in various newspapers. Despite the meticulous revisions, Naubakht expressed his dissatisfaction with the negotiated terms and voted against the ratification of the protracted treaty, alongside a handful of other deputies.[27]

The vehemence of the opposition sent ripples beyond the Majles, prompting Axis sympathisers in the country to make contact with the parliamentary deputy from Fasa. Opposition to the ratification in the Majles was interpreted by many – especially by German agents hiding in Iran – as a clear indication of Naubakht's anti-British stance. They therefore extrapolated from this that he must have pro-German sympathies. In his private diaries, the young fugitive German SS agent Franz Mayer recorded that 'the deputy Naubakht was the one who protested most', highlighting Naubakht as a person of interest in his pro-German agenda.[28] Yet while Naubakht's dissent seemed to some to be a sign of his pro-German stance, in reality his anti-colonial diatribe was not necessarily an expression of support for the Axis powers. In spite of Naubakht's protests, the Tripartite Agreement was finally signed by Ali Soheili, M. Smirnoff, and Reader Bullard, the representatives of the three governments, on 29 January 1942. The Americans became party to the treaty several months later. Although Naubakht's opposition in the Majles seemed a somewhat inconsequential event at the time, its broadcast and publication brought him to the attention of Axis supporters in Iran and triggered a series of new arrests.

---

27 Majles, 5 Bahman 1320/25 January 1942.
28 Franz Mayer, Comments on the Diary and Documents, 1943, British National Archives, KV 2-/1482 – 1–7 files include important commentary on Iranian nationals targeted by the German intelligence officers in Iran.

Naubakht's Opposition Speech and the Axis Approach

The Japanese legation in Iran viewed Naubakht's speech as a sign that he could be persuaded to work on behalf of the Axis in Iran. Accordingly, a Japanese delegation paid a semi-informal visit to Naubakht's house shortly after his public opposition to the Tripartite Agreement, and only two weeks before their official expulsion from the country. No doubt the Japanese delegation wished to recruit Naubakht as a pro-Axis ally in their absence, and even suggested that he meet clandestinely with a German agent, which Naubakht refused to do at the time. According to British archival documents, in April 1943, the Japanese intelligence services reported that its embassy gave two wireless telegraph sets and all their connections to Franz Mayer, the German agent who they wanted Naubakht to meet. These two American-made sets were used to try to communicate with Ankara.[29]

While Naubakht claims that he refused to meet with the German agent, Mayer made sure that he ran into the parliamentarian at an opportune moment on the street. As we now know, many Germans living in Iran after the invasion were shipped off to internment camps in Australia.[30] However, a handful of Germans – Franz Mayer, Friedrich Kümmel, Roman Gamotta, Berthold Schulze-Holthus, and Constantin Jakob (Kassakowski) – went underground at the time when their compatriots were evacuated and interned. At this time, Mayer – who was renowned as a 'master of disguise', using soot to darken his complexion and dressing in rags to masquerade as a vagrant on the streets of Tehran and Isfahan – formed a friendship with Naubakht. Mayer met him on a number of occasions and solicited his help in securing the safe passage of his countrymen, who were now considered fugitives in Iran. As Naubakht represented Fasa in the south, which was not too far from the rebellious Boir Ahmadi, Lur, Mamasani, and Qashqai tribes, he was able to facilitate the flight from

---

29 British National Archives, KV /-2/1486, Schulze-Holthus, Pirwanka, Harbers, Kurmes, 6 June 1944. This file contains multiple documents and reports about Schulze-Holthus's activities during the war in Iran.

30 Pedram Khosrownejad has interviewed their descendants and curated exhibits about Germans who were forced to leave Iran for Australia. See, https://www. german-civilians-of-persia-wwii.com/. This project concerns the life stories of Germans living in Iran before the occupation and those who were taken to Australia's concentration camps during the war.

the country of Berthold Schulze-Holthus, the *Abwehr* (German military foreign intelligence service) agent who had acted as the German consul in Tabriz, into southern Qashqai territories. In fact, Naser Khan Qashqai, who had worked with the Germans during the First World War, offered employment to Schulze-Holthus at this time.[31] In turn, Naubakht and his friends provided transportation from Tehran to Firuzabad for the German fugitive to join the Qashqais.

It took British authorities almost a whole year to put the puzzle together, however imperfectly; they duly arrested Naubakht, notwithstanding his immunity as a Majles deputy, took him to the internment camp in Sultanabad (Arak), and held him in solitary confinement.[32] In a letter from Bullard to British Foreign Secretary Anthony Eden on 22 September 1943, the British envoy wrote:

> In order to test the sincerity of the Prime Minister's recent offer to
> me to arrest anybody against whom I might be able to produce proper
> evidence, I at the same time in a letter of the 5th August requested
> him to withdraw Naubakht's parliamentary immunity to enable him
> to be arrested and sent to Sultanabad for detention and interrogation
> in accordance with the Anglo–Persian Agreement of 1942. After the
> usual delays the interpellation was finally fixed for the 24th August,
> but Naubakht, undoubtedly scenting danger and realising how weak
> his hand had become, particularly in view of the arrest of certain
> Germans in Tehran, failed to put in an appearance. The Government
> did not feel themselves strong enough to ask the Majles to remove his
> immunity, and it is now reported that he and his son have fled to the
> Shiraz district.

According to a British report: 'Because of the late nature of the arrest

---

31 G. F. Magee, *The Tribes of Fars*, 1948, 17. For more about Nasir Khan, see Abbas Milani, *Eminent Persians: The Men and Women Who Made Modern Iran, 1941–1979*, vol. 2, 2008, 261–266.

32 Ext5001/41 'PERSIA – INTERNAL (Miscellaneous dispatches).' [80v] (160/248). Ref: IOR/L/PS/12/564. On Naubakht's immunity: the British requested to withdraw Naubakht's immunity so he could be arrested and sent to Sultanabad (Arak). The British knew that these arrests would 'annoy' the American government.

of Habibollah Naubakht, he remained in solitary confinement for a longer time while others were either released or sent to other internment camps.'[33]

Prior to the arrests of Naubakht and Franz Mayer, law enforcement had detained Friedrich Kümmel, an Austrian geologist who had technical command over Iran's railroads, along with his accomplice Erwin Weissrock, who was arrested on his way to Turkey. While Kümmel denied under interrogation having worked for the Nazi government, and supposedly maintained a calm composure throughout, the British authorities were fully aware of his membership of the Nazi party and his training as a saboteur before being posted to Iran. In his confession, Kümmel divulged that he had been hiding in a well in the German summer legation in Shemiran for a considerable period of time.[34] The British document states:

> [Kuemel] [sic] went to Persia originally to carry out certain geological surveys on behalf of the Germans. It was while he was in Persia that he was recruited for intelligence work.[35]

Persian documents in the Iranian Ministry of the Interior's law enforcement archives include a letter written to the foreign ministry indicating Kümmel's arrest in Kashan in the spring of that year, before being taken to the Sultanabad camp.[36] Nonetheless, the German/Austrian geologist continued to deny his involvement with the Nazis.

British documents reveal:

> When the British Security Authorities began to investigate subversive activities at the beginning of January 1942, an apparently philanthropic body called 'The Workman's Aid Society' almost immediately came

---

33 A secret telegram on 7 September 1943, Coll 28/109 'Persia. Anglo–Soviet–Persian Treaty of Alliance, 1942', British Library: India Office Records and Private Papers, IOR/L/PS/12/3520, in Qatar Digital Library: https://www.qdl.qa/archive/81055/vdc_100000000648.0x000050 [accessed 15 May 2022].
34 British National Archives, KV 2/1473, Kuemel, Friedrich, document 85.
35 British National Archives, KV 2/1473, Kuemel, Friedrich.
36 NLAI 5570-4400, 9 Mehr 1320/1 October 1941, 29. Confidential letter from the interior ministry to the foreign ministry; and British National Archives, KV 2/1473, Kuemel, Friedrich. Kümmel was interrogated by CSDIS, PAIFORCE in 1942 and this file includes important information about the geologist's role in Iran.

to their notice, especially as Franz Mayer was said to have attended its meetings. One of its members, Mahmud Mushaver, was a contact of Abbas Mazda who was already under suspicion. Another member, Habibollah Kheltash, was found to be hiding the German Friedrich Kumel [sic] in his house. The latter was eventually arrested along with his collaborators, Erwin Weissrock, and certain Persian accomplices. Their interrogations revealed that Franz Mayer, Berthold Schultze and Roman Gamotta were in hiding and that they were called by certain code names in an enemy organization.[37]

The British also found that Germans who took refuge in the German Legation were adamant that within a month or two German troops would enter Persia and that they would once again be free. So confident were they of this outcome that some even paid their house rent in advance. Others went into hiding to await the great day.[38]

After preliminary interrogations in the Sultanabad (Arak) camp, Friedrich Kümmel was later transferred to Palestine and then to Egypt as an internee. British interrogators wrote that 'Friedrich Kumel is mentioned throughout this report [Mayer's report] and proves he was not only spying but was interested in sabotage on behalf of the Germans in Persia.'[39] But Kümmel never broke down under interrogation, and all we know of his activity was conveyed by Franz Mayer.[40]

As a fugitive himself, Franz Mayer anxiously tried to locate Friedrich Kümmel and Erwin Weissrock, whom he believed were in hiding somewhere in Iran. He was unaware that they had already been captured in the

37 Coll 28/109 'Persia. Anglo–Soviet–Persian Treaty of Alliance, 1942', British Library: India Office Records and Private Papers, IOR/L/PS/12/3520, in Qatar Digital Library: https://www.qdl.qa/archive/81055/vdc_100000000648. 0x000050 [accessed 15 May 2022].
38 Coll 28/109 'Persia. Anglo–Soviet–Persian Treaty of Alliance, 1942', British Library: India Office Records and Private Papers, IOR/L/PS/12/3520, in Qatar Digital Library: https://www.qdl.qa/archive/81055/vdc_100000000648.0x000050 [accessed 15 May 2022].
39 British National Archives, KV 2/1482, Franz Mayer (comments on diary and documents), May 1943. In this document Kümmel's code name is given as Leo.
40 British National Archives, KV 2/1482, Franz Mayer (comments on diary and documents), May 1943.

spring of 1942 and taken to the internment camp at Sultanabad. Kümmel provided his captors with several Iranian names, the same ones that he had previously given to Mayer. After receiving this information, British authorities formally requested that the Iranian government detain these individuals. In fact, the first set of people arrested in Sultanabad (Arak) were detained in conjunction with Kümmel, who was arrested in 1942, and handed over to the British authorities in July of that year.[41]

German fugitives tried to forge links with Iranian nationalists, many of whom had no clue about their political significance for the Germans, nor did they consider that they were cooperating with Germans, or saboteurs for that matter. Franz Mayer had also assiduously sought out those individuals out on Kümmel's list, based on the scientist's instructions, and met with several of the Iranians on Kümmel's list, with the help of his Iranian point man Hessam al-din Vaziri from Irantours. It would later be revealed that Vaziri acted as a double agent for the Germans as well as the Soviets.[42] British authorities requested the detention of named individuals, even before they discovered Mayer's special notebook with codes and names of Iran's potential nationalist factions.

The discovery of Mayer's documents, left behind after his location was divulged, was a significant coup for the British officials. Their informant, Moses Gasparian, an Armenian accomplice of Mayer's, divulged the whereabouts of the German agent to the British. According to the reports, Moses Gasparian engaged in a gunfight with Mayer in the middle of the historic city of Isfahan, but Mayer fled the scene before he could be captured.[43] Gasparian, however, revealed the location of Mayer's notebooks, very odd material for a spy on the run to keep. In the notebooks, Mayer kept detailed information about his meetings with several named personalities, and he wove stories about them, which sometimes seemed more like fantasy than reality.[44]

---

41 British National Archives, KV 2/1482, Franz Mayer (comments on diary and documents), May 1943.
42 British National Archives, KV-2/1317, Mohammed Hussein Hissam Vaziri, 13 January 1943, 41.
43 British National Archives, KV 2/1477 (files 1–3), Franz Mayer and his codes; and O'Sullivan, *Nazi Secret Warfare in Occupied Persia (Iran)*, 110.
44 Franz Mayer uses the code name Fathullah for Naubakht.

The Iranian Government and the Qashqais

While the British government requested that the Iranian government detain and hand over German fugitives and their alleged accomplices, the Iranian government remained sceptical as to the legality of such detention.[45] In fact, Sardar Radsar (Adib al-Saltanah), the maternal uncle of the future prime minister Amir Abbas Hoveyda, who was appointed as Chief of the Imperial Persian Police Force during the war (replacing Rokn al-din Mokhtari), wrote to his supervisors to question the legality of the arrests. The letter from the Chief of Police Authorities, Sar Pas Radsar, to the interior ministry reads:

> Recently Soviet or British political or military officials in provinces request through governors to arrest individuals and dispatch them to other places, and police officials, based on the requests they have from governors, have executed orders and dispatch individuals escorting them to the centre while the reason for their arrest and dispatch is not certain and the main office of police cannot arrest them without legal adjudication and is uncertain what to do and if they make the arrest it is possible that the prosecutor would protest and if they free them it is possible that the Soviet and British representatives find difficulties. I ask you to issue what you would order to do in such instances, so that they would obey those orders.[46]

As many of the detainees on the list were quite familiar with the judicial process and knew that the police could not legally detain them without an official arrest warrant signed by an Iranian prosecutor, subduing many of them remained a challenge for the police, who themselves did not know whom to obey.[47] The interior ministry also received letters saying that

---

45 Coll 28/118 'Persia. Shiraz – Consular diaries.' [57r] (115/728), British Library: India Office Records and Private Papers, IOR/L/PS/12/3531, in Qatar Digital Library. https://www.qdl.qa/en/archive/81055/vdc_100063052005.0x000074.
46 NLAI 10948-1910, Interior Ministry Files, confidential letter, 10 Shahrivar 1322/2 September 1943, 5.
47 Coll 28/118 'Persia. Shiraz – Consular diaries.' [92r] (185/728), British Library: India Office Records and Private Papers, IOR/L/PS/12/3531, in Qatar Digital Library [accessed 8 July 2020], 76.

such arrests were motivated by personal vendettas rather than security concerns.[48] Several on the list resisted arrest or fled Iranian police officers, and some even escaped from the Sultanabad camp.[49]

On 5 September 1942, Anthony Eden wrote to Sir Reader Bullard: 'Sir, The Soviet Ambassador discussed with me on the 1st of September the difficulties arising from our recent request to the Persian Government that they should arrest some forty-five suspected Axis agents and hand them over to our military authorities for internment.' He continued:

> I gave M. Maisky some account of the back history of this question, explaining that our previous experience had shown only too clearly that, if we allowed suspected Axis agents to be guarded by the Persian police alone, many of them succeeded in escaping. When it became necessary to request the Persian Government to arrest these forty-five suspects, we therefore asked that they should be handed over to the British military authorities for internment. It was true that the Persian Government, while agreeing to hand over the foreign suspects, had objected to sending Persian subjects to be interned at Arak, and that the Persian Prime Minister had even spoken of resigning. But you had reported on the 29th of August that the Prime Minister and Minister for Foreign Affairs had both assured you that they accepted our view and agreed that our military authorities should begin to make arrangements for the reception of the suspects at Arak.[50]

Allied forces were especially concerned about the security of the southern areas, where rebellious tribes could jeopardise or disrupt the so-called 'bridge to victory' mission. Naubakht, for whom Mayer used the code name 'Fathullah', had provided the link between Berthold Schulze-Holthus and Naser Khan Solati, the Qashqai khan, whose father Solat

---

48 NLAI 10948-1910, Interior Ministry Files, Confidential letter, 28.
49 Coll 28/109 'Persia. Anglo–Soviet–Persian Treaty of Alliance, 1942.' [2r]
(3/442), British Library: India Office Records and Private Papers, IOR/L/
PS/12/3520, Qatar Digital Library, https://www.qdl.qa/archive/
81055/vdc_100061616228.0x000004. Sajjad Ra'i Golujeh ed., *Asnadi az Eshghal-e Iran dar Jang-e Jahani-ye Dovvom*, 1389, 167.
50 Coll 28/109, confidential letter from Eden to Sir Reader Bullard, 5 September 1942.

al-Dawlah had been killed in prison before the war, and who had an axe to grind with the Iranian government. As mentioned earlier, Naubakht introduced Schulze-Holthus to Naser Khan, who in turn offered a security job to the German *Abwehr* agent. The Qashqais still remembered the German diplomat and spy Wilhelm Wassmuss from the First World War, who supported them throughout the conflict, supplied them with arms, and became known as 'Wassmuss the Persian'. Welcoming their foreign guest, the Qashqais put themselves in a precarious political position by supporting Schulze-Holthus and later a group of German parachutists. Tribal rules and borders were different from those drawn by the Iranian government, and the conflict in the south could potentially jeopardise the Allied operations. The Qashqais were not alone, but the Boir Ahmadis, Mamassanis, and other Lur and Kurdish tribes in the south each had centuries of rights and privileges in the region to protect, and they each claimed the right of rule in those territories, many of which were fought over throughout Reza Shah's rule. Now, with the departure of Reza Shah, the southern tribes saw an opportunity to reclaim those lands. In the British documents, the report on Naubakht details this relationship:

> The opposition of the Qashqai tribe to the Government grew in the summer and autumn of 1942 and the tribal question was heatedly debated in the Majlis. Qavam-es-Sultaneh, who was then Prime Minister, sent for Naubakht and asked him to go down to the South to persuade Nasir Khan Qashqai to come to Tehran to negotiate a settlement. He was also to arrange the surrender, by the Qashqai, of certain arms they had recently taken from Government troops. Naubakht was sceptical of his chances of success, but eventually agreed and went to Firuzabad to see Nasir Khan. He stayed there a week and made a trip to Shiraz in connection with his mission.[51]

---

51 British National Archives, KV 2/3405, Habibullah Naubakht, 15, Appendix A. Interrogation report in Persian 6–7 July 1944 by Capt. R Thistlewaite and Lieut. H.G. Navarra. This interrogation report includes Naubakht's meeting with the Japanese, with Mayer, meeting in the house of Sayid Naghibzadeh Mushayekh, Naubakht's acquaintance with Kashani, the attempt to bring Naubakht and Zahedi together, the journeys to the South, Mayer's arrest and Naubakht's flight, and other Iranians incriminated by Naubakht, among other issues.

In his memoir, *Daybreak in Iran*, Berthold Schulze-Holthus recounts how the southern tribes – the Qashqais, the Boir Ahmadis, and the Mamasanis – fought against the Allied forces and the Iranian government to keep their hold on certain territories.[52] In this detailed and colourful book, the author provides a remarkable semi-fictional account of his days as a fugitive in Iran, beginning from his life as a German Consul in Tabriz and as a fugitive who took refuge with the Qashqais during the war. His accounts of the British security forces after his arrest in 1943 seem authentic and believable, although years later they discovered that Schulze-Holthus had managed to conceal his real name throughout his interrogations, possibly along with many other secrets.[53] Schulze-Holthus writes of his escape from the Swedish embassy in Tehran on the day that he was to be handed over to the Allied forces, going underground in the Shemshak/ Meygun area, his days in hiding with his wife on Qazvin Street, his wife's daring escape to Turkey, and his acquaintance with Naubakht, as well as the time he spent working for the Qashqai, the arrival of the Anton parachutist group, and finally their arrest, which led to him being handed over to the British forces at Sultanabad (Arak) camp.

This highly romanticised account of Schulze-Holthus's fugitive days in Iran was ghostwritten by a German professor (Paul Weymar) after the war, in 1954, but the raw material for it can be found in the pages of his interrogation now kept in the British archives.[54] Schulze-Holthus, the former German consul in Tabriz, who had led a group of German parachutist saboteurs with the Qashqai tribes, remained a valuable asset for the British, and in order to continue his interrogation he was transferred from Sultanabad (Arak) to the Monastery Camp near Jerusalem, where he was detained alongside Franz Mayer and General Fazlollah Zahedi.

---

52 Berthold Schulze-Holthus, *Daybreak in Iran: A Story of the German Intelligence Service*, 1954.
53 British National Archives, KV 2/1478, (File 2) Mayer, Franz.
54 On Schulze-Holthus, see British National Archives files KV 2/1485 and KV 2/1486. There are several documents here pertaining to Schulze-Holthus's activities in the south.

Operation Pongo: Fazlollah Zahedi Kidnapped and Taken to Sultanabad (Arak)

Fazlollah Zahedi was captured and detained in Sultanabad (Arak) as a fifth-columnist, even though he held one of the highest-ranking military positions as Head Commander of Forces (troop 9) in Isfahan. Zahedi was one of the last appointments made by Reza Shah before his resignation, just before he left for Isfahan. General Zahedi (Bassir Divan), who had been educated and trained in the Cossack Brigade, had been appointed to extremely sensitive positions during Reza Shah's rule: he was the chief of police in Mashhad during the Gowharshad massacre (1935), and before that he served as chief of police in Tehran. Zahedi had also married into the influential Qajar family of the Pirniyas, but soon divorced. The British SAS officer Fitzroy Maclean wrote a suspenseful account of his mission to travel from Baghdad to Isfahan. His primary purpose was to track down Zahedi, kidnap him, and hand him over to the British forces.

According to Maclean's account, he gained entry to Zahedi's house by posing as a British envoy, but within minutes drew his revolver, stuck it in Zahedi's side, and forced him to walk to his car without saying a word. The rationale for his abduction was that, following the Anglo-Soviet invasion, Zahedi's role as commander in the south of Iran, outside the control of British and Soviet forces, and in proximity to many influential tribal chiefs, would have placed him in a vital location vis-à-vis the so-called Persian Gulf Corridor. Any tribal instability, local insurgency, or arms supply to hostile tribes could have jeopardised the lend-lease supply corridor. The Allied forces had also received intelligence that the general had met German agents in Isfahan, negotiated with tribal chiefs, and hoarded substantial amounts of wheat. These actions and his general hostility towards the occupation were interpreted as pro-German, and caused the British to suspect him of subversive activities.

Fitzroy Maclean's superiors told him that there were signs that trouble might be brewing in southern Iran. They were worried about potential uprisings by the Qashqai or Bakhtiari tribes, fomented by German agents who were thought to be living among them, just as they had in 1916, when tribal rebellions caused a great deal of difficulty for the British occupiers. The main concern of the British was that the rebellion might cause the supply route to the Persian Gulf to be cut. As Maclean explained

There was also discontent in Isfahan and other towns, caused by
the hoarding of grain by speculators, which we were unable to
prevent. This discontent might at any moment flare up into open
rebellion. Worse still, if there were trouble, the Persian troops in south
Persia were likely to take the side of the rioters.[55]

The British were convinced that General Zahedi, whom they believed
was acting in conjunction with the tribal leaders, was playing a key role
in encouraging insurrection.[56] They saw Isfahan being placed in a precarious position. The nearest British troops were two hundred miles north of
the city, in Qom. Any movement of Allied troops in south Iran could have
caused an uprising and would have been in violation of their agreement
with the Iranian government, but the British believed that if they 'allowed
events to take their course, the results would be equally disastrous'. It was
necessary 'to nip the trouble in the bud', as Maclean recalls being told
when he was charged with the task of removing General Zahedi. The idea
was to seize Zahedi before he and his men could do anything to threaten
the British position. Only two conditions were imposed on Maclean: first,
Zahedi must be taken alive; and second, his arrest should be carried out
without creating a disturbance.[57]

Over dinner, the British Consul John Gault provided Maclean with
some information about General Zahedi. He said, 'though pleasant to me,
[he] was... a really bad lot: a bitter enemy of the Allies, a man of unpleas-
ant personal habits, and, by virtue of his grain-hoarding activities, a source
of popular discontent and an obstacle to the efficient administration of
south Persia.'[58] The consul had heard that Zahedi was plotting with both
the Germans and the tribal leaders, as one of his opening moves was a plan
to liquidate the British consul in Isfahan, a piece of news that completely

---

55 Fitzroy Maclean, *Eastern Approaches*, 1949, 214.

56 Maclean, *Eastern Approaches*, 214. According to the senior British officer,
Henry Maitland 'Jumbo' Wilson, the decision to arrest Zahedi was his and achieved
its goal: '... the possibility of others being treated in a like manner put a complete
damper on any further activities of the plotters.' Henry Maitland Wilson, *Eight years
overseas, 1939–1945*, 146.

57 Maclean, *Eastern Approaches*, 214.

58 Maclean, *Eastern Approaches*, 214.

'outweighed all the General's personal charm, as far as he was concerned'.[59]

To execute his secret mission, Maclean sent a telegram with instructions on 'Operation Pongo', the name given to the operation to take out Zahedi, asking 'to be given authority to assume for the occasion a Brigadier's badges of rank', and 'a platoon of British infantry to lend a hand in case anything went wrong'. The plan was 'approved in principle' and the captain was instructed to go ahead with preparations. However, Maclean also scathingly condemned the British authorities with his claim that what 'stuck in the throats of the well-trained staff officers at the other end' of his 'highly unorthodox programme' was the fact that it 'was not (repeat: not) possible, they said, to authorise an officer of [his] age and seniority to masquerade, even for a day, as a Brigadier.'[60] Accordingly, the British sent an actual Brigadier (and not a fake one) to travel from Qom for the 'highly unorthodox' Trojan Horse plan.

The captain also extracted from the authorities, 'permission to shoot the General' should he be 'armed and resist capture'. Maclean narrates that

> After a copious lunch we took our places in the staff car which was flying
> a large Union Jack. A reliable N.C.O., armed to the teeth, occupied the
> seat next the driver, while Guardsman Duncan, and a Seaforth Highlander,
> both carrying tommy-guns, crouched in the luggage compartment at
> the back, under a tarpaulin. Gault followed in his own car.

In front of Zahedi's house, there were two trucks, 'their tarpaulin covers concealing the battle-hungry Seaforths'.[61]

Maclean arrived in front of Zahedi's mansion. 'At the gate, the Persian sentry was deep in conversation with Laurence Lockhart, a Persian linguist from RAF Intelligence,'[62] whose services he had enlisted for the occasion. For Maclean, everything had gone according to plan. They drove up to the house, when a couple of minutes later, General Zahedi appeared, 'a dapper figure in a tight-fitting grey uniform and highly polished boots.' When he

---

59 Maclean, *Eastern Approaches*, 215.
60 Maclean, *Eastern Approaches*, 218.
61 Maclean, *Eastern Approaches*, 220.
62 Maclean, *Eastern Approaches*, 220.

entered the room, he found himself looking down the barrel of Maclean's Colt automatic. 'There was no advantage in prolonging a scene which might easily become embarrassing,' the captain had thought. Maclean then asked the general 'to put his hands up' informing him that he had 'instructions to arrest him and that, if he made any noise or attempt at resistance, he would be shot'. Then he took away his pistol and 'hustled him through the window into the car which was waiting outside with the engine running'.

Maclean was surprised that there had been no bodyguards, but as

they passed the guardroom, the sentry interrupted their conversation to present arms, and the General, sitting bolt upright, with the pistol pressed against his ribs and Duncan breathing down his neck, returned the salute. The whole convoy swept at a brisk pace over the bridge and into the main avenue leading out of Isfahan.[63]

They passed large barracks full of Iranian troops in Isfahan, and to their good fortune 'the telephone wire from the town had duly been cut by the wire-cutting party, and there was no sign of the alarm having been given.' Zahedi, who was a military man, kept his calm, and while still sitting 'bolt upright', he assured his captors that there were good explanations for all aspects of his conduct, which might at first sight have seemed suspicious. However, the officers were only tasked with arresting him; they were not interested in his explanations at that time, so they proceeded to take him to the Allied internment camp at Sultanabad (Arak) before transferring him to the Monastery Camp in Palestine.

Operation Pongo successfully abducted one of the most feared, decorated, and powerful Iranian officials, and took him not only out of Isfahan, to Arak, but eventually entirely out of Iran and into British internment in Palestine. A man who had been known to be pro-British had now been arrested by the British as an enemy combatant on the unproven suspicion of working as a fifth columnist, an accusation that even his enemies would not have found credible.

---

63 Maclean, *Eastern Approaches*, 220.

Sayyed 'Abol-Qassem Kashani: The Grand Mufti of Jerusalem and the Failed Coup in Iraq by Rashid Ali al-Guilani

Fazlollah Zahedi had already left the camp when Sayyed 'Abol-Qassem Kashani, the only religious authority to be detained, was arrested. Out of respect for his religious status and his popularity, the British held Kashani in better quarters in Sultanabad, despite what they referred to as the 'crafty tricks' he had played escaping from them.[64] The British official had reported months earlier that

> Deputy Naubakht and his son are now known to be with Qashgai.
> Mullah Kashani still at large. [I] have authorized our security
> authorities to arrest them if they can. Police allowed Kashani to escape
> by a crafty trick.[65]

In fact, Kashani evaded arrest by hiding around the village of Ushan in the north of Tehran but was eventually arrested near Golabdareh, Darband/ Pas Qale.[66]

Until recently, the real reason for Kashani's arrest was shrouded in mystery. However, the declassified British archives offer some clarity. Kashani was arrested by the British because of the discovery of signed letters in possession of Franz Mayer, who had the intention of dispatching them to his contacts in Germany. Kashani had written to Rashid Ali al-Gailani, the toppled prime minister of Iraq, and Amin al-Hosseini, the ex-Grand Mufti of Jerusalem, after they had left their refuge in Tehran. Both had been accepted as political refugees by Reza Shah shortly before his resignation, and Kashani had found an ally in spreading the religious word beyond the borders of Iran. But both refugees had strong

---

64 QDL 81055 A secret telegram on 7 September 1943. Ext 5001/41 'PERSIA – INTERNAL (Miscellaneous despatches).' [80v] (160/248), British Library: India Office Records and Private Papers, IOR/L/PS/12/564, in Qatar Digital Library, https://www.qdl.qa/archive/81055/vdc_100042321849.0x0000a1 [accessed 15 May 2022].

65 Sir Reader Bullard, 7 September 1943, 'Anglo–Soviet–Persian Treaty of Alliance, 1942', IOR/L/PS/12/3520.

66 Golujeh ed., *Asnadi az Eshghal-e Iran*, 169. Document no. 63/6, Pasyar Seyf's secret letter to Prime Minister on 27 Khordad 1323/17 June 1944.

pro-German and anti-British ideologies, which made Kashani guilty by association.[67]

They were especially alarmed when they discovered a letter written by Kashani professing his allegiance. The translation of the letter was reproduced in Kashani's file, and read:

Esteemed Grand Mufti and Esteemed Mr. Rashid Ali:

Since our aims are the same, you occupy a special place in my heart. We also are working here at the same thing and hope that we shall reach the goal as we perceive it. If there is anything to be sent to Mesopotamia, please say so and I will have the orders sent there through my special messenger. We all hope that Islam and the Islam[ic] world will be freed from the yoke of our unmerciful foes through your tireless endeavour and our spirit of sacrifice and that we shall all once more achieve true freedom.

Abol-Qassem-al-Hosseini- al-Kashani.[68]

Despite repeated denials from Kashani that he had written the letter, the British believed that its content provided sufficient evidence of Kashani's pro-German activism in Persia.

The terms of the agreement setting up the internment camp at Sultanabad stipulated that the interrogation of Persian suspects should be carried out by a joint Anglo–Persian commission. Due to the sensitive nature of the arrests of Sayyed 'Abol-Qassam Kashani, whose detention had caused the bazaar to close in protest, and Naubakht, who was a sitting parliamentarian with immunity, the British made sure that they worked together with the Iranian officials. It was important for them to convince the Iranian officials of the detainees' guilt in order to justify the arrests. The British reports about these two detainees are very telling and amusing,

---

67 Ext 5001/41 'PERSIA – INTERNAL (Miscellaneous dispatches).' Ref: IOR/L/ PS/12/564.
68 British National Archives, KV 2-/1482, Franz Mayer, Comments on the Diary and Documents, 1943, 4.

even contemptuous, containing as they do several ad hoc comments such as describing Naubakht's entering the room 'as proud as a peacock'. Likewise, when describing Kashani's agility, the writer compares him to 'Rumpelstiltskin', in reference to the way in which he jumped off his chair to leave the room.[69]

At first, Kashani flatly denied that he had written letters to the pro-German leader of Iraq and the ex-Mufti of Jerusalem, but under pressure, and in front of the Iranian officials, he admitted to having signed the letters himself. Based on what they viewed as damning evidence of pro-German activity, the British Security Office decided to hand Kashani over to the Soviets in Rasht for further interrogation. In a memo sent on 27 October 1944, the Defence Security Office (DSO) wrote:

Closer collaboration in matters of mutual interest is reported between the Soviet and British Security authorities. The anti-British mullah [Sayid Abul Qasim] Kashani, and the deputy Habibullah Naubakht, at present held in Sultanabad, are to be handed over to the Soviet authorities for interrogation at Rasht, after which they will be returned to British custody. The chief Soviet interrogating officer from Rasht has held brief interrogations of four Persians in the internment camp at Tehran, in the presence of officers of C.I.C.I.[70]

Interrogation documents in the British archives show why the Allied forces were sensitive about Kashani's interactions. As a member of the clergy with stature and popularity, his contact with the Iraqi Rashid al-Gailani and the ex-Mufti of Jerusalem may have had the potential to generate a wave of popular sympathy for the German cause. But was it the case that Kashani harboured pro-German sympathies? He did not confess to anything of that sort, and later in Malayer, he once again denied his authorship of the two letters, describing them as forgeries. However, Kashani's affiliations were called into question after the war, as reported in a top-secret memo from the Defence Security Office, C.I.C.I. Persia, Tehran, dated 15 February 1945:

---

69 KV 2/3405, Habibullah Naubakht.
70 KV 2/3405, Habibullah Naubakht.

The Russians may think we have suborned Naubakht and Kashani and that we have plans to use them in the future. In this connection, it is of interest that rumours circulated some time ago among members of the left-wing Tudeh party that the British were on the point of discarding Sayid Zia and using Kashani in his place. Recently, also, Sosnin protested to us about the articles Danesh Naubakht was publishing in his paper '*Aftab*'. These could be interpreted as being pro-British but anti-Russian. The Russians may therefore be blackening Naubakht and Kashani in case we intend to use them… Another explanation may be that the Russians themselves have suborned Naubakht and Kashani during their interrogation at Rasht. The possibility of this occurring was mentioned in paragraph 16 of our last report. In this case, the remarks in the '*Pravda*' article, the rumours among Tudeh members and the complaint Danesh Naubakht might all be so much camouflage.[71]

Interestingly, Kashani was elected to the Fourteenth Majles while he was in Allied captivity, but his *itibarnamah* (accreditation) was disqualified as he remained in Allied confinement until the very end.

One question worth considering here is how history might have changed had Kashani not been pursued by the Allied forces during the war. Would he have become the spiritual leader of a militant group such as Fadayian Islam, or any other subversive group, for that matter, if he had not been incarcerated? We will never know. But what we do know is that Kashani's subsequent trajectory in life was strongly influenced by the occupation. These experiences led him to adopt strong anti-colonial sentiments. In the years following his return to Iran, he became a spiritual mentor of Ruhollah Khomeini. After the Iranian Revolution, a major highway crossing in Tehran was named after Kashani, paying tribute to his revolutionary and anti-colonial stance, but for a variety of reasons, including the question of whether he supported or undermined Mohammad Mosaddeq, Kashani is still a controversial figure in contemporary Iran.

---

71 KV 2/3405, Habibullah Naubakht, 34.

The Railroad and Ja'far Sharif-Emami

Alongside Kashani and Naubakht, several high-ranking railroad officials were held by the British in the Sultanabad camp, including Ja'far Sharif-Emami, the deputy chief of the Railway Company of Iran. Sharif-Emami later held many prestigious offices, such as the head of the Senate, and was prime minister on two occasions, the final time just before the revolution of 1979. According to Nurollah Larudi, Sharif-Emami entered the internment camp in company of several other railroad officers. In the memoirs of a young engineer employed by the railway, named Abbas Mazda, Sharif-Emami's arrival on 7 Aban 1322/30 October 1943 is highlighted as a significant event during their detention.[72] In a later interview, Sharif-Emami described his detention in Sultanabad after the occupation, which he believed had come about as a result of his insistence on pursuing the Americans and the British for payment of taxes, fees, and customs duties owing to the Iranian railway system. The Allied forces refused to pay the full amount due to the Iranian authorities, and also tried to shroud their transport of supplies in secrecy, concealing details of the kind of goods, and the quantities, they were carrying.[73] As the official in charge of the railway and its finances, Sharif-Emami insisted on the payment of these dues. For the British, removing him from his sensitive position allowed them to install individuals who would do their bidding.

In captivity, Sharif-Emami mingled with some of the highest-ranking Iranian officials, along with some of the brightest journalists, lawyers, and judges. It became increasingly clear that his employment at the Iranian Railway Company undermined the Allied operation. When the time came for Sharif-Emami and fellow railway employees to be freed, the Defence Security Office (DSO) tabled its objection to their release, and the author of the report stated, 'I am also protesting strongly to the Prime Minister at the release on his personal instructions of a number of internees before we had obtained the Persian Government's written assurance for which we had asked that they would not be re-employed on the railway.'[74] Clearly,

---

72 Abbas Mazda, *Daftar-e Yadegar-e Zendan 2*, unpublished notebook in Majles library, catalogue number 18916.
73 Sharif-Emami interview, Iranian Oral History Collection, transcript 3.
74 KV 2/3405, Habibullah Naubakht, 33.

blocking their employment on the railways was seen as a pre-emptive move to remove any potential obstacle to the war mission at hand.

While in detention, one of the railway engineers, Abbas Mazda, called for a 'radical transformation' of Iranian society. Mazda, who was also a poet and later became a Majles deputy, had been arrested in connection with Kümmel's case. During his captivity he compiled four notebooks, which are still unpublished and are currently held by the Majles Library in Iran. In them, Mazda wrote of his vehement opposition to the prevailing political system in Iran, and advocated a 'total transformation', a radical statement for the time.[75] The need for revolutionary change was a feeling that was shared by many of his fellow inmates, who encouraged him with poems and messages of support recorded in his notebooks.

Sharif-Emami's traumatic experience of confinement, alongside many other railway employees (over sixty-five of them), raises the question of how trauma experienced during occupation affected the ideological outlook of detainees. Can we see a relation between the experience of occupation and the subsequent stance they took regarding interference in Iranian affairs by foreign powers?

*

In the end, Iranian citizens who were seized and detained during the occupation were found innocent of any crimes, even though the Allied forces chose not to make this public and even tried to suggest their guilt had been established. For example, one British report stated,

> All remaining Persian internees, including both those interned in
> Persia and those interned in Palestine, were released on the 15th
> August or a few days later. In order to anticipate any manifestation
> in their favour, representing them as Persian patriot martyrs, a
> communique was published at the same time in the press by His
> Majesty's Embassy, emphasising their complicity in the German
> conspiracy against the Allies and reproducing in facsimile, the letter

---

75 Mazda, Abbas. *Yadegar-e Zendan 3*, unpublished notebook in Majles library, catalogue number 18916.

addressed by the Sayyid Abul Qasim Kashani to the Grand Mufti and Rashid Ali in Berlin.[76]

In other words, there was a deliberate attempt to ensure that the internees, who had endured an unspeakable injustice, would not re-emerge as heroes in the public eye.

The injustice these prisoners suffered during captivity at the hands of the Allied forces was not only not forgotten, but also impacted many future decisions pertaining to Iran's military and foreign policy. What emerged out of this traumatic experience of captivity and occupation was the incidental formation of a political network of activists and potential revolutionaries that might have never existed otherwise. It is thus important to understand how bonds were strengthened in this eclectic network of likeminded individuals, some of whom became influential political figures in the decades and years leading up to the Iranian Revolution.

As Matin-Daftari noted in his farewell speech, Sultanabad put him in touch with a cadre of 'high-achieving' and 'passionate social and political activists'.[77] The names of many prominent people arrested and interrogated by the Allied forces appear in Iran's modern history as movers and shakers of the post-war era, during Mohammad Reza Pahlavi's reign. Two of the principal detainees of the Allied forces, Fazlollah Zahedi and Ja'far Sharif-Emami, were appointed prime minister at critical junctures, while Sayyed 'Abol-Qassem Kashani at one point became the president of the controversial Seventeenth Majles. He remained a stalwart supporter of Islamic radical and revolutionary causes, and a spiritual leader implicated in the assassinations of several high-ranking figures. Meanwhile, Habibollah Naubakht's political aspirations almost ended during this time, but he became a prolific writer, composing one of the longest modern Shahnamehs, about the reign of the Pahlavis in Iran.[78] While the roles played by leftist individuals and Islamic fundamentalism in the gestation of the Iranian Revolution have been exhaustively examined in recent academic studies, the existence of a network of anti-colonial activists who came

---

76 Ext 5001/41 Persia – Internal (Miscellaneous dispatches), [14r] (27/248).
77 Larudi, *Asiran,* 281; and Matin-Daftari, *Khaterat,* 218.
78 Habibullah Naubakht, *Shahnameh* or *Pahlavi-namah,* 2016.

together in Sultanabad (Arak), through no choice of their own, but who remained active as lawyers, judges, generals, and intellectuals over the following thirty-seven years, has not received due scholarly attention.

In retrospect, the process of decolonisation began soon after the occupation and was tied to the fate of these captives in one way or another. Yet while the Tripartite Agreement sought to guarantee the departure of all Allied forces from Iran after the war, the intended decolonisation process was never fully realised. Only a year before the 1979 revolution, the shah wrote an account of the Tripartite Agreement in a state-sponsored historical document about *Shahrivar 20*, entitled, *Darbareh-ye Sevvom Shahrivar va Naqsh-e Iran dar Jang-e Jahani Dovvom* ('About the Third of Shahrivar and the Role of Iran in the Second World War'), which included a foreword by Amir Abbas Hoveyda.[79] In this document he maintained, 'According to the Tripartite Agreement, the Allied forces pledged that the existence of their soldiers in my country would never be considered as a military occupation (even though all Iranians considered this situation a military occupation.)' The shah's account shows the conflicting views of the people of Iran and the occupying Allied forces that had invaded a territory with little respect for its sovereignty, hatching plans to use the roads and railroads of the country to their own advantage with little by way of compensation – a situation that fostered resentment in both the short and long term. Highlighting the duplicity of the invaders, the shah further added, 'They also pledged to respect our country's territorial integrity and political leadership, and to leave Iran six months after the end of the war with German forces.' The shah ruefully admits that decisions taken by the Iranian parliament after the occupation were mainly for the benefit of the Allied forces. 'We ended our political relations with Japan', he wrote, 'and on 9 September 1943 declared war against Nazi Germany'. Iranians bowed to the will of the Allied forces during the war and their resentment of the occupiers grew. The fact that such an historical document was prepared just a year before the revolution proves the lingering traces of a traumatic experience that needed to be recounted and processed.

Is it therefore possible to extrapolate from this that the Iranian Revolution

---

79 *Darbareh-ye Sevvom Shahrivar va Naqsh-e Iran dar Jang-e Jahani-ye Dovvom,* 1356.

of 1979, with its anti-colonial slogans and ideological view, was partly a response to the trauma of the colonial occupation? Can we identify the Tripartite Agreement, as an expression of colonialism, as one of the roots of the Iranian Revolution of 1979? Many people from different social classes endured the hardships and humiliations of colonialism during this time, so how might this shared traumatic experience, less than forty years earlier, have affected the revolutionary fervour? How did a cadre of like-minded individuals in an internment camp, in Sultanabad, form an activist network that 'found its provenance', as Matin-Daftari noted, in the Allied (mis)treatment? Furthermore, how did those affected personally by the trauma of colonialism change the course of Iranian history? This is an open inquiry, therefore, to question the role of the Iranian captives of the Second World War, and to investigate their life stories, as a prelude to one of the most monumental transformations of modern global history, the Iranian Revolution.

Acknowledgements

I want to extend my deepest gratitude to Professor Firoozeh Kashani-Sabet for the invitation to present at the Decolonisation symposium, in May 2021, the findings of my research into the captives of Sultanabad (Arak) during the Second World War, and the Tripartite Agreement. This study would not have been completed had it not been for her constant encouragement, friendship, and astute suggestions. Her research on the Second World War provided a solid background for this chapter.

I also want to thank Dr Robert Steele for co-organizing the symposium, and editing this volume, in such a collegial and professional manner. He went above and beyond in identifying documents, providing feedback, and suggesting future topics.

I am also very grateful to Adrian O'Sullivan, who sent me various digitized documents in his personal library, especially very crucial ones with regard to Habibollah Naubakht. This research would not have started had it not been for his authoritative books and outstanding articles on German espionage and counter-espionage in Iran. His books on intelligence and counter-intelligence during the war in Turkey and Iraq are equally important for the understanding of the war landscape in Iran.

I also want to thank various readers of early drafts of this paper, whose comments certainly gave me new perspectives.

The tribulations of the captives of Sultanabad (Arak) who were subjected to a series of injustices is the main impetus for this work. I would not have come to this research without having heard vague stories as a child relating to my great-grandfather's incarceration in Sultanabad (Arak), after having been an outspoken attorney in Tehran. As I unearthed more material about Sheykh Abdul Majid's life and involvement during the Second World War, in the declassified confidential documents of the British and Iranian archives, I discovered a treasure trove of unknown connections, historical realities, and the existence of an influential network of notables who came together in captivity and defined the politics of Iran for the next thirty-seven years (1941–1978). I believe this study, at its nascent stage, uncovers some seminal aspects regarding the roots of the Islamic Revolution. A crucial question here is thus, how did the network of captives by the Allied forces constitute a prelude to the Iranian Revolution?

Bibliography

Abrahamian, E. *A History of Modern Iran*, Cambridge, 2012.

Asnadi az Matbu'at-e Iran, 1320–1340, Tehran, 1378.

Entezam, N. *Shahrivar 1320 az didgah-e darbar*, Tehran, 1371.

Golujeh, Sajjad Ra'i ed., *Asnadi az Eshghal-e Iran dar Jang-e Jahani-ye Dovvom*, Tehran, 1378.

Jackson, A. *Persian Gulf Command: A History of the Second World War in Iran and Iraq*, New Haven, 2018.

Larudi, N. *Asiran*, Tehran, 1953.

Maclean, F. *Eastern Approaches*, London, 1949.

Magee, G. *The Tribes of Fars*, India, 1948.

Majd, M.G. *Iran Under Allied Occupation in World War II: The Bridge to Victory & A Land of Famine*, Lanham, 2016.

Mazda, A. *Yadegar-e Zendan 3*, unpublished notebook in Majles library, catalogue number 18916.

Matin-Daftari, A. *Khaterat Yek Nakhost Vazir*, Tehran, 1992.

Milani, A. *Eminent Persians: The Men and Women Who Made Modern Iran, 1941–1979*, vol. 2, Syracuse, USA, 2008.

Naubakht, H. *Shahnameh* or *Pahlavi-namah*, Tehran, 2016.

O'Sullivan, A. *Nazi Secret Warfare in Occupied Persia (Iran): The Failure of the German Intelligence Services, 1939–45*, New York, 2014.

O'Sullivan, A. *Espionage and Counterintelligence in Occupied Persia (Iran): The Success of the Allied Secret Services, 1941–45*, New York, 2015.

O'Sullivan, C. *FDR and the End of Empire. The World of the Roosevelts*, New York, 2012.

Qodsi, J. *Daftar-e Ayyam: Khaterate Dr. Jafar Qudsi*, Tehran, 1381.

Schulze-Holthus, B. *Frührot in Iran: Abenteuer im deutschen Geheimdienst*, Esslingen, 1952.

Schulze-Holthus, B. *Daybreak in Iran: A Story of the German Intelligence Service*, London, 1954.

Schulze-Holthus, B. *Aufstand in Iran: Abenteuer im Dienste der deutschen Abwehr*, Munich, 1980.

Seydi, S. 'Intelligence and Counter-Intelligence Activities in Iran during the Second World War', *Middle Eastern Studies* 46/5, 2010, 733–752.

Seyfpour Fatemi, N. *Gazand-e Roozegar: Khaterati az Tahavollat-e Fars dar Astaneh Jang-e Jahani-ye Dovvom*, Tehran, 2007.

Sreberny, A. and Torfeh, M. *Persian Service: The BBC and British Interests in Iran*, London, 2014.

Stewart, R. *Sunrise at Abadan: the British and Soviet invasion of Iran, 1941*, New York, 1988.

Tabara'iyan, Safa' al-din ed. *Iran dar Eshqal-e Mottafeqin: Majmu'eh Asnad va Madarek 1318–1324*, Tehran, 1371.

Wilson, H. *Eight years Overseas, 1939–1945*, New York, 1950.

3

Iranian Oil Nationalisation as Decolonisation: Historiographical Reflections, Global History, and Postcolonial Theory

Mattin Biglari

> Now that by God's will, and through the attempts of the deputies of the
> two Houses, the country's major national resources have been restored,
> we all feel confident that if this overflowing wealth is utilised properly,
> our nation will be enabled to enjoy a prosperous and comfortable
> life, and in line with the progressive nations, accomplish its duty in
> contributing towards universal civilization.[1]

These were the words of Mohammad Mosaddeq, the newly appointed
prime minister of Iran, addressing the country's population over radio. His
message referred to the government's decision to nationalise oil operations
in the southwestern province of Khuzestan, thereby expelling the British-
owned Anglo–Iranian Oil Company (hereafter AIOC). His message not
only conveyed the hope that national sovereignty over oil would provide
the necessary basis for Iran's future internal development, but also that in

---

1 'Prime Minister's Message Broadcast on the Radio', *Ettela'at*, 30 April 1951, BP
Archive (hereafter BP) 54458.

doing so it would help create a path for other countries to follow. In this way, Mosaddeq's vision aligned with those of many contemporary anti-colonial figures across the Global South who saw decolonisation as an opportunity for 'worldmaking', helping to realise universalist aspirations for a more egalitarian post-war world.[2]

In this reading, Iran's nationalisation of oil in 1951 was part of a much broader story of global decolonisation. The Iranian government received messages of congratulation from leaders of the Non-Aligned movement, such as Nehru, as well as the former Mexican president Cardeñas, who oversaw the nationalisation of oil in Mexico in 1937. Such messages of solidarity also extended below the level of government. For example, in September 1951 some 30,000 Mexican oil workers sent a message to oil workers in Khuzestan to share lessons they had learned from their own experience of nationalisation: 'in the beginning we were also intimidated by nations who exploited us and we were told we could not administer our oil industry, but for nearly twenty years we have been running our oil industry'.[3] Proponents of nationalisation in Iran were well aware of the global attention they had garnered. For instance, in March 1951 the newspaper *Keyhan* proudly rejoiced that Iranian oil had 'become the talk everywhere in the world', especially in Muslim countries like Pakistan.[4] Such transnational imagination 'sought not only to disrupt colonial rule in one colony, but to attack colonialism everywhere as a systemic, worldwide problem in need of eradication'.[5]

In particular, Iranian oil nationalisation helped usher in a new era when governments across the Global South increasingly wrested control of natural resources from foreign governments and firms on the path towards

---

2 Adom Getachew, *Worldmaking after Empire: The Rise and Fall of Self-Determination*, 2019. However, as Getachew shows, 'worldmaking' envisaged self-determination beyond the limits of the nation-state framework.
3 Telegram from Tehran embassy to US Secretary of State, 5 September 1951, Box 5505A, RG 59, Central Decimal File 888.2553/7-195 – 888.2553/9-1951, NARA. On the role of oil workers in Mexican oil nationalisation see Myrna I. Santiago, *The Ecology of Oil: Environment, Labor, and the Mexican Revolution, 1900–1938*, 2006.
4 'Reflection of the Iranian Oil Question in the World', *Keyhan*, 29 March 1951.
5 Heather Streets-Salter, 'International and Global Anti-Colonial Movements', in *World Histories from below: Disruption and Dissent, 1750 to the Present*, ed. Antoinette M. Burton and Tony Ballantyne, 2016, 47–74, at 47.

securing postcolonial sovereignty. In June 1951, one Pakistani newspaper hoped

> that Iran would not fail. For possession of the oilfields, vital as they are
> to Iran's economy, vindicate a principle of far greater importance to
> the people of Asia... the rubber of Malaya, the oil of Iran, the control
> of the Suez Canal, these belong without reservation to the people
> who inhabit these regions... no one doubts, or laments, the end of an
> Empire that had dominated the world for over a hundred years.[6]

As international historians have recently stressed, such resource nationalism animated various ventures across several postcolonial countries to build or take over national oil industries, laying the foundations for the establishment of OPEC in 1960 and its ascendancy in subsequent decades.[7] Likewise, for some time historians of the British empire have suggested that the events of 1951 in Iran emboldened the Free Officers in Egypt in their seizure of power in January 1952 and inspired Nasser's decision to nationalise the Suez Canal in 1956.[8]

Indeed, it has long been acknowledged in the historiography of Iran's oil nationalisation that the expropriation of AIOC promoted among Global South countries the 'sovereignty of nations and their right to control their natural resources'.[9] The very first history of this subject written in 1956, Mostafa Fateh's magisterial *Panjah Sal Naft-e Iran* ('Fifty Years of Iran's Oil'), situated it within a broader context of awakening in the 'East' and

---

6 'Great Britain and Iran', *Civil and Military Gazette*, 19 June 1951, FO 248/1527, the National Archives of the UK (hereafter TNA).
7 Christopher R. W. Dietrich, *Oil Revolution: Sovereign Rights and the Economic Culture of Decolonization, 1945 to 1979*, 2017.
8 William Roger Louis, *The British Empire in the Middle East 1945–1951: Arab Nationalism, the United States, and Postwar Imperialism*, 1984. For a recent study on Mosaddeq's influence in Egypt see Lior Sternfeld, 'Iran Days in Egypt: Mosaddeq's Visit to Cairo in 1951', *British Journal of Middle Eastern Studies* 43/1, January 2016, 1–20.
9 As quoted in one of the most comprehensive English-language account of Iranian oil nationalisation, Mostafa Elm, *Oil, Power, and Principle: Iran's Oil Nationalization and Its Aftermath*, 1992, 341.

liberation from Western impositions.[10] Today, oil nationalisation occupies a central place in Iranian national memory, heralded as a triumph of democratic popular will and a marker of the country's stand against imperialism, marked each year on its 29 Esfand (20 March) anniversary both within Iran and amongst the Iranian diaspora. As will be elucidated, several rich historical accounts have been written in English and Persian, especially highlighting the role of the pro-nationalisation coalition, the National Front (*jebhe-ye melli*), and its figurehead, Mosaddeq, who has been likened to other leading anti-colonial and Non-Aligned leaders. For instance, in his recent textbook of modern Iran, Abbas Amanat writes that Mosaddeq

> was quick to learn the populist politics of the post-war era and quicker
> to grasp and indigenize its anti-imperialist message as it circulated
> throughout the non-Western milieu, from China, India, and Southeast
> Asia to Africa and Latin America. In this and other respects, Mosaddeq
> represented a new face of postcolonial leadership pioneered by the
> likes of Mahatma Gandhi and later by Sukarno in Indonesia and
> Gamal Abdel Nasser in Egypt.[11]

However, despite recognising the anti-colonial nature of the oil nationalisation movement, historians have stressed its importance for decolonisation outside Iran more so than within. This is because, as is commonly pointed out, Iran was not formally colonised or governed by Western powers. In this chapter I make an historiographical and conceptual contribution to consider oil nationalisation as an instance of decolonisation in Iran, and therefore also as a window to the usefulness of postcolonial theory in the study of modern Iranian history more generally. In the first section, I survey the literature to show how historians have long acknowledged the anti-colonialism of oil nationalisation but have not fully accounted for the colonial context from which it emerged. In the second section, I suggest that oil nationalisation should be grounded in everyday life in the centre of oil operations, Khuzestan, to fully illuminate how oil was imbricated

---

10 Mostafa Fateh, *Panjah Sal Naft-e Iran*, 1335/1956, 448.
11 Abbas Amanat, *Iran: A Modern History*, 2017, 531.

in global networks of colonialism and racial capitalism. I elaborate why through discussing the burgeoning field exploring the social history of the Iranian oil industry. In the final section, I outline how conditions in Khuzestan translated to the political sphere in Tehran to reappraise how oil nationalisation was an act of decolonisation. Incorporating insights from postcolonial theory, I conclude how oil nationalisation provides a vantage point to consider the nature of colonial modernity in Iran and can be generative of new research agendas in wider Iranian historiography.

Oil Nationalisation in Iran: An Historiographical Overview

Works on Iranian oil nationalisation fall into three main categories. First, there are studies in the field of international history that have focused on the Cold War dimensions of nationalisation and its place in global decolonisation. These are mostly concerned with the events that precipitated the 1953 coup and less with the reasons for the initial emergence of the oil nationalisation movement, and so they are less the focus of attention in this chapter.[12] Second, there are histories from the perspective of oil companies that offer detailed accounts of negotiations between AIOC and the Iranian government, as well as the global oil industry's reaction to the expulsion of the British company.[13] Though very informative about the motivations behind major oil companies, especially AIOC's management, they rely on documents from archives in the West, especially the UK

---

12 William Roger Louis, *The British Empire in the Middle East*; Mary Ann Heiss, *Empire and Nationhood: The United States, Great Britain, and Iranian Oil, 1950–1954*, 1997; Steven G. Galpern, *Money, Oil, and Empire in the Middle East: Sterling and Postwar Imperialism, 1944–1971*, 2009; James Bill and William Roger Louis, eds. *Musaddiq, Iranian Nationalism and Oil*, 1988. A recent exception is Gregory Brew, *Petroleum and Progress in Iran: Oil, Development, and the Cold War*, 2022, which does assess why nationalisation happened and makes ample use of Persian language sources. Dietrich's *Oil Revolution* is also concerned with reasons for nationalisation but situates Mossadeq's motivations within a global context of resource nationalism across the Global South.

13 These include company histories such as J. H. Bamberg, *The History of The British Petroleum Company: vol. 2, The Anglo–Iranian Years, 1928–1954*, 1994; and also global histories of oil as in Daniel Yergin, *The Prize: The Epic Quest for Oil, Money, and Power*, 1991.

National Archive and BP Archive. As a result, they provide a one-sided account and reveal little about Iranian perspectives except when quoted in foreign correspondence.

The third type, which will be the focus of this survey, relates to histories of oil nationalisation written by historians of Iran, written in Persian and English. While often relying on the same diplomatic archive as the types above, they provide much greater insight by also incorporating Persian language sources such as memoirs, newspapers and, more recently, archival documents.[14] These studies offer more comprehensive accounts of the oil nationalisation movement and its internal tensions beyond Mosaddeq, especially the National Front (*jebhe-ye melli*) and other prominent proponents of nationalisation such as Hoseyn Makki, Mozaffar Baqai, Allahyar Saleh, Hoseyn Fatemi, and Ayatollah Kashani. They also highlight the position of the Left, including the Tudeh Party and Khalil Maleki's Non-Aligned 'Third Force'.[15] For instance, they point out that Tudeh cofounder Abbas Eskandari made the first calls for oil nationalisation heard in the Majles in August 1948 and again in January 1949.[16] In addition, there are several notable histories written by figures who were directly involved in government or the oil industry at the time of nationalisation and became important figures in oil policy, combining personal recollections with a rich primary source base.[17] Finally, there has been a recent

---

14 The most notable of these works published in English include Richard W. Cottam, *Nationalism in Iran*, Rev. edn, 1979; Mostafa Elm, *Oil, Power, and Principle*; Fakhreddin Azimi, *Iran: The Crisis of Democracy*, 1989; Homa Katouzian, *Musaddiq and the Struggle for Power in Iran*, 2nd edn, 1999; Ervand Abrahamian, *The Coup: 1953, the CIA, and the Roots of Modern U.S.–Iranian Relations*, 2013; and, in Persian, Fateh, *Panjah Sal*; Fu'ad Rowhani, *Tarikh-e Melli Shodan-e Ṣanʿat-e Naft-e Iran*, 1352/1973; Mohammad Ali Movahed, *Khab-e Ashofte-ye Naft: Doktor Mosaddeq va Nahzat-e Melli-ye Iran, Jald-e 1 va 2*, 1378/1999; Qobad Fakhimi, *Si Sal-e Naft-e Iran: Az Melli Shodan-e Naft ta Enqelab-e Eslami*, 1387/2008; and Mansur Mahdavi, *Tarikh-e Nahzat-e Melli-ye Naft*, 1396/2017.

15 Katouzian, *Musaddiq*, is particularly strong in this regard.

16 Elm, *Oil, Power, and Principle*, 52; Katouzian, *Musaddiq*, 68; Movahed, *Khab-e Ashofte-ye Naft*, 154.

17 Fateh, *Panjah Sal*; Rowhani, *Tarikh-e Melli Shodan*; Hossein Makki, *Ketab-e Siyah, Jald-e Sevvom: Khalʿ-e Yad az Sherkat-e Naft-e Inglis va Iran*, 1360/1981; Mohammad Mosaddeq, *Musaddiq's Memoirs*, ed. Homa Katouzian, 1988; Manucher

proliferation of memoirs in Iran written by former oil workers, residents, and onlookers present in Khuzestan at the time of nationalisation.[18]

Many of these works have long acknowledged that Iranian oil nationalisation must be understood within a global context. For instance, Fateh provides a long overview of Mexican oil nationalisation in 1938, and Rowhani compares the Iranian case to various nationalisations across the world in the post-war period, including Britain, France, and Egypt.[19] Several authors have also drawn parallels between Iranian oil nationalism and anti-colonial movements elsewhere, especially India, even comparing Mosaddeq to Gandhi.[20] Movahed goes as far as asserting that oil nationalisation was a 'revolutionary act in the struggle against colonialism'.[21]

Nevertheless, there has arguably been a general tendency towards methodological nationalism in the above works. Many situate nationalisation within a longer tradition of struggle in Iran, beginning with foreign concessions and the Constitutional Revolution.[22] Of course, some leading figures actively took part in the Constitutional Revolution and often referred to it at the time of nationalisation. But it is not particularly helpful to include such events taking place so many years apart in one linear narrative. If read superficially, it might create the impression that oil nationalisation was merely the completion of Iran's long march to democracy.

Farmanfarmaian, *Blood and Oil: Memoirs of a Persian Prince*, 1997. In addition to these, Fakhimi, *Si Sal-e Naft-e Iran* and Movahed, *Khab-e Ashofte-ye Naft* both include eyewitness accounts of the authors.

18 Iraj Valizadeh, *Anglo va Bangolo Dar Abadan*, 1390/2011; Heidar Dehqani, *Nim Qarn-e Khedmat Dar San'at-e Naft-e Iran*, 1394/2015; Majid Javaherizadeh, *Palayeshgah-e Abadan dar 80 Sal Tarikh-e Iran 1908–1988*, 1396/2017; Nosratallah Bakhturtash, *Chand Yademan az San'at Melli Shodan-e Naft Dar Abadan va Qeireh*, 1396/2017; Hassan Kamshad, *Hadith-e Nafas: Khaterat-e Resteh az Faramushi*, 1396/2017.

19 Fateh, *Panjah Sal*, 133–42; Rowhani, *Tarikh-e Melli Shodan*, 5–15.

20 Abrahamian, *The Coup*, 5; Fakhimi, *Si Sal-e Naft-e Iran*, 129.

21 Movahed, *Khab-e Ashofte-ye Naft*, 154.

22 For instance, the narrative begins with the 1872 Reuter concession in Elm, *Oil, Power, and Principle*. Similarly, Fateh opens his section on the oil nationalisation movement by referring back to previous mass movements in Iran such as the Tobacco rebellion and the Constitutional revolution in Fateh, *Panjah Sal*, 515. Likewise, Movahed considers the nationalisation movement as one of three mass movements in modern Iran, alongside the Constitutional Revolution and 1979 revolution, in Movahed, *Khab-e Ashofte-ye Naft*, 51.

Furthermore, most of these accounts focus on elites, which is perhaps an underlying reason for methodological nationalism. To be sure, they are mostly political histories and so focus on the actors directly involved in negotiations between AIOC and the Iranian government. As such, they provide very valuable chronologies of the events leading up to the oil nationalisation bill in March 1951.[23] In addition, some scholars such as Katouzian and Movahed make particularly good use of the press to offer extremely rich accounts of the National Front and its various constituent parties, also acknowledging the importance of public opinion as a driving force.[24] For example, Katouzian argues that public opinion was already against the supplemental agreement of July 1949, which would replace the 1933 concession, and it was to this that figures such as Makki and Baqai 'owed their success... to public opinion which they themselves had helped arouse. The press had been alerted to the oil issue more than ever before, the bazaar leaders had become active, students were drawn into the campaign, and public meetings were frequently held in support of the Majles opposition'.[25]

Nevertheless, in adopting a political history approach, they have left lacunae about exactly how public opinion emerged from below. Indeed, despite being a huge mass movement, illustrated by images of enormous crowds carrying placards bearing various anti-imperialist slogans, there has been remarkably little research on the mass base of the nationalisation movement.[26] The actors involved represented a much wider cross-section of Iranian society than the notable figures of the National Front, most of whom were wealthy men. For instance, we know little about the role of women in the nationalisation movement, despite women having long been integrated into the historiography of other popular movements.[27] Like-wise, there is much to learn about nationalisation from the perspectives of

---

23 This is exemplified by Elm, *Oil, Power and Principle*.

24 For example, Katouzian, *Musaddiq*; and Movahed, *Khab-e Ashofte-ye Naft*.

25 Katouzian, *Musaddiq*, 71.

26 One exception is the role of university students in Tehran; for example, see Katouzian, *Musaddiq*, 224–226, 233–234.

27 However, we know that women were active in fighting for suffrage at the time of oil nationalisation, as shown in Firoozeh Kashani-Sabet, *Conceiving Citizens: Women and the Politics of Motherhood in Iran*, Oxford, 2011, 177.

ethnically-minoritised groups. In short, there is ample room to unpack the 'nation' in 'nationalisation'.

Above all, and understandably given their focus, these histories are told fundamentally from the vantage point of Tehran rather than Khuzestan. Of course, they reference the malpractices of the oil company in Khuzestan and pay close attention to the implementation of nationalisation there from April 1951, detailing how AIOC was expelled. Some, such as Fateh, even highlight the earlier significance of the oil workers' movement in making colonialism visible to the outside world.[28] More recently, histories written by former oil workers have re-centred nationalisation in Khuzestan, with Fakhimi even asserting that Abadan was the 'heart' of the nationalisation movement.[29] On the whole, though, most have underplayed the direct role played by workers in shaping oil nationalisation from below and challenging how it was implemented from above.[30] As an illustrative example, just after the oil nationalisation bill was passed in March 1951 there was a general strike across all operations in Khuzestan, and yet this receives only passing reference in most studies of oil nationalisation.[31] Moreover, in these studies, workers and residents are mostly invisible beyond episodic mobilisations and formal labour organisations – a problem in common with traditional labour histories. So very little is known about how oil nationalisation was connected to daily life in between the two major strikes of 1946 and 1951.[32]

---

28 Fateh long ago acknowledged the importance of the 1946 general strike in this regard, outlining it and workers' demands in detail in Fateh, *Panjah Sal*, 438–444. Most other historians of nationalisation briefly reference the 1946 strike to illustrate the malpractice of the oil company, for example Katouzian, *Musaddiq*, 65–66.
29 Fakhimi, *Si Sal-e Naft*, 43. Abrahamian's *The Coup* is also grounded in labour activism in Khuzestan.
30 This reflects a general tendency to neglect oil workers in history-writing, as argued in Touraj Atabaki, Elisabetta Bini, and Kaveh Ehsani, eds. *Working for Oil: Comparative Social Histories of Labor in the Global Oil Industry*, 2018.
31 This point is made in Abrahamian, *The Coup*, 72; Abrahamian provides the only detailed account of the strike on 64–74. In other studies of nationalisation, the strike only receives passing mention, for example Elm, *Oil, Power, and Principle*, 84; Fateh, *Panjah Sal*, 409; Movahed, *Khab-e Ashofte-ye Naft*, 57; and Rowhani, *Tarikh-e Melli Shodan*, 117.
32 On the need to examine everyday life in critique of traditional labour history, see Hanan Hammad, *Industrial Sexuality: Gender, Urbanization, and Social Transformation in Egypt*, 2016.

Demonstration in Tehran in favour of oil nationalisation, 1951.

These intervening years coincided with great social upheaval across the Global South in the wake of the Second World War. By the end of the decade, anti-colonialism had brought about the near-total collapse of European empires in Asia. Apart from partition in South Asia, countries in Southeast Asia such as Vietnam and Indonesia saw labour mobilisations, the sudden rise or return of communist parties, and the public outpouring of popular nationalism.[33] This is not to mention the upsurge of anti-colonial labour activism in colonial Africa.[34] Beyond messages of solidarity, the direct transnational linkages between these movements and Iran should not be overstated. But the striking parallels force us to consider possible historical contingencies that Iran shared with much of the decolonising world at this time. They alert us to the fact that Iran's experience was

33 Christopher Alan Bayly and Timothy N. Harper, *Forgotten Wars: Freedom and Revolution in Southeast Asia*, 2010.
34 Frederick Cooper, *Decolonization and African Society: The Labor Question in French and British Africa*, 1996.

Women at protest in support of oil nationalisation, 2 July 1951.

not necessarily exceptional and warn us against viewing nationalisation as being simply the result of endogenous political processes, whether the rise of Iranian nationalism or democratic politics. Although the anti-colonial nature of oil nationalisation has been long acknowledged, its full extent has yet to be elucidated. In the next section, I argue that this requires a detailed grounding in the social history of the oil industry in Khuzestan, which can help us more comprehensively appreciate the colonial attitude of the oil company.

The Oil Company as a Colonial Presence

Of course, although the British government had a majority share in AIOC, the company had its own commercial interests that were sometimes at odds with the British empire. There were often tensions between the British government and the company in the years immediately leading up to nationalisation, especially over labour and living conditions in Khuzestan. Nevertheless, as growing scholarship on the history of the Iranian oil industry has shown, by closely examining the company's operations in Khuzestan it is possible to detect several features and practices on the ground that were imbricated in global networks of colonialism.

First, the assembly of operations in Khuzestan was predicated on dispossession of local populations. As Kaveh Ehsani shows, upon finding oil in Masjed-e Soleyman in 1908, the Anglo–Persian Oil Company (APOC, as AIOC was then known) soon began to secure territory at the expense of existing populations who were living and utilising this land. The company undertook cadastral surveys to make claims to private property, abstracting land from its seasonal, communal, and fluid use by pastoral nomads, especially the Bakhtiari confederation.[35] These served as bases for contracts with local khans for the company to lease territory for its pipelines and hire private security to protect them, exercising a form of corporate sovereignty.[36] Moreover, its selected site for a refinery on the island of 'Abbadan – more locally known as Jazirat al-Khizr – consisted of a mostly Arab population of 24,000, and was under the administrative authority of the Sheikh of Mohammerah (then Sheikh Khaz'al). The company worked to frame the land as 'wasteland' despite its cultivation by the local population for date farming, which underpinned new contracts that simplified a pre-existing complex configuration of land rights into its own private property.[37] This process ultimately helped erase the island's history, including the name of the island changing from its local Arabic version to 'Abadan' (although this was also the Persianised name that many Iranians used as

---

35 Kaveh Ehsani, 'The Social History of Labor in the Iranian Oil Industry: The Built Environment and the Making of the Industrial Working Class (1908–1941)', Ph.D. Dissertation, Leiden University 2015; Katayoun Shafiee, *Machineries of Oil: An Infrastructural History of BP in Iran*, 2018, 21–55. On these contracts also see Stephanie Cronin, *Tribal Politics in Iran: Rural Conflict and the New State, 1921–1941*, 2007; and Arash Khazeni, *Tribes & Empire on the Margins of Nineteenth-Century Iran*, 2009.

36 Joshua Barkan, *Corporate Sovereignty: Law and Government under Capitalism*, 2013. There are parallels here to the British East India Company, as shown in Philip J. Stern, *The Company-State: Corporate Sovereignty and the Early Modern Foundation of the British Empire in India*, 2011.

37 As Ehsani demonstrates in detail, this process also involved representing the island as desolate and wasted by 'Arab apathy'. See Ehsani, 'The Social History', 134–139; cf. Shafiee, *Machineries of Oil*, 36.

well).[38] In this regard, the very foundations of the Iranian oil industry shared central features with settler colonialism.[39]

Second, the company's workforce structure was based on a racialised division of labour. In initial operations, white European geologists and drillers oversaw teams of manual labourers consisting mostly of seasonal and lower-status pastoral nomads. Company managers most often conceptualised these workers as 'coolies' as late as the 1930s, reflecting the prevailing colonial discourse that they were intimately familiar with through their colonial service (especially in India).[40] As historians of the colonial world have shown, in areas such as India and the Persian Gulf, the term 'coolie' carried the meaning not just of a manual labourer, but specifically one uprooted from home and thus devoid of any traditional skills, merely serving as a temporary hired hand for a particular job.[41] For skilled labour positions, however, the company recruited Indian workers.[42] Well into the 1930s, managers maintained that Indians were inherently more suited for such work thanks to their docile nature and technical competence compared to local workers, drawing on stereotypes from British colonial tradition about Indians having some degree of technical competence compared to other 'races'.[43] Of course, this stratification was more reflective of wider trends in corporate capitalism towards dividing workforces along racial lines while maintaining the supremacy of white management.[44] This was

---

38 Willem M. Floor, 'The Early Beginnings of Modern Abadan', Abadan:Retold, 2016, http://www.abadan.wiki/en/the-early-beginnings-of-modern-abadan/.

39 For example, see Patrick Wolfe, 'Settler Colonialism and the Elimination of the Native', Journal of Genocide Research 8/4, December 2006, 387–409.

40 Ehsani, 'The Social History', 46. Fateh suggests that the company's managers brought colonial attitudes with them from India, which were then reproduced by junior technicians arriving from Britain; see Fateh, Panjah Sal, 424.

41 Jan Breman and E Valentine Daniel, 'Conclusion: The Making of a Coolie', Journal of Peasant Studies 19/3, 1992, 268–295.

42 Touraj Atabaki, 'Far from Home, But at Home: Indian Migrant Workers in the Iranian Oil Industry', Studies in History 31/1, 2015, 85–114.

43 Michael Adas, Machines as the Measure of Men: Science, Technology, and Ideologies of Western Dominance, 1989. This was acknowledged as early as Fateh, Panjah Sal, 424.

44 As is well established by scholars of racial capitalism, influenced especially by Cedric Robinson, Black Marxism: The Making of the Black Radical Tradition, 1983.

especially pronounced in the world's oil and mineral frontier, with Khuzestan being no exception.[45]

Third, following from the above, racialisation extended into spatial segregation at work and beyond. Around its refinery at Abadan, the company initially built bungalows for its European staff in the area of 'Braim', as well as more basic accommodation for its Indian workers in the area known as 'Coolie Lines'. At the same time, the 'sheikh's bazaar' area spontaneously grew into a boomtown by the 1920s as people migrated to Abadan for work from other parts of the country. The refinery was located in the middle of the city, functioning as a *cordon sanitaire* separating these areas.[46] Abadan quickly resembled a colonial city, both physically in its spatial segregation between 'indigenous' and European areas, and discursively through references to 'bungalows' and 'coolies'.[47] Scholars have pointed out that the presence of Indian labour complicates the classic colonial 'dual city' model, making Abadan more of a 'tripartite' or 'quartered' city.[48] Nevertheless, Europeans living in Abadan conceptualised the Iranian areas as sources of disease and disorder.[49] As such, from the late 1920s the company resolved to intervene increasingly in the town through the destruction of the bazaar and the creation of new neighbourhoods like Bahmanshir, aimed at socially engineering populations architecturally and infrastructurally.[50] For its urban planning the company even hired James

---

45 Similar racialised divisions of labour and attendant segregation elsewhere in the global oil industry also drew on Jim Crow, as famously shown in Robert Vitalis, *America's Kingdom: Mythmaking on the Saudi Oil Frontier*, 2007; cf. Miguel Tinker Salas, *The Enduring Legacy: Oil, Culture and Society in Venezuela*, 2009; Santiago, *The Ecology of Oil*.

46 Mark Crinson, 'Abadan: Planning and Architecture under the Anglo–Iranian Oil Company', *Planning Perspectives* 12/3, January 1997, 341–359, at 345.

47 Indeed, there are remarkable parallels here to Delhi as set out in the classic study Anthony D. King, *Colonial Urban Development: Culture, Social Power and Environment*, 1976, 83–84, 90–91.

48 Kaveh Ehsani, 'The Social History, 15; Atabaki, 'Far From Home', 100. The concept of 'dual city' was popularised through Janet Abu-Lughod, *Rabat, Urban Apartheid in Morocco*, 1981.

49 Crinson, 'Abadan', 342.

50 Kaveh Ehsani, 'Social Engineering and the Contradictions of Modernization in Khuzestan's Company Towns: A Look at Abadan and Masjed-Soleyman', *International Review of Social History* 48/3 December 2003, 361–399; Crinson, 'Abadan'.

M. Wilson, who had served as an assistant to the famous British architect Edwin Lutyens in the reconstruction of Delhi.[51] The infrastructural disparities between management areas and predominantly Iranian ones like Abadan Township and Ahmadabad, not to mention shantytowns such as the notorious Kaghazabad, became a major source of political grievance by the 1940s. Likewise, the persistence of segregated social clubs, transport and leisure facilities had striking similarities to the 'global colour line'.[52] The colonial nature of such segregation was not lost on visitors and residents at the time: after his first visit in 1941 Manuchehr Farmanfarmaian likened it to a 'British colony', and the writer Hassan Kamshad later reflected that the system was a form of 'apartheid'.[53]

Fourth, the company's training programme drew on practices from the wider colonial education system. From the late 1920s, and especially after the 1933 concession agreement mandated the promotion of Iranians to more senior positions (known as 'Iranianisation'), the company introduced training schemes for apprentices and students.[54] This included sending Iranians to trade schools and universities in Britain to study engineering and petroleum technology. Within Iran, the most ambitious project was the Abadan Technical Institute, established in 1939, which was nominally designed to train Iranians to become genuine oil experts and future managers. However, the institute and its hostel most closely resembled colonial boarding schools in their architecture, curricula and extra-curricular activities, aimed at socially engineering students into becoming disciplined, professional employees.[55] This was best exemplified by the sports

51 On the social engineering of urban planning in colonial Delhi see Legg, *Spaces of Colonialism*.
52 Marilyn Lake and Henry Reynolds, *Drawing the Global Colour Line: White Men's Countries and the International Challenge of Racial Equality*, 2008; cf. Carl Husemoller Nightingale, *Segregation: A Global History of Divided Cities*, 2012.
53 Kamshad, *Hadith-e Nafs*, 92. Farmanfarmaian, *Blood and Oil*, 87–88.
54 Mattin Biglari, 'Making Oil Men: Expertise, Discipline and Subjectivity in the Anglo–Iranian Oil Company's Training Schemes', *Life Worlds of Oil in the Middle East: Histories and Ethnographies of Black Gold*, ed. Nelida Fuccaro and Mandana Limbert, 2023, 221–48.
55 Sanjay Srivastava, *Constructing Post-Colonial India: National Character and the Doon School*, 1998; and Heather J. Sharkey, *Living with Colonialism: Nationalism and Culture in the Anglo–Egyptian Sudan*, 2003.

programme, which focused on 'character building' much like the games ethic tradition of the wider British empire.[56] Yet like colonial boarding schools elsewhere, the institute could produce anti-colonial subjectivities by bringing together boys from different and disparate parts of the country and defining them against British management, especially when they faced barriers to promotion.[57] These were 'tensions of empire' common to many colonial contexts.[58]

Fifth, like the rest of the country during the Second World War, Allied forces occupied Khuzestan and implemented a series of measures to redirect resources and fix wages to aid the war effort.[59] This contributed to inflation, famine, and disease throughout the country, but the situation was especially pronounced in Abadan, where the cost of living increased by 900 per cent during the war.[60] In taking full control of food matters, the company effectively expropriated existing sources of food provision and replaced them with its own, in the process making the population dependent.[61] At the same time, the refinery's importance as a source of aviation fuel led to heightened securitisation and a 1941 Order-in-Council that severely restricted freedom of movement, followed by martial law in 1942 as the company and British government turned Khuzestan into a 'special military zone'. As Elling and Razak conclude, 'the wartime militarisation of the oil complex exposed the true face of the Company as not just an extension of but a critical component to British imperialism'.[62]

---

56 See J. A. Mangan, *The Games Ethic and Imperialism: Aspects of the Diffusion of an Ideal*, 1986.

57 Biglari, 'Making Oil Men'. For a similar account charting the rise of anti-colonialism among colonial school students see Sharkey, *Living with Colonialism*.

58 For comparison see Frederick Cooper and Ann Laura Stoler, eds., *Tensions of Empire: Colonial Cultures in a Bourgeois World*, 1997.

59 Touraj Atabaki, 'Chronicles of a Calamitous Strike Foretold: Abadan, July 1946', *On the Road to Global Labour History*, ed. Karl Heinz Roth, 2017, 93–128.

60 Atabaki, 'Chronicles', 99.

61 Then, the local population could be cast as lacking the knowledge and experience to produce its own food, requiring education; David Nally, 'The Biopolitics of Food Provisioning', *Transactions of the Institute of British Geographers* 36/1, January 2011, 37–53, at 43.

62 Rasmus Christian Elling and Rowena Abdul Razak, 'Oil, Labour and Empire: Abadan in WWII Occupied Iran', *British Journal of Middle Eastern Studies*, July 2021, 1–18.

Mud huts in the shantytown of Kaghazabad, 1948.

It was in this context that resource nationalism emerged and gave birth to the first calls for oil nationalisation. As Touraj Atabaki shows in detail, these factors coalesced to underpin the sudden ascendance of the communist Tudeh Party during the 1946 general strike, which halted nearly all oil operations.[63] The party had been active in Khuzestan clandestinely since 1943, but through its affiliated trade union federation (CCFTU) now played a central role in a resurgence of labour activism.[64] In the months

---

63 Atabaki, 'Chronicles'.
64 Fateh, *Panjah Sal*, 437; Atabaki, 'Chronicles', 94. On the Khuzestani labour movement in 1946 also see Ervand Abrahamian, 'The Strengths and Weaknesses of

leading up to the strike, Tudeh activists appealed to local opposition towards the oil company as a colonial entity, manifested in a grassroots resource nationalism that saw even fourteen-year old children talking about how 'liquid gold' should belong to Iranians and not the British.[65] The Tudeh Party, along with the CCFTU and its organ *Zafar*, positioned oil as a source of wealth that needed to be reclaimed not only for Iran, but as part of an 'economic revolution' in which the masses in Khuzestan were part of a 'worldwide democratic movement'.[66] It was in this moment, as Abrahamian finds, that the first known calls for oil nationalisation were heard in Khuzestan, made by a woman named Maryam at a public meeting on 20 May 1946.[67] Thus, Iranian oil nationalisation was rooted in very similar conditions to those in other parts of the Global South also affected by the Second World War, meaning it should be viewed as part of a broader global moment in which labour activism and anti-colonialism were intricately linked.[68] This fact should also counterbalance narratives that treat the emergence of post-war resource nationalism as deriving exclusively from a transnational milieu of anticolonial elites.[69]

Moreover, by examining local politics in Khuzestan, we observe how labour activism extended beyond a methodological nationalist framework.

---

the Labor Movement in Iran, 1941–1953', *Modern Iran: The Dialectics of Continuity and Change*, ed. Michael E. Bonine and Nikki R. Keddie, 1981, 211–232; and Habib Ladjevardi, *Labor Unions and Autocracy in Iran*, 1985), 117–147; Rasmus Elling, 'A War of Clubs: Inter-Ethnic Violence and the 1946 Oil Strike in Abadan', *Violence and the City in the Modern Middle East*, ed. Nelida Fuccaro, 2016, 189–210; and Nimrod Zagagi, 'An Oasis of Radicalism: The Labor Movement in Abadan in the 1940s', *Iranian Studies* 53/5–6, November 2020, 847–872.

65 Abrahamian, *The Coup*, 20; J. H. Jones, 'My Visit to the Persian Oilfields', *Journal of The Royal Central Asian Society* 34/1, January 1947, 56–68, at 65.

66 'Abadan Labour Movement', *Zafar*, 10 May 1946. On Tudeh propaganda during the 1946 strike see Atabaki, 'Chronicles'; Abrahamian, *The Coup*, 20.

67 Abrahamian, *The Coup*, 19.

68 For a classic account of this moment see Cooper, *Decolonization and African Society*.

69 As is presented in Dietrich, *Oil Revolution*. On the contribution of labour to post-war resource nationalism see Peyman Jafari, 'Labour in the Making of the International Relations of Oil: Resource Nationalism and Trade Unions', *Handbook of Oil and International Relations*, ed. Roland Dannreuther and Wojciech Osrowski, 2002, 206–20.

Through the construction company Solel Boneh, there had been over 200 hundred Jewish employees working at the Abadan refinery since 1942. As early as 1944 AIOC management expressed concern that these employees were attempting to sabotage installations to undermine British imperial interests, especially as the Jewish offensive in Palestine intensified in 1947.[70] Meanwhile, the politics of Indian partition played out amongst the company's South Asian workforce, such that there were soon separate social clubs for Indians and Pakistanis and some outbreaks of communal violence. Independence had emboldened many workers to mobilise for better terms, with Indian workers sending 'shoals of telegrams' to the Indian ambassador and helping spread anti-company propaganda in the Indian newspaper *Blitz*, much as Indian migrant workers were doing from Bahrain using the prevailing post-war discourse of international human rights.[71] At other times, as in the 1946 May Day demonstrations, workers from different ethnicities articulated a multi-lingual, cosmopolitan anti-colonialism based on class unity, although there were also ethnic divisions due to the mobilisation of Arab tribes against the labour movement.[72] Through transnational labour networks, then, Abadan was imbricated in the post-war reconfiguration of international politics more than just through its place in Iranian oil nationalisation.

Oil Nationalisation and Colonial Modernity

Having accounted for the colonial context out of which oil nationalisation emerged, we may more fully appreciate how nationalisation was an act of decolonisation within Iran. At the same time, like many other instances

---

70 Elling and Razak, 'Oil, Labour and Empire: Abadan in WWII Occupied Iran', 14. V.W.D. Willoughby, 'Report for the Quarter April–June 1947 on the affairs of the Anglo–Iranian Oil Company', 17, LAB 13-519, TNA.

71 V.W.D. Willoughby, 'Report for the Quarter January–March 1948', 9–11, LAB 13-519, TNA; Andrea Grace Wright, 'Migratory Pipelines: Labor and Oil in the Arabian Sea', Ph.D. Thesis, University of Michigan, 2015, 42. On the globalisation of human rights discourse at this time, especially through labour politics, D. Maul, *Human Rights, Development and Decolonization: The International Labour Organization 1940–70*, 2014.

72 Atabaki, Chronicles of a Calamitous Strike Foretold', 107. On ethnic divisions in the strike see Elling, 'A War of Clubs'.

of decolonisation across the Global South, it was capable of reproducing colonial modernity. In this section I indicate several ways this happened through a postcolonial analysis. As such, I argue, oil nationalisation shows how postcolonial theory may be applied to Iran despite the country not being formally colonised and opens a window to the nature of colonial modernity in the country more generally.

First, the translation of events in Khuzestan into Tehran's political discourse reproduced modern ontologies separating technology from politics. Following an invitation from AIOC, from 1947 onwards journalists from Tehran began visiting Khuzestan to investigate the reasons for the general strike the previous year and learn more about the workings of the oil industry. In their findings, they framed technical installations as a discrete, objective domain separate from local society, much as the oil company had done through its public relations machinery.[73] In doing so, they were drawing on the cultural capital of Tehran's middle classes about how Western science and technology could be utilised to modernise the country and civilise its population.[74] They contrasted the Abadan refinery to the squalor and lawlessness of the town's Iranian neighbourhoods, which they saw as emblematic of the nation's cultural backwardness and company's colonial nature. In delineating between technology and culture as separate domains, these writers displayed a common feature of anticolonial nationalism that positioned Western science as a source of emulation.[75] Even *Shahed*, one of the leading newspapers in favour of nationalisation, claimed that despite its disgust for AIOC, its administrative and technical

---

73 Mattin Biglari, *Refining Knowledge: Labour, Expertise and Oil Nationalisation in Iran, 1933–1951*, forthcoming 2024, Ch. 5.
74 Cyrus Schayegh, *Who Is Knowledgeable, Is Strong: Science, Class, and the Formation of Modern Iranian Society, 1900–1950*, 2009; Bianca Devos, 'Engineering a Modern Society? Adoptions of New Technologies in Early Pahlavi Iran', *Culture and Cultural Politics under Reza Shah: The Pahlavi State, New Bourgeoisie and the Creation of a Modern Society in Iran*, ed. Bianca Devos and Christoph Werner, 2014, 266–287.
75 As famously argued in Partha Chatterjee, *The Nation and Its Fragments: Colonial and Postcolonial Histories*, 1993. Parallels can be drawn here to another country that was not formally colonised, China, as evident in Edmund S. K. Fung, *The Intellectual Foundations of Chinese Modernity: Cultural and Political Thought in the Republican Era*, 2010.

organisation was amongst 'the most perfect in the world'.[76] Postcolonial scholarship has shown that Iran was far from unique in reproducing colonial modernity through such scientific rationality at the time.[77]

Second, in the public discourse that emerged surrounding oil, a pervasive developmentalism took shape that was premised on the externalisation of 'Nature' as an ontological domain separate from humanity.[78] In the late 1940s, journalists, politicians, and members of the public engaged in debates about how Iran could exploit its own oil as part of the country's development planning. After their investigations, they tended to arrive at the conclusion that knowledge of oil should be produced via its measurement, abstraction, and calculation from afar, and this knowledge could be applied regardless of local particularities.[79] In this reordering of the world, in which the 'Nature'/'the Environment' could be objectified, calculated, and utilised, space opened up for the production of expertise and new forms of transnational governance, especially through development projects across the postcolonial world in the twentieth century.[80]

Hence, foreign expertise occupied a privileged position in the Tehran-based oil nationalisation movement, such that the leading proponents of oil nationalisation consulted 'experts' who had never even visited Khuzestan over oil workers who had been there for decades. When enquiring into the feasibility of nationalisation in early 1951, Mosaddeq drafted a questionnaire enquiring into the feasibility of nationalisation, which explicitly delineated 'technical' considerations from 'political' ones.[81] He sent the questionnaire to the engineers of the Iran Oil Company, who had either been consulted by Western oil experts or had trained in centres

---

76 'Our Honour and Prestige at Stake', *Shahed*, 7 June 1951.

77 For example, see Omnia S. El Shakry, *The Great Social Laboratory: Subjects of Knowledge in Colonial and Postcolonial Egypt*, 2007.

78 On the colonial origins of this separation, see Walter Mignolo and Catherine E. Walsh, *On Decoloniality: Concepts, Analytics, Praxis*, On Decoloniality, 2018, 153–176. On the centrality of this binary to modernity see Bruno Latour, *We Have Never Been Modern*, trans. Catherine Porter, 1993.

79 Biglari, *Refining Knowledge*, Ch. 5.

80 Timothy Mitchell, *Rule of Experts: Egypt, Techno-Politics, Modernity*, 2002, especially Ch. 1.

81 'Views expressed in respect of questions H. E. Dr Mussadiq', folder 'AIOC, vol. 3', FO 248/1526, TNA.

of standardised oil expertise. In response to the questionnaire, the engineers advised that nationalisation would not be possible without retaining AIOC's existing foreign experts, especially in refining. This high modernist judgment framed oil expertise as an exclusively abstract and disembodied set of knowledge removed from embodied, in-situ experiences.[82] As such, it overlooked oil workers' daily contestations of AIOC's expertise on the ground in Khuzestan.[83] For instance, in 1950 workers highlighted toxic exposure in the refinery through reference to sensory experience and their own corporeal damage, despite the company dismissing such claims based on the disembodied measurement of dangerous gases.[84] Thus, in contrast to the oil nationalisation movement in Tehran, these workers challenged the ontological dualisms underpinning colonial modernity that separated mind and body, reason and Nature. The marginalisation of these workers' expertise reflects a wider trend of 'epistemic violence' brought forth by colonial modernity, especially through the global oil industry.[85]

Third, the oil company's expertise was reproduced through centres of knowledge production. In the company's training schemes, oil expertise was defined as scientific knowledge and distinguished from manual dexterity. This created aspirations amongst students at the Abadan Technical Institute, and from the Iranian government, to gain access to this knowledge rather than redraw the boundaries delimiting what knowledge constituted legitimate expertise. As a result, these students gradually distinguished themselves from 'simple workers' in the refinery, disavowing

---

82 The 'high modernism' of state development projects, as James C. Scott calls it, was premised on the marginalisation of embodied, local knowledge (what he terms *metis*) in favour of abstract and disembodied knowledge (*techne*) James C. Scott, *Seeing like a State: How Certain Schemes to Improve the Human Condition Have Failed*, 1998. Talal Asad observes a similar transformation wrought by colonial modernity, away from embodied to disembodied knowledge as a basis for authority; see Talal Asad, 'Reconfigurations of Law and Ethics in Colonial Egypt', in *Formations of the Secular: Christianity, Islam, Modernity*, 2003, 205–256.
83 Biglari, *Refining Knowledge*, Ch. 4.
84 Petition written by representatives Ali Mohamad Daneshmand and Gholam Ali Salehi to Majles 'on behalf of the sick workers of the AIOC', undated (ca. 1950–51), document no. 2109236, Library and Archive of the Majles, Tehran; cf. Biglari, *Refining Knowledge*, Ch. 4.
85 Timothy Mitchell, *Carbon Democracy: Political Power in the Age of Oil*, 2011, 192; cf. Shafiee, *Machineries of Oil*.

manual dexterity and demanding to be treated as oil experts as had been defined through the company's own knowledge production.[86] As in the words of Frantz Fanon, the company had 'deeply implanted in the minds' of a native elite the 'essential qualities of the West'.[87] Together with students whom the company had sent to study in the UK – especially the 'Birminghamers' (*birminghami-ha*) who had studied Petroleum Technology at Birmingham University – many of these individuals took up prominent positions in the post-nationalisation period, either in the National Iranian Oil Company or in other departments of the Iranian government. Yet they also played a leading role in driving AIOC out of the country, organising the general strike of 1951. Here colonial domination did not come up against an autonomous indigeneity, but rather produced the very subjects that fought for its downfall.[88]

At the same time, the company's system of knowledge production deeply influenced wider society. Newspapers such as *Ettela 'at* took great interest in the number of students from Tehran going to study at the Abadan Technical Institute, regularly publishing articles on entrance exam results and even reporting on trips that had been arranged for Tehrani students to visit the oil installations in Abadan. This enthusiasm perhaps explains why the University of Tehran was so receptive to assistance from the oil company: in fact, AIOC helped establish its Engineering Faculty through provision of laboratory equipment worth £150,000 as well as three full-time British lecturers, a laboratory supervisor and a training shop supervisor.[89] Of course, this faculty became one of the most important centres of knowledge production for Iran's modernisation and development projects in the second half of the twentieth century. The foundations were set, then, for the reproduction of AIOC's expertise long after its expulsion from the country in the form of 'epistemic coloniality'.[90]

---

86 Biglari, *Refining Knowledge*, Ch. 6.
87 Frantz Fanon, *The Wretched of the Earth*, trans. Constance Farrington, 2001, 36.
88 On this point, drawing on a Foucauldian analysis, this case aligns more with the postcolonial tradition concerning Africa and Asia rather than Latin America; see Achille Mbembe, *Out of the Dark Night: Essays on Decolonization*, 2021, 74.
89 'Education and Training in Iran, 1928–1951', 11, BP 142640.
90 As decolonial scholars argue in relation to the Global South more generally; see Mignolo and Walsh, *On Decoloniality*.

Fourth, the position of subalterns in oil nationalisation challenges nationalist and Eurocentric frameworks. In late March 1951, just after the oil nationalisation bill had been passed, a general strike erupted and swept across oil operations in Khuzestan. The timing of the strike was no coincidence: workers and trainees who led the strike had been emboldened by the oil nationalisation bill and used the spotlight shone on them to highlight their everyday grievances, which they had raised through industrial relations mechanisms for several years but hoped nationalisation would now redress. Demands included raising the minimum wage, improved infrastructure, ending segregation, ensuring pathways to promotion, and for trainees, lower exam pass marks. However, most leading newspapers such as *Ettela'at*, *Keyhan*, *Bakhtar-e Emruz*, and *Shahed*, condemned the strike and circulated a conspiracy theory that it was initiated as part of a British plot to undermine nationalisation. Moreover, local authorities clamped down brutally on the strike, blockading the Abadan Technical Institute because it was supposedly a centre of intrigue and killing several protestors in Abadan and Bandar Mahshahr.[91] Through the strike, then, subaltern actors put forward a vision of what nationalisation should entail concretely on the ground in ways that did not neatly conform to the discourses and tactics of the nationalist elite.[92]

Finally, we observe how 1951 did not necessarily mark a rupture from the centralising tendencies of the Pahlavi dynasty, but rather a continuation of its ongoing civilising mission and modernisation programmes, albeit in an increasingly technocratic form.[93] Thus, we are reminded of

---

91 Biglari, *Refining Knowledge*, Ch. 6.

92 The Subaltern Studies Group of South Asia long ago made this intervention to critique Eurocentric and nationalist historiographies of Indian independence, exemplified by Ranajit Guha and Gayatri Chakravorty Spivak, eds. *Selected Subaltern Studies*, 1988. It is in this area that Iranian studies have perhaps most benefited from the postcolonial tradition; for example, see Stephanie Cronin, *Soldiers, Shahs and Subalterns in Iran: Opposition, Protest and Revolt, 1921–1941*, 2010; and, more recently, Stephanie Cronin, *Social Histories of Iran: Modernism and Marginality in the Middle East*, 2021, which connects subaltern and global history approaches. However, so far there have been no subaltern studies of oil nationalisation.

93 On centralisation under Reza Shah see Cronin, *Soldiers, Shahs and Subalterns in Iran*.

Marashi's argument that even though Iran was not formally colonised, the Iranian government acted as a 'surrogate colonial state', enacting many of the same practices of colonialism within the borders of Iran.[94] Nevertheless, the nationalist middle class from which the government drew its base could still forge alliances with subaltern groups. During the 1951 strike, workers and students appealed to the National Front and chanted pro-Mosaddeq slogans in attempts to fraternise with the army. When faced with local repression in Bandar Mahshahr, workers sent a petition to the Majles demanding that the government intervene to protect their 'human rights'.[95] Thus, nationalist elites could forge an alliance with subaltern groups around national liberation because of an external colonial presence in the oil company. Indeed, oil workers regularly appealed in petitions to the Iranian government and Majles well before the emergence of the National Front, contradicting Eurocentric models about the rise of class consciousness occurring independently from state formation.[96] As postcolonial scholarship on the Middle East indicates, rather than searching for the liberal subaltern subject endowed with autonomous consciousness, we should examine how workers and politics were co-constitutive. [97]

---

94 Afshin Marashi, 'Paradigms of Iranian Nationalism: History, Theory, and Historiography', in *Rethinking Iranian Nationalism and Modernity*, ed. Kamran Scot Aghaie and Afshin Marashi, 2014, 3–24, at 18.

95 Mattin Biglari, *Refining Knowledge,* Ch. 6.

96 For example, see Stephanie Cronin, 'Popular Politics, the New State and the Birth of the Iranian Working Class: The 1929 Abadan Oil Refinery Strike', *Middle Eastern Studies* 46/5, September 2010, 699–732; Ehsani, 'The Social History of Labor in the Iranian Oil Industry'; Atabaki, 'From 'Amaleh (Labor) to Kargar (Worker)'. Studies on the post-nationalisation period reveal a similar relationship; see Maral Jefroudi, '"If I Deserve It, It Should Be Paid to Me": A Social History of Labour in the Iranian Oil Industry 1951–1973', Ph.D. Thesis, Leiden University 2017; and Peyman Jafari, 'Oil, Labour and Revolution in Iran: A Social History of Labour in the Iranian Oil Industry, 1973–83', Ph.D. Thesis, Leiden University 2018.

97 Postcolonial scholarship has shown how the history of labour in the Global South cannot be separated from modern state formation, pre-capitalist structures of power and negotiations over democratic rights in the political sphere. On the pitfalls of searching for the autonomous liberal subject see Rosalind O'Hanlon, 'Recovering the Subject: Subaltern Studies and Histories of Resistance in Colonial South Asia', *Modern Asian Studies* 22/1, 1988, 189–224; Timothy Mitchell, 'Everyday Metaphors of Power', *Theory and Society* 19/5, October 1990, 545–577.

Troops deployed to put down strike in Abadan, April 1951.

*

The importance of the Enlightenment in shaping Iran is well established in Iranian historiography. From the ideas that animated the Constitutional Revolution to those that were inherited by the Left, and from the reforms of Reza Shah to the constitution of the Islamic Republic, the 'modern' is pervasive. To what extent this was also colonial has been asked much less. Certainly, many postcolonial scholars would argue that modernity cannot be viewed as endogenous to a hermetically-sealed Europe, but rather was the result of global connections and power relations forged through colonialism.[98]

While in agreement with this argument, in this chapter I have made the case that the question of whether modernity can be equated to colonialism

---

98 For instance, see Timothy Mitchell, 'The Stage of Modernity', *Questions of Modernity*, ed. Timothy Mitchell, 2000, 1–34.

should not determine the usefulness of postcolonial theory to Iran. This is because although Iran was not formally colonised in the same way many parts of Asia and Africa were, and Latin America much earlier, there was still an actual colonial presence in the country: the Anglo-Iranian Oil Company. I demonstrated this through an overview of how the oil company's practices drew on wider colonial networks, including dispossession of local populations, racialised divisions of labour, spatial segregation, colonial education, and military occupation. As a result, many developments in Khuzestan closely mirrored those in other colonial contexts, culminating in the rise of anti-colonialism that was manifested in calls for oil nationalisation. It is by rooting oil nationalisation in this context that we more fully appreciate it as an act of decolonisation *within* Iran, even if existing scholarship has already acknowledged its anti-colonial nature and significance for global decolonisation.

Moreover, I argued that oil nationalisation offers a window to examine the reproduction of colonial modernity in Iran beyond Khuzestan. Incorporating the insights of postcolonial theory, I proceeded to show how events in Khuzestan had profound effects on the oil nationalisation movement in Tehran, shaping anti-colonialism in a way that reproduced several features of colonial modernity. In exhibiting many of the common paradoxes of decolonisation, oil nationalisation shows the usefulness of postcolonial theory in relation to Iran in the decades after nationalisation, even if there were important differences with the decolonising world.

Bibliography

Abrahamian, E. 'The Strengths and Weaknesses of the Labor Movement in Iran, 1941–1953', *Modern Iran: The Dialectics of Continuity and Change*, ed. M.E. Bonine and N.R. Keddie, Albany, 1981, 211–232.

——. *The Coup: 1953, the CIA, and the Roots of Modern U.S.-Iranian Relations*, New York, 2013.

Abu-Lughod, J. *Rabat, Urban Apartheid in Morocco*, Princeton, 1981.

Adas, M. *Machines as the Measure of Men: Science, Technology, and Ideologies of Western Dominance*, Ithaca, 1989.

Amanat, A. *Iran: A Modern History*, New Haven, 2017.

Asad, T. *Formations of the Secular: Christianity, Islam, Modernity.*
Stanford, 2003.

Atabaki, T. 'Far from Home, But at Home: Indian Migrant Workers in
the Iranian Oil Industry', *Studies in History* 31/1, February 2015,
85–114.

——. 'Chronicles of a Calamitous Strike Foretold: Abadan, July 1946', *On
the Road to Global Labour History*, ed. Karl Heinz Roth, Leiden,
2017, 93–128.

——. 'From 'Amaleh (Labor) to Kargar (Worker): Recruitment, Work
Discipline and Making of the Working Class in the Persian/Iranian Oil
Industry', *International Labor and Working-Class History* 84, 2013,
159–75.

Atabaki, T., E. Bini, and K. Ehsani, eds. *Working for Oil: Comparative
Social Histories of Labor in the Global Oil Industry*, Cham, 2018.

Azimi, F. *Iran: The Crisis of Democracy*, London, 1989.

Bakturtash, N. *Chand Yademan az San 'at Melli Shodan-e Naft Dar
Abadan va Qeireh*, Tehran, 1396/2017.

Bamberg, J.H. *The History of The British Petroleum Company: vol. 2,
The Anglo-Iranian Years, 1928–1954*, Cambridge, 1994.

Barkan, J. *Corporate Sovereignty: Law and Government under
Capitalism*, Minneapolis, 2013.

Bayly, C.A., and T.N. Harper. *Forgotten Wars: Freedom and Revolution
in Southeast Asia*, Cambridge, USA, 2010.

Biglari, M. 'Making Oil Men: Expertise, Discipline and Subjectivity in
the Anglo–Iranian Oil Company's Training Schemes', *Life Worlds of
Oil in the Middle East: Histories and Ethnographies of Black Gold*,
ed. Nelida Fuccaro and Mandana Limbert, Edinburgh, 2023, 221–48.

——. *Refining Knowledge: Labour, Expertise and Oil Nationalisation in
Iran, 1933–1951*, Edinburgh, forthcoming 2024.

Bill, J., and W.R. Louis, eds. *Musaddiq, Iranian Nationalism and Oil*,
London, 1988.

Breman, J., and E.V. Daniel. 'Conclusion: The Making of a Coolie',
Journal of Peasant Studies 19/3, 1992, 268–295.

Brew, G. *Petroleum and Progress in Iran: Oil, Development, and the
Cold War*, Cambridge, 2022.

Chakrabarty, D. 'Labor History and the Politics of Theory: An Indian Angle on the Middle East', *Workers and Working Classes in the Middle East: Struggles, Histories, Historiographies*, ed. Z. Lockman, Albany, 1994.

Chatterjee, P. *The Nation and Its Fragments: Colonial and Postcolonial Histories*, Princeton, 1993.

Cooper, F. *Decolonization and African Society: The Labor Question in French and British Africa*, Cambridge, 1996.

Cooper, F., and A.L. Stoler, eds. *Tensions of Empire: Colonial Cultures in a Bourgeois World*, Berkeley, 1997.

Cottam, R.W. *Nationalism in Iran*, Pittsburgh, 1979.

Crinson, M. 'Abadan: Planning and Architecture under the Anglo-Iranian Oil Company'. *Planning Perspectives* 12/3, January 1997, 341–359.

Cronin, S. 'Popular Politics, the New State and the Birth of the Iranian Working Class: The 1929 Abadan Oil Refinery Strike', *Middle Eastern Studies* 46/5, September 2010, 699–732.

——. *Soldiers, Shahs and Subalterns in Iran: Opposition, Protest and Revolt, 1921–1941*, Basingstoke, 2010.

——. *Tribal Politics in Iran: Rural Conflict and the New State, 1921–1941*, London, 2007.

——. *Social Histories of Iran: Modernism and Marginality in the Middle East*, Cambridge, 2021.

Dehqani, H. *Nim Qarn-e Khedmat Dar San 'at-e Naft-e Iran*, Tehran, 1394/2015.

Devos, B. 'Engineering a Modern Society? Adoptions of New Technologies in Early Pahlavi Iran', *Culture and Cultural Politics under Reza Shah: The Pahlavi State, New Bourgeoisie and the Creation of a Modern Society in Iran*, ed. B. Devos and C. Werner, London, 2014, 266–287.

Dietrich, C.R.W. *Oil Revolution: Sovereign Rights and the Economic Culture of Decolonization, 1945 to 1979*, Cambridge, 2017.

Ehsani, K. 'Social Engineering and the Contradictions of Modernization in Khuzestan's Company Towns: A Look at Abadan and Masjed-Soleyman', *International Review of Social History* 48/3, December 2003, 361–399.

——. 'The Social History of Labor in the Iranian Oil Industry: The Built Environment and the Making of the Industrial Working Class (1908–1941)', Ph.D. Thesis, Leiden University, 2015.

Elling, R.C. 'A War of Clubs: Inter-Ethnic Violence and the 1946 Oil Strike in Abadan', *Violence and the City in the Modern Middle East*, ed. Nelida Fuccaro, Stanford, 2016, 189–210.

Elling, R.C., and R.A. Razak. 'Oil, Labour and Empire: Abadan in WWII Occupied Iran', *British Journal of Middle Eastern Studies*, July 2021, 1–18.

Elm, M. *Oil, Power, and Principle: Iran's Oil Nationalization and Its Aftermath*, Syracuse, USA, 1992.

El Shakry, O.S. *The Great Social Laboratory: Subjects of Knowledge in Colonial and Postcolonial Egypt*, Stanford, 2007.

Fakhimi, Q. *Si Sal-e Naft-e Iran: Az Melli Shodan-e Naft ta Enqelab-e Eslami*, Tehran, 1387/2008.

Fanon, F. *The Wretched of the Earth*, trans. C. Farrington, London, 2001.

Farmanfarmaian, M. *Blood and Oil: Memoirs of a Persian Prince*, London, 1997.

Fateh, M. *Panjah Sal Naft-e Iran*, Tehran, 1335/1956.

Floor, W.M. 'The Early Beginnings of Modern Abadan'. *Abadan:Retold*, 2016. http://www.abadan.wiki/en/the-early-beginnings-of-modern-abadan/.

Fung, E.S.K. *The Intellectual Foundations of Chinese Modernity: Cultural and Political Thought in the Republican Era*, Cambridge, 2010.

Galpern, S.G. *Money, Oil, and Empire in the Middle East: Sterling and Postwar Imperialism, 1944–1971*, Cambridge, 2009.

Getachew, A. *Worldmaking after Empire: The Rise and Fall of Self-Determination*, Princeton, 2019.

Guha, R., and G.C. Spivak, eds. *Selected Subaltern Studies*, Oxford, 1988.

Hammad, H. *Industrial Sexuality: Gender, Urbanization, and Social Transformation in Egypt*, Austin, 2016.

Heiss, M.A. *Empire and Nationhood: The United States, Great Britain, and Iranian Oil, 1950–1954*, New York, 1997.

Jafari, P. 'Oil, Labour and Revolution in Iran: A Social History of Labour in the Iranian Oil Industry, 1973–83', Ph.D. Thesis, Leiden University, 2018.

—. 'Labour in the Making of the International Relations of Oil: Resource Nationalism and Trade Unions', *Handbook of Oil and International Relations*, ed. Roland Dannreuther and Wojciech Osrowski, Cheltenham, 2022, 206–20.

Javaherizadeh, M. *Palayeshgah-e Abadan dar 80 Sal Tarikh-e Iran 1908–1988*, Tehran, 1396/2017.

Jefroudi, M. '"If I Deserve It, It Should Be Paid to Me": A Social History of Labour in the Iranian Oil Industry 1951–1973', Ph.D. Thesis, Leiden University, 2017.

Jones, J.H. 'My Visit to the Persian Oilfields'. *Journal of The Royal Central Asian Society* 34/1, January 1947, 56–68.

Kamshad, H. *Hadith-e Nafs: Khaterat-e Resteh az Faramushi*, Tehran, 1396/2017.

Kashani-Sabet, F. *Frontier Fictions: Shaping the Iranian Nation, 1804–1946*, Princeton, 1999.

—. *Conceiving Citizens: Women and the Politics of Motherhood in Iran*, Oxford, 2011.

Katouzian, H. *Musaddiq and the Struggle for Power in Iran*, London, 1999.

Khazeni, A. *Tribes & Empire on the Margins of Nineteenth-Century Iran*, Seattle, 2009.

King, A.D. *Colonial Urban Development: Culture, Social Power and Environment*. London, 1976.

Ladjevardi, H. *Labor Unions and Autocracy in Iran*. Syracuse, USA, 1985.

Lake, M., and H. Reynolds. *Drawing the Global Colour Line: White Men's Countries and the International Challenge of Racial Equality*, Cambridge, 2008.

Latour, B. *We Have Never Been Modern*, trans. C. Porter, Cambridge, USA, 1993.

Legg, S. *Spaces of Colonialism: Delhi's Urban Governmentalities*, Oxford, 2007.

Louis, W.R. *The British Empire in the Middle East 1945–1951: Arab Nationalism, the United States, and Postwar Imperialism*, Oxford, 1984.

Mahdavi, M. *Tarikh-e Nahzat-e Melli-Ye Naft*, Qom, 1396/2017.

Makki, H. *Ketab-e Siyah, Jald-e Sevvom: Khal'-e Yad Az Sherkat-e Naft-e Inglis va Iran*, Tehran, 1360/1981.

Mangan, J.A., *The Games Ethic and Imperialism: Aspects of the Diffusion of an Ideal*, Harmondsworth, 1986.

Marashi, A. 'Paradigms of Iranian Nationalism: History, Theory, and Historiography', *Rethinking Iranian Nationalism and Modernity*, ed. K.S. Aghaie and A. Marashi, Austin, 2014, 3–24.

Maul, D. *Human Rights, Development and Decolonization: The International Labour Organization 1940–70*, Basingstoke, 2014.

Mbembe, A. *Out of the Dark Night: Essays on Decolonization*. New York, 2021.

Mignolo, W., and C.E. Walsh. *On Decoloniality: Concepts, Analytics, Praxis*, Durham, USA, 2018.

Mitchell, T. 'Everyday Metaphors of Power', *Theory and Society* 19/5, October 1990, 545–577.

——. 'The Stage of Modernity', *Questions of Modernity*, ed. T. Mitchell, Minnesota, 2000, 1–34.

——. *Rule of Experts: Egypt, Techno-Politics, Modernity*, Berkeley, 2002.

——. *Carbon Democracy: Political Power in the Age of Oil*, London, 2011.

Movahed, M.A. *Khab-e Ashofte-Ye Naft: Doktor Mosaddeq va Nahzat-e Melli-Ye Iran, Jald-e 1 va 2*, Tehran, 1378/1999.

Mosaddeq, M. *Musaddiq's Memoirs*, ed. H. Katouzian, London, 1988.

Nally, D. 'The Biopolitics of Food Provisioning'. *Transactions of the Institute of British Geographers* 36/1, January 2011, 37–53.

Nightingale, C.H. *Segregation: A Global History of Divided Cities*, Chicago, 2012.

O'Hanlon, R. 'Recovering the Subject: Subaltern Studies and Histories of Resistance in Colonial South Asia', *Modern Asian Studies* 22/1, 1988, 189–224.

Robinson, C. *Black Marxism: The Making of the Black Radical Tradition*, London, 1983.

Rowhani, F. *Tarikh-e Melli Shodan-e San'at-e Naft-e Iran*, Tehran, 1352/1973.

Santiago, M.I. *The Ecology of Oil: Environment, Labor, and the Mexican Revolution, 1900–1938*, Cambridge, 2006.

Schayegh, C. *Who Is Knowledgeable, Is Strong: Science, Class, and the Formation of Modern Iranian Society, 1900–1950*, Berkeley, 2009.

Scott, J.C. *Seeing like a State: How Certain Schemes to Improve the Human Condition Have Failed*, New Haven, 1998.

Shafiee, K. *Machineries of Oil: An Infrastructural History of BP in Iran*, Cambridge, USA, 2018.

Sharkey, H.J. *Living with Colonialism: Nationalism and Culture in the Anglo-Egyptian Sudan*, Berkeley, 2003.

Srivastava, S. *Constructing Post-Colonial India: National Character and the Doon School*, London, 1998.

Stern, P.J. *The Company-State: Corporate Sovereignty and the Early Modern Foundation of the British Empire in India*, Oxford, 2011.

Sternfeld, L. 'Iran Days in Egypt: Mosaddeq's Visit to Cairo in 1951', *British Journal of Middle Eastern Studies* 43/1, January 2016, 1–20.

Streets-Salter, H. 'International and Global Anti-Colonial Movements', *World Histories from below: Disruption and Dissent, 1750 to the Present*, ed. A.M. Burton and A. Ballantyne, London, 2016, 47–74.

Tinker Salas, M. *The Enduring Legacy: Oil, Culture and Society in Venezuela*, Durham, USA, 2009.

Valizadeh, I. *Anglo va Bangolo Dar Abadan*, Tehran, 1390/2011.

Vitalis, R. *America's Kingdom: Mythmaking on the Saudi Oil Frontier*, Stanford, 2007.

Wolfe, P. 'Settler Colonialism and the Elimination of the Native', *Journal of Genocide Research* 8/4, December 2006, 387–409.

Wright, A.G. 'Migratory Pipelines: Labor and Oil in the Arabian Sea', Ph.D. Thesis, University of Michigan, 2015.

Yergin, D. *The Prize: The Epic Quest for Oil, Money, and Power*, New York, 1991.

Zagagi, N. 'An Oasis of Radicalism: The Labor Movement in Abadan in the 1940s', *Iranian Studies* 53/5–6, November 2020, 847–872.

4

Iran and the Dominican Republic, 1958–1961: Trade and Intelligence Cooperation during Leland Rosemberg's Mission to Tehran

Fernando Camacho Padilla[1]

Iran's relations with the Caribbean during the late Pahlavi period appear at first glance to have been non-existent. The small size of the Caribbean countries, as well as the extent of political relations between Iran and other states overshadowed contacts and tensions between Iran and this region. However, within the context of the Cold War, the Caribbean had been a region of great importance since 1959 due to political developments in Cuba and the Dominican Republic. Fidel Castro's revolution in particular and his approach to the Soviet Union had come to have a significant impact

1 This chapter is part of the results of the project: 'Nuevos actores en las relaciones internacionales contemporáneas durante los procesos de descolonización de África, Asia y América Latina (1810–1990). Redes políticas, alianzas y cooperación Sur-Sur', funded by *Comunidad de Madrid* through a multi-year agreement with *Universidad Autónoma de Madrid*, V PRICIT (Reference: SI1/PJI/2019-00493). My gratitude to José Manuel Díaz, from the Dominican National Archive, and Morteza Tafreshi for their support.

on the balance of power within the international system. Likewise, during
the last two years of the Rafael Leónidas Trujillo regime, the Dominican
Republic also became an important international actor due to Trujillo's
negotiations with the Soviet Union, his concern about the Cuban Revolution and his troubled relations with Venezuela. Despite the enormous
geographical distance that separated Iran from the Caribbean, attempts to
engineer relations were made in these years, especially on the initiative of
the Dominican Republic, something unusual because up to that date, Iran
had always been the party to take the initiative with the countries of Latin
America.[2] Trujillo opened a diplomatic representation in Tehran, but the
shah could not reciprocate for several reasons, most importantly the lack
of diplomats in Iran's Ministry of Foreign Affairs with expertise of Latin
America but also because of the bad political relations between the United
States and the Dominican Republic during these years.

Cuba–Dominican Republic bilateral relations had a notable impact
on their respective links to Iran. It was significant that the Dominican
Republic had established ties with Iran in 1958, before Castro's revolution, and Trujillo sought to use his influence with the shah's regime to try
and prevent any collaboration taking place between Havana and Tehran.
As this chapter will show, this strategy was remarkably successful and
although Cuba did try to establish bilateral relations with Iran during this
period, the requests fell on deaf ears. Trujillo was helped by the fact that
the shah was already suspicious of Cuba due to its increased collaboration with the Soviet Union, and considered the Dominican Republic to
be a more favourable ally in the Caribbean. Trujillo was also fortunate
that his ambassador in Tehran, the Swiss-born Leland Rosemberg, already
had familial ties to the shah, so was able to establish a strong position
for himself among the Pahlavi political elite. In fact, as this chapter will
demonstrate, these personal connections played a significant role in the
development of political ties between Iran and the Dominican Republic
at this time.

---

2 Fernando Camacho Padilla and Fernando Escribano Martín, 'Introducción', *Una
vieja amistad. Cuatrocientos años de relaciones históricas y culturales entre Irán y
el mundo hispano*, ed. Fernando Camacho Padilla and Fernando Escribano Martín,
2020, 15–21.

Despite their short duration, relations between the two countries were intense and assumed considerable importance; more importance even than Iran's relations with the two largest economic powers in Latin America, Argentina and Brazil, with which Tehran maintained an older political and economic partnership. The Dominican Republic was unique during this short period between 1958 and 1961 because, aside from the big economies of Latin America, Iran's interactions with countries in Central and South America were negligible. The partnership was certainly driven by geopolitical realities, particularly in the context of the development of the Cold War in the Caribbean and the Middle East, but both sides also sought to develop a commercial link, primarily in the trade of sugar and petrol.

Given that the shah had shown little interest in the Caribbean both before and after Trujillo's regime, this chapter examines the reasons for and nature of the short surge in his relations with Trujillo between 1958 and 1961. As well as investigating the various areas of cooperation between the two sides, including in the fields of trade and intelligence, the chapter explores the crucial role of the chargé d'affaires, Rosemberg, and additionally how the Trujillo regime sought to extend its relations with neighbouring countries, such as Iraq, through its legation in Tehran. Because of the complete absence of historical literature on this subject and the severe restrictions in gaining access to documents in Iran, this chapter incorporates a wide range of primary source materials from around the world, most importantly from archives in the Dominican Republic, but also from Spain, France and the United States.

Until quite recently, Iran's foreign relations with countries of the Global South had been a somewhat neglected subject in late Pahlavi historiography. The few studies that do exist are related to foreign relations during the 1960s and 1970s with Africa,[3] but comparatively little work has been done on Latin America.[4] These types of studies are extremely important;

---

3 Houchang E. Chehabi, 'South Africa and Iran in the Apartheid Era', *Journal of Southern African Studies* 42/4, 2016, 687–709; Robert Steele, 'Two Kings of Kings: Iran–Ethiopia Relations Under Mohammad Reza Pahlavi and Haile Selassie', *The International History Review* 43/6, 2021, 1375–1392; and Robert Steele, 'The Keur Farah Pahlavi Project and Iranian–Senegalese Relations in the 1970s', *Iranian Studies* 54/1–2, 2020, 169–192.

4 Fernando Camacho Padilla, 'Las relaciones entre Latinoamérica e Irán durante la

first, because they illuminate the global character of Iran's foreign policy during this period, and second, because they demonstrate that relations with countries of the Global South shaped the shah's interactions with the United States and the Soviet Union. Iran–Dominican Republic relations during the end of the 1950s and the beginning of the 1960s highlight the shah's growing interest in Latin American political developments, especially in matters of geopolitics and the oil industry. By focusing on this short, but intriguing episode, this chapter offers new perspectives on Iran's interaction with the Global South in the era of decolonisation, and seeks to open up new areas of investigation for future research.

The Genesis of Iran–Latin American Relations

Historically, Latin America had always had a place in Iranian foreign policy, though this place was relatively minor, and engagement was mainly limited to the biggest or most developed countries of the region. The first Persian ambassador to visit South America was Mirza ʿAbdol Hasan, who arrived in 1810 aboard a British vessel. He was travelling with the new British ambassador to Persia under the rule of Fath Ali Shah (1797–1834). ʿAbdol Hasan had travelled to London the year before to elicit the support of King George III against the Russians. Prince John of Portugal hosted the entourage in Rio de Janeiro for almost two weeks before they continued sailing towards the Persian Gulf.[5] Two hundred years earlier, in the seventeenth century, dozens of Persian–Armenians had travelled from Isfahan to Spanish America, sailing along the Pacific and the Atlantic trade routes, but the community had already disappeared by the time of ʿAbdol Hasan's visit.[6]

última década de la dinastía Pahleví', *Anuario de Historia de América Latina* 56, 2019, 66–96.

5 Anita Correia Lima de Almeida, 'Relatos da passagem da embaixada persa pelo Rio de Janeiro Joanino', *Portugal no Golfo Pérsico. 500 anos*, ed. Miguel Castelo-Branco, 2018, 277. Prince John was living in Brazil due to the French occupation of his country during the Napoleonic wars. In 1821 he returned to Portugal.

6 The Persian–Armenian community from New Julfa (Isfahan) created an important commercial network across practically the entire globe, especially in Europe and Asia, and even reaching the main Spanish colonial cities in North and South America.

Diplomatic relations between Iran and some Latin American countries began in earnest in the late nineteenth and early twentieth centuries. The Iranian ambassador to the United States, Isaac Khan, negotiated treaties of friendship, commerce, and navigation with Mexico, Brazil, Uruguay, Argentina, and Chile in the first decade of the twentieth century.[7] The first limited political contacts were also made with Cuba, Haiti, Paraguay, and Guatemala at this time.[8] Also, during this period, a small migration from Iran, consisting mainly of Christians (Assyrians and Armenians) but also some Jews and Muslims, began to arrive in Latin America, travelling primarily to Argentina but also to other countries such as Mexico, Brazil, and Cuba.[9] However, many of the political relations that were established during this time were not long-lasting and when the Iranian diplomatic representative to the United States, Morteza Khan, left Washington in 1909, Iran's political contact with Latin America vanished. It was not until the early decades of the reign of Reza Shah (r. 1925–1941) that Iran regained an interest in the region. An Iranian diplomatic representation was opened for the first time in Buenos Aires in 1935 by Nader Arasteh to promote trade between the two countries. But again, these ties did not last long. In 1937 Arasteh was posted to Berlin, and nobody was sent to replace him because the Argentinian government had not responded with reciprocity.[10]

For the remainder of Reza Shah's rule, South America featured little in Iran's foreign policy, but this began to change again under his successor, Mohammad Reza Pahlavi (r. 1941–1979).[11] Diplomatic relations

---

7 Fernando Camacho Padilla, 'Las relaciones diplomáticas entre Persia y América Latina durante las últimas décadas de la Dinastía Qajar (1895–1925)', *Una vieja amistad*, ed. Camacho Padilla and Escribano Martín, 50–120.

8 In September 1902, soon after gaining independence, the president of Cuba, Estrada Palma, had informed the Persian ambassador to the United States, Isaac Khan, of his interest in formalising diplomatic relations. Document GH1321-K30-P21-32, Archive of the Ministry of Foreign Affairs of Iran.

9 Fernando Camacho Padilla, 'El éxodo de los cristianos de Persia tras la Primera Guerra Mundial. De la acción humanitaria española a su llegada a Latinoamérica', *Miradas de Irán. Historia y cultura*, ed. Fernando Camacho Padilla, Fernando Escribano Martín, Nadereh Farzamnia Hajardovom, and José Luis Neila Hernández, 2021, 48–76.

10 Camacho Padilla, 'Las relaciones diplomáticas entre Persia y América Latina', 19.

11 In spite of these weak political connections, Reza Shah had initially hoped to go

were re-established with Brazil in 1943, Chile in 1944 and Argentina in 1946. Shortly after, Iran opened diplomatic legations in Rio de Janeiro and Buenos Aires, and Brazil and Argentina sent permanent diplomatic representatives to Tehran. But Chile was the first Latin American country to send a representative, Manuel Garretón, who was accredited in Ankara between 1945 and 1950, to present credentials in Iran.[12] However, Chile did not open an embassy in Tehran until 1974, and during this period, the closest Iranian diplomatic representation to Santiago was in Buenos Aires.

When Prime Minister Mohammad Mosaddeq nationalised the oil sector in 1951 and had to face a British embargo, Mexico was the only Latin American country to support this decision and to express solidarity. The former president of Mexico, Lázaro Cárdenas, expressed support for Mosaddeq through political demonstrations and press articles, and the Mexican government began a national campaign to send professionals from its oil sector to Iran to collaborate with the shah's opponents in order to soften the impact caused by the departure of British technicians from the Abadan refineries.[13]

During the first half of the twentieth century, although connections had been intermittently nurtured with countries in South America, Iran had shown very little interest in the Caribbean. While there was some minor engagement with Cuba, the largest country in the Caribbean, there had been no engagement with the second largest country, the Dominican Republic. This situation changed in 1958, when the first attempts were made to establish formal diplomatic ties.

Iran–Dominican Republic Relations (1958–1961)

In July 1958, the first official contact between Iran and the Dominican Republic was made on the initiative of the Dominican government, whose

---

to Argentina after the British invasion of 1941, but he was never authorised.
Mohammed Reza Pahlavi, *Answer to History*, 1980, 68; Shaul Bakhash, *The Fall of Reza Shah: The Abdication, Exile, and Death of Modern Iran's Founder*, 2021.
Another one of his preferred destinations was Canada.
12 Camacho Padilla and Escribano Martín, 'Introducción', 20.
13 Mostafa Elm, *Oil, Power, and Principle: Iran's Oil Nationalization and Its Aftermath*, 1994, 172.

ambassador to Germany, Salvador Ortiz, had met and discussed the prospect with the Iranian chargé d'affaires, Ali Fotuhi.[14] The Iranian government gave the green light to the idea of establishing diplomatic relations in early September.[15] The decision to open a diplomatic legation in Tehran was soon made, and Leland Rosemberg, a Swiss-born Dominican diplomat serving as trade attaché in Bern, who enjoyed a close friendship with General Rafael Leónidas Trujillo Jr. (alias Ramfis), the son of the dictator, was immediately appointed chargé d'affaires in Iran.[16] In 1955, Rosemberg had married the shah's former sister-in-law, Princess Minu Dowlatshahi.[17] It is probable that it was Rosemberg himself who, after visiting Iran and studying different economic sectors, mostly the sugar industry, convinced Trujillo that Iran could be a valuable economic partner.[18]

On 16 October 1958, Rosemberg and Princess Minu arrived in Tehran to commence their new duties and on 20 October, Rosemberg presented his credentials to the Iranian government.[19] For one month, Rosemberg

14 At that moment, the Iranian ambassador Khalil Esfandiary (Queen Soraya's father) was absent because he was in the process of being replaced. Letter no. 250 from the Embassy of the Dominican Republic in Bonn to Secretary of State, Bonn, 17 July 1958, Ref. 3114528, Archivo General de la Nación de República Dominicana (hereafter AGN).

15 Letter no. 839 from Embassy of Iran to Germany to Embassy of Dominican Republic to Germany, 8 September 1958, Ref. 3114105, AGN.

16 Rosemberg was a cosmopolitan Jewish businessman who moved to the United States in 1946. In 1954 he was granted Dominican citizenship by Trujillo, but only lived for a short time on the island because in 1955 he was appointed trade attaché to Switzerland. He had also worked in Germany and at the Dominican consulate in New York, and was a close friend of Porfirio Rubirosa, one of the closest advisers of dictator Leónidas Trujillo. Letter from the Embassy of the Dominican Republic in Bonn to the Vice-President of the Republic, Bonn, 26 September 1958, Ref. 3114105, AGN.

17 In 1954, Princess Minu divorced Prince Hamid Reza Pahlavi after being married for three years. Hamid Reza Pahlavi was son of Reza Shah and Queen Esmat. According to Queen Soraya, Princess Minu met Leland Rosemberg while she was travelling in Europe and decided to divorce Hamid Reza Pahlavi because of his difficult personality. Soraya Esfandiary-Bakhtiari, *The Autobiography of Her Imperial Highness*, 1964, 71–72.

18 Queen Soraya confirms in her memoirs that Rosemberg and Princess Minu had already visited Tehran on several occasions. Esfandiary-Bakhtiari, *The Autobiography*, 71–72.

19 Memorandum no. 4938 from the Secretary of Foreign Affairs to the President of

operated from the Keyan Hotel in central Tehran before a diplomatic legation was finally opened on 15 November.[20] During his first weeks, Rosemberg established contact with Iranian political authorities and Latin American diplomats and residents to expand his networks in the country. At this point, only one Dominican woman was living in the country, Elena Ariza de Wheelock. She was married to a senior Canadian executive from the World Bank who was working as a financial advisor to the Iranian government.[21] Very soon after Rosemberg's arrival, the Iranian government requested that the Dominican Republic support their candidates at the upcoming United Nations elections.[22]

The Iran–Dominican Republic bilateral relationship developed during a very tense period for the Trujillo regime. Relations between Santo Domingo and Washington had deteriorated quickly due to the complicity of the Trujillo regime in the kidnapping of political opponents abroad and even the assassination of US citizens. The Cuban Revolution also worried Trujillo, who felt that a similar process could take place in his country with the support of Fidel Castro. Cuba's former dictator, Fulgencio Batista, went into exile in the Dominican capital in January 1959 when the situation in Cuba became ungovernable. But he had a difficult relationship with Trujillo, who demanded large sums of money to allow him to stay in the country and kept him under strict surveillance. Batista was even briefly imprisoned on the order of Trujillo.[23]

Political repression in the Dominican Republic increased enormously

---

the Republic, Santo Domingo, 16 October 1958, Ref. 3114528, AGN; and Memorandum no. 5002 from the Secretary of Foreign Affairs to the President of the Republic, Santo Domingo, 21 October 1958, Ref. 3114528, AGN.
20 Letter no. 22195 from the Secretary of State for Finance to the Budget director, Santo Domingo, 30 November 1958, Ref. 3114528, AGN.
21 Letter no. 00115 from the Legation of the Dominican Republic to Iran to the Secretary of Foreign Affairs, Tehran, 5 November 1958, Ref. 3114528, AGN.
22 Memorandum no. 5009 from the Secretary of Foreign Affairs to the President of the Republic, Santo Domingo, 14 November 1958, Ref. 3114528, AGN.
23 Roberto Batista Fernández, *Hijo de Batista. Memorias*, 2021, 65. After several efforts, Batista managed to leave Dominican Republic and settle on the island of Madeira (Portugal). Trujillo's poor reception of Batista was due to old political grudges dating from the 1930s. Hans Paul Wiese Delgado, *Trujillo, amado por muchos, odiado por otros, temido por todos*, 2000, 397.

in the following months, provoking great agitation and fear among Trujillo's opponents, a significant number of whom left the island seeking refuge in different countries. Among those who offered protection to these political émigrés was the president of Venezuela, Rómulo Betancourt, who had been a long-time critic of Trujillo. The support of Betancourt for the Dominican opposition enraged Trujillo, to the extent that on 24 June 1960 he tried to have him assassinated.[24] As a result of this assassination attempt, the Organization of American States (OAS) condemned the Trujillo regime in August, and the United Nations approved a series of economic sanctions in September on petrol and machinery imports, among other products, which further deepened his international isolation. Because of the situation, Trujillo began to seek new foreign allies, and even considered the establishment of relations with the Soviet Union. In response to these developments, the government of Iran informed Rosemberg that it would support the Dominican Republic at the United Nations Assembly if and when it was needed.[25]

For various reasons, Iran was unable to reciprocate the Dominican Republic's mission to appoint a diplomatic representative there in 1958 or 1959.[26] The initial idea was that the Iranian representative would be based in Washington DC, but probably due to the deterioration of relations between Trujillo and the Kennedy administration, an alternative was considered. In September 1960, Iran's ambassador to Brazil, Mahmud Forughi, was finally recognised as Iran's representative to the Dominican Republic, having first been put forward by his government in February of that year.[27] After the confirmation of Iran's representative to the

24 For details of this episode, see: Edgardo Mondolfi Gudat, *El día del atentado: el frustrado magnicidio contra Rómulo Betancourt*, 2013.

25 Letter no. 321 from the Legation of the Dominican Republic to Iran to the Secretary of Foreign Affairs, Tehran, 4 August 1960, Ref. 3114961, AGN.

26 Mu-Kien Adriana Sang, *La Política Exterior Dominicana 1844–1961 Tomo II. La política exterior del dictador Trujillo, 1930–1961*, 2000, 120–121. See also: Letter no. 343 from the Legation of the Dominican Republic to Iran to the Secretary of Foreign Affairs, Tehran, 19 July 1959, Ref. 3114528, AGN.

27 Letter no. 1697 from the Secretary of the Presidency to the Secretary of Foreign Affairs, Santo Domingo, 3 February 1960, Ref. 3114961, AGN; Letter no. 321 from the Legation of the Dominican Republic to Iran to the Secretary of Foreign Affairs, Tehran, 4 August 1960, Ref. 3114961, AGN; Letter no. 386 from the Legation of the

Dominican Republic, Rosemberg suggested to Trujillo that his position be elevated from chargé d'affaires to minister plenipotentiary so that he could present his new credentials to the shah.[28] Because of the Iranian government's interest in Latin America, the idea of creating a department for Latin America at the Iranian Ministry of Foreign Affairs was also discussed with Rosemberg in August 1960.[29]

Sugar and Security

One of the main objectives of Rosemberg was to expand exports of Dominican raw and refined sugar to Iran without the use of intermediaries.[30] At that time, Iran imported more refined sugar than any other nation in the world, and its Caribbean sugar was primarily imported from Cuba.[31] Sugar exports to Iran from the Dominican Republic began in 1956, shortly before the first political interactions between the two countries took place, when 10,176 metric tons of sugar were sold.[32] The political and economic instability of Cuba, both during the tumultuous period of 1956 to 1959 and the years immediately following the revolution, directly affected Cuban sugar exports. Trujillo sought to take advantage of the situation to expand its international market and at the same time, Iran was open to diversifying its sources of sugar.

In October 1959, the first Iranian delegation arrived in Santo Domingo for a three-day visit to begin negotiations about sugar supply, after

---

Dominican Republic to Iran to President Rafael L. Trujillo, Tehran, 6 September 1960, Ref. 3114961, AGN. After his term in Brazil had ended in August 1961, Foroughi was sent to Switzerland for a short time. Then he became ambassador in Washington from 1963 to 1965, and during that time, he also was accredited as ambassador to Mexico and Venezuela. After the Iranian Revolution, he moved to the United States.

28 Letter no. 386 from the Legation of the Dominican Republic to Iran to President Rafael L. Trujillo, Tehran, 6 September 1960, Ref. 3114961, AGN.

29 Letter no. 321 from the Legation of the Dominican Republic to Iran to the Secretary of Foreign Affairs, Tehran, 4 August 1960, Ref. 3114961, AGN.

30 Memorandum no. 5772 from the Secretary of Foreign Affairs to the President of the Republic, Santo Domingo, 29 November 1958, Ref. 3114528, AGN.

31 *Kayhan*, 27 February 1960.

32 Wiese Delgado, *Trujillo*, 274.

having participated in the latest meeting of the Central Treaty Organization (CENTO) in Washington.[33] Although the trip was organised in haste,
giving little time to make proper arrangements, the Iranian delegation held
talks with the agriculture minister and the director and deputy director
of the Central Bank.[34] President Trujillo and the Dominican minister of
foreign affairs, Porfirio Herrera Báez, also met the Iranian delegates at a
lunch reception organised in their honour.[35] The delegation was clearly
concerned with more than just sugar exports, as it included the head of
Iran's security services (SAVAK), Teymur Bakhtiar, and the deputy minister of foreign affairs, Amir Khosrow Afshar. Indeed, Bakhtiar and Afshar
were taken to visit the San Isidro Air Base, the most important military
facility in the country, which was also used as a torture and interrogation centre, along with a weapons factory and the Navy Academy of San
Cristobal.[36] In order not to generate suspicions of a potential collaboration
between the secret services of the two countries, details of these visits were
absent in press reports in the Dominican Republic and Iran.[37] It is likely
that discussions over intelligence cooperation did indeed take place.

   During the visit, the president of the national sugar cooperation and
business administrator of Azucarera Haina, Hans Wiese Delgado, participated in negotiations with the Iranian delegation. According to Wiese's
memoirs, the Iranian delegation visited the refinery Ingenio Provenir,
which impressed Bakhtiar with its size and large number of employees.[38]
Wiese also states that Iran, which sought to become a self-sufficient sugar

---

33 Letter of the French Embassy in Dominican Republic to the French Minister of
Foreign Affairs. Santo Domingo, 26 October 1959, Ref. 367QO/21, Centre des
Archives diplomatiques de La Courneuve (hereafter CADC).
34 Memorandum no. 56743 from the Secretary of Foreign Affairs to the President
of the Republic, Santo Domingo, 14 October 1959, Ref. 3114961, AGN.
35 Wiese Delgado, *Trujillo*, 275–276.
36 Letter of the French Embassy in Dominican Republic to the French Minister of
Foreign Affairs. Santo Domingo, 26 October 1959. Reference: 367QO/21, CADC.
37 In fact, the Iranian press did not publish anything about this trip until four
months later. See *Kayhan*, 27 February 1960. In the 1970s, the SAVAK also
collaborated with Pinochet's intelligence agency, Dirección de Inteligencia Nacional
(DINA). For more details, see: Mónica González, 'El día en que Manuel Contreras
le ofreció al Sha de Irán matar a "Carlos, El Chacal"', *Centro de Investigación
Periodística*, 6 August 2009.
38 Wiese Delgado, *Trujillo*, 276.

producer in the future, was trying to increase its sugar production by switching from cane to beet cultivation, which would generate a higher yield. They discussed the idea of establishing a sugar refinery as a joint venture with fifty per cent Iranian and fifty percent Dominican capital. Moreover, it was agreed that Iran would buy around 100,000 tons of raw sugar starting in 1961, rising to 200,000 in 1962 and 300,000 in 1963.[39] But it seems that sugar imports were significant by then because already in July 1960, the Canadian legation in Tehran reported that 'the Dominican Republic and the Republic of China (Formosa – represented in Iran by a resident ambassador) are said to command the Iranian imported sugar market.'[40]

Soon after the departure of the Iranian mission, Dominican authorities invited the shah to visit the island on his next trip to Washington. However, the shah's next trip to Washington did not take place until 1962, by which point Trujillo had already been killed and Iran's relations with the Dominican Republic suspended.[41]

Back in Iran, Rosemberg was able to use his personal relationships with the Imperial Court and high officials of the government to access privileged information and gain entrance to social circles not normally accessible to members of the diplomatic corps in Tehran.[42] Just days after his arrival in Tehran, he wrote:

> On October 28 I had the honour of being invited to a private dinner
> by His Majesty the Shah and I was the only diplomat present. It was a
> very small dinner, which only friends and the Shah's family attended.

---

39 Wiese Delgado, *Trujillo*, 276. Due to the assassination of Trujillo on 30 May 1961, the agreements were unfulfilled.

40 Letter from the Canadian Legation in Iran to the Under-Secretary of State for External Affairs, Tehran, 18 July 1960, Ref: 5/3-40-PT-2. vol. 5018. Library and Archives Canada.

41 Letter of the French Embassy in Dominican Republic to the French Minister of Foreign Affairs, Santo Domingo, 26 October 1959, Ref. 367QO/21, CADC.

42 In his reports he also gives an account of some of his meetings with the shah's siblings, for example Prince Gholam Reza Pahlavi and Princess Ashraf Pahlavi, with whom he also discussed the purchase of sugar. Memorandum no. 6043 from the Secretary of Foreign Affairs to the President of the Republic, Santo Domingo, 16 December 1958, Ref. 3114528, AGN.

I had the opportunity to discuss with His Majesty various issues. There is no doubt that we can count on His Majesty's help, especially regarding sugar, since he is the owner of one of the most important refineries in this country. [...] He will be absent for a few days, and even though I will meet with him on several occasions before his departure, he has proposed to leave this matter until his return, which is convenient for me because it will give me the opportunity to finish protocol visits and to arrange the legation.[43]

As his letters show, Rosemberg had strong sympathies for the Iranian monarchy, which led him to openly express his full support even on sensitive moral issues, such as the Pahlavi regime's application of the death penalty for communist activists. In early May 1960, for example, Rosemberg wrote:

unfortunately, in Latin America, contrary to what happens in Iran, there only seems to be democracy where there is a communist party. While in Iran the communists are shot, in Latin America it would be necessary to decorate them to show the existence of a pseudo-democracy.[44]

For the duration of his mission, Rosemberg also kept his government abreast of political developments in neighbouring countries, such as the 1960 military coup in Turkey against Prime Minister Adnan Menderes.[45] He also became an active member of the diplomatic corps in Tehran and held talks with other foreign legations, including those of Iraq,[46]

---

43 Letter no. 0099 from the Legation of the Dominican Republic to Iran to the Secretary of Foreign Affairs, Tehran, 2 November 1958, Ref. 3114528, AGN.
44 Letter no. 171 from the Legation of the Dominican Republic to Iran to the Secretary of Foreign Affairs, Tehran, 5 May 1960, Ref. 3114528, AGN.
45 Letter no. 217 from the Legation of the Dominican Republic to Iran to the Secretary of Foreign Affairs, Tehran, 8 June 1960, Ref. 3114961, AGN.
46 Given the geographical distance of the Dominican Republic from the Middle East and especially given the lack of diplomatic relations with other countries in the region, representatives of neighbouring nations and Rosemberg initiated negotiations. Thus, in late June 1960 the Iraqi ambassador, General Amin, proposed to initiate diplomatic relations between both countries because Baghdad wanted both

Afghanistan,[47] the Soviet Union, and the Vatican.[48] However, he appears to have had very limited contact with other diplomats from Latin America, which perhaps gives a good sense of his priorities.[49] Rosemberg had a much closer relationship with the Iranian authorities than Argentinian and Brazilian diplomats did at that time. Indeed, Rosemberg was so trusted by the Iranian authorities that he was able to negotiate intelligence cooperation between Iran and the Dominican Republic.

From mid-1959 onwards, Trujillo's diplomats and intelligence service had begun collaborating with SAVAK, particularly regarding Cuban and Venezuelan foreign policy in the Middle East.[50] As Rosemberg wrote on 20 June:

> General Bakhtiar has been extremely grateful for the cooperation of the authorities of the [Dominican] Republic and especially for

---

to expand its relationships in Latin America and to import Dominican sugar. Final negotiations were planned to take place in late October 1960. See Letter no. 253 from the Legation of the Dominican Republic to Iran to the Secretary of Foreign Affairs, Tehran, 30 June 1960, Ref. 3114961, AGN; Letter no. 435 from the Legation of the Dominican Republic to Iran to the Secretary of Foreign Affairs, Tehran, 22 September 1961, Ref. 3114961, AGN; Letter no. 13205 from the Secretary of State to the Secretary of Foreign Affairs, Santo Domingo, 5 September 1960, Ref. 3114528, AGN.

47 In January 1961, Rosemberg also met the Afghan ambassador to Tehran to discuss the establishment of bilateral relations. See Letter no. 13205 from the Secretary of State to the Secretary of Foreign Affairs, Santo Domingo, 5 September 1960, Ref. 3114528, AGN; Memorandum no. 443 from the Secretary of Foreign Affairs to the President of the Republic, Santo Domingo, 2 February 1961, Ref. 3114961, AGN.

48 Many reports were written regarding apostolic nuncio Lino Zanini, who was appointed in Tehran until 1959 and later assigned to the Dominican Republic. From the beginning of his stay in Santo Domingo he maintained his distance from the government, and on 21 May 1960 Trujillo declared him persona non grata. Thereafter, he left the country. For more details, see: Bernardo Vega, *Los Estados Unidos y Trujillo. Los días finales, 1960–61. Colección de documentos del Departamento de Estado, la CIA y los archivos del Palacio Nacional*, 2000.

49 Very few documents show any contact with either the other Latin American diplomatic legations in Iran (Argentina and Brazil) or with the Spanish embassy.

50 During the early days of SAVAK, intelligence agencies of western countries, including CIA and Mossad, cooperated also in training and improvement programmes. Yves Bomatim, and Houchang Nahavandi, *Mohammad Réza Pahlavi*, 2019, 329.

the efficiency and the speed shown by the Foreign Ministry under
your charge. [...] He pointed out that he has given orders to quickly
terminate the list of subversive people, which he will provide to our
government, and once again demonstrated his interest in receiving a
list of the agents of International communism and other subversive
people prepared by the Dominican authorities. [...] During our
conversation, General Bakhtiar also informed me that he has already
given instructions to his agents to follow the movements of the
Venezuelan missions in the Middle East.[51]

This document confirms the existence of an early security cooperation
between Iran and the Dominican Republic during these years, motivated
by fears from each side about the danger of revolution taking place in their
own country. In the same document Iran's concern about Castro's foreign
relations is discussed:

General Bakhtiar has expressed to me his concern about the tour of
a Cuban delegation around countries of the Middle East, and he is
surprised that Commander Guevara has been received by General
Nasser in Cairo. General Bakhtiar has immediately sent a new
telegram to all Iranian diplomatic missions with clear instructions
deny him entry visas to Iran. He also informed me that he is go   to
notify friendly countries about Commander Guevara.[52]

Rosemberg's critical views on Venezuela likely in   .ced how Bakhtiar regarded Caracas's foreign policy in the reg￼   Iran felt that Venezuela could eventually also become a comm   st state and considered
how that might affect its oil production.[53] In   .tion, the shah was worried

---

51 Confidential letter no. 303 from th   .gation of the Dominican Republic to
Iran to the Secretary of Foreign A   . , Tehran, 20 June 1959, Ref. 3114528,
AGN.
52 Confidential letter no. 30   .m the Legation of the Dominican Republic to Iran
to the Secretary of Forei   .fairs, Santo Domingo, 20 June 1959, Ref. 3114528,
AGN.
53 Letter no. 321   .i the Legation of the Dominican Republic to Iran to the
Secreta-   Tehran, 4 August 1960, Ref. 3114961, AGN.

that Venezuela would be pressured by the Soviet Union to nationalise its oil industry.[54] After the creation of OPEC in September 1960, during the Baghdad Conference, the director of Shell in Iran, Mr. Jochen, told Rosemberg:

> the situation in Venezuela is risky and the high percentage of communist employees in the oil sector could represent an immediate threat. A new Fidel Castro could emerge, and therefore, oil companies are trying to take advantage of their relations with the present government to safeguard their capital in case such an event occurs.[55]

Due to the shah's concern regarding Caracas's attitude at the OPEC meeting in Baghdad, the Venezuelan delegation that visited Iran in September 1960, after being invited by the National Iranian Oil Company (NIOC), was not received by any member of the Iranian government.[56]

In response to the US boycott of Trujillo's regime, diplomatic negotiations with Moscow began to take place through conversations between Dominican and Soviet representatives at the United Nations headquarters in New York, Brussels, Cairo, and other capitals of the world, including Tehran, which also confirms the importance of Rosenberg's diplomatic position. Then, in late April 1961, the Soviet ambassador to Iran, Nikolai Pegov, requested a formal meeting with Rosemberg to propose both the establishment of diplomatic relations and the inauguration of several Soviet cooperation programmes in the Dominican Republic. The only condition impossed by Moscow to the Dominican goverment was to improve

---

54 Letter no. 318 from the Legation of the Dominican Republic to Iran to the Secretary of Foreign Affairs, Tehran, 4 August 1960, Ref. 3114961. AGN.
55 Letter no. 446 from the Legation of the Dominican Republic to Iran to the Secretary of Foreign Affairs, Tehran, 29 September 1960, Ref. 3114961, AGN. Manucher Farmanfarmaian's memoirs regarding the creation of the OPEC are interesting to see the Venezuela–Iran connection. See Manucher Farmanfarmaian and Roxanne Farmanfarmaian, *Blood & Oil: A Prince's Memoir of Iran, from the Shah to the Ayatollah*, 2005, 344–345.
56 Letter no. 418 from the Legation of the Dominican Republic to Iran to the Secretary of Foreign Affairs, Tehran, 18 September 1960, Ref. 3114961, AGN. The delegation included Venezuelan oil Minister, Juan Pablo Pérez Alfonso, Venezuela's ambassador in Cairo, and an oil expert.

relations with Havana, for which they should contact Cuban officials.[57] Despite his openly critical stance towards Moscow, Rosemberg acknowledged in reports that the Soviet embassy in Tehran was more professional and knowledgeable than that of the United States, which he criticised for its limited interest in Iran and for its diplomats living in complete isolation from Iranian society. Rosemberg added that he considered this attitude to be a serious mistake, since it could promote greater sympathies for the Soviet Union, which might ultimately result in Iran switching allegiance toward its northern neighbour.[58]

Oil Trade Negotiations between the Shah and Trujillo

As a result of the economic and commercial sanctions imposed on the country at the Sixth Meeting of Foreign Ministers of the OAS, held in San José, Costa Rica, from 16 to 20 August 1960, the Dominican Republic had to look for new trade partners. Iran did not miss the opportunity and offered oil to Rosemberg at a reasonable rate. This possibility was tabled for discussion for the first time in early August 1960, when Rosemberg met Iran's ambassador to the United States, Ardeshir Zahedi, and the director of the department of the Americas at the Ministry of Foreign Affairs, Parviz Hushang Safinia.[59] A few days later, one of the shah's deputies, Ahmad Mehbod, also proposed to Rosemberg that Iran import all of its sugar needed for domestic consumption from the Dominican Republic.[60] This proposal was positively received by the Dominican political authorities, which ordered Rosemberg to continue with the negotiations, and to arrange the arrival of an economic delegation in Tehran.[61]

---

57 Letter no. 143/61 from the Legation of the Dominican Republic to Iran to the Secretary of Foreign Affairs, Tehran, 25 April 1961, Ref. 3114961, AGN.
58 Letter no. 262 from the Legation of the Dominican Republic to Iran to the Secretary of Foreign Affairs, Tehran, 13 July 1960, Ref. 3114961, AGN.
59 Letter no. 321 from the Legation of the Dominican Republic to Iran to the Secretary of Foreign Affairs, Tehran, 4 August 1960, Ref. 3114961, AGN. Ambassador Zahedi also expressed to Rosemberg his interest in visiting Santo Domingo.
60 Letter no. 354 from the Legation of the Dominican Republic to Iran to the Secretary of Foreign Affairs, Tehran, 21 August 1960. Ref. 3114961, AGN.
61 Document, no. 12680 from Oscar Guaroa Ginebra Henríquez, Secretary of State

Only one month after this notification, the shah agreed to invite a Dominican delegation to Iran to discuss the cooperation project, but due to the international isolation of Trujillo, he wanted to keep the conversations top secret. The shah's offer was to exchange petrol for sugar, and he charged the prime minister, Ja'far Sharif-Emami, with the task of beginning negotiations. The main problem Iran faced was securing enough refined petrol to trade because it lacked the capacity to export such large quantities. Therefore, they planned to send Iranian crude first to a refinery in Italy, and then to the Dominican Republic. They also considered the possibility of building a refinery on the island with Iranian and Dominican capital.[62] The Dominican mission headed by minister Oscar Guaroa Ginebra Henríquez and Salvador Ortiz, from the Central Bank of the Dominican Republic, stayed in Tehran from 13 to 17 September. During these days, they had several official receptions and meetings with several high-ranking representatives of the Iranian government, including Ahmad Mehbod and ministers Mohammad Sadjadi and Mohammad Reza Vishkai. No information was given either to foreign diplomats or to the press about the conversations due to the shah's own instruction to keep them top secret.[63]

In late September 1960, during the opening ceremony of the academic year at the University of Tehran, Rosemberg and the shah had a conversation regarding the political situation in Latin America and the acquisition of Dominican sugar. According to Rosemberg, the shah gave the order to the general director of the Pahlavi Foundation, Mohammad Ja'far Behbahanian, to procure from the Dominican Republic all the sugar required for a new refinery currently under construction. In his report of this meeting, Rosemberg added:

> During the ceremony, I was the only member of the Diplomatic
> Corps called to speak with his Majesty the Shah [...]. I would like to
> highlight the king's gesture of expressive and close friendship toward

---

to the Legation of the Dominican Republic to Iran, Santo Domingo, 23 August 1960, Ref. 3114961, AGN.

62 Letter no. 386 from the Legation of the Dominican Republic to Iran to President Rafael L. Trujillo, Tehran, 6 September 1960, Ref. 3114961, AGN.

63 Memorandum, no. 3735, Santo Domingo, 27 September 1960, Ref. 3114961, AGN.

the [Dominican] Republic, remarkable considering that this fifteen-minute conversation took place in front of thousands of people and in circumstances particularly unrelated to the topic of the event, which shows the true interest of the Iranian king in strengthening relations with the [Dominican] Republic.[64]

Negotiations were carried out quickly and in late October, Rosemberg and Ahmad Mehbod travelled together to Santo Domingo.[65] Because the Iranian crude that would be sent to the Dominican Republic would have to be refined in Italy first, these discussions also included Italian authorities, including the president of the Italian National Oil Company, Enrico Mattei.[66]

Iran's political support was also enlisted at this time to ensure that the Dominican Republic's oil supply was not disrupted. In January 1961, during the OPEC meeting in Caracas, the Venezuelan government prepared a proposal to block the supply of oil to the Dominican Republic. Hearing this, Rosemberg quickly contacted the ambassadors of Iraq and Saudi Arabia in Tehran, who reiterated their support. In addition, he met with various senior Iranian political authorities to discuss the problem, including the deputy foreign minister, Amir Khosrow Afshar, president of the NIOC, 'Abdollah Entezam, vice president, Fuad Ruhani, and even the shah himself. All of them reaffirmed their solidarity with Trujillo and insisted that they would deliver all of the necessary oil. They also stressed that such a decision was outside the framework of OPEC and pledged to move forward with the negotiations of the sugar-for-oil exchange.[67]

In late January, Rosemberg travelled to Paris and to Santo Domingo for almost three weeks to accompany a French economic mission with staff

---

64 Letter no. 451 from the Legation of the Dominican Republic to Iran to the Secretary of Foreign Affairs, Tehran, 30 September 1960, Ref. 3114961, AGN.
65 Document no. 23051 from Secretary of Foreign Affairs to State Secretary, Santo Domingo, 11 October 1960, Ref. 3114961, AGN.
66 Document no. 16698 from Secretary of the Presidency to the Legation of the Dominican Republic to Iran, Santo Domingo, 18 November 1960, Ref. 3114961, AGN.
67 Secret letter no. 21/61 from the Legation of the Dominican Republic to Iran to the Secretary of Foreign Affairs, Tehran, 10 January 1961, Ref. 3114961, AGN.

of the Credit Lyonnais and ENSA (from Schneider Electric) who oversaw preliminary plans to set up an oil refinery.[68] In early March 1961, Rosemberg returned to Paris to discuss the results of their survey.[69] A few days later, another French mission went back to Santo Domingo for final discussions.[70] In late April 1961, Rosemberg sent the agreed conditions with a series of documents confirming the French government's authorisation to carry out the oil refinery construction project, and ENSA's official commitment to carry it out.[71] French diplomats remarked: 'As for Iran, the activity of the Dominican Chargé d'Affaires in Tehran, Mr. Leland Rosenberg, seems to lead to the establishment of economic ties not with the country where he is accredited, but with France.'[72]

Meanwhile, Rosemberg did not miss an opportunity to continue doing business in other sectors. In March 1961, for instance, he organised an exhibition of wood houses built by a Dominican–Swiss company in Switzerland in Tehran. General Mohammad Amir Khatami, chief of staff of the imperial air force, first travelled to Basel to see the different models of the houses and decided to acquire 2,000 units for the Iranian air force. The shah loaned the land on which the houses were laid out in the capital.[73]

As US–Dominican relations deteriorated further, Rosemberg expressed an extremely critical view of the role of Washington in Iran's economy, but also in relation to its national politics. He alerted the Dominican foreign secretary that sugar and petrol trade negotiations could be affected by Washington, in spite of Iran's interest in the project and its good relations with the Dominican Republic, as demonstrated through its support of

68 Letter from Leland Rosemberg to Secretary of the Presidency, Santo Domingo, 12 February 1961, Ref. 3114961, AGN.
69 Secret letter no. 77 from the Legation of the Dominican Republic to Iran to the Secretary of Foreign Affairs, Tehran, 28 February 1961, Ref. 3114961, AGN.
70 Memorandum no. 785 from the Secretary of Foreign Affairs to the President of the Republic, Sango Domingo, 2 March 1961, Ref. 3114961, AGN.
71 Letter no. 140/61 from the Legation of the Dominican Republic to Iran to Ambrosio Álvarez Aybar, Legal Consultant of the executive branch, Tehran, 2 March 1961, Ref. 3114961, AGN.
72 Letter no. 70 from the Embassy of France to Dominican Republic to the French Minister of Foreign Affairs, Tehran, 28 February 1961, Ref. 108QO/19, CADC.
73 Letter no. 88 from the Legation of the Dominican Republic to Iran to the Secretary of Foreign Affairs, Tehran, 2 March 1961, Ref. 3114961, AGN.

Trujillo during the OPEC meeting in Caracas in January 1961. According to Rosemberg:[74]

> However, we must consider the situation of Iran as a country subjected to the US economic and military system, a fact that decisively influences its policy, and which must always serve the interests of the United States. This restricts the intention of the Shah to achieve independence of action that allows him to carry out a national policy for his country [...]. The North American influence is enormous and fully determines Iran's policy to its own interests, creating a climate of instability which delimitates the government's capacities to their mercy as soon as they do not comply with Yankee imports.
>
> [...] There is obviously a great amount of administrative corruption in Iran. Two sides are always necessary for corruption; here in Iran, America is always one of them. They are the most generous corrupters. And this fact, unfortunately, is a daily occurrence.[75]

A more pressing concern at this time was American attempts to block Iran's purchase of Dominican sugar, agreed during the Iranian mission to the Dominican Republic in 1959. The US embassy in Tehran sent a note to the Iranian government informing it that the funds it received from the International Cooperation Administration could not be used to buy Cuban or Dominican sugar. At the same time, Washington also pressured Iran to use these resources to buy sugar from other partners, which, under the conditions of the US–Iran cooperation treaty, had to be transported using US ships. This would have increased the costs enormously. In spite of protestations from the United States, the Iranian authorities informed Rosemberg that they would not be influenced by Washington and would try to dispense the transactions with other funds to respect the agreement.[76]

---

74 Secret Memorandum no. 46/61 from the Legation of the Dominican Republic to Iran to the Secretary of Foreign Affairs, Santo Domingo, 20 January 1961, Ref. 3114961, AGN.
75 Secret Memorandum no. 46/61 from the Legation of the Dominican Republic to Iran to the Secretary of Foreign Affairs, 6 May 1960, Ref. 3114961, AGN.
76 Letter no. 87 from the Legation of the Dominican Republic to Iran to the Secretary of Foreign Affairs, Tehran, 2 March 1961, Ref. 3114961, AGN.

When Ali Amini became prime minister of Iran in early May 1961, the news was received by Rosemberg, now in Santo Domingo, with great enthusiasm not only because Amini was a close friend, but also because he had some knowledge of the Dominican Republic, having visited there on an official mission while serving as Iran's ambassador to the United States. Another positive characteristic of Amini, according to Rosemberg, was his critical views towards Washington.[77] For these reasons, he felt that Amini would fully support sugar imports to Iran and would help to intensify bilateral relations.[78] The sudden collapse of the Trujillo regime made all these hopes disappear completely.

The Assassination of Leónidas Trujillo and its Impact on Iranian–Dominican Relations

In early April 1961, a new diplomatic attaché was chosen to replace Rosemberg in the Dominican legation in Tehran, named Andrés Julio Espinal.[79] Rosemberg had planned to return to the Dominican Republic in the following weeks, probably after considering that the objectives of his mission in Iran were already achieved and that it was easier for him to closely supervise the construction of the oil refinery from Santo Domingo. Espinal was operating from Beirut when Trujillo was murdered on 30 May, which meant that he had no time to discuss any important issues with the shah.[80] The assassination was carefully organised secretly by the Central Intelligence Agency (CIA) during the Kennedy administration to increase

---

77 At this time, in Iran the position of the United States was not as consolidated as it became later, and there were still people in positions of relative power with ideas which were closer to Third Worldism than to United States capitalism. Amini was one of them, which could explain the overtures of Iran towards the Dominican Republic. For more details, see Ramin Nassehi, 'Domesticating Cold War Economic Ideas: The Rise of Iranian Developmentalism in the 1950s and 1960s', *The Age of Aryamehr, Late Pahlavi Iran and Its Global Entanglements*, ed. Roham Alvandi, 2018, 35–67.
78 Letter from the Chargé d'Affaires of the Dominican Republic to Iran to the Secretary of Foreign Affairs, Santo Domingo, 6 May 1961, Ref. 3114961, AGN.
79 *La Nación*, 5 April 1961, 3.
80 Andrés J. Espinal, *Trujillo, Bosh y yo: el desafío*, 1970, 129.

political stability on the island and, possibly, to avoid the risk of a new revolution that eventually could establish another Cuba in the Caribbean.

Arturo R. Espaillat Rodríguez,[81] former head of the Military Intelligence Service, was officially appointed trade attaché to Iran on 17 July 1961,[82] though his appointment had been first announced in the diplomatic guide of the Secretary of Foreign Affairs published in February of that year. To date, no documents have been found confirming whether he ever took over the post before the assassination. Most of the records indicate that he was in the Dominican Republic at the time and had only travelled on secret missions to Europe, Canada, and Cuba to try to improve political relations.[83] Given his long experience as head of the Dominican intelligence services, Espaillat was most probably among the Dominican officers who received Bakhtiar during his visit to the military installations in October 1959. It was possibly due to his position within military intelligence that he was seen as a suitable figure for the role, which suggests that had Trujillo not fallen, this would have been an area of increased cooperation.[84]

When Trujillo was murdered, Rosemberg was on a business trip in France with Trujillo's son, Ramfis. Upon hearing the news, both men travelled quickly to Santo Domingo to take control of the succession.[85] Rosemberg was a key figure in helping the Trujillo family maintain political control of the country during the first months following the assassination. Later, Rosemberg went to Paris to help the family with the necessary

---

81 Espaillat (1921–1967) was the first Dominican officer to graduate from West Point, and had in the previous year been complicit in the violent suppression of the opponents of the Trujillo regime in the United States. See Memorandum From Joseph J. Montllor of the Office of Middle American Affairs to the Acting Assistant Secretary of State for Inter–American Affairs (Rubottom) Washington, 3 April 1957, *Foreign Relations of the United States (FRUS), 1955–1957, American Republics: Multilateral; Mexico; Caribbean, vol. 6,* doc. 323. See also Alan A. Block, *Space, Time and Organized Crime,* 1994, 192–194.

82 Memorandum no. 2325 of the Secretary of Foreign Affairs to the President of the Republic, Santo Domingo, 17 July 1961, Ref. 3114102, AGN.

83 Vega, *Los Estados Unidos y Trujillo.*

84 On the evening of the assassination of Trujillo, Arturo R. Espaillat was actually having a drink very close to the crime scene, thus he was among the first people to see the body of the dictator and was suspected by the police of being involved in his murder.

85 *La Nación,* 3 June 1961, 1.

procedures to bury the body in France, where he arrived on 30 November 1961.[86] Weeks later, Rosemberg briefly returned to Iran just to close the legation, and on 5 February 1962 he bade farewell to the shah. According to the French chargé d'affaires in Tehran:

> [Rosemberg] told the press that he was renouncing his nationality because of his opposition to the new regime instituted in his country. [...] Before his departure, Mr Rosemberg, who passes here for having been a close friend of the Dominican dictator and who was in any case closely linked with the Trujillo family, severely criticised the policy of the United States regarding his country, as far as accusing President Kennedy's administration of promoting the assassination of General Trujillo. Moreover, what seems more surprising is that he also criticises American policy towards the regime of Fidel Castro, which, he says, has the support of a large part of the Cuban population. It should be noted that in Tehran this diplomat was often considered to have a bizarre attitude.[87]

Trujillo's successor as president, Joaquin Balaguer, who served until January 1962, did not continue to pursue relations with the shah for several reasons, not least because an important part of the ties with Iran was intelligence cooperation, a sensitive aspect of Trujillo's reign that he believed should be curtailed. In addition, relations with Iran had always been managed by an intimate group close to the Dominican dictator. No one from the opposition seemed to have contact with Iran, nor demonstrated any interest in Iran, since the shah's regime employed similar repressive practices as Trujillo's. Likewise, once relations with the United States and the other Latin American countries were normalised following the death of Trujillo, traditional commercial networks were re-established, and the

---

86 *La Nación*, 30 November 1961, 1.

87 Letter from the French Chargé d'Affaires in Iran to the French Minister of Foreign Affairs, Tehran, 6 February 1962, Ref. 367QO/34, CADC. Rosemberg's bizarre attitude described by the French diplomat mostly referred to his extravagant behaviour in public and his arrogant attitude due to his personal connections with the Iranian nobility. Regarding his Dominican citizenship, it was in fact revoked by the Dominican Republic's new council of state.

Dominican Republic resumed trading sugar and oil. There was simply no longer any need to pursue relations with such a faraway country. The incoming government, headed by the leftist Juan Bosh, demonstrated a similar lack of interest in re-establishing relations with either Iran or other countries in the Middle East. It appears as though there was little attempt from the Iranian side to reach out to revive the relationship, either.

*

Iran and the Dominican Republic were not natural allies, yet they were drawn together during this short period almost by accident. However, once the relationship had been established, each side recognised the benefits of it. The shah found a partner that could help to keep an eye on Cuban encroachment and also on the political evolution of other Latin American countries, mostly Venezuela, which was becoming a major international player in the politics of oil. The Dominican Republic, for its part, found a new market to sell sugar to and from which to purchase oil, which was particularly crucial at the time, when its ties with both Latin American countries and the United States were rapidly deteriorating.

In his efforts to attain a better position on the international sugar market, Trujillo explored the possibility of promoting exports to countries where there was a high demand for sugar, such as Iran. By sheer coincidence, one of Trujillo's allies, the Swiss-born Leland Rosemberg, not only had an Iranian wife, but one with close links to the Pahlavi court, having been previously married to the shah's brother. He was the ideal person to lead a mission to Iran; indeed, it was possibly Rosemberg himself who convinced Trujillo to pursue relations with Iran. These connections, coupled with his business and diplomatic background, meant that he was able to navigate the world of Iranian business and politics with some success. Indeed, it could be argued that without Rosemberg, there would have been no relationship between Iran and the Dominican Republic at this time.

Iranian–Dominican relations were limited to cooperation in two fields; first, trade in sugar and oil, and second, cooperation in the field of intelligence, best understood in the context of a shared anxiety about communist subversion. Initially, the Dominican strategy focused solely on the export of sugar to Iran. The possibility of importing oil was never discussed in the early days of the bilateral relationship. However, in a matter of a few months, it became one of the main points because of the sanctions imposed on the Trujillo regime for the attempted assassination of the president of Venezuela, Rómulo Betancourt, as well as for its repressive practices against the opposition in other countries. Unusually, and in spite of the possible negative consequences for himself, the shah did not follow Washington's directives to block the Trujillo regime. Most likely this was due to Rosemberg's handling of the situation and his personal relationship with the shah.

The dictator Trujillo saw Cuba as his main political rival in the region and competitor for the export of sugar to Iran. For this reason, from the first moment of the triumph of the Cuban Revolution, Trujillo tried to isolate Fidel Castro through his representatives abroad. In this sense, Rosemberg's role was essential, due to his own capacity to persuade Iranian diplomats, and indeed SAVAK, to reject the arrival of different Cuban delegations that were committed to establishing relations with the shah. Collaboration with SAVAK, especially regarding the exchange of lists of political activists from the respective countries, likely had little impact since Iran was not a destination of interest for the Trujillo opposition nor the Dominican Republic for the detractors of the shah. It is highly probable that no other accredited representative in Tehran had such a clear and direct impact on their country's relations with Iran as Rosemberg.

The assassination of the dictator Trujillo marked an abrupt end of relations between Iran and the Dominican Republic. From that moment on, Rosemberg focused his efforts on ensuring that the Trujillo family could stay in power. When this proved impossible, he helped them flee the country. He was relieved of his diplomatic duties by the new Dominican government and settled in Europe. Given the involvement of the United States in the assassination of Trujillo, Rosemberg adopted a decidedly anti-American stance, and, in addition, began to express sympathy for Fidel Castro for his implacable enmity toward Washington. Rosemberg also maintained some contact with the shah and even managed to meet him in New York in August 1967.[88]

---

88 Letter from Iran's Royal Court, Asadollah Alam, to Leland Rosemberg. Tehran, 4 May 1967. Records of the Foreign Service Posts of the Department of State, 1788

Both the fall of Batista and the assassination of Trujillo orchestrated by the CIA were viewed with concern in Iran. It became evident to the shah that a close relationship with Washington, as Batista and Trujillo had, did not guarantee that one would necessarily remain in power in either the medium or the long term. Therefore, he reformulated his strategy and his relationship with the White House to avoid the same fate by implementing policies such as the White Revolution and adapting judiciously to the recommendations given by the different presidents of the United States over the following years. Although the shah's exposure to the politics of the Caribbean was brief, it left a lasting impression on the Pahlavi monarch, as he too tried to navigate a path for his country in the final two decades of his rule.

Bibliography

Archives

Archivo General de la Administración (Spain)
Archive of the Ministry of Foreign Affairs (Iran)
Archivo General de la Nación (Dominican Republic)
Centre des Archives diplomatiques de La Courneuve (France)
National Archives and Records Administration (United States)
Library and Archives Canada

Published Sources

Almeida, A.C.L. de. 'Relatos da passagem da embaixada persa pelo Rio de Janeiro Joanino', *Portugal no Golfo Pérsico. 500 anos*, ed. M. Castelo-Branco, Lisbon, 2018, 15–25.
Bakhash, S. *The Fall of Reza Shah: The Abdication, Exile, and Death of Modern Iran's Founder*, London, 2021.

– ca. 1991 (RG84). Ambassador's Subject Files, 1965–1969 (P 353), of United States. Federal Records (1967), Box 3, Ambassador Armin Henry Meyer Files
– Tehran – April–May 1967. National Archives and Records Administration.

Balcácer, J.D. *Trujillo: el tiranicidio de 1961*, Santo Domingo, 2007.

Batista Fernández, R. *Hijo de Batista. Memorias*, Arganda del Rey, 2021.

Block, A.A. *Space, Time and Organized Crime*, New Brunswick, 1994.

Bomatim Y., and Nahavandi, H. *Mohammad Réza Pahlavi*, Paris, 2019.

Camacho Padilla, F. 'El éxodo de los cristianos de Persia tras la Primera Guerra Mundial. De la acción humanitaria española a su llegada a Latinoamérica', *Miradas de Irán. Historia y cultura*, ed. F. Camacho Padilla, F. Escribano Martín, N. Farzamnia Hajardovom, and J.L.N. Hernández, Madrid, 2021, 48–76.

Camacho Padilla, F. 'Las relaciones diplomáticas entre Persia y América Latina durante las últimas décadas de la Dinastía Qajar (1895–1925)', *Una vieja amistad. Cuatrocientos años de relaciones históricas y culturales entre Irán y el mundo hispano*, ed. F. Camacho Padilla and F. Escribano Martín, Madrid, 2020, 50–120.

Camacho Padilla, F. and Escribano Martín, F. 'Introducción', *Una vieja amistad. Cuatrocientos años de relaciones históricas y culturales entre Irán y el mundo hispano*, ed. F. Camacho Padilla and F. Escribano Martín, Madrid, 2020, 11–28.

Camacho Padilla, F. 'Las relaciones entre Latinoamérica e Irán durante la última década de la dinastía Pahleví', *Anuario de Historia de América Latina* 56, 2019, 66–96.

Chehabi, H.E. 'South Africa and Iran in the Apartheid Era', *Journal of Southern African Studies* 42/4, 2016, 687–709.

Elm, M. *Oil, Power, and Principle: Iran's Oil Nationalization and Its Aftermath*, New York, 1994.

Esfandiary-Bakhtiari, S. *The Autobiography of Her Imperial Highness*, New York, 1964.

Espaillat, A.R. *Trujillo: anatomia de un dictador*, Barcelona, 1963.

Espaillat, A.R. *Trujillo: The last Caesar*, Chicago, 1963.

Espinal, A.J. *Trujillo, Bosh y yo: el desafío*, Santo Domingo, 1970.

Farmanfarmaian, M. and Farmanfarmaian, R. *Blood & Oil: A Prince's Memoir of Iran, from the Shah to the Ayatollah*, New York, 2005.

Foreign Relations of the United States (FRUS), 1955–1957, American Republics: Multilateral; Mexico; Caribbean, vol. 6.

Gómez Bergés, V. *Balaguier y yo: la historia*. vol. 1, Santo Domingo, 2006.

González, M. 'El día en que Manuel Contreras le ofreció al Sha de Irán matar a "Carlos, El Chacal"', *Centro de Investigación Periodística*. 6 August 2009. https://www.ciperchile.cl/2009/08/06/el-dia-en-que-manuel-contreras-le-ofrecio-al-sha-de-iran-matar-a-%E2%80%9Cel-chacal%E2%80%9D/

Mondolfi Gudat, E. *El día del atentado: el frustrado magnicidio contra Rómulo Betancourt*, Caracas, 2013.

Nassehi, R., 'Domesticating Cold War Economic Ideas: The Rise of Iranian Developmentalism in the 1950s and 1960s', *The Age of Aryamehr, Late Pahlavi Iran and Its Global Entanglements*, ed. R. Alvandi, London, 2018, 35–67.

Reza Pahlavi, M. *Answer to History*, Toronto/Vancouver, 1980.

Sang, M-K.A. *La Política Exterior Dominicana 1844–1961 Tomo II. La política exterior del dictador Trujillo, 1930–1961*, Santo Domingo, 2000.

Steele, R. 'Two Kings of Kings: Iran–Ethiopia Relations Under Mohammad Reza Pahlavi and Haile Selassie', *The International History Review* 43/6, 2021, 1375–1392.

Steele, R. 'The Keur Farah Pahlavi Project and Iranian–Senegalese Relations in the 1970s', *Iranian Studies* 54/1–2, 2020, 169–192.

Vega, B. *Kennedy y los Trujillo*, Santo Domingo, 1991.

Vega, B. *Los Estados Unidos y Trujillo. Los días finales, 1960–61. Colección de documentos del Departamento de Estado, la CIA y los archivos del Palacio Nacional Dominicano*, Santo Domingo, 2000.

Wiese Delgado, H.P. *Trujillo, amado por muchos, odiado por otros, temido por todos*, Santo Domingo, 2000.

5

Iran's Foreign Policy and the Algerian War of Independence, 1954–1962

Thomas Bédrède

On the night of 31 October–1 November 1954, a series of attacks across Algeria by a new organisation, the National Liberation Front (FLN), marked the beginning of the Algerian War of Independence. On 3 July 1962, following a referendum in which the Algerians voted for freedom, France finally recognised the loss of its former colony, more than 130 years after the beginning of its conquest.

Before the war ended, Ferhat Abbas, the head of the GPRA (Provisional Government of the Algerian Republic) insisted that 'the armed struggle [was] essential, while the diplomatic struggle [was] intended to complement the armed struggle'.[1] Indeed, Algeria won its independence at the cost of numerous human lives. However, as Matthew Connelly has shown in his magisterial interpretation of this liberation struggle, it is as much on the diplomatic front that one must look to comprehend the reasons for this

---

1 Abderrahmane Kiouane, *Les débuts d'une diplomatie de guerre (1956–1962): journal d'un délégué à l'extérieur*, 2000. In the book's epigraph, Abbas shared his perspective of a meeting with Zhou En Lai, prime minister of State Affairs of the People's Republic of China in Beijing on 3 October 1960.

victory.[2] From Cairo to Tunis, from the UN headquarters to the Bandung Conference, Algerian nationalists pleaded their case and played on the tensions of the Cold War to oust the French from Algeria. What echo did these initiatives, and the conflict as a whole, find in Tehran? Given that the Iranians themselves had encountered several serious challenges from the imperialist powers since the start of the Cold War, the question of how Iran reacted to the decolonisation struggle of another large Muslim country during the same period strikes us as of particular interest. Yet this question has so far hardly attracted any attention in the literature. Connelly mentions Iran only four times, and the historiography of modern Iran invokes the Algerian War merely through references to Shariati and to the Iranian student movement.[3] Recent works on the foreign relations of Pahlavi Iran have rather focused on other periods and/or matters, such as the Cold War.[4]

As French diplomats and military officials in Iran noted at the time, Iranian politicians regularly discussed the Algerian War of Independence in parliament, in the Senate, and in the press.[5] This chapter therefore explores how Iran's foreign policy makers perceived this decolonisation conflict and how they reacted to it. It draws on French military and diplomatic records, as well as on memoirs published by Iranian and Algerian officials. It also considers Iranian newspaper coverage. Relying on French archival material to address this unexplored angle of the Algerian War of Independence requires awareness of the fact that at the time, successive French governments were obsessed with this conflict and focused the

---

2 Matthew James Connelly, *A Diplomatic Revolution: Algeria's Fight for Independence and the Origins of the post-Cold War Era*, 2002.

3 Ervand Abrahamian, *Iran Between Two Revolutions*, 1982; Ervand Abrahamian, *A History of Modern Iran*, 2018; Ali Rahnema, *An Islamic Utopian: A Political Biography of Ali Shari'ati*, 1998.

4 See, for example, Roham Alvandi, 'Flirting with Neutrality: The Shah, Khrushchev, and the Failed 1959 Soviet–Iranian Negotiations', *Iranian Studies* 47/3, 2014, 419–440; Roham Alvandi 'The Shah's Détente with Khrushchev: Iran's 1962 Missile Base Pledge to the Soviet Union', *Cold War History* 14/3, 2014, 423–444; and Ramin Nassehi, 'Domesticating Cold War Economic Ideas: The Rise of Iranian Developmentalism in the 1950s and 1960s', *The Age of Aryamehr*, ed. Roham Alvandi, 2018, 35–69.

5 Ali Rahnema, *The Rise of Modern Despotism in Iran: The Shah, the Opposition, and the US, 1953–1968*, 2021, 94–95.

bulk of their diplomatic efforts on it. The sheer volume of related reports sent from Iran by both military and diplomatic representatives reflects this preoccupation. Hence, any researcher faced with this relative abundance of French sources runs the risk of overestimating the importance of the Algerian War of Independence for a country like Iran.

Still, this correspondence helps to understand how Iran, as a member of the Afro-Asian group at the UN and of the Baghdad Pact, but also as a state that maintained strong economic and cultural ties with France, became involved, *nolens volens*, in the diplomatic battle between the Algerians and the French. Iran did so at a time when its foreign policy faced serious regional and global challenges. Throughout this period, Iran's relations with Egypt, where the monarchy had been overthrown in 1952, were diffi-cult, with the Iranian monarch developing a hatred of its president, Gamal Abdel Nasser, that would soon become obsessive. In July 1958, the shah and his government had to deal with the fall of the Hashemite dynasty in neighbouring Iraq, which had been a fellow member of the Baghdad Pact. Also in 1958, the Qarani affair resulted in a severe loss of Iranian confidence in the United States as an ally, and a year later, a *rapproche-ment* with the Soviets did not yield the hoped-for results. This challenging regional and global context, which coincided with the shah's active role in the conduct of Iranian foreign policy, shaped and conditioned Iran's reac-tion to the Algerian War of Independence.

1955–1958: The Spirit of Bandung, the Baghdad Pact, and Islamic Solidarity

The beginning of the war led to public protests in Iran, 'where the Muslim population, despite the reserve and prudence of its government, [was] still ready to show its solidarity with its brothers outside the country at the call of the Mullahs' according to François Coulet, the French ambassador in Tehran.[6] This reaction did not come as a total surprise to the French. During the premiership of Mohammad Mosaddeq, not only his foreign

---

6 Centre des Archives diplomatiques de La Courneuve (hereafter CADC), 367QO/16, François Coulet, ambassadeur de France à Téhéran, Télégramme 1173/ AL.

minister Hoseyn Fatemi,[7] but also Ayatollah 'Abol-Qassem Kashani had already voiced their opposition to France's colonial presence in North Africa.[8] But, this was the first time since Mosaddeq's removal that such a public protest had taken place.

Ayatollah Kashani was again at the forefront of the protests, calling on the Shi'ite clergy to reference the Algerian problem during sermons. Meanwhile his son, a Majles deputy, denounced French policy in North Africa in parliament and requested that the Iranian representative at the UN be given instructions in line with the opinion of the Iranian people.[9] As the Security Council session was approaching, the Iranian minister of foreign affairs, 'Abdollah Entezam, stated in an interview with a local newspaper that Iran, the representative of the Afro-Asian group at the Council, would adopt a pro-Arab line of conduct.[10]

In January 1955, Iran's representative at the UN, 'Abdollah Entezam's brother Nasrollah, refused to follow up on a Saudi initiative to bring the Algerian Question before the Security Council – an initiative he had declared 'perfectly absurd'.[11] If his decision pleased the French,[12] it was also aligned with the policy stated by his brother, as it seemed to have been based on the lack of support for the Saudi initiative on the part of the other Arab states.[13] This first defeat on the diplomatic stage for the Algerians was soon followed by their first victory, which occurred during the Bandung Conference in April 1955.

---

7 CADC, 130QO/29, Coulet, 881/AS, 24 October 1952; 130QO/37, Coulet, Télégramme 426/28, 15 August 1953.
8 CADC, 367QO/16, Coulet, 283/AL, 19 January 1954.
9 CADC, 367QO/16, Coulet, 1173/AL, 24 November 1954.
10 CADC, 367QO/16, Coulet, 624, 29 November 1954.
11 Connelly, *Diplomatic Revolution*, 75.
12 CADC, 367QO/16, Direction Générale des Affaires politiques Direction d'Afrique Levant Service du Levant 1/AL, 27 January 1958. Generally speaking, the French authorities were pleased with Nasrollah Entezam's actions at the UN since he was 'elevated to the rank of Grand Officer of the Legion of Honour for his action in favour of France at the United Nations' in January 1958.
13 Connelly, *Diplomatic Revolution*, 75.

The Bandung Conference, April 1955

The Bandung Conference, which met from 18 to 24 April 1955 and brought together twenty-nine Afro-Asian countries, welcomed as observers the representatives of the Algerian, Tunisian, and Moroccan peoples. Iran was among those invited. However, the Algerian question was not a priority for the Iranian delegation, and in general the shah did not seem particularly interested in Iran's participation in this conference.[14] Ali Amini had been designated to head the Iranian delegation, but he finally renounced it, preferring to stay in Tehran after the fall of the Zahedi government.[15] Jalal 'Abdoh, a member of the delegation, was appointed in his place and it was he who received the shah's instructions just before his departure for Bandung. According to 'Abdoh, the Iranian monarch doubted that the conference would have any effect on the course of world affairs and wanted his representatives to refrain from taking any extreme position.[16]

'Abdoh obeyed his instructions. Upon his arrival in Bandung, he declared

it is necessary to avoid submitting subjects that would bring out differences between countries. The Bandung Conference should not be used to promote political ideologies, but the negotiations should be

---

14 Jalal 'Abdoh, *Chehel sal dar sahneh-ye qaza'i, siyasi diplomasi-ye Iran va jahan: khaterat-e Doktor-e Jalal 'Abdoh*, 1368 [1989], 441. The Western countries were responsible for the disinterest the shah showed towards the Bandung conference. Darwis Khudori, *La France et Bandung*, 2020, 276–282. By early 1955, France, Great Britain and the United States, after having initially opposed the idea of such a conference, were actually encouraging the countries that they supported to join it to counterbalance the communist voices. Khudori, *La France et Bandung*, 183, The British government, in a memorandum dated from 10 January 1955, considered Turkey's attendance at the conference essential and hoped that Prime Minister Zahedi and his Iraqi counterpart Nuri Said could represent their countries at it.

15 *Majalleh-ye Taraqqi*, 640, 28 Farvardin 1334/18 April 1955, 4. According to *Taraqqi*, Ali Amini was supposed to head the Iranian delegation. 'Abdoh, *Chehel sal*, 441. 'Abdoh in his memoirs explains that because of the fall of the Zahedi government, Ali Amini had decided not to go to Bandung and that 'Abdoh was named as head of the delegation in his place.

16 'Abdoh, *Chehel sal*, 443.

conducted in a calm atmosphere so that satisfactory solutions to Asian economic and political problems emerge.[17]

'Abdoh attacked the Soviet Union and 'praised the United States' aid to Iran'.[18] While condemning colonialism and 'recognising the legitimate aspirations of the peoples of North Africa, [he] openly expressed understanding for [France].'[19] The final declaration of the conference clearly drew attention to the case of the North African countries, as did the statement of Iraq's foreign minister, Mohammad Fadhil Jamali.[20] However, 'Abdoh was careful not to refer to either France or North Africa in his closing statement.[21] Although he indicates in his memoirs the presence of North African delegates at the conference, he does not say if he had any exchanges with any of them. Furthermore, he mistakenly mentions Ferhat Abbas as having been one of the two Algerian representatives (the other one was Ait Ahmed) while in fact it was M'hammed Yazid.[22]

The opposition to French policy in North Africa voiced in the Majles, in the Senate, in the press or in the mosque finally found an echo in Iran's foreign policy.[23] On 26 July 1955, Iran, along with countries such as Afghanistan,

---

17 *Seda-ye Vatan*, 30 Farvardin 1334/20 April 1955, 4.
18 Rouhollah Ramazani, *Iran's Foreign Policy, 1941–1973: A Study of Foreign Policy in Modernizing Nations*, 1975, 277; *A'ineh-ye Eslam*, 348, 2 Ordibehesht, 1334/23 April 1955, 16.
19 Letter from General Ely, French Commissioner General in Indo-China to Antoine Pinay, French Foreign Minister on the Bandung Conference, Saigon, 28 April 1955. https://www.cvce.eu/en/obj/letter_from_general_ely_to_antoine_pinay_ on_the_bandung_conference_saigon_28_april_1955-en-f71582f5-0631-4b0d-a1a9- 4d7a75eeffdb.html%5D (accessed 28 March 2022).
20 *A'ineh-ye Eslam*, 348, 2 Ordibehest 1334/23 April 1955, 16.
21 'Abdoh, *Chehel sal*, 468, 471; *Asian-African Conference Bulletin*, June 1955, 10, Jalal 'Abdoh closing statement, 9–10.
22 'Abdoh, *Chehel sal*, 446. Natalya Vince, *the Algerian War, the Algerian Revolution*, 2020, 59.
23 CADC, 367QO/21, Dossier Algérie Juin 1955–Mai 1958, Jacques-Emile Paris, ambassadeur de France à Téhéran, 858/AL, 21 June 1955. In June 1955, Ambassador Paris linked an upsurge of 'fairly violent articles against French policy in North Africa' to the context of a recent 'outbreak of anti-Bahai Muslim fanaticism', which to him created a fertile ground for this sort of hostile press coverage. 367QO/16, 977/AL, 26 June 1956. In 1956, according to him, the Iranian government allowed the publication of violent articles to placate the religious

Saudi Arabia, Burma, Egypt, India, Indonesia, and Iraq, proposed that the 'Algerian Question' be placed on the agenda of the tenth regular session of the United Nations General Assembly. The memorandum accompanying this request noted that the 'unanimous conclusions [of the Bandung Conference] of twenty-nine countries whose populations represent just under 50% of humanity show how anxious the international community is to see the Algerian question resolved without delay'. On 30 September 1955, Iran voted with its fellow members of the Afro-Asian group in favour of putting the Algerian question on the agenda, and thus helped to defeat the motion defended by France by one vote (twenty-eight votes to twenty-seven).[24] Although the UN did not ultimately take any binding decision against France, the Algerians saw the vote as an unprecedented victory, while France regarded it as an affront it could hardly bear. The French delegation to the UN was recalled, and the French government threatened to leave the organisation.

In Tehran, the French ambassador obtained a meeting with Prime Minister Hoseyn 'Ala, who confirmed 'with warmth that Iran's attitude had no unfriendly intention towards France'.[25] He explained it was impossible for his government to resist the pressure of its friends and to refuse its support to co-religionists who were demanding their freedom. He also expressed reservations about the thesis that Algeria was part of the metropolitan territories. 'Ala was worried that the French government would retaliate, but the ambassador reassured him by stating that

it was not his intention to undermine solidly established relations such as those existing in the economic field. Nothing had changed with regard to the upcoming visit to Tehran of the French delegation responsible for negotiating the renewal of the trade agreement.[26]

leaders in a context of strong discontent in religious circles. Rahnema, *Rise of Modern Despotism*, 94. Rahnema explains that if 'the Iranian could not condemn its own domestic oppressors; it took great pleasure in condemning foreign oppressors'.
24 CADC, 372QO/546, Hervé Alphand, France permanent representative at the UN, New York, 2.175, 30 September 1955.
25 CADC, 372QO/546, J-E Paris, 1381/AL, a/s démarche au sujet du vote iranien à l'ONU, 7 October 1955.
26 CADC, 372QO/546, J-E Paris, 1381/AL, a/s démarche au sujet du vote iranien à l'ONU, 7 October 1955.

The trade agreement was then indeed renewed for one more year.[27]

The next year saw another initiative made by the Afro-Asian group at the UN. In May 1956, in a meeting with the French ambassador, Iran's minister of foreign affairs, ʿAliqoli Ardalan, warned that Iran, as the only representative of the group at the UN Security Council, was under a lot of pressure from the Arab countries, mainly Egypt and Iraq, to take action over Algeria. The minister explained that 'its government [could not] shirk the obligations imposed on it by Islamic solidarity', whatever action might have to be taken. He then assured the French ambassador 'of his desire to exert a moderating influence on the other members of the Arab-Asian group and to avoid making France's task more difficult'.[28] On 13 June, thirteen countries signed a letter in which they asked the Security Council to take up the Algerian problem.[29] Jalal ʿAbdoh, then the Iranian permanent representative at the UN, was among the signatories. In his memoirs, ʿAbdoh explains that, as the only Afro-Asian member of the UN Security council, he had to 'face up to sensitive tasks especially after the Bandung Conference when the Afro-Asian group [members] were cooperating with more force and confidence when it came to the matters of colonialism', encouraged by 'the bold actions of the Algerian independence seekers'.[30]

ʿOmar Lotfi, the Egyptian representative at the UN, and Ait Ahmed, one of the leaders of the Algerian nationalists, met ʿAbdoh several times to discuss Algeria.[31] The French government was not pleased with the initiative and asked its representative to express its disappointment to the Iranian authorities.[32] The minister of court, Manuchehr Eqbal, who was known to the French as having some influence on the shah, told Jacques-Emile Paris that he did not approve of the actions of the Iranian representative to the UN and that he would speak to the Iranian monarch about it.[33]

---

27 CADC, 367QO/24, Direction des Affaires Economiques et Financières, 22 November 1955.

28 CADC, 367QO/16, J.E. Paris, 748 AL, 8 May 1956.

29 CADC, 372QO/548, Paris, Secrétariat des Conférences, 466/69, 14 June 1956.

30 ʿAbdoh, Chehel sal, 516.

31 ʿAbdoh, Chehel sal, 519.

32 CADC, 372QO/548, Paris, Secrétariat des Conférences, 466/69 Téhéran, 14 June 1956.

33 CADC, 372QO/548, dossier réactions arabes, JE Paris, 81/83, pour Téhéran 475/76, 17 June 1956.

As for Ardalan, at the request of the French ambassador, he said he would consider the possibility of instructing 'Abdoh to postpone the delivery of the letter of 13 June to the president of the Security Council.[34] Ultimately, however, the delivery of the letter was not delayed and Kazemi, the under-secretary for foreign affairs, confirmed that instructions ordering a delay had actually been sent but had not arrived on time in New York. For his part, 'Abdoh explains in his memoirs that he only presented the Afro-Asian request at the UN Security Council after having received the approval of his government.[35] The shah admitted to the French ambassador that

> recourse to the Security Council could have propaganda value and that it provided moral encouragement to the Algerian rebels. But it was to be understood that Iran's action was imposed on it by the obligations deriving from Muslim solidarity.

The shah also insisted that the Arab countries put constant pressure on the Iranian permanent representative at the UN.[36]

Iran and the Baghdad Pact

According to Jacques-Emile Paris, the shah was all the more reluctant to shift the Iranian position in a direction that was less antagonistic towards France because he still resented France's attitude toward the Baghdad Pact.[37] As soon as the Iraqi-Turkish pact was signed on 24 February 1955, according to British and French sources, Mohammad Reza Pahlavi showed interest in joining it, against the advice of some of his close associates.[38] By joining the Baghdad pact in October 1955, Iran not only abandoned

---

34 Dossier réactions arabes, JE Paris, 81/83, pour Téhéran 475/76, 17 June 1956.
35 'Abdoh, *Chehel sal*, 519.
36 CADC, 367QO/16, JE Paris, 973/AL, Audience du Chah, 24 June 1956.
37 CADC, 367QO/16, JE Paris au MAE, 977/AL, 26 June 1956.
38 Behçet Kemal Yeşilbursa, *The Baghdad Pact: Anglo-American defence policies in the Middle East, 1950–1959*, 2005, 110; CADC, 367QO/15, 21 September 1955; Yeşilbursa, *Baghdad Pact*, 119; and Rahnema, *Rise of Modern Despotism*, 75. Rahnema explains it was 'the shah's first significant foreign policy move'.

Mosaddeq's negative neutralism,[39] but also chose Iraq's side in the battle raging against Egypt for hegemony over the Arab world.

The French authorities, as well as their Egyptian counterparts, opposed the Baghdad Pact. Worried about the threat posed by Iraq to the independence of Syria, where it hoped to retain its influence, the French government could not accept the creation of a pact that would strengthen the Iraqi position. The desire to find a solution to the war being waged by Algerian independence fighters led the French to approach Nasser in March 1956. The Egyptians agreed to act as intermediaries. They tried to extract maximum benefits from France, including limiting military aid to Israel and reaffirming its opposition to the Baghdad Pact, which Guy Mollet, the president of the French Council, did publicly. When the French refused to limit their support for Israel, Nasser turned away from France and threw his weight behind the Algerian independence movement.[40]

The shah stressed the importance of economic ties between his country and France. At the time, France was the biggest importer of Iranian cotton, a French bank had agreed to finance the Iran seven-year plan in 1954, and the Iranian government had awarded the contract for the building of the *Sefid Rud* Dam to French companies.[41] Nonetheless, the Iranian monarch did not hesitate to express his dissatisfaction with French opposition to the Pact, at least twice: first, in June 1956 during an audience given to the French ambassador; and a second time, in 1957, during a conversation with Maurice Faure, the French secretary of state for foreign affairs.[42] France's inability to settle the Algerian problem also embarrassed the shah as it hampered his desire to reinforce simultaneous links with France and the Pact.[43]

---

39 Yeşilbursa, *Baghdad Pact,* 119.

40 Sofia Papastamkou, 'France and the Middle East in 1958: Continuity and change through crisis', *Middle East in 1958: Reimagining a Revolutionary Year,* ed. Jeffrey Karam, 2020, 34–42; 'La France au Proche-Orient, 1950–1958. Un intrus ou une puissance exclue?', *Bulletin de l'Institut Pierre Renouvin* 1/25, 2007, 177–188.

41 CADC, 367QO/24, Lettre de H. Camerlynck au ministre des Affaires étrangères, 17 April 1957. Sébastien Fath, *L'Iran et de Gaulle: chronique d'un rêve inachevé,* 1999, 26.

42 CADC, 367QO/16, JE Paris, 973/AL, Audience du Chah, 24 June 1956.

43 CADC, 367QO/15, Roux au MAE, 1074/AL, Entretien du shah avec Maurice Faure, 6 October 1957.

The consolidation of the Baghdad Pact seemed to be at the centre of the shah's concerns. Like the other signatories, he wanted the United States to join the Pact formally and envisioned that Saudi Arabia and Jordan would also join it. He hoped to rally the countries of North Africa or, failing that, to see the formation of 'a Mediterranean pact [with France, Italy, and Spain] which would link up with the Baghdad Pact and leave Egypt and Syria isolated, thus forcing them, sooner or later, to turn their backs on the USSR and show feelings that were more reasonable and more in line with their true interests'.[44] He therefore expected France to find a solution in Algeria as quickly as possible, even if it meant, as he said to Maurice Faure, 'going, as of now, to the extreme limit of the liberal concessions that [France] would inevitably be led to make one day or another, given the constant and inescapable deterioration, according to him, of the situation in Algeria'.[45] He went so far as to propose welcoming to Iran French colonists who would be forced to leave Algeria if they were prepared to get involved in developing the northern regions of his country.[46]

The French secretary of state for foreign affairs was not caught off guard by the shah's comments. Henri Roux, the French ambassador, had warned him of the atmosphere in Tehran regarding Algeria. According to Roux, Ahmed Balafrej, the Moroccan foreign minister, had made a strong impression on Iranian officials, including the shah, whom he had met during his stay in Tehran in August 1957:

[Balafrej] had emphasised the very serious repercussions that the prolongation of the current situation could have for Morocco and Tunisia and, by extension, for the West and its supporters. He [had] stressed to his interlocutors that if France did not rapidly take the

---

44 Entretien du shah avec Maurice Faure, 6 October 1957.
45 Entretien du shah avec Maurice Faure, 6 October 1957.
46 Entretien du shah avec Maurice Faure, 6 October 1957; Memorandum of a Conversation, Department of State, Washington, 19 November 1957, Foreign Relations of the United States (FRUS), 1955–1957, Near East Region; Iran; Iraq, vol. 12, doc. 276. This seemed to have been a feature of the Iranian diplomacy at the time. In a meeting held in Washington on 19 November 1957, gathering the ambassadors of the members of the Baghdad Pact, Ali Amini, the Iranian representative, offered Iran's help to resettle Palestinian refugees.

initiative of a show of goodwill, it would be outvoted at the United
Nations and would suffer a failure which would constitute for the bad
Arabs, Egypt and Syria, and for the USSR which supports them, an
undeniable success.[47]

Balafrej's visit reciprocated, according to the French ambassador, that
of the Iranian foreign minister, Entezam, of the previous year when he
attended the celebration of Morocco's independence.[48] Entezam had taken
this opportunity to make a tour of the Maghreb that had also taken him to
Tunisia and Libya, a journey during which he had been tasked to sound
out North African leaders on the Baghdad Pact.[49] It does not seem, though,
that the Iranian authorities had tried to engage with the Algerian militants.

Algerian Diplomatic Efforts in Iran

In his memoirs, 'Abdoh mentions having met two of the leaders of the
Algerian independence movement, Ait Ahmed and M'hammed Yazid, in
New York, but does not give many details of these encounters.[50] As for the
activities of the Algerian militants in Iran, while waiting for an eventual
access to Algerian sources, we must make do with French sources and
memoirs from Algerian officials.

In both 1955 and 1956, the French ambassador, Jacques-Emile Paris,
informed his government of visits to Tehran by North African students
and young Algerians.[51] During the summer of 1955, 'Abdolaziz Khalifa,

---

47 CADC, 367QO/21, Dossier Algérie Juin 1955–Mai 1958, Henri Roux,
ambassadeur de France à Téhéran, 934/AL, 19 August 1957.
48 CADC, 367QO/21, Dossier Algérie Juin 1955–Mai 1958, Imbert de Laurens-
Castelet chargé d'affaires, 311/AL, a/s : Voyage de M. Entezam en Afrique du Nord,
26 February 1957.
49 CADC, 367QO/25, Dossier général sur le pétrole janvier 1953–novembre 1959,
Henri Roux, ambassadeur de France à Téhéran, 644/AL, 25 May 1957.
50 'Abdoh, Chehel sal, 519, 540.
51 CADC, 367QO/16, J.E. Paris, 1254/AL, 10 September 1955. The French
Ambassador refers to a previous telegram (1195/AL) sent on 30 August of the same
year where he had mentioned the arrival of four North African students in Tehran. I
have not been able so far to locate the aforementioned telegram. CADC, 367QO/21,
Dossier Algérie Juin 1955–Mai 1958, J.E. Paris, 1186/AL, 25 August 1956.

al-'Akhzar Bu al-Tamin, Muhammad Sa'id al-Jaza'eri and Tohami al-Wakili arrived from Baghdad, where they were pursuing their studies. They presented themselves as the 'representatives of the committee of student supporters of the movement for the liberation of North Africa'. During the month they had spent in Tehran, they had attempted to raise awareness among the Iranian youth and the Iranian students about the struggle for independence led by their people.[52] In 1956, Jacques-Emile Paris reported that 'MM. Mohammed Cherif Djavad [Sherif Javad], Abul-Gasem Baghdadi, Mohamed Saleh Bowiyah [Muhammad al-Saleh Bawiya] and Akhtar Idris [al-'Akhdar 'Idris]' had come from Kuwait and introduced themselves as 'propagandists of Algerian nationalism'.[53] The French ambassador minimised the importance of these visits. Nevertheless, he recognised that Ayatollah Mohammad Behbahani 'a prominent Shiite figure' in Tehran had granted the second group an audience but added that Grand Ayatollah Hoseyn Borujerdi had refused. However, their presence in Tehran found an echo in *Keyhan*, one of Iran's most influential newspapers at the time.[54]

In May 1957, two senior FLN members, Ahmed Francis and Abderrahmane Kiouane, made a short visit to Iran as part of a tour of the countries in the region.[55] According to the French military attaché in Iran, Lieutenant-Colonel Aubinière, the visit was organised by Egypt and led by the Saudi ambassador in the absence of his Egyptian counterpart. Aubinière detailed four requests made by the Algerian delegates:

---

52 *Ettela'at*, 31 Mordad 1334/23 August 1955, 12.

53 *Al-Basa'ir,* 262, vol. 6, 12 March 1953. *Al-Basa'ir* was the magazine of the Jam'iyyat al-'Ulama' al-Muslimin al-Jaza'iriyyin (Association of Algerian Muslim Ulema), an association whose aim was the defence of the Arab-Islamic identity of Algeria. It secured scholarships for its students in other Arab countries. In this issue of *Al-Basa'ir* the lists of the students benefiting from these scholarships were published. I would like to thank Dr al-Rashoud for having provided me the digitized version of *Al-Basa'ir* and told me where I could find these lists.

54 CADC, 367QO/21, Dossier Algérie Juin 1955–Mai 1958, JE Paris, 1186/AL, 25 August 1956.

55 Archives du Service Historique de la Défense à Vincennes (hereafter ASHDV), GR 14 S 329, Dossier contacts avec le FLN [déclassifié par décision 502296 du 8 avril 2021], Aubinière, 2 June 1957. Kiouane, *Diplomatie de guerre (1956–1962)*, 27–29.

- The organisation of 'Algerian days' in Iran with a collection for the benefit of the FLN.
- The creation of a propaganda office in Tehran.
- Financial support from the Iranian government.
- Support of Iran at the UN.

The military attaché commented that

it already seems certain that on the first two points the Algerians will be politely rejected, the Iranian government having decided not to tolerate any hotbeds of agitation on its territory. He also doubted that Iran, which was in financial difficulties and whose interest was to maintain cordial relations with France, would finance the FLN, but he did not think that it would prohibit private financing.[56]

In a book devoted to the financing of the FLN, Colin-Janvoine and Derozier wrote, however, that 'as early as 1957, Iran recognised a principled support for the Algerian cause' adding that

military archives show that at the same time a government subsidy of 70 million francs had been granted to the cause. This information cannot be verified, however, government aid is attested.[57]

In addition, according to the authors, collections were made amongst the public, notably during a week dedicated to the Algerian cause held in 1958, which the Iranian government sought to control. On the other hand, recently declassified archives show that the French military attaché

---

56 ASHDV, GR 14 S 329, Dossier contacts avec le FLN [déclassifié par décision 502296 du 8 avril 2021], Aubinière, 2 June 1957.
57 Emmanuelle Colin-Janvoine and Stéphanie Derozier, '2. Les ressources financières du FLN', *Le financement du FLN pendant la guerre d'Algérie 1954–1962*, ed. Emmanuelle Colin-Janvoine and Stéphanie Derozier, 2008, 37–88, https://www.cairn.info/le-financement-du-fln-pendant-la-guerre-d-algerie – 9782356760029-page-37.htm.

in Tehran indicated in 1957 that rumours of financing of the 'Algerian rebellion' by Iranians seemed unfounded.[58]

As for organising an Algeria Week in 1958, French diplomatic sources mention that Mostafa Rahnama, an Iranian journalist and political activist close to the religious leaders, founder and head of the movement Moslem-e Azad and director of the newspaper *Hayat-e Moslemin*, tried to promote such an event in Iran.[59] Rahnama, who claimed to be the provisional representative of the Algerian Partisans of Independence in Iran, wanted to emulate similar kinds of events that had been organised in other Afro-Asian countries.[60] In April 1958, he sent a leaflet to Iranian newspapers in which he announced that 10 Farvardin (30 March) had been inaugurated 'Algeria Day' by the peoples of Asia and Africa.[61] The press did not reprint the leaflet and Prime Minister Eqbal promised the French representative to prevent what he described an 'imbecilic initiative'.[62] In a telegram dated 30 September 1958, Henri Roux, the French ambassador, mentioned this episode in order to confide that the Iranian government had actually prevented the organisation of the planned Algeria Week and that the activity of the FLN was limited to fundraising, which, according to him, was largely unsuccessful.[63] Moreover, Kiouane, while pleased with the welcome that he had received in Tehran as well as with the 'total support' that he had

---

58 ASHDV, GR 14 S 329, Dossier contacts avec le FLN [déclassifié par décision 502296 du 8 avril 2021], Aubinière, 132 AM./IR. Objet : financement de la rébellion algérienne, 30 March 1957.

59 CADC, 367QO/21, Dossier Algérie Juin 1955–Mai 1958, Roux, 388/AL, 9 April 1958. Henri Roux describes *Moslem-e Azad* as a 'political-religious movement of negligible importance'. Mostafa Rahnama appears a few times in the French sources that present him as a vocal defender of the Algerian cause. Mostafa Rahnama, *Khaterat va Asnad-e Sheykh Mostafa Rahnama*, 1390, 40. Rahnema, *Rise of Modern Despotism*, 76. He is the nephew of the Vahedi brothers, members of the *Fedayan-e Eslam* who were arrested after the assassination attempt on Hoseyn 'Ala in November 1955.

60 CADC, 367QO/21, Dossier Algérie Juin 1955–Mai 1958, Roux, 388/AL, a/s: journée de l'Algérie, 9 April 1958.

61 *El Moudjahid*, Vol 1. 1962, 256. 15, 1 January 1958. The date for the celebration of the solidarity of the Afro-Asian people with the Algerians was set at the African Asian Peoples' Solidarity Conference in Cairo in December 1957.

62 CADC, 367QO/16, Roux, 103/106, 21 May 1958.

63 CADC, 372QO/556, Roux, 237/40, 30 September 1958.

been offered by officials, from Prime Minister Eqbal to Minister of the Court 'Ala and the 'Imam Djome Sayyed Hassan Imamy', does not specify any concrete benefits arising from his visit. However, he mentions that the foundations had been laid for the visit of

> a second delegation that could come after the Pilgrimage but would have to deal more specifically with contacts and action on the Islamic level. Islam plays a very important role here and its representatives have a great influence on both government and public opinion.[64]

French sources do mention the arrival of Algerians with Iraqi passports in May 1958. However, it is unclear whether they were members of the delegation announced by Kiouane. According to the French ambassador, their activity provoked an upsurge in attacks by the Iranian press against French policy in Algeria.[65] Kiouane's assessment was consistent with the reports sent by the French representatives; apart from Front National veterans, the Algerian cause was promoted mainly in religious circles at this point, where figures such as Kashani, Behbahani, and Taleqani[66] called for support for their Algerian Muslim brothers.

1958–1959: A Franco-Iranian Rapprochement on the Algerian Question? The Shah, Nasser, de Gaulle and the GPRA

The year 1958 witnessed major upheavals in the Middle East including the creation of the United Arab Republic in February, and the coup in July that put an end to the Iraqi monarchy. *The Middle East in 1958: Reimagining a Revolutionary Year*, edited by Jeffrey Karam, offers an exploration of the revolutionary character of that year. In it, Sylvie Thénault devotes an article to the Algerian War of Independence that questions the relevance of this characterization.[67] She recognises that in each of the two camps,

---

64 Kiouane, *Diplomatie de guerre (1956–1962)*, 26–29.
65 CADC, 367QO/21, Dossier Algérie Juin 1955–Mai 1958, Roux, 523/AL, a/s: Propagande favorable aux rebelles algériens, 8 May 1958.
66 Yann Richard, *l'Islam Chiite, Croyances et Idéologie*, 1991, 220.
67 Sylvie Thénault, 'How about 1958 in Algeria? A transnational event in the

Algerian and French, the year 1958 was indeed a watershed year. For the relations between France and Iran regarding Algeria, it was also a turning point.

The bombing of the Tunisian village of Sakiet Sidi Youssef, on the border with Algeria, by the French air force on 8 February 1958 triggered international disapproval. The stated target of the attack was an Algerian ALN (National Liberation Army) camp, but it caused many civilian casualties. The event provoked heated reactions in the Iranian press. Violent criticism first appeared in the newspaper *Jahan* on 10 February and then in *Seda-ye Mardom* on 11 February.[68] Criticism was also voiced in the Senate.[69] According to the French ambassador, the two most important Iranian dailies, *Keyhan* and *Ettela'at* remained, at first, measured, in accordance with the reaction of the Iranian authorities. But the political crisis in France triggered by the bombing worried them greatly, as they feared 'first of all that the French Communist Party, through the Algiers movement, would succeed in promoting a popular front that would have compromised the Western alliance and strengthened the Soviet camp'.[70]

Over time, the attacks against France became more numerous. The French Fourth Republic was reaching the end of the line, and governments came and went with ever greater frequency. In Algiers, the army ruled and would no longer tolerate government attempts to establish links with FLN representatives. The crisis culminated in the organisation of a demonstration by supporters of French Algeria, which turned into a riot and was then joined by the high command. The return to power of Charles de Gaulle on 27 May put an end to the crisis and was 'welcomed in Iranian official circles with particular favour'. Both the prime minister and the minister of foreign affairs expressed their congratulations to the French ambassador in this regard in 'unambiguous terms'.[71]

De Gaulle's return to power was not the only factor in the changing attitude of the shah towards the Algerian question. Nasser's growing influence

context of the war of independence', *The Middle East in 1958: Reimagining a Revolutionary Year,* ed. Jeffrey Karam, 2020, 122–130.

68 CADC, 367QO/16, Henri Roux au MAE, 207/AL, 17 February 1958.

69 Henri Roux au MAE, 207/AL, 17 February 1958.

70 CADC, 367QO/16, Roux au MAE, 114–115, 5 June 1958.

71 Roux au MAE, 114–115, 5 June 1958.

in the Arab world after the Suez crisis had him worried, since he believed that the Algerian case was being used by the Egyptian leader to rally the other Arab countries around him.[72] Times had surely changed since the Bandung Conference in 1955, when Jalal ʿAbdoh had handed Nasser an invitation from the shah to visit Iran, an invitation that the Egyptian leader declined.[73] With the proclamation of the United Arab Republic (UAR) – the political union between Egypt and Syria – on 1 February 1958, the Iranian authorities were even more alarmed.[74] According to Henri Roux, the shah, his prime minister and foreign minister expressed similar concerns over the USSR's growing influence in Cairo and Damascus. In their view, the union had only been made possible with the assent of the Soviets. The ultimate goal, according to the shah and his foreign minister, was the fusion of all the Arab countries under Nasser's leadership. In a meeting with the president of the United States, Dwight Eisenhower, on 1 July 1958, the shah added that Nasser was a conspirator whose 'primary interest was obviously to control oil', an interest he shared with the Soviet Union.[75] The shah also feared that the Baghdad Pact might not be strong enough to cover the new fronts, especially since Iraq seemed ever more ready to detach itself from it. The brutal fall of the Hashemite dynasty in Iraq on 14 July might have been perceived in Tehran as the final nail in the Pact's coffin. Deeply shocked, the shah questioned the effectiveness of the Baghdad Pact.[76]

The announcement, on 19 September 1958, from Cairo, of the creation of the Provisional Government of the Algerian Republic (GPRA) was therefore unlikely to be well received. The shah informed the French ambassador in early October through his under secretary of state for foreign affairs

---

72 CADC, 372QO/556, Roux, 262/26, 15 September 1957.
73 ʿAbdoh, *Chehel sal*, 475.
74 CADC, 367QO/17 Dossier relation avec l'Egypte, Henri Roux au MAE, 205/ AL, 16 February 1958.
75 *FRUS, 1958–1960, vol. XII*, 242. Memorandum of Conversation, Washington, 1 July 1958, 1851–1863. During this conversation, the shah, after John Foster the US Secretary of State had compared Nasser's pan-Arabism to Hitler pan-Germanism, even answered that indeed Nasser 'was trying to follow in the footstep of Hitler'.
76 Gholam Reza Afkhami, *The Life and Times of the Shah*, 2009, 292.

that he had never thought of recognising the GPRA.[77] Moreover, relations with Egypt worsened. According to Henri Roux, the French ambassador, the Iranians were concerned about the evolution of the situation in Kurdistan following the regime change in Iraq. They held 'a very negative view of [the return from exile of] Kurdish elements whose hostility towards Iran was in no doubt'.[78] The welcome the Kurds received in Cairo from Nasser did nothing to improve the shah's opinion of the Egyptian president whom he resented for his opposition to the Baghdad Pact and his attitude during the Suez Crisis, despite Iran's official show of support. Roux added that the Iranians also 'reproached him for the hostile attitude that he adopted toward the project of a pact of the Aryan countries grouping Iran, Pakistan, Afghanistan and possibly Turkey, envisaged in the aftermath of the coup d'état of Baghdad [...] the Radio of Cairo had denounced in advance the imperialist character of such an alliance.'[79]

Meanwhile, on 26 September, during a conversation with Henri Roux on the occasion of the inauguration of the new Faculty of Literature at the University of Tehran, the shah 'expressed [...] in very friendly terms, all his warm wishes for the future of our country, for the success of the referendum [on the new constitution] and for the stability of the French Government'.[80] After the referendum on 28 September in France and therefore in Algeria, the newspapers celebrated de Gaulle's victory and the defeat of the Algerian nationalists. The newspaper *Ettela'at* in its editorial indicated that 'if the constitution of the free government of Algeria had been a blow to the referendum of de Gaulle, the referendum was, in turn, a blow to the free government of Algeria'.[81]

The proposal the French president made to the FLN during a press conference on October 23 of a 'paix des braves' was received favourably by the shah, who made this known to Roux during a dinner. According to Roux, the shah 'returned several times to the idea that if this policy succeeded in putting an end to the territorial war, it would constitute a failure

---

77 CADC, 372QO/559, Roux, 6 October 1958.
78 CADC, 367QO/17, Dossier relation avec l'Egypte, Roux, 1078/AL, 16 October 1958.
79 Dossier relation avec l'Egypte, Roux, 1078/AL, 16 October 1958.
80 CADC, 367QO/16, Roux, 234, 26 September 1958.
81 CADC, 367QO/16, Extrait de l'éditorial d'*Ettela'at*, 28 September 1958.

of such gravity for Colonel Gamal Abdel Nasser that he would not recover because North Africa would lean entirely towards the West.'[82] Meanwhile at the UN, on 13 December 1958, Iran nevertheless voted with the other countries of the Afro-Asian group in favour of a draft resolution concerning Algeria.

The Franco-Iranian rapprochement became more evident the following year, when in May 1959, the French president received the shah. Articles in the Iranian press celebrated the proximity of the two countries. In the newspaper *Iran-e Ma* on 22 May 1959, an editorial entitled 'The Shahanshah and the President of the French State – the deep spiritual influence of the French in our country' noted how the political and military elite had been largely trained in France. It also supported France's right to retain oil from the Sahara, an issue that poisoned negotiations with the Algerians.[83] An article in *Jahan* of 25 May explained that

General de Gaulle, by stabilising power in France, not only did his country a favour by removing the Communist party, but by strengthening the position of France, he strengthened the Western camp at the same time... It is for this reason that we attach great importance to the friendship of France, and we have always been opposed to the demagogic recognition of the Free Government of Algeria created by Cairo.[84]

As the date of the UN General Assembly drew near, the French ambassador was asked to sound out Iranian intentions. At first, the Iranian authorities did not want to disassociate themselves from the Afro-Asian group. French representatives, both civil and military, engaged in propaganda efforts in Iran, as requested by de Gaulle's prime minister, Michel Debré, in March.[85] Inspired by the talking points prepared by the French

---

82 CADC, 367QO/16, Roux, 273, 28 October 1958.

83 ASHDV, GR 14 S 329, dossier relation franco-iranienne, 190 AM/IR Note d'information, 26 May 1959.

84 Dossier relation franco-iranienne, 26 May 1959.

85 CADC, 372QO/565, Laurens-Castelet, 271/72, 13 August 1959; CADC, 372QO/565, Laurens-Castelet, 279/280, 19 August 1959; Connelly, *Diplomatic Revolution*, 200–201.

delegation at the UN, Laurens-Castelet, the French chargé d'affaires, sent a document to sixty prominent Iranians. In it, he argued that Iran, Iraq, Turkey, and the USSR would refuse any legitimacy to the United Nations if it decided to put the question of Kurdistan on the agenda under the pretext that it was a minority with a vocation to independence. Only a few months after the collapse of the Iran-Soviet negotiations, he also stressed that a show of support to the FLN would mean the support of increasing communist influence in the world.[86]

On 16 September 1959, de Gaulle announced the principle of recourse to self-determination by referendum for the Algerians. A month later, in an audience with the French ambassador, Henri Roux, the shah said that 'General de Gaulle's decision concerning Algeria seemed to him the most reasonable and the best that France could promote.' He added that he was convinced that no other French personality could have proposed such a wise solution. For his part, he approved it entirely. The shah promised Roux that his country would do all that it could to support France at the UN but added that Iran, as a Muslim country, was limited in the help it could provide to France on this matter.[87] In *Iran-e Ma* on 23 November, an article which echoed Laurens-Castelet's position insisted on the strong Franco-Iranian friendship, and explained that a vote at the UN against de Gaulle's France, which was proposing a referendum to the Algerians, meant voting with Nasser and Khrushchev.[88]

The French military attaché learned from a trusted source that at a CENTO meeting in Karachi in November 1959, Iran and Turkey had refused Pakistan's request to discuss the Algerian question. The French military attaché indicated that the argument used by the shah was that France was invoking its sole competence, Algeria being an integral part (until further notice) of the French Republic. It was therefore dangerous to vote in favour of UN interference because this could create a precedent which, later on, might possibly work against Iran (in Khuzestan and Kurdistan), another talking point pushed by Laurens-Castelet.[89]

---

86 CADC, 372QO/565, Laurens-Castelet, 12 August 1959.
87 CADC, 367QO/16, Roux, 367/69, 24 October 1959.
88 CADC, 367QO/16, Roux, 1006, 26 November 1959.
89 ASHDV, GR 14 S 329, [déclassifié par décision 502296 du 08/04/2021], dossier relation franco-iranienne, 133 AM/IR, 11 February 1960.

According to the same report, this argument proved decisive in deter-mining the vote in the UN General Assembly on the Algerian case. Thus, in December 1959, the Iranian representative abstained from voting.[90] The minister of foreign affairs, Abbas Aram, informed Henri Roux that the abstention had put the Iranian government under a lot of pressure from the other Muslim countries of the Afro-Asian group. He added that 'the Iranian government hopes that the French government will still show goodwill to stop the bloodshed as soon as possible and find a reasonable solution for its Algerian affairs.'[91]

1960–1962: Iran Between the Afro-Asian Group and GPRA

The UN General Assembly of 1959 was the only time Iran abstained from a vote concerning the Algerian cause. From 1960 on, Iran resumed voting against French interests on the Algerian question. From 24 January to 1 February 1960, the 'Week of the Barricades' took place, during which part of the European population of Algiers blocked major roads in the city. This ended in violent clashes between demonstrators and the gendarmes, with deaths on both sides. These events, condemned by the Iranian press, tested the Iranian officials' resolve. They feared that they had not made the right choice in siding with France at the last UN General Assembly, particularly after the criticism Iran's authorities had sustained from the other members of the Afro-Asian group. According to the report from the military mission, the speech de Gaulle gave soon after reassured them. For the shah and Eqbal's government, the French president still represented the guarantee that France would manage to find a solution to preserve the political, social, and economic rights of the Muslim majority.[92] The test detonation in Algeria of the first French atomic bomb on 13 Febru-ary 1960 did nothing to weaken the confidence they had in de Gaulle. On the contrary, according to the military attaché, 'the Iranians, both civilian and military, have been sensitive to France's act of political and moral

---

90 Dossier relation franco-iranienne, 11 February 1960.
91 CADC, 372QO/565, Téhéran, Roux, 468/70 Communiqué à ONU sous 6271/73 par les soins du département.
92 ASHDV, GR 14 S 324, Note d'information, 98 AM/IR, Réaction iranienne à la crise d'Alger, 3 February 1960.

independence, to the prestige of the force that we have conferred upon ourselves'. Aware of their own dependency on American aid, Iranians could not fail to see the analogy to their own situation and hope to emulate the French, he explained.[93]

Up until 23 July 1960, the Iranian government seemed ready to stick to the position it had taken at the General Assembly in December 1959.[94] A few days later though, the atmosphere had totally changed. After the shah had replied to a question from a foreign correspondent on 24 July that 'Iran had recognised Israel long ago', Nasser cut diplomatic ties with Iran on 26 July and Iran reciprocated the following day. Aram explained to Henri Roux that the rupture with Egypt and Nasser's violent attacks would surely force the government in Tehran to show increased Islamic solidarity, which would be to the detriment of France if by then there had been no resumption of cease-fire talks in Algeria.[95]

In August 1960, the military attaché, Guillot, explained that the diplomatic rupture between Iran and the UAR was a decisive factor in the modification of Iran's behaviour at the UN. According to him, Iran was 'seeking not to provoke the Arab countries, and especially Iraq, to align themselves with Nasser'. In order to do so, the Iranian government would tend to satisfy the imperatives of Islamic solidarity, and, in the first place, join the majority of Afro-Asians hostile to France over Algeria at the UN.[96] French ambassador, Henri Roux, confirmed Guillot's comments. Aram, the Iranian minister of foreign affairs, had told him that Iran might not be able to resist pressure from the Arab countries. Guillot noticed that 'Turkey's new attitude towards this problem' could also have weighed on the Iranian decision. If, according to him, the Ministry of Foreign Affairs advocated voting for the motion tabled by the Afro-Asian group, everything would depend on the shah.[97] Guillot cultivated the good graces of the military chiefs who had the ear of the shah and were favourable to the French position.

---

93 ASHDV, GR 14 S 324, Note d'information, 162 AM/IR, 18 February 1960.
94 CADC, 517INVA/1067, Dossier Guerre d'Algérie, Roux, 330/332, 3 August 1960.
95 Dossier Guerre d'Algérie, Roux, 330/332, 3 August 1960.
96 ASHDV, GR 14 S 329, Dossier relation franco-iranienne, 708 AM/IR, 15 August 1960.
97 Dossier relation franco-iranienne, 15 August 1960.

The Arab League conference in Chtaura, Lebanon, a few days later validated Guillot's analysis. The Arab countries refused to align themselves with Egypt. Iran, for its part, had to renounce officially any normalisation with Israel.[98] Relations with Iraq were improving after a crisis in December 1959 had erupted because of the frontier issue on the Shatt al-Arab waterway. On 14 July 1960, an Iranian delegation had attended celebrations for the second anniversary of the Iraqi revolution and Iraq, according to Henri Roux, had showed the greatest understanding after the Iran-Egyptian diplomatic rupture and had stopped its attacks broadcast on radio. Azadi, the Iranian ambassador in Iraq, became the new minister of foreign affairs and Iran participated in the conference in Baghdad from 10 to 14 September during which OPEC was founded. In addition to Iraqi and Iranian representatives, the conference brought together those of Kuwait, Saudi Arabia, and Venezuela. The French military attaché noted that 'Bahrain was not invited to be represented in Baghdad, which [was] a remarkable concession made to Iran.'[99]

In November, Henri Roux confirmed Guillot's report about Turkey, whose change in attitude had surprised everyone in Iran. The most surprising was the fact that the National Union Committee was more favourable to the GPRA than the Menderes government. An Algeria Week was even organised in Turkey with the approval of the government. Iran was isolated from the other Muslim members of CENTO. The ambassador regretted that 'the efforts in providing information' were not reflected in a press that was more and more understanding of the theses defended by the GPRA. Roux even noted that the *rapprochement* with the Soviet Union and Communist China was no longer used as a repellent but, on the contrary, as an argument to accelerate the inevitable process towards Algerian independence.[100] The argument was taken up again in *Keyhan* on 17 December 1960, which evoked the risk of Nasser's penetration of Algeria, on par with that of communism.[101] The General Assembly session concluded on 19

---

98 CADC, 367QO/62, Roux, 1018/AL, 10 September 1960.

99 ASHDV, GR 14 S 324, Note d'information, 787 AM/IR, 22 September 1960.

100 CADC, 367QO/52, [dossier Guerre d'Algérie] Henri Roux au MAE, 1280/AL, 12 November 1960.

101 CADC, 367QO/52 [dossier Guerre d'Algérie] Henri Roux au MAE, 1464/AL, 22 December 1960.

December with a vote recognising Algeria's right to independence, a vote in which the Iranian representative sided with the Afro-Asian group.[102] The next day, de Gaulle proposed a referendum on his Algerian policy that was to be held on 8 January 1961.

A few days after these two major events, the French military attaché in Tehran proposed an evaluation of the evolution of the 'Iranian climate as far as the Algerian question was concerned'. He defined three main trends. The military, which he believed had a direct influence on the shah, was more inclined to accept French arguments such as 'the danger of a communist installation on the southern shores of the Mediterranean, or of a Soviet or Nasserite influence on the Maghreb'. At the Ministry of Foreign Affairs, Iranian officials were more apt to 'consider the political implications, as far as Iran was concerned, of a conflict which, for some, weakened Europe and the West, or for others, called into question Afro-Asian solidarity'. This trend was also present in the press. The third trend was represented by religious circles which denounced 'the "oppression" of a Muslim people, the collusion of France and Israel, and even attacked those Iranians who, openly or secretly, were in favour of this collusion'. The government, he explained, inspired by these three tendencies, was worried about 'anything that might promote Arab unity or Nasserite dynamism, anything that might provide support for Soviet penetration of Africa', but refused to risk being attacked for failing to show Islamic solidarity. He concluded: 'For the moment, the fear that the presence of the GPRA on its soil serves as a conduit for dangerous activities carried out by agents of the UAR prevented him from recognising the GPRA.'[103]

For this reason, the demonstrations 'which at the call of religious leaders [...] had happened in the mosques, in the form of public prayers and mourning, were authorised under the express condition of not spilling into the street'. These gatherings had brought together in mid-December members of the National Front such as Hossein Makki and Mozaffar Baqa'i, as well as Ayatollah Behbahani and the ambassadors of Saudi

---

102 Henri Roux au MAE, 22 December 1960. Roux understood that this vote was a sign that Iran was heavily influenced by the new position of the Turkish government towards the Algerian cause.

103 ASHDV, GR 14 S 329, 1112 AM/IR Note d'information [déclassifié par décision 502296 du 8 avril 2021] Objet Iran et Algérie, 29 December 1960.

Arabia and Morocco.[104] As the Franco-Algerian conflict dragged on, calls for the recognition of the GPRA appeared in Iranian newspapers. An article in *Khandaniha* on 26 August 1961 read that

> the Algerian nationalists urge Iran to recognise the GPRA, as Pakistan
> had done, because, among the Muslim countries, only Iran has not
> yet done it. Pakistan lends moreover a material help to Algeria.
> The GPRA complains that Iran has not defended the interests of the
> Algerian people... In Algeria, in addition to the Sunnis, there is a
> large number of Shi'ites who are part of the nationalist supporters of
> independence.[105]

Mostafa Rahnama quoted this article in an open letter to the government calling for the recognition of the GPRA, which the people want, reiterating a request he had made the previous year along with nineteen mullahs.[106] Two months later, *Vazifeh*, a small-circulation newspaper, called on the Ministry of Foreign Affairs to recognise the GPRA and thus 'stop offending Iranian Muslims'.[107] Criticism of France and calls for the recognition of the GPRA did not prevent the Iranian ruler from making an official visit to France that took place between 11 and 14 October 1961.[108]

In November, students demonstrated to express their solidarity with the GPRA. The military attaché, while admitting 'the tendency of youth to identify with Afro-Asian concepts', explained that 'after investigation [...] the students [had] taken the pretext of an opportune subject to authorize the meetings whose ultimate goal remained to demonstrate against the Amini government.'[109] These multiple calls were not heard. In November, Amini, who had the support of the court on this matter, according to the French military attaché, expressed his desire to avoid a useless gesture:

---

104 Note d'information, 29 December 1960.

105 CADC, 367QO/52, dossier Guerre d'Algérie, Lescot, 1017/AL, 31 August 1961.

106 Dossier Guerre d'Algérie, 31 August 1961.

107 CADC, 367QO/52, dossier Guerre d'Algérie, Lescot, 1141/AL, 9 October 1961.

108 Fath, *L'Iran et de Gaulle*, 28.

109 ASHDV, GR 14 S 329, 856 AM/IR, Note d'information, Objet : Manifestations d'étudiants iraniens en faveur du GPRA à Téhéran, 5 November 1961.

'the recognition of a state must help with the solution of a problem; this does not seem to be the case at present with regard to Algeria.'[110]

On 18 March 1962, representatives from both the French government and the GPRA signed a peace agreement, the *Accords d'Évian*. In Iran, the critics of the Iranian government on the Algerian matter did not fall silent with the end of the war, however. *Ettela'at*, which celebrated the agreement as the victory of the Algerian Muslim nation,[111] continued to blame the Iranian government for its lack of support for the Algerian people through its special envoy to North Africa, Mansur Taraji.[112] Taraji reported that the Iranian ambassador in Tunis, 'Abdol Hoseyn Meftah,[113] had told him that he had asked the Ministry of Foreign Affairs and the Red Lion and Sun Society several times to send aid to the Algerian people, but to no avail.[114] Taraji also relayed the words of an Algerian official, Hadj Cherchali. The latter had explained to him that he had gone to Iran in 1959 to obtain food and medicine for his people, but had only been allowed to stay for two days.[115]

The campaign led by *Ettela'at* and its owner Abbas Mas'udi, in support of the Algerian people materialised with the creation of a committee in charge of organising, collecting, and delivering the help the Iranian people would provide to their Algerian 'Muslim brothers' *(Komiteh-ye melli bara-ye komak-e mardom-e al-Jazayir)*; money and clothes were collected, and Iranian doctors were sent to North Africa to take care of the Algerian refugees. It culminated in the invitation of an official representative of the

---

110 Note d'information, 5 November 1961.

111 *Ettela'at*, 28 Esfand 1340/19 March 1962, 3.

112 *Ettela'at*, 19 Khordad 1341/9 June 1962, 1, 23; 20 Khordad 1341/10 June 1962, 5, 7. Gholam Hoseyn Salehyar, the international desk's chief editor explains that this was the first time that the newspaper had sent a special correspondent abroad.

113 'Abdolreza Hushang Mahdavi, *Siyasat-e Khareji-ye Iran dar Dowran-e Pahlavi*, 1375, 533. Meftah was Iran's ambassador to Tunis from Azar 1340 (December 1961) to Mordad 1341 (August 1962).

114 *Ettela'at*, 8 Khordad 1341/29 May 1962, 23.

115 *Ettela'at*, 16 Khordad 1341/6 June 1962, 18. In this article, this official is named Shushali and introduced as Ben Khedda's chief of staff. I was unable to identify anyone named Shushali but Hadj Cherchali was Ben Khedda's chief of staff when Ben Khedda was minister of social affairs. Benjamin Stora, *Dictionnaire Biographique de Militants Nationalistes Algériens: E.N.A., P.P.A., M.T.L.D., 1926–1954*, 1985, 280.

GPRA to Iran. According to an article published in *Ettela'at*, Taraji was the originator of this initiative. While in North Africa, he had advised the Algerian nationalists to send a representative to Iran to strengthen and develop relations between the two countries and to raise awareness among the Iranian people of the struggles of the Algerian nation. The GPRA had agreed and decided to send Mas'ud Ait Sha'lal, the head of the Algerian diplomatic mission in Beirut. *Ettela'at* covered the cost of the travel and completed the administrative process so Sha'lal could be the first Algerian to enter Iran with an official passport issued by the Algerian government.[116]

The visit to Iran in June 1962 of the GPRA representative was not a sign of changes to come regarding the attitude of Amini's government towards the GPRA. Although this three-day visit benefitted from an extended coverage,[117] few details got out of the only meeting Sha'lal had with a member of the Iranian government, a forty-five-minute talk with Amini at his personal residence. At a press conference that took place after this meeting, the Algerian representative said he was pleased with Amini's interest in Algeria's success, but when asked if diplomatic relations between Algeria and Iran would be established, he answered that only the GPRA could make these kinds of decisions.[118] According to the French representative, Sha'lal had assured Amini that his country would remain neutral in the dispute between Egypt and Iran and in return, Amini had promised that Iranian recognition of the new Algerian government would take place immediately after independence.[119] Although the Iranian authorities recognised Algeria as an independent state on 3 July 1962,[120] they never recognised the GPRA. Iran was one of only two Muslim countries – the other being Turkey – to act in this manner. Official diplomatic relations were only established after the defeat of the GPRA by the Bureau Politique.[121]

---

116 *Ettela'at*, 2 Tir 1341/23 June 1962, 17.

117 *Ettela'at*, Sha'lal was on the front page of the *Ettela'at* during 5 days starting from 2 Tir 1341 (23 June 1962) and long articles were devoted to his speeches and meetings.

118 *Ettela'at*, 4 Tir 1341/25 June 1962, 16.

119 CADC, 367QO/59, dossier Algérie, Renaud Sivan, ambassadeur de France en Iran, 358/59, 25 June 1962.

120 CADC, 367QO/52, Sivan, 387, 5 July 1962, 367QO/59, dossier Algérie, Sivan au MAE, 358/59.

121 CADC, 367QO/59, Sivan, 663, 29 October 1962. On this date, a month and a

According to 'Abolhasan Ebtehaj, the ambiguous attitude of successive Iranian governments towards the Algerian cause was perceived as a sign of hostility by the Algerians and could even have cost the shah his life. In his memoirs, Ebtehaj, whom the World Bank had appointed to be its representative in Algeria,[122] recalls that Ahmed Ben Bella, the Algerian president at the time, had told him over lunch that some young Algerian freedom fighters had come to him to seek his approval for an assassination attempt on the shah during one of his trips to Europe. Ben Bella had then explained to Ebtehaj that although Algerian nationalists were opposed to the shah, he could not have possibly condoned such an act.[123]

*

A constellation of circumstances brought the Algerian War of Independence to the forefront of Iranian politics. Iran's economic and cultural relations with France, its geographic position, its membership in the Afro-Asian group at the United Nations, and the Baghdad Pact combined to assign it a position in a diplomatic battle that it might have preferred to avoid: namely, a position that opposed both the Algerian FLN and French colonial power. At the UN, where the FLN and its supporters pleaded the cause of Algerian independence, Iran voted in favour of Algeria from 1955 to 1958 while the shah was eager to welcome the North African countries into the Baghdad Pact. Nevertheless, the French repeatedly praised Iranian diplomats for their tact and restraint at the UN on the Algerian question. In return, Iranian authorities appreciated France's respect for their decisions, stating regularly that their representative would act in a measured way. Despite French hostility towards the Baghdad Pact, Iranian authorities

---

half after the defeat of the GPRA, the French ambassador mentioned that Iran would be sending a diplomatic mission to Algeria for the independence celebrations, a mission that would have conversations about the exchange of diplomatic representatives. 367QO/59, Sivan, 342/AL, 2 March 1963. An article published in the *Donya* newspaper on 2 March 1963 indicates the opening of an Iranian embassy in Algeria later that year.

122 CADC 367QO/59 Dossier Algérie, Sivan, 286/88, 21 April 1964.

123 'Abolhasan Ebtehaj, beh kushesh-e 'Alireza 'Aruzi, *Khaterat-e 'Abolhasan Ebtehaj*, vol. 2, 524.

adamantly pursued relations with France on the economic level. However, religious circles, and members of both the Senate and the Majles, regularly raised their voices to take a stand in favour of the Algerian people. The Algerians also benefitted from the support of the representatives of Arab countries in Iran to make their voice heard.

In 1958, with the return to power of de Gaulle, the Iranian government grew closer to the French and more weary of Nasser, whom it suspected of using the war in Algeria to rally the Arab countries around him. The creation of the UAR in February 1958 and the fall of the Hashemite dynasty in Iraq in July 1958 made the threat posed by Nasser even more acute in the eyes of the Iranian authorities. Thus, when the FLN announced the creation of the GPRA from Cairo, it could not be well received in Iran. The shah refused to recognise the new government. With the collapse of Iranian-Soviet negotiations in February 1959, the shah felt surrounded and isolated in the face of the dual threat of Nasserism and communism. The French propaganda regarding Algeria echoed the shah's insecurity and Iran even went as far as to abstain from a vote on the Algerian question at the UN General Assembly in 1959.

Finally, from 1960 to 1962, although Iran's representatives at the UN resumed voting in favour of Algerian independence, the shah never accepted recognition of the GPRA despite growing opposition to his reluctance within Iran. One might consider that after the French government had finally signed a peace agreement with the GPRA, the shah could have, at this point, also recognised the latter, thereby bringing an end to the protests that were raised against him on this matter, but he did not. The reason for this was not so much his desire to maintain good relations with France but his visceral hatred of Nasser, whom he had identified with the GPRA.

Thus, during the course of the almost eight-year decolonisation war that pitted the Algerian nationalists against the French colonial power, the Iranian authorities' support for Algeria never really went beyond voting in its favour at the UN. The shah, who at that time began to assert his grip over Iran's diplomacy, had not yet theorised his transactional vision of foreign policy but acted accordingly when it came to this conflict. He considered first and foremost the interests of his country – not unlike countries such as Egypt and Tunisia, which also conducted their policy towards the war according to their own best interests. The shah was 'embarrassed', to quote a French diplomat, by the situation. He expected the conflict to end quickly so that he could develop Iran's relations with both France and the countries of North Africa, to draw new partners into the Baghdad Pact and away from the Egyptian sphere of influence. His neighbours and allies in the region exerted pressure on the Iranian government for it to take a more aggressive stance towards France, but Iran considered its relations with France too important to sever over this conflict, especially as Iran became increasingly isolated after 1958. De Gaulle's policy of independence from the United States, both in terms of diplomacy and defence, must also have appealed to the shah. French officials' arguments to justify their desire to keep Algeria as an integral part of France echoed his concerns over Bahrain; his fears of a communist penetration of the region; and of Nasserism. For the shah, the Algerian nationalist leaders were at best tools in Nasser's hands, and at worst close allies of the Egyptian leader.

Bibliography

Archival Material

Archives du Service Historique de la Défense, Vincennes (ASHDV).
Centre des Archives diplomatiques de La Courneuve (CADC).
FRUS, 1955–1957, Near East Region; Iran; Iraq, vol. 12, Washington D.C., 1991.

Memoirs

'Abdoh, J. *Chehel sal dar sahneh-ye qaza'i, siyasi diplomasi-ye Iran va jahan: khaterat-e Doktor-e Jalal 'Abdoh*, virayesh va tanzim az Majid Tafreshi, Tehran, 1368 [1989].
Ebtehaj, A. *Khaterat-e 'Abolhasan Ebtehaj*, vol. 2, Tehran, 1371 [1992].
Rahnama, M. *Khaterat-e Sheykh Mostafa Rahnama beh damimeh-ye yaddasht-ha-ye sal-e 1333*, Tehran, 1393.
Kiouane, A. *Les débuts d'une diplomatie de guerre (1956–1962): journal d'un délégué à l'extérieur*, Algiers, 2000.

Newspapers

A'ineh-ye Eslam
Al-Basa'ir
Ettela'at
El Moudjahid
Majalleh-ye Taraqqi
Seda-ye Vatan

Secondary Sources

Abrahamian, E. *Iran between Two Revolutions*, Princeton, 1982.

Abrahamian, E. *A History of Modern Iran,* Cambridge, 2018.

Afkhami, G. *The Life and Times of the Shah*, Berkeley, 2009.

Alvandi, R. 'Flirting with Neutrality: The Shah, Khrushchev, and the Failed 1959 Soviet– Iranian Negotiations', *Iranian Studies* 47/3, 2014, 419–440.

Alvandi, R. 'The Shah's Détente with Khrushchev: Iran's 1962 Missile Base Pledge to the Soviet Union', *Cold War History* 14/3, 2014, 423–444.

Colin-Jeanvoine, E. and Derozier, S., ed. *Le Financement du FLN pendant la Guerre d'Algérie 1954–1962*, Saint-Denis, 2008, 37–88, https://www.cairn.info/le-financement-du-fln-pendant-la-guerre-d-algerie--9782356760029-page-37.htm.

Connelly, M.J. *A Diplomatic Revolution: Algeria's Fight for Independence and the Origins of the Post-Cold War Era*, New York, 2002.

Fath, S. *L'Iran et de Gaulle: Chronique d'un Rêve Inachevé*, Neuilly-sur-Seine, 1999.

Khudori, D. *La France et Bandung*, Paris, 2020.

Mahdavi H. 'Abdolreza, *Siyasat-e Khareji-ye Iran dar Dowran-e Pahlavi,* Tehran, 1375.

Nassehi, R. 'Domesticating Cold War Economic Ideas: The Rise of Iranian Developmentalism in the 1950s and 1960s', *The Age of Aryamehr*, ed. R. Alvandi, London, 2018, 35–69.

Papastamkou, S. 'La France au Proche–Orient, 1950–1958 Un intrus ou une puissance exclue?', *Bulletin de l'Institut Pierre Renouvin* 1/25, 2007, 177–188.

Papastamkou, S. 'France and the Middle East in 1958: Continuity and change through crisis,' *Middle East in 1958: Reimagining a Revolutionary Year,* ed. J. Karam, London, 2020, 34–42.

Rahnema, A. *An Islamic Utopian: A Political Biography of Ali Shari'ati,* London, 1998.

Rahnema, A. *The Rise of Modern Despotism in Iran: The Shah, the Opposition, and the US, 1953–1968,* London, 2021.

Ramazani, R.K. *Iran's Foreign Policy, 1941–1973: A Study of Foreign Policy in Modernizing Nations,* Charlottesville, 1975.

Richard, Y. *L'Islam Chiite, Croyances et Idéologie,* Paris, 1991.

Stora, B. *Dictionnaire Biographique de Militants Nationalistes Algériens: E.N.A., P.P.A., M.T.L.D., 1926–1954,* Paris, 1985.

Stora, B. and de Rochebrune, R. *La Guerre d'Algérie vue par les Algériens, 1, Le Temps des Armes: des Origines à la Bataille d'Alger,* Paris, 2011.

Stora, B. and de Rochebrune, R. *La Guerre d'Algérie vue par les Algériens, 2, Le Temps de la Politique: de la Bataille d'Alger à l'Indépendance,* Paris, 2016.

Thénault, S. 'How about 1958 in Algeria? A transnational event in the context of the war of independence', *The Middle East in 1958: Reimagining a Revolutionary Year,* ed. J. Karam, London, 2020, 122–130.

Vince, N. *The Algerian War, the Algerian Revolution,* Basingstoke, 2020.

Yeşilbursa, B.K. *The Baghdad Pact: Anglo-American defence policies in the Middle East, 1950–1959,* London, 2005.

6

Iranians and the Vietnam War: Cold Warrior Enmities or Anti-Colonial Solidarities?[1]

Arash Azizi

On 28 December 1965, an American diplomat had a tense meeting with a Third World leader who was accusing the West of racial prejudice. This sounds like an unsurprising event but its details might prove less predictable. The complaint came from the shah of Iran. Meeting in Tehran with the ambassador of the United States, Armin H. Meyer, the shah complained about how the 'white' European allies of the United States supported it over Berlin but 'are conspicuously absent' when it came to backing the US war effort in Vietnam.[2] Urging the United States to 'stand by its commitments' to its Vietnamese allies and refrain from withdrawal, the Iranian

---

1 This paper started in a seminar led by Chen Jian at NYU and has gone through many iterations following its presentation at various fora. For their comments, wisdom and sharing of original documents, I am indebted to Zachary Lockman, Sara Pursley, Arang Keshavarzian, Masha Kirasirova, Roham Alvandi, Firoozeh Kashani-Sabet, Kathryn Statler, Salim Yaqub, Rob Steele, Afshin Matin-Asgari, Rohan Advani, William Figueroa, Lorenz M. Lüthi, Nima Mina, Cyrus Schayegh, Stephanie Cronin, and Ayse Lokmanoglu.
2 Telegram from the embassy in Tehran to the Department of State, 18 December 1965, National Archives and Records Administration (hereafter NARA).

monarch even expressed concern over the peace appeal by Pope Paul VI. A few months later, in June 1966, when the shah visited Bucharest to meet with Romanian communist leader Nicolae Ceausescu, he sounded a different tone by claiming (in private) that 'if Vietnamese communists win in South Vietnam, this is the problem of Vietnamese' and 'nobody has the right to meddle in there'.[3] Shortly after the Bucharest trip, the Iranian ambassador to the United States, Khosrow Khosravani, boasted to US officials that the shah had actually helped 'water down' a sharp Romanian communique on Vietnam, thus proving its status as 'America's closest friend in the Middle East'.[4]

These were not unimportant vacillations of a marginal leader; the shah's positions on the Vietnam War were closely watched by leaders in the United States, the Soviet Union, and others who attempted to sway Tehran to their side. Iranian actors made tangible contributions to both sides of the conflict in Vietnam. Additionally, for both the shah and the Iranian opposition, the Vietnam War was a central event that helped define their political identity. Basing itself on a study of Iranian ties to the Vietnam War, this chapter makes two broad arguments in two sections. First, I chart the development of the shah's Vietnam policy to show that while it had a serious ideological component as part of the Cold War, it was also much more complex than caricatures of the 'US-backed anti-communist despot' allow.[5] His declared foreign orientation of 'national independent policy' (*siyasat-e mostaqel-e melli*) was intent on establishing Iranian sovereignty and bolstering his regime while also gaining a prideful place for Iran among the community of nations, just as decolonisation was giving a new meaning to this concept.[6] I will demonstrate this by showing how the

---

3 Quoted in Roham Alvandi and Eliza Gheorghe, 'The Shah's Petro-Diplomacy with Ceausescu: Iran and Romania in the era of Detente', CWIHP Working Paper No. 74, 2014, 6.

4 Lyndon B. Johnson Library, National Security File, Country File, Iran. Memos & Miscellaneous, vol. II 1/66/1/69.

5 For a critique of such simplistic analyses see Arash Azizi, 'Review of America and Iran: A History, 1720 to the Present, by John Ghazvinian', *The Middle East Journal* 75/3, 2021, 473–475.

6 For more on the shah's foreign policy see Roham Alvandi, 'Introduction: Iran in the Age of Aryamehr', *The Age of Aryamehr: Late Pahlavi Iran and Its Global Entanglements*, ed. Roham Alvandi, 2018; Amin Saikal, *The Rise and Fall of The*

shah used his contributions to the Vietnam War to increase his influence in Washington, how he also cultivated serious relationships in the Eastern Bloc, how he could appear to share a Vietnam position with a fellow maverick in the Eastern Bloc (Ceausescu), and how in the post-1973 period, he went out of his way to appear neutral between Hanoi and Saigon.

In the second part of the paper, I argue that the Vietnamese revolutionary project had a decisive effect on the Iranian opposition to the shah and was unique in gathering support from all of its diverse quarters. The Vietnamese example of successfully resisting and finally defeating their US-backed enemies did much to animate the Iranian opposition. The Iranian connection to Vietnam was not only aspirational and included attempts at making material links with the Vietnamese communists.[7] Furthermore, the Iranian opposition's understanding of the Vietnam War and how it defined itself in relation to it was crucial to shaping how the oppositionists came to see themselves in the theatre of the global anti-imperialist struggle.[8] As such, Vietnam and its representations are an integral part of the development of Iranian revolutionary subjects in the long 1960s. The chapter concludes by pointing out some troubling consequences of revolutionary transnationalism, often elided in celebratory accounts.

Shah: Iran from Autocracy to Religious Rule, 2009; and Rouhollah K Ramazani, *Iran's Foreign Policy, 1941–1973: A Study of Foreign Policy in Modernizing Nations*, 1974.

7 I owe this distinction between aspirational and material connections to Victoria Langland, 'Transnational Connections of the Global Sixties as seen by a Historian of Brazil', *Routledge Handbook of the Global Sixties*, ed. Chen Jian et al., 2018, 15–26. In his discussion of Third Worldism in West Germany, Quinn Slobodian discusses how consequential the existence of real, material links can be in a solidarity action. He argues that the West German solidarity with African and Iranian progressive movements was qualitatively different from their later solidarity with the 'Vietnamese revolution', due to the fact that the former was characterised by the partnership that West German students had built with students from Africa and Iran whereas this was absent in the Vietnamese case. See Quinn Slobodian, *Foreign Front: Third World Politics in Sixties West Germany*, 2012.

8 For an account of Palestinian revolutionary activism that shows the central place of Vietnam in this global theatre see Paul Thomas Chamberlin, *The Global Offensive: The United States, the Palestine Liberation Organization, and the Making of the Post-Cold War Order*, 2012.

The Global Turn

Few fields of history have benefitted from the 'global turn' as much as the Cold War,[9] an era that lends itself quite well to the study of global links and transnational entanglements. The Cold War *was,* after all, a struggle waged all over the globe, during which parties at any one location were often interested in developments elsewhere.[10] But as Nile Green has recently pointed out, in the different context of Indian Ocean histories, it is one thing to want to write multi-country, global histories and another thing to actually do it.[11] Following up transnational aspects of a history often means extensive research, in places often inaccessible and in a range of languages beyond the reach of any one particular scholar. As a result, various global links of many Cold War histories remain unexplored, providing a rich research agenda for scholars in years to come.

A growing body of literature in Iranian studies on Iran's transnational ties in the twentieth century[12] has gone beyond its neighbours and more obvious candidates like the United States and European countries to include the Soviet world,[13] and even nations in Sub-Saharan Africa,[14]

---

9 On the 'global turn' and rise of Global History see Sebastian Conrad, *What is Global History?*, 2016.

10 Among the notable recent examples of transnational Cold War histories Taomo Zhou, *Migration in the Time of Revolution: China, Indonesia and the Cold War*, 2019; Renata Keller, *Mexico's Cold War: Cuba, the United States and the Legacy of Mexican Revolution*, 2015.

11 See Nile Green, 'Lost Voices from the Indian Ocean', *Los Angeles Review of Books*, 20 January 2017.

12 For pioneering examples of transnational Iranian histories see Firoozeh Kashani-Sabet, *Frontier Fictions: Shaping the Iranian Nation, 1804–1946*, 2000; H.E. Cheahbi ed., *Distant Relations: Iran and Lebanon in the Last 500 Years*, 2006; Nikki R. Keddie and Rudi Matthee ed., *Iran and the Surrounding World: Interactions in Culture and Cultural Politics*, 2002

13 See, for example, Masha Kirasirova, 'My Enemy's Enemy: Consequences of the CIA Operation against Abulqasim Lahuti, 1953–4', *Iranian Studies* 50/3, 2017, 439–465; and Timothy Nunan, '"Doomed to Good Relations": The USSR, the Islamic Republic of Iran, and Anti-Imperialism in the 1980s', *Journal of Cold War Studies* 24/1, 2022, 39–77.

14 See, for example, H. E. Chehabi, 'South Africa and Iran in the Apartheid Era', *Journal of Southern African Studies* 42/4, 2016; Robert Steele, 'The Keur Farah Pahlavi Project and Iranian–Senegalese Relations in the 1970s', *Iranian Studies* 54/1–2, 2021, 169–192; Steele, 'Two Kings of Kings: Iran–Ethiopia Relations Under

although Iran's ties to Southeast Asia remain largely unexplored.[15] On the other side, the historiography of the Vietnam War, even in its laudably global and international accounts, has so far largely managed to ignore not only Iran, but other Middle Eastern countries, too.[16]

This account attempts to fill this lacuna by pointing out a number of ways in which Iranians were linked to the Vietnam War. This includes diplomatic, military, and auxiliary contributions of the Iranian government and state institutions to one side of the war, most notably the dispatch of dozens of Iranian doctors and medics to South Vietnam. It will also chart the attitude and practice of the Iranian opposition toward the Vietnam War. Another dimension pertains to Iranian civilians whose lives were shaped by the Vietnam War, such as the journalists and photographers who covered the war.[17]

Mohammad Reza Pahlavi and Haile Selassie', *International History Review* 43/6, 2021, 1375–1392.

15 An example that should not be overlooked is Houchang Chehabi's comparison of Iranian and Thai histories in Chehabi, 'The Cats That Did Not Meow: An Historian of Iran Discovers Thailand', *Mizan Project*, 11 March 2020. https://mizanproject. org/the-cats-that-did-not-meow/.

16 See R. B. Smith, *An International History of the Vietnam War*, 3 volumes, 1983; Jeffrey Kimball, *Nixon's Vietnam War*, 1998; Kimball, *The Vietnam War Files: Uncovering the Secret History of Nixon-Era Strategy*, 2004; Lien-Hang T. Nguyen, *Hanoi's War: An International History of the War for Peace in Vietnam*, 2012; Lewis Sorley, *A Better War: The Unexamined Victories and Final Tragedy of America's Last Years in Vietnam*, 1999; Frederick Logevall, *Embers of War: The Fall of an Empire and the Making of America's Vietnam*, 2013.

17 For reasons of space, this dimension will not be pursued here but an example of a subject for study is the career of Abbas Attar, often known simply as Abbas. Born in 1944 in the small city of Khash in the peripheral areas of south-eastern Iran, he rose to become an internationally well-known photographer. Attar travelled to Vietnam twice in 1973 and 1975, just as the war was coming to a close, and took some of the most memorable photos of the conflict. He passed away in April, 2018. For a recognition of his Vietnam work in the Iranian press see Faradid, '(Tasavire) Yek Irani Dar Jang-e Vietnam', *Faradeed.ir*, May 2016. Attar's career is best studied as part of the history of rise of international journalism and how various Third World journalists saw, reported on and recorded various Cold War conflicts around the globe.

Tehran–Saigon Ties in the Age of Cold War

The end of the Second World War in 1945 soon brought about another global conflict known as the Cold War. Iran's place in the post-war world reflected its double historical reality. On the one hand, it was one of the very few non-Western countries never to have been formally colonised, reflected in its status as a sovereign founding member of the United Nations and as the only state in the Middle East to have been a founding member of the League of Nations (Afghanistan, Iraq, and Turkey joined in 1932–1934). On the other hand, Iran had been under imperialist domination by European countries for much of its contemporary history.[18]

The safeguarding of Iran's sovereignty was one of the hot issues of the early Cold War, subject to the first ever resolution of the United Nations Security Council which helped secure the withdrawal of Soviet forces from Iranian territory.[19] As the Cold War continued into the 1950s, Iran's progressive prime minister, Mohammad Mosaddeq (1951–1953), stood for a pioneering neutralism that was a precursor to the global non-aligned movement.[20] Mosaddeq's overthrow in a CIA-backed coup in August 1953 paved the way for Iran's close identification with the United States in the Cold War under the authoritarian rule of the bolstered shah.

The first post-war diplomatic contacts between Vietnam and Iran,

---

18 Following scholars of the Marxist school, such as Vivek Chibber, I define imperialism as distinct from colonialism, with the latter consisting of mechanisms of direct control and the former relying on more informal means of advancing dominance. For Chibber's discussion of imperialism see Vivek Chibber, 'The Return of Imperialism to Social Science,' *European Journal of Sociology* 45/3, 2004, 427–441. For a classical defence of this understanding of imperialism (as informal control) in the field of history see John Gallagher and Ronald Robinson, 'The Imperialism of Free Trade', *The Economic History Review* 6/1, 1953, 1–15. For an understanding of (and challenges to) Edward Said's understanding of imperialism vis-à-vis colonialism see 'Edward Said's Culture and Imperialism: A Symposium,' *Social Text* 10, Autumn 1994.

19 See Louise Fawcett, *Iran and the Cold War: The Azerbaijan Crisis of 1946*, 2009. For an account of the early Cold War era that centres Iran alongside Turkey and Greece, see Bruce Kuniholm, *The Origins of the Cold War in the Near East*, 1980.

20 For an account of Mosaddeq's pioneering neutralism and its global effect see Lior Sternfeld, 'Iran's days in Egypt: Mosaddeq's visit to Cairo in 1951', *British Journal of Middle Eastern Studies* 43/1, 2016, 1–20.

however, date back to the pre-Mosaddeq period. In 1945, Vietnamese anti-colonial nationalists under the leadership of Ho Chi Minh had formed the Democratic Republic of Vietnam (hereafter DRV) which soon found itself in control of much of the country while battling the forces of French colonialism. In response, France's allies in Vietnam gathered under the leadership of Bao Dai, the final emperor of the Nguyen dynasty, the last ruling family of precolonial Vietnam, who formed the State of Vietnam (hereafter SV) in 1949, following a series of provisional governments.[21]

Bao Dai's SV was recognised by the United States in 1950, which was a boon for its attempts at gaining further recognition. In January 1953, SV's ambassador to the United States, Tran Van Kha, wrote to his Iranian counterpart (and close Mosaddeq ally), Allahyar Saleh, to remind him that Canada had recognised 'the independent state of Viet-Nam and the Government of His Majesty Bao Dai', implying that Iran should follow suit. Iran's then foreign minister, Hoseyn Fatemi, raised the matter with Prime Minister Mosaddeq, but before it could be pursued further, Mosaddeq was overthrown, Saleh was in jail, and Fatemi was executed.[22] Shortly after the 1953 coup in Iran, Vietnam also saw monumental changes. In 1954, an international conference in Geneva divided the country along the seventeenth parallel, with DRV forming a government in Hanoi known as North Vietnam and Bao Dai forming a government in Saigon known as South Vietnam. A year later, Bao Dai fell after a rigged referendum organised by his prime minister, Ngo Dinh Diem, resulted in the creation of the Republic of Vietnam. The new South Vietnamese republic energetically pursued diplomatic ties with countries around the world, including Iran.[23] Tehran had voted for South Vietnam's membership of the UN in 1957 and, in 1960, it recognised the Saigon government following requests made by Vu Van Mau, South Vietnam's deputy foreign minister and separately by its envoys in Tokyo and Paris (all in 1955) and by its envoy in Washington (in 1959). The 1960 recognition was followed by a trip to Iran by Do Vang Ly, South Vietnam's envoy to India. Shortly after this visit, Do Vang wrote

21 Ellen J. Hammer. 'The Bao Dai Experiment', *Pacific Affairs* 23/1, 1950, 46–58.
22 Hoseyn Ebrahimkhani, *Tarikh-e Ravabet-e Iran va Viyetnam*, 2007, 12.
23 Sean Fear, 'Saigon Goes Global: South Vietnam's Quest For International Legitimacy in the Age of Détente', *Diplomatic History* 42/3, 2018, 453.

to the Iranian embassy in New Delhi as the 'Personal Representative' of South Vietnam's foreign minister and requested an expansion of ties, highlighting his country's 'desperate struggle against Communist invasion and subversion.... [a] problem which Vietnam is convinced is common with the two countries.'[24]

By mentioning communism, Do Vang had found just the right device to attract Iranian interest. While the shah's Iran paid little attention to the distant state of Vietnam in the 1960s, anticommunism remained a framework for the two countries' relations. On 31 March 1962, South Vietnam's President Diem wrote a personal letter to the shah, which was answered on 14 August by the monarch with anti-communist solidarity being the main theme of the correspondence. In the very first line of his reply, the shah thanked Diem for 'elucidating the activities of communist elements'.[25]

For the same reason, North Vietnamese attempts at establishing relations were rebuffed by Tehran in this period. On 20 July 1955, Hanoi's envoy in Czechoslovakia wrote to his Iranian counterpart in Prague asking to establish ties, followed by a similar request in 1957 by Hanoi's envoy in Warsaw. On both counts, the Iranian foreign ministry urged envoys not to respond to these letters since 'Iran does not recognise the communist government of Indochina'.[26] A 1961 letter by North Vietnam's foreign minister, Ung Van Khiem, to his Iranian counterpart, Hussein Ghods Nakhai, and a 1964 note by Hanoi's foreign ministry to its counterpart in Tehran went similarly unanswered.[27]

By contrast, Iran continued to maintain ties to South Vietnam, even following the 1963 coup that brought down Diem. The new regime in Saigon continued to emphasise a common anticommunist cause which it successfully leveraged to solicit aid from Iran. On 18 July 1964, the new foreign minister, Pham Huy Quat, wrote to his Iranian counterpart, Abbas Aram, with a list of what his country needed: industrial machinery, agricultural goods, human resources, and armaments. In response, Iran promised to send 1,000 tons of petroleum, some animal serum, and a number of

---

24 Facsimile of the letter printed in Ebrahimkhani, *Tarikh-e Ravabet-e Iran va Viyetnam*, 35.
25 Ebrahimkhani, *Tarikh-e Ravabet-e Iran va Viyetnam*, 44.
26 Ebrahimkhani, *Tarikh-e Ravabet-e Iran va Viyetnam*, 158.
27 Ebrahimkhani, *Tarikh-e Ravabet-e Iran va Viyetnam*, 165.

veterinary experts. These were shortly delivered to Saigon together with a delegation headed by Hormoz Qarib, Iran's ambassador to Tokyo.[28]

Tehran's commitment to anticommunism included its taking part in the World Anti-Communist League (hereafter WACL), the right-wing organisation founded by Chinese nationalist Chiang Kai-Shek in 1952, whose headquarters were based in Saigon from 1957 to 1964 and from 1967 to 1975. Iran's foreign ministry paid the relatively high cost of dispatching an Iranian delegation to WACL's gatherings in the Far East. In December 1968, WACL's second conference in Saigon was attended by delegates from more than fifty countries including an Iranian delegation headed by Senator Parviz Kazemi.[29] The conference was chaired by none other than Phan Huy Quat and it was shortly followed by the 14th conference of the Asian People's Anti-Communist League, where Iran joined India in submitting 'a resolution condemning Russian imperialism and expressing support of the struggle for national independence of subjugated peoples'.[30] On 21 December, the delegates also had a chance to visit the battlegrounds of the war to, according to a sympathetic account, 'see for themselves the fighting spirit of the Vietnamese army [and] how the American army is unjustly condemned for so-called cruelty while barbarisms perpetrated by the Viet Cong and the armies of Ho Chi Minh on the defenseless population go unnoticed'.[31]

'We do not fight alone'

Iran's anticommunist sympathies meant that it soon went on to make contributions to Saigon's cause, as highlighted in the propaganda material of the time. In 1975, as the war was coming to an end, the US Department

---

28 Ebrahimkhani, *Tarikh-e Ravabet-e Iran va Viyetnam*, 68.
29 Putting his Vietnamese experience to use, Kazemi went on to write a review of the South Vietnam's constitution for the journal of Iran's bar association. See Parviz Kazemi, 'Nazari be Qanun-e Asasi-ye Jomhuri-ye Vietnam va Tahavolat-e An Keshvar', *Kanun-e Vokala*, issues 110 and 111, 1969.
30 *ABN Correspondence: Bulletin of the Antibolshevik Bloc of Nations*, 20/1, January–February 1969.
31 *ABN Correspondence: Bulletin of the Antibolshevik Bloc of Nations*, 20/1, January–February 1969.

of the Army published a pamphlet as part of its 'Vietnam Studies' series, which highlighted the nations that had supported the anti-communist side.[32] It celebrated the 'more than forty nations' that had 'provided assistance to the Republic of [south] Vietnam in its struggle against North Vietnam'. In addition to countries that had given major military assistance, the pamphlet listed those that gave other kinds of help, including, from the Middle East, Iran, Israel, and Turkey.[33] It went on to explain that Iran had 'extended significant assistance' to Saigon and in response to requests by President Lyndon B. Johnson, had 'promised petroleum products and one thousand tons of gasoline were delivered in July of 1965'. Iran had also sent a 'medical team of high quality', consisting of twenty doctors, technicians, and nurses from the Red Lion and Sun Society (hereafter RLSS), Tehran's version of the Red Crescent.[34] More accurate numbers are found in American and Iranian foreign ministry archives, according to which, a first team of 21 Iranian doctors, nurses, and technicians left for South Vietnam on 11 January 1966 and were stationed in a 300-bed hospital in the war-torn province of Kien Hoa (today's Ben Tre), southwest of Saigon, where the Viet Cong (the guerrilla allies of the North Vietnamese communists active in South Vietnam) were known to be particularly active. The costs of the Iranian delegation were shared by Saigon (which paid for housing), US Aid (which paid for furniture), and Tehran (which paid for the rest). To thank Iran, a large Imperial Iran flag was installed in the centre of Saigon and also in the large central square in Kien Hoa.[35]

The Iranian medical team was praised by both US and South Vietnamese officials. An American diplomat visiting the Iranian team in February 1966 praised its 'excellent work' and the fact that its members had 'already established themselves firmly with the population'. The presence of several women in the group (such as Farideh Javadi, Puran Ostovari, Mohtaram Dadkhah, Farzaneh Alavi, and Pari Valikhani) and the fact that they had agreed to remain in Vietnam beyond their term also repeatedly impressed

32 Lieutenant General Stanley Robert Larsen and Brigadier General James Lawton Collins Jr, *Allied Participation in Vietnam*, 2005 (first printed in 1975).
33 Larsen and Collins Jr, *Allied Participation in Vietnam*, 160.
34 Larsen and Collins Jr, *Allied Participation in Vietnam*, 163.
35 Ebrahimkhani, *Tarikh-e Ravabet-e Iran va Viyetnam*, 69.

the American officials.[36] The US State Department soon asked Iran to send
another medical team to Vietnam, a request which was repeated in the fall
of 1966 during a visit to Iran by South Vietnam's health minister, Nguyen
Ba Kha. When the RLSS complained to the Iranian foreign ministry that
it did not have the budget for its Vietnamese operations, the shah personally intervened to reassure the group of state support. The RLSS was also
worried that its principled autonomy might be tarnished by having to work
under the supervision of the Saigon authorities but American officials
promised that the group would be 'self-contained and self-directing'.[37]
In the next few years, at least 150 Iranian medical professionals were
sent to South Vietnam, acting with such distinction that they went on to
be decorated. In the spring of 1969, the South Vietnamese embassy in
Ankara wrote to its Iranian counterpart to note that Saigon's Health Ministry intended to confer its medals of merit on the head and deputy head of
the Iranian medical delegation.[38] In March 1970, Saigon wrote to Tehran
to ask for the decoration of eight Iranian health professionals (five doctors,
one radiologist, and two paramedics) working in South Vietnam.[39]

The fact that the far-away country of Iran was giving support to Saigon
was an important psychological boost, highlighted by propaganda leaflets
produced in the Vietnamese language at the time. One such leaflet showed
pictures of Iranian surgeons in a hospital in South Vietnam and introduced
Iran as 'a country in the Middle East which is [one of the 31 countries] also
actively helping the victims of Communism in South Vietnam'.[40] There
was also a propaganda poster entitled 'Medical Aid for the Vietnamese,'
which showed doctors from Iran, Australia, the United States, and the Philippines.[41] Another leaflet showed a map of the world under the title 'We
Do Not Fight Alone,' with dots indicating the '31 countries of the Free

---

36 NARA, Department of State, Telegram, From Tehran Embassy to State, 20
December 1966.
37 Iranian Foreign Ministry Archives (hereafter IRFMA), report by the foreign
ministry's Seventh Political Department, 8 October 1969, doc. 7/731.
38 IRFMA, letter from Iranian embassy in Ankara to the foreign ministry in Tehran,
24 November 1969, doc. 4886.
39 Ebrahimkhani, *Tarikh-e Ravabet-e Iran va Viyetnam*, 76.
40 A reprint of the leaflet (undated), along with English translation, is reproduced in
Herbert A. Friedman, 'Allies of the Republic of Vietnam'. http://psywarrior.com/.
41 Friedman, 'Allies of the Republic of Vietnam'.

World' which had provided Saigon with economic, military, agricultural, medical, and educational support. 'Having the wholehearted support of the peace-loving countries in the world, we will surely win. The Communists will surely be defeated', the leaflet promised.[42]

These propaganda materials help us understand a crucial aspect of what is at stake in writing global histories of the Cold War; the fact that there were significant transnational contributions to conflicts of the Cold War, and that they were justified in ideological terms, possibly coloured the way Cold Warriors saw themselves at every juncture. Thus, writing a history of 'Iran and the Vietnam War' is not about merely adding one more country to a crowded theatre, but rather emphasising the global impact of the Vietnam War.

Iran's Military Intervention in Vietnam? Fact and Fiction

The exact scale of Iran's military participation in Vietnam has often been elided in official narratives, not least because the shah's government did much to hide it at the time. It does not help that some fabrications also exist on the topic. After the fall of the Pahlavi regime in 1979, a cottage industry developed in Iran publishing completely fake and made-up memoirs from figures of the Pahlavi regime. To make things worse, statements of these fake memoirs have been often quoted in newspapers of note, the national broadcaster, and even academic works.[43] One such statement, attributed to Farah Pahlavi, the shah's wife, has the shah complaining about the lack of US support in his hour of need 'even though I had given them Iranian warplanes in South Vietnam'.[44] Another fake memoir, purportedly written by the shah's mother, makes the false claim that the United States had even taken planes from Iran to Vietnam without the shah's knowledge.[45]

---

42 Friedman, 'Allies of the Republic of Vietnam'.

43 For a discussion of this problem in Iranian historiography see Robert Steele, *The Shah's Imperial Celebrations of 1971: Nationalism, Culture and Politics in Late Pahlavi Iran*, 2020, 9.

44 Quoted in major daily *Keyhan*, 2 March 2014 and also cited in Mohammadreza Chitsazian, 'Aya Iran dar Jang-e Viyetnam Mosharekat Dasht?', *Institute for Iranian Contemporary Historical Studies*, July 2016. https://bit.ly/3kZXytk

45 Quoted in *Keyhan*, 18 February 2003. This was part of the Islamist government's propaganda which aimed to show how Tehran was supposedly run by the United States under the shah.

A more tactful example is found in a documentary about the life of the last major prime minister of the Pahlavi era, Amir Abbas Hoveyda, which includes footage of an interview from the 1970s with an Iranian military officer in Vietnam. In the documentary the narrator claims that the Hoveyda government had broken the law by sending Iranian military forces to Vietnam without the permission of the parliament. The officer, interviewed in the 1970s, says:

> Those officers who finished serving in Vietnam will now go back
> to Tehran. These men have served with honour and distinction in
> difficult conditions. Some officers will remain here and I wanted
> to tell the families of all those who are here that there is nothing to
> worry about. Myself and Major General Sodeifi, the deputy head of
> Iranian contingent, are also remaining here. Despite what you hear in
> newspapers, nothing threatens our officers here.[46]

When the documentary aired in 2017, this was widely reported to have been evidence of Iranian officers giving military support to Saigon but, as shown below, Sodeifi's name proves that this delegation was part of a neutral Iranian contingent, tasked with supervising the ceasefire, not engaging in warfare. The only actual case of Iranian military contribution to the Saigon side of the Vietnam War involved a re-transfer of military equipment to the United States in the final period of the war in 1972. This episode complicates our understanding of Iranian–American Cold War relations and illuminates Tehran's positioning in the war.

In 1972, the United States was in the midst of Operations Enhance and Enhance Plus, which aimed to transfer as much military equipment as they could to aid the South Vietnamese government in anticipation of an end to direct American involvement. On 20 October Washington cabled its embassy in Tehran to ask Ambassador Joseph S. Farland to 'request [an] immediate appointment with shah' to tell him that President Nixon was 'seeking… Iranian cooperation on [a] matter of highest urgency and importance which may materially advance prospects for early peaceful

---

46 Mostafa Showghi, director, *Hoveyda*, 2017.

settlement in Southeast Asia'.[47] Farland was to ask the shah to turn over the 'entire Iranian Force [estimated at 90 aircraft] of F-5As for immediate disassembly and delivery to Vietnam by fastest possible US carriers'. This was part of the air force that the shah had been able to acquire from the Americans after much tortuous negotiation, which characterised the process in which the shah moved from being a marginal client to emerging as a key partner of United States in the region.[48] The telegram said that Washington did recognise the 'unprecedented nature' of the request but that this was only done 'for reasons of unparalleled importance' and 'certain other countries' were also being asked. It also said that an answer was needed 'by tomorrow'.[49]

Tehran was to act quickly. One day later, on 21 October, Farland cabled Washington to report on the three-hour meeting he had held with the shah at Niavaran Palace, just after the latter's return from a trip to the Soviet Union. According to Farland, the shah had announced that he 'fully appreciated the US position in making every effort to bring about a peaceful settlement of the Vietnam War for all the obvious reasons'. The shah was therefore happy to immediately provide two squadrons of F-5As, 'a total of 32 aircraft'; about one-third of what Washington had requested. Farland pressed further but was refused. The shah ended by asking him to pass on to Nixon his 'personal hope for success of this or subsequent undertakings leading toward peace in Southeast Asia'. In his diary, the shah's court minister, Asadollah 'Alam, confirms the basic elements of this account.[50]

Five days later, Farland wrote to Washington again to ask for a better approach to the shah 'should we decide to ask for additional F-5As'. The ambassador said the shah's 'prompt response' did show how valuable 'his sense of close relationship' with Nixon was to him, but that the Iranian needs, for instance for their airforce training programmes, would also need

47 Telegram 192358, from the Department of State to the Embassy in Iran, 20 October 1972, 2246Z.

48 See Roham Alvandi, *Nixon, Kissinger, and the Shah*, 2014; Stephen McGlinchey, 'Lyndon B. Johnson and Arms Credit Sales to Iran 1964–1968', *Middle East Journal* 67/2, Spring 2013, 229–247.

49 Telegram 192358, from the Department of State to the Embassy in Iran, 20 October 1972, 2246Z.

50 'Alinaqi 'Alikhani ed., *Yaddashtha-ye 'Alam*, vol. 2, 1993, 317.

to be acknowledged. Since Iranians were 'keenly interested' in increasing the number of their airforce trainees in the United States, to persuade the shah, the Iranian quota at US military schools should be increased six-fold, the ambassador recommended.[51]

A few weeks later, another cable from Tehran expressed serious concern over what appeared to have been a faux pas by the Pentagon. A spokesperson for Pentagon had told the media that Iran, along with Taiwan and South Korea, had agreed to give its F-5As to Operation Enhance Plus. The 'spirit of good will and cooperation' shown by the shah's granting of his planes for the Vietnam War had been 'badly shattered by what from here [Tehran embassy] appears to be [an] astonishing violation of the Shah's confidence and [the] understanding we had urged on the Shah', the cable read. Farland reported that 'Alam had told him that 'the Shah was greatly disturbed over this development'.[52] In his diary, 'Alam remembered the shah's shock that this 'very confidential' issue had been leaked. 'He became very angry and ordered me to quickly call the US ambassador', 'Alam wrote.[53] Farland told Washington about his embassy's 'shock and consternation' at the Pentagon's mistake. He stressed that such actions put the US 'in [an] extremely awkward position... at a time when we are seeking strengthening [the] sense of collaboration in our military and other relations with Iran'.[54]

Taken together, these communications show how the shah had achieved his status as a favoured partner of the United States after years of difficult negotiations. Vietnam had coloured Johnson's relationship with the shah, who actively used the Cold War framework to pursue his goal of increasing arms purchases from the United States and attaining the status of a more significant power. In May 1965, when the shah briefly stopped in New York City on his way to Brazil and Argentina, he received a call from President Johnson who said he was 'certainly grateful to you for your Dominican and Vietnamese positions' and expressed his concern about

---

51 Telegram 6417 from the Embassy in Iran to the Department of State, 27 October 1972, 1355Z.
52 Telegram 6611 from the Embassy in Iran to the Department of State, 4 November 1972, 1405Z.
53 'Alikhani ed., *Yaaddashtha-ye 'Alam*, 327–8.
54 Telegram 6611 from the Embassy in Iran to the Department of State, 4 November 1972, 1405Z.

the coming Afro–Asian summit in Algiers (which ended up being can-celled due to a coup in Algeria).[55] One year later, in February 1966, the shah wrote to Johnson to warn against Iran falling victim to the 'evils of aggression,' as had happened in Vietnam, an assessment the US president sympathised with in his reply.[56]

But the shah only half-agreed to Nixon's request in 1972, and his insist-ence on keeping the help secret shows both the degree to which Iran had gained autonomy and the shah's aim to appear neutral and to take on the role of a mediator, not simply a loyal member of one camp in the Cold War. This had been already evident in October 1967 when the shah sug-gested to President Johnson that he could mediate between North and South Vietnam, using the services of his intellectual-cum-diplomat Fer-eydoun Hoveyda who, as a founder of the French film journal *Cahiers du Cinema*, was known to have many links on the French and international left and could presumably easily connect to Hanoi. With American agree-ment, Hoveyda was hurriedly summoned to Tehran from New York, where he was in the midst of the UN General Assembly proceedings, as a chief negotiator for the G-77 in discussions with the West.[57] Meetings followed in Paris between Hoveyda and a representative of the North Vietnamese and was later followed by the Iranian embassy in Moscow. The Americans do not seem to have taken the shah's mediation very seriously, just as when they turned down his offer to act as a broker between Israel and the PLO.[58] But to the shah and Hoveyda, the fact that Johnson had accepted Tehran's offer of mediation only spoke to Iran's growing influence, even before the Americans came to request Iran's help in Vietnam.

---

55 US officials repeatedly thanked the shah for his position on Vietnam while the shah would constantly complain about the Americans not being grateful. In July 1966, for instance, he told Kermit Roosevelt (who was visiting in a personal capacity) that 'the United States has shown no gratitude for his support in South Vietnam'. Quoted in Johnson Library, White House Central Files, EX FO–5, 6/30/66–8/31/66.

56 McGlinchey, 'Lyndon B. Johnson', 235–236.

57 Fereydoun Hoveyda, 'A Contribution to History: My Secret Mission During the Vietnam War', *American Foreign Policy Interests* 23, 2001, 243–252.

58 Milani, Abbas, *Negahi be Shah*, 2013, 412–414.

From Tehran to Bucharest: Cold War Mavericks and Vietnam

The shah's staunch anticommunism did not prevent him from establishing extensive ties with the Soviet Union, some of whose thinkers praised his domestic reforms,[59] just as an earlier generation of Soviets had lauded those of his father, the founding Pahlavi monarch Reza Shah.[60] Additionally, the shah had established diplomatic relations and paid official visits to Romania, Yugoslavia, Bulgaria, Poland, Hungary, and Czechoslovakia. Following Nixon's rapprochement with the People's Republic of China, the shah also established diplomatic relations with Beijing in 1971 and received a high-level delegation from the country in 1978.[61] If these connections were not enough to establish his maverick status in the Cold War, the nativist and anti-Western turn he took in the latter years of his rule similarly supported this stance.[62]

The shah discussed the Vietnam War with Romania's Nicolae Ceausescu, who was something of a maverick of the Eastern Bloc since his communist country had had its spats with Moscow and asserted independence from it.[63] In summer 1966, the shah paid a visit to Bucharest, during which he held comprehensive discussions with Ceausescu. The Romanian leader considered the meeting to have been very successful and the shah to have been anything but a pliant tool of Washington. When briefing the Viet Cong ambassador in early June 1966, the Romanian leader said that the shah had conceded that 'if Vietnamese communists win in South Vietnam, this is the problem of Vietnamese' and that 'nobody has the right to meddle in there.'[64] Later in the same month, Ceausescu met the Soviet ambassador, Alexander Vasilievich Basov, and the record shows that Moscow welcomed Bucharest's new diplomatic channel with the shah and the

---

59 Mikhail Sergeevich Ivanov, *Iran seogdnya*, 1969.

60 Kayhan A. Nejad, 'To Break the Feudal Bonds: The Soviets, Reza Khan, and the Iranian left, 1921–25', *Middle Eastern Studies* 57/5, 2021, 758–776.

61 William Figueroa, 'China and the Iranian Revolution: New Perspectives on Sino–Iranian Relations, 1965–1979', *Asian Affairs* 53/1, 2022, 106–123.

62 For an exploration of the Shah's nativist, anti-Western discourse, see Ali Mirsepassi, *Iran's Quiet Revolution: The Downfall of the Pahlavi State*, 2018.

63 Roham Alvandi and Eliza Gheorghe, 'The Shah's Petro-Diplomacy with Ceausescu: Iran and Romania in the era of Détente', *Cold War International History Project*, working paper 74, 2014.

64 Alvandi and Gheorghe, 'The Shah's Petro-Diplomacy', 6.

revelation that even America's close allies were not happy with how the war was going in Vietnam (Beijing had a similar position to Moscow).[65]

When meeting the Romanian ambassador to Tehran in April 1967, the shah spoke more openly against Washington's actions in Vietnam and criticised their support for the coup that had overthrown the president of South Vietnam, Ngo Dinh Diem. The shah is reported in Romanian cables to have said: 'What did they achieve through this, other than anarchy and war in Vietnam, a war which they cannot even end and from which they cannot pull out either?'[66] While this statement betrays the Iranian monarch's unease in seeing how easily the superpower could overthrow a Cold War ally, it also showed open exasperation at the mess the United States was making in Asia.

Two years later, in 1969, it was Ceausescu's turn to visit Tehran. Once more, Vietnam was a topic of conversation between the two leaders. The shah spoke of Ho Chi Minh's poor health and old age before affirming that, even if he died, 'Vietnamese people are the ones to decide [their fate].' The shah applauded Nixon's supposed plan for getting out of Vietnam and when Ceausescu said that 'the only way [out] is for the US to withdraw its troops from Vietnam', the shah not only agreed but asserted that he had 'told Nixon to do this a long time ago'.[67] The fact that two leaders on opposite sides of the Iron Curtain had such close relations (not least based on their common oil interests) and could take a common stance on such important international issues like the Vietnam War should surely do something to change rigid narratives of the Cold War. Different actors in the Cold War had many motivations which often competed with each other. Domestic political considerations, geostrategic designs, and ideological commitments were sometimes at odds with each other and often made for strange bedfellows.

In making this argument, I do not intend to go as far as some scholars who have maintained that the Cold War lens does not apply to the Global South. In introducing this literature, Jeremi Suri speaks of a 'group of scholars' who have 'questioned the very utility of the Cold War as an

---

65 Alvandi and Gheorghe, 'The Shah's Petro-Diplomacy', 6.
66 Alvandi and Gheorghe, 'The Shah's Petro-Diplomacy', 24.
67 Alvandi and Gheorghe, 'The Shah's Petro-Diplomacy', 31.

analytical concept' by pointing to 'the ways in which this geopolitical term privileges state actors in the United States and Europe and neglects local forces of change, many of which had little apparent connection to the basic issues and personalities of the Cold War'.[68] But this is a fundamental mis-reading of the Cold War as it was understood by the Cold Warriors of the time. There is nothing in the 'analytical concept' of the Cold War that needs to privilege state actors in Washington and Moscow. Many Cold Warriors in the Global South, like the shah or, for that matter, Chairman Mao, did not see the Cold War in such light. They saw themselves as taking part in nothing less than a global struggle over the future of humanity. To show that they were not merely foot soldiers in this war is not to assert that there was no such war to speak of.

Iranians as Mediators

If the shah's initiatives did not bring peace to Vietnam, the Paris peace process led by Henry Kissinger and Le Duc Tho ultimately resulted in the Agreement on Ending the War and Restoring Peace in Vietnam, commonly known as Paris Peace Accords, in January 1973. The treaty included the governments of the United States, North and South Vietnam as well as the Viet Cong-led provisional government of South Vietnamese Communists. The United States pledged to withdraw all its forces and the International Control Commission was now replaced by an International Commission of Control and Supervision (ICCS). Tasked with overseeing the ceasefire, ICCS initially consisted of Canada, Indonesia, Poland, and Hungary with two seats going to each sides of the Cold War.[69] Canada's presence was marred from the beginning and, when one of its soldiers was killed in action, Ottawa declared that it would withdraw from the commission by July 1973, setting off a search for a replacement. As late as 13 July 1973, when the Dutch envoy to Saigon brought up the issue with the Iranian ambassador to Thailand, the Iranians (including the shah himself) said

---

68 Jeremi Suri, 'The Cold War, Decolonization, and Global Social Awakenings: Historical Intersections', *Cold War History* 6/3, 2006, 354.

69 For general terms of the ICCS and its headquartering in Saigon (although not its composition) see 'Protocol Concerning the International Commission of Control and Supervision', *The American Journal of International Law* 67/2, 1973, 412–418.

they had never heard of a proposal for Iranian inclusion in the ICCS. But later that month, when the shah made an official trip to the United States, Nixon requested that Iran replace Canada in the ICCS. The shah accepted swiftly. Iranian archives show that this was seen by Tehran as a sign of Iran's growing international stature. For example, Iran's ambassador to the United States, Ardeshir Zahedi, boasted in an internal circular that the request proved that the shah was 'a global personality and high-ranking leader who not only helped to keep stability and peace in the Middle East and South Asia but safeguarded global peace'.[70]

Membership of the ICCS required the approval of all four parties of the Paris Peace Accords including the two communist signatories, North Vietnam and the Viet Cong government, which meant Iran had to break precedent and officially recognise them, something that the Canadians had never done. The shah's Iran, however, was quick in this regard. Iran recognised Hanoi on 4 August 1973 and Viet Cong shortly thereafter (in the latter case, first de facto and then de jure).[71]

The Iranian ICCS contingent was headed by Major General Rassoul Sodeifi, who reportedly had 'the authority to select the best officers in [the] army'. The contingent went on to include dozens of Iranian officers with ranks ranging between major and full colonel.[72] The first Iranian delegation arrived on 29 August 1973, consisting of five officers. A further 137 officers were sent in October and November. Following a dispute between the Iranian joint chief of staff and the foreign ministry, the control of the ICCS file was delegated to the latter which formed a dedicated Office for ICCS and dispatched Asadkhan Sadri, a seasoned diplomat, as the head of the Iranian ICCS delegation. On 16 November 1973, the delegation, along with that of the other three ICCS members, visited the Viet Cong's seat of provisional government in Dong Ha and met its foreign minister Nguyen Thi Binh (a pioneering female diplomat). This was followed by a trip to Hanoi on 30 January 1974, which included a meeting with the DRV's

---

70 Ebrahimkhani, *Tarikh-e Ravabet-e Iran va Viyetnam*, 114.
71 Ebrahimkhani, *Tarikh-e Ravabet-e Iran va Viyetnam*, 173.
72 Richard Helms telegram dated 24 September 1973, WikiLeaks Cable 1973TEHRAN06780_b. https://www.wikileaks.org/plusd/cables/1973TEHRAN06780_b.html.

prime minister, Pham Van Dong.[73] Evidence of Iran's participation in the ICCS suggests that the shah went out of his way to appear as a neutral party, confirming both his ambitions and his maverick Cold War status.

Disputes soon arose in the work of ICCS, with Hanoi complaining that Iran and Indonesia were violating the Paris Accords by unilaterally dispatching observers to areas where Poles and Hungarians were not present.[74] Iranians complained that the Eastern Bloc representatives on the ICCS simply did not participate in the commission's activities, which made its functioning difficult. But when the issue came to the shah's desk, he ordered Sadri to 'keep within the limits of the Paris Accords'.[75] When the dispute remained unresolved, Sadri was replaced in April 1974 by Mohsen Sadeq Esfandiari, Iran's ambassador in Bangkok (who was also accredited as Iran's envoy to South Vietnam). When Sadri suggested issuing scholarships for students from Iran's South Vietnamese allies, the foreign ministry, approved by the shah, requested an equal number of scholarships to be given to South and North Vietnamese students.[76] In the spring of 1975, Iran broke with US policy in co-sponsoring a resolution for North Vietnamese membership in the Geneva-based World Meteorological Organization. Iran was now helping to advance the membership of a communist state in a specialized agency of the United Nations; a classic Cold War confrontation in which Tehran took an unexpected side.

These good relations between Tehran and Hanoi meant that the fall of Saigon on 30 April 1975 was not as cataclysmic an event for Iran as it was for the United States and some of its other Cold War allies. To be sure, most of the Iranian delegation was evacuated out of Saigon prior to the city's fall and its remaining three members made it to the French embassy followed by a short stay in the US embassy and then an evacuation by helicopter to

---

73 Ebrahimkhani, *Tarikh-e Ravabet-e Iran va Viyetnam*, 122.

74 *Ayandegan*, 14 May 1974.

75 IRFMA, Letter from Abdolkarim Ayadi to Foreign Minister Khal'atbari, 3 January 1974, doc. 29/24866.

76 The offer was sent to the embassies of South Vietnam and China in Tehran, the latter as representative of Hanoi's interests, for two scholarships for each of the two nations, but neither made use of it, Ebrahimkhani, *Tarikh-e Ravabet-e Iran va Viyetnam*, 176–7.

the US fleet nearby.[77] But Iran collaborated with Hanoi and the Viet Cong to solve outstanding issues. An Iranian officer with the rank of captain had been captured by the Viet Cong alongside an Indonesian comrade. Tehran quickly pursued the matter with both the Hanoi and Viet Cong embassies in Beijing and also in the first meeting between the North Vietnamese ambassador accredited to Iran and Foreign Minister Abbas Khal'atbari. The Iranian captain was released shortly after.[78] On 29 April 1975, exactly one day before the fall of Saigon, Iran's ambassador to China, Ahmad Ali Bahrami, was actually in Hanoi to meet with North Vietnamese officials, who accepted his accreditation as ambassador to their government. Shortly thereafter, Hanoi's deputy education minister came to Tehran for an international meeting. In 1976, a three-person Iranian delegation was allowed to visit Saigon to assess the damage to its properties which had occurred during the fall of the city to the Viet Cong the previous year. The delegation was received warmly by the highest Viet Cong officials, who allowed it to access the funds in the frozen bank account of the Iranian embassy in Saigon, take pictures of lost documents, and visit the residence of ambassador and Iranian diplomats.[79]

As the Viet Cong government and Hanoi joined up in 1976 to establish the Socialist Republic of Vietnam (hereafter SRV), the new administration was instantly recognised by Tehran, which continued to have surprisingly good relations with it. Even when potential problems arose, Tehran was determined not to exacerbate them. On 3 February 1977, when the Vietnamese news agency published a message of congratulation from the Tudeh party's first secretary, Iraj Eskandari, to Le Duan on his election as the general secretary of the Communist Party of Vietnam, the Iranian embassy in Beijing asked Tehran if a protest should be lodged against this action. The shah decided that there was no need.[80] In May, Iran's ambassador to Beijing, Mahmud Esfandiari, visited Hanoi to meet Vice-President Nguyen Huu Tho and be accredited as ambassador to the SRV.[81] Esfandiari, whose extensive trip included a visit to Saigon, also met the foreign

---

77 Ebrahimkhani, *Tarikh-e Ravabet-e Iran va Viyetnam*, 142–4.
78 Ebrahimkhani, *Tarikh-e Ravabet-e Iran va Viyetnam*, 142–8.
79 Ebrahimkhani, *Tarikh-e Ravabet-e Iran va Viyetnam*, 143–4.
80 Ebrahimkhani, *Tarikh-e Ravabet-e Iran va Viyetnam*, 199.
81 *Daily Report: Asia and Pacific*, Issue 94, 1977, 15.

minister and his deputy, the agriculture minister, deputy education and trade ministers, and Hanoi's mayor.[82] Tehran had managed to establish good ties with Hanoi, just as it had with Moscow and Beijing.

'Many Vietnams'

While the shah's Vietnam policy underwent changes over time, things could hardly have been more different in the case of the Iranian opposition, which consistently backed the North Vietnamese and the Viet Cong throughout the Vietnam War. In fact, while the opposition endured many splits and was riven by harsh internal bickering, backing of the Vietnamese revolutionary project was a rare point of agreement among supporters of the Tudeh, Maoists, new leftist guerrillas, and various brands of Islamists. This was rooted in the flexibility of Vietnamese communists themselves, who maintained a broad front of various progressive and leftist forces and avoided taking definitive sides in the global rifts of the left such as the Sino–Soviet split.[83] Remarkably, even when the Vietnamese entered peace negotiations with the United States, they retained the unified support of most of the global left.

In 1973, as the Confederation of Iranian Students (CIS)[84] got ready for its fourteenth world congress, its various sections boasted of their support for the Vietnamese left. In its message to the congress, the leadership of the North America-based Iranian Student Association (ISA) attacked the shah's regime for 'doing a favour for its masters by using the arms that it has bought with the blood of the toilers from its imperialist masters to oppress the Vietnamese people'. While the full details of Iran's contribution to the war was not yet clear, the ISA attacked Iran's 'giving of Phantom jets to the mercenary army of Saigon' and 'sending of the Savak agents to torture the brave offspring of Vietnam' (no evidence was ever

82 Ebrahimkhani, *Tarikh-e Ravabet-e Iran va Viyetnam*, 200–201.
83 For Vietnam's place in the Cold War see Lorenz Lüthi, *Cold Wars: Asia, the Middle East, Europe*, 2021, 138–162; Lorenz Lüthi, *The Sino–Soviet Split*, 2008, 302–340.
84 For a history of CIS see Afshin Matin-Asgari, *Iranian Student Opposition to the Shah*, Costa Mesa, CA, 2002.

offered for the latter's claim).[85] In April 1973, the confederation's section in Italy held its eleventh congress in Florence with students attending from Rome, Florence, Bologna, Padua, and Ferrara. Students in Florence (numbering between thirty-five and fifty) reported about a 'Vietnam committee' they had formed, tasked with engendering solidarity.[86] A year earlier, CIS's research publication, *Nameh-ye Parsi*, had published a special issue dedicated to liberation movements, most of which consisted of material on Vietnam and Cambodia, featuring Persian translations of statements by North and South Vietnamese communist figures such as Ly Van Chan, Nguyen Minh, and Pham Van Dong.[87]

Still, while all strands of opposition did their part in showing support to the Vietnamese struggle, each would draw wildly different conclusions from it and attempt to use it differently in ideological debates. The Iranian Maoists, who split from the Tudeh Party of Iran in 1964 to form the Revolutionary Organization of the Tudeh Party of Iran (hereafter ROTPI), saw the Vietnamese struggle as a confirmation of their strategy of 'surrounding the cities from the countryside' and a refutation of 'Trotskyism and revisionism'.[88] Those close to the New Left-inclined People's Fada'iyan guerrilla movement, on the other hand, praised the 'epic of the heroic people of Vietnam' as the 'most glorious epic of the century' while pointing to its 'tactical flexibility' and 'nonsectarianism' to argue that, for Iranian conditions, the urban guerrilla struggles of Latin America, particularly Brazil and Uruguay, were more relevant.[89]

Among many Islamists, too, the godless Vietnamese communists were praised as exemplary anti-imperialists. In 1977, the Freedom Movement of Iran, a liberal-Islamist split off Mosaddeq's National Front, published a Persian translation of Michael T. Klare's *War Without End: American*

---

85 'Payam-e Heyat Dabiran-e Sazman-e Amrika be Chahardahomin Kongereh-ye Konfedrasion-e Jahani', *Bultan-e Konfedrasion-e Jahani-ye Mohasselin va Daneshjuyan-e Irani* 7, July–August 1973, 2.
86 'Gozaresh-e Yazdahomin Kongereh-ye Federasion-e Italia', *Bultan-e Konfedrasion-e Jahani-ye Mohasselin va Daneshjuyan-e Irani* 7, July–August 1973, 13.
87 *Nameh-ye Parsi* 2/11, October–November 1972.
88 *Tarikh-e Mokhtasar-e Hezb-e Zahmatkeshan-e Viyetnam*, n.p., 1973, 6.
89 Siamak Azadeh, 'Az Viyetnam ta Orugue va dars-hayi az anha', *Asr-e Amali*, Issue 2, n.d., published in Karlsruhe, West Germany.

Planning for the Next Vietnams with a preface that included verses from the Quran.[90] Sayed Mohsen, a founder of a major left–Islamist organization, the People's Mojahedin Organisation of Iran (hereafter PMOI), dedicated some of his defence trial to support of Vietnam and other revolutionary struggles, which even if fought under the banner of atheistic Marxism, were still 'realisation of Ali's far-sighted thought'.[91]

'When in China, they've reached the cultural revolution', Mohsen said, 'when in Cuba and Vietnam, some movements answer the call of conscience and morals and reach toward a higher goal, when the epic of the twentieth century history is being made by sacrifice of human for human, we can see the thought of Ali over the high peaks of history'.[92] This was not left on the level of 'aspirational' contacts as PMOI contacted the North Vietnamese embassies in Europe and tried to make material links with Hanoi.[93]

What these diverse groups had in common was attacking the Soviet Union and the Tudeh Party for their policy of 'peaceful coexistence'. Thus, when *Bakhtar-e Emruz,* published by a Marxist-inclined section of the National Front, described the Vietnam War as 'a war of ideologies, a war between good and evil', it also attacked the 'Soviet leaders who drink in joy with Nixon and speak of "global peace" just when the Vietnamese ports are being bombarded'.[94]

Yet the Tudeh Party and its allies in the world communist movement

---

90 Nehzat-e Azadi-ye Iran (edited and translation), 'Jang-e Bi Payan: Amrika va Tadarok-e Viyetnamha-ye digar', 1977.

91 Ali was a cousin and son-in-law of the Prophet Mohammad; the fourth Caliph; and the first Shia Imam.

92 Reza Rezai, *Ghesmati az Defa'iyat-e Sazman-e Mojahedin-e Khalq-e Iran*, 1972, 32.

93 Political Studies and Research Institute (PSRI), *Sazman-e Mojahedin-e Khalq-e Iran: Paydari ta Farjam (1344–1384)*, 2006, 373. More research needs to be done on this but Hanoi does not seem to have been much interested in building material links with the revolutionary forces around the world as it left PMOI's calls unanswered. This was in marked contrast to the Egyptian, Chinese, and Cuban governments, which all hosted and trained Iranian revolutionaries at some point. The same was also done by Palestinian revolutionary organisations, which hosted Iranian fighters in their camps in Jordan, Syria, and Lebanon. Memories of people in those camps affirm that they often spoke glowingly of the Vietnamese struggle.

94 *Bakhtar-e Emruz* 2/28, June–July 1972.

also did much to support the Vietnamese struggle. The communist-aligned International Union of Students (IUS), which had inaugurated the tradition of celebrating International Students' Day on 17 November to commemorate the students killed by the Nazis during their occupation of Czechoslovakia, changed the day to a 'week of friendship and solidarity with Vietnam', which was also celebrated by the Tudeh. In 1971, the Tudeh successfully fundraised from its supporters to help rebuild the Nguyen Van Troi hospital in Hanoi that had been bombarded by the United States. The Tudeh may also have dispatched some of its members to North Vietnam. Parviz Hekmatju, a Tudeh activist who was later killed in one of the shah's prisons, claimed to have travelled to Hanoi in October 1962 to teach Persian to North Vietnamese diplomats – a claim that was disputed by Savak, which believed this was a cover for Hekmatju's trips to Iraq.[95] Ironically, while the Tudeh was attacked for its allegedly soft position on Vietnam, it seems to have had more direct links to Vietnamese communists. ROTPI, which had trained its members in Cuba and China, formulated its objection as follows: 'The internationalist duty of Iranian communists is not to send volunteers to Vietnam but to start the national liberation war in Iran so that US imperialism is surrendered by the revolutions of the oppressed peoples.'[96]

To ward off criticisms from the groups to its left, which had helped to divide the vast majority of the party's youth and student base, the Tudeh published a pamphlet entitled 'Testimonies of Friends About the Soviet Help to National Liberation Movements', which highlighted quotes by revolutionary leaders in Vietnam, Cuba, and the Middle East that praised the Soviet Union as a loyal and consistent anti-imperialist power.[97] The pamphlet published quotes by the likes of Ho Chi Minh and Pham Van Dong, who lauded the Soviets as a loyal ally.

The high standing of Tudeh and pro-Moscow communists was also evident in January 1966, when Fidel Castro played host to the Tricontinental

---

95 Savak document no. 2/3/222/380, 315/195 published online by the Center for Study of Historical Documents: https://historydocuments.org/sanad/ ?page=show_document&id=4xvbb7vfmkwso.
96 Vo Nguyen Giap, *Vietnam Pish Miravad*, 1965, 4.
97 Hezb-e Tudeh-ye Iran, *Govahi-ye Dustan Darbareh-ye Komakha-ye Shoravi be Jonbesh-ha-ye Azadibakhsh-e Melli*, 1970.

Conference in Havana, which welcomed more than 500 representatives from around eighty-two countries. Among those attending the conference were two competing delegations from Iran: one representing the Iranian government, which, as an Asian state, had been able to make its way to Havana; and another representing the Tudeh-aligned Iranian Anti-Colonial Society (hereafter IACS), which heavily protested the presence of the shah's envoys and pointed to their lack of support for the North Vietnamese as the ultimate evidence of their being out of tune with the spirit of Havana. The head of IACS, the Iranian-Jewish communist activist Rahim Namvar, spoke against the Tehran delegation on Cuban national radio and the Tudeh Party's organ *Mardom* subsequently reported on the whole episode.[98] Vietnam was a central theme of Castro's speech to the conference and the Organization of the Solidarity of the Peoples of Africa, Asia, and Latin America that came out of it regularly featured Vietnam, most famously by publishing Che Guevara's 'Message to the Tricontinental', published before he left Cuba for clandestine revolutionary work in Bolivia.

This short pamphlet was to be translated into dozens of languages around the world and it became a mini-bible for many revolutionaries. The title picked by most versions was a phrase that had not actually occurred in the original text: 'Create One, Two, Three Vietnams.' Nevertheless, Che had dedicated much of this pamphlet to Vietnam, a struggle that he considered to be central to what he saw as a united worldwide struggle against imperialism. Bijan Hirmanpur, a supporter of the People's Feda'iyan, translated Che's pamphlet into Persian with the title 'Payam beh Konferans-e Seh Qareh', which became popular with revolutionaries of all hues.[99]

The pamphlet had to be published as a clandestine document as it would have been suppressed by the authorities. Still, the controversies of Vietnam would sometimes make it to the legal Iranian press. In 1967, the literary magazine *Negin* published an anthology of 'US poets on the Vietnamese war'.[100] It reviewed *Where is Vietnam? American Poets Respond*, an

---

98 A. Moravej, 'Konferans-e Havana, Mazhar-e Hambastegi-ye Mobarezan-e Zed-e Este'mar-e Seh Qareh', *Mardom* 6/11, 1966.
99 Torab Haqshenas, '48 sal Pas Che Guevara: Az u va Darbareh-ye u', 2015.
100 'Shora-ye Amrikai va Jang-e Viyetnam', *Negin* 26, 1967.

anthology that had recently come out in the United States. There was no doubt as to where the book's sympathies lay, since it was edited by Walter Lowenfels, a member of the US Communist Party and an editor of the communist press in Pennsylvania. The journal did not mention this, of course, even as it published translations of many of the poems from the book. In fact, it strangely credited the American interest in Vietnam to US poets 'being heavily influenced by Asian ideas, especially Buddhism'. 'For them, the Asian philosophy is a glorious ideal and absolute beauty confronting the destructive mechanism of the new civilisation', *Negin* wrote. *Negin*'s caution was wise since more overtly pro-Hanoi literature would have been censored. Indeed, this is exactly what happened to the Persian translation of *Return from Vietnam*, a book by French left-wing journalist Jean Lacouture. In banning the book, Savak noted that it 'contained criticism of Western states' policy in Vietnam'.[101]

But support for the North Vietnamese cause could not be easily contained as leftist ideas spread around Iran. Even some of the doctors dispatched to Vietnam were leftist sympathisers. For instance, Majid Jamshidi, who had been sent to Vietnam as a medic, was later arrested in Mashhad as a Marxist sympathiser. When he was transferred to Tehran, Jamshidi spoke to his fellow political prisoners of his time in Vietnam and, according to one of them, condemned the 'CIA-manufactured regime of the shah who spent the money of toiling people of Iran on fuel for US jets who killed the innocent people in Vietnam ... and sent trained doctors and nurses and medicine for wounded American soldiers and officers in Vietnam'. He also claimed to have treated an inspiring teenaged Viet Cong guerrilla who knew, in impressive detail, the history of the leftist struggle in Iran, from the Constitutional Revolution of 1905 to the execution of communist Tudeh officers following the 1953 coup.[102]

101 Savak documented cited in Ali Reza Kamari, 'Parvandeh-ye Kotob-e 'Mazarreh-ye Mazhabi', *Mo'aseseh-ye Motale'at va Pazhuheshha-ye Siyasi*, 2018.
102 Albert Sohrabian, *Khaterat-e Albert Sohrabian, Bargi az Jonbesh-e Kargari Komonisti-ye Iran*, 2000, 78.

The Enduring Impact of Vietnam in Iran

Following the 1979 revolution, the memory of the actions of the United States in Vietnam remained central to how Iranians perceived the Western superpower. Speaking in the Iranian parliament in 1980, Ebrahim Yazdi, the first foreign minister of the Islamic Republic and a leading member of FMI, retold the story of when he and Mehdi Bazargan, his close comrade and the first prime minister under the new regime, met US National Security Advisor Zbigniew Brzezinski for negotiations. 'The first thing Mr Brzezinski said was that "we both believe in God and our two governments can work together"', Yazdi remembered.

> We asked Mr Brzezinski: Where was your God and your Bible in these 27 years [i.e., since the US-backed 1953 coup in Iran]? Where was your God when you bombed Vietnam?[103]

This striking exchange shows that many Islamists did not prioritise an abstract Islam in their worldview. They would rather ally with the atheist Hanoi than the Christian Washington.

In the years to come, when Islamists were to engage in the suppression of Marxists, their former allies against the shah, the topic of Vietnam was often brought up as a reminder of the time when the Islamists had been happy to follow the call of atheist revolutionaries in Hanoi. Hoseyn Riyahi, leader of a failed Maoist uprising in the northern city of Amol in 1982, chose to dwell at length on Vietnam in his trial, arguing that, at the time, becoming a Marxist was seen as genuinely anti-imperialist, as solidarity with the struggle in Vietnam showed.[104] Torab Haqshenas was a leading figure of PMOI who had led the organisation's 1975 'ideological change', when it openly declared that it had replaced Islam with Marxism as the only true revolutionary ideology. In the midst of post-revolutionary clashes, Haqshenas addressed Mohammad Montazeri, a cleric with close links to Qaddafi's Libya, to remind him of a time when Islamists had

---

103 Quoted in Serge Baresghian, 'Bazargan beh Brejenski Che Goft?' *Shahrvand*, September 2009, Issue 67.
104 Film of Sarbedaran trial, taking place in Tehran in early 1983, broadcast on IRIB Mostanad, March 2016.

looked to the Marxists as the most militant fighters. It was not surprising that the subject of Vietnam came up again.

> Have you forgotten how, in 1973, you came and asked me to introduce a few of your friends to the Vietnamese comrades? Or how I arranged a meeting in the Southern Vietnamese Liberation Front [official name of Viet Cong] embassy in Baghdad for you to go and show your support for the struggle of the Vietnamese people?[105]

Shortly after writing these lines, Haqsehnas became one of the many Marxist revolutionaries who fled into exile to escape Islamist repression. He passed away in 2016, but to the end of his life, opposition to 'US imperialism' centred around Vietnam remained fundamental to his political identity. In 2014, Haqshenas decried the 'crimes of capitalism and ignorance [that] have covered every corner of the globe...today in Syria and elsewhere, yesterday in Vietnam and Yugoslavia'.[106] He would have thus been proud of one of the eulogies he received following his death. Behrooz Mo'azami, an old comrade of Haqshenas, remembered the first time he had met him. Mo'azami recalled that Haqshenas was compared to the Vietnamese revolutionaries for his discipline and seriousness. 'Most obvious in [Torab's] behaviour was how he defined himself in terms of an organisational "We". I attributed this to him being "Vietnamese"'.[107]

Vietnam was also a perennial reference in the cultural products of the Iranian opposition. Sayed Soltanpur, the notable Marxist poet and playwright, wrote one of the most iconic revolutionary plays of the time, *Abbas Agha, a worker at Iran National Automobile Manufacture Company*. The play depicts the life of a factory worker who stands up to his employers (the national automotive manufacture company) and their accomplices. The plays of the 'worker against the bosses' genre habitually focus on capitalist exploitation at work. Soltanpur's play was no exception as one of Abbas's struggles was around workplace issues like the closure of

---

105 Quoted in *Peykar* 69, 25 August 1980, 14–15.
106 Torab Haqshenas, 'Man Faryad Mikesham Pas Hastam,' *Hafteh*, 19 July 2014.
107 Behrooz Mo'azami, 'Dar Sug-e yek Nasl,' *Andisheh va Peykar* website, 9 February 2016.

bathrooms after 11 pm. But since, in the given context of Iran, the anti-imperialist struggle was to be of seminal importance, this theme had to also be somehow weaved into the play. Soltanpur did this by bringing a fictional and somewhat fantastical Vietnam connection to the play: the factory owners demand that the workers give blood so that it can be sent to Vietnam to save the lives of US soldiers requiring transfusions, a demand that Abbas vehemently opposes.[108]

When comrades of Soltanpur organised mass activities in the early post-revolutionary years after 1979, they often cued in Vietnam. For example, where they organised peasants in the north-eastern areas of Iran, which are home to the country's Turkmen ethnic minority, a particular social-ist culture was disseminated among the peasants that included prominent Vietnam references. A report from the time tells us about some of the visual presentations made for the largely illiterate peasants. These included Soviet films such as the 1944 production 'Rainbow', concerning life in a Nazi-occupied village in Ukraine or the 1926 title 'Mother', based on a popular 1906 novel by Maxim Gorky, which depicted women's struggle against Tsarist rule. One of the other visual presentations was a slideshow on Vietnam, which was shown to the local scouts, the local university, and the local high school and 'attracted hundreds of people'.[109] From students in Tehran to peasants in the northeast, to be a progressive in the Cold War Iran meant to celebrate the Vietnamese struggle.

Problems of Internationalism

Recent works of global and transnational history are written against a tradition of methodological nationalism. In an era of rising nativism and nationalism, they also often voice opposition to these ideologies. As such, they are often celebratory of and even enthusiastic about global links and transnational entanglements that bind the revolutionaries of the 1960s to one another. This can be to the detriment of a more critical stance showing

---

108 Sayed Soltanpur, *Abbas Agha Kargar-e Iran Nasional*, 1979.
109 PSRI, 'Negahi beh Jangha-ye Gonbad va Naghsh-e Fadaiyan-e Khalq-e Torkaman va Setad-e Monhaleh-ye Khalq-e Torkaman', n.d. http://ir-psri.com/?Page =ViewArticle&ArticleID=1801.

how problematic the 'travel of ideas' might be. A good example of such a critical stance is Slobodian's differentiation between West German solidarity action with Middle Eastern movements and those they professed with the Vietnamese revolutionaries (which he considers a problem).[110]

I suggest a critique of the approach of Iranian revolutionaries toward the Vietnamese struggle (that has some similarities to, but many differences from, the West German case). As noted before, more research needs to be done to establish what actual links existed between the Iranians and the Viet Cong. Haqshenas's memory of contacts with the Viet Cong embassy in Baghdad shows that such links did exist with 'the Vietnamese comrades'. But it is nevertheless true that Iranian revolutionaries had an idealised image of Vietnam and its conditions, often passed on to them through the translation of European books on the topic.

A scene from the 2001 film *Hidden Half* does much to portray the troubling aspects of Iranian revolutionary internationalism of the era. The film depicts the life of a young Marxist woman in the immediate post-1979 period. In a memorable scene, Fereshteh, the young Marxist, is confronted by Ms Pahlavan, an older progressive, probably associated with the Tudeh, whom Fereshteh acknowledges with respect – 'I know you have been in prison for five years', she says. Ms Pahlavan criticises Fereshteh for lacking 'political wisdom' and accuses her generation of being 'more about excitement and sensation than conscious struggle'. Fereshteh, in turn, accuses the old political prisoner of being 'like the middle class in the Soviet Union who opposed the revolution in the past'. The conversation takes a sharp turn, when Pahlavan asks Fereshteh about the books she has read. She mentions titles on Chile and, of course, 'the war in Vietnam'. Pahlavan erupts in protest. How is it that young Fereshteh reads all about Russia, Chile, and Vietnam when she wants to make revolution in Iran?

'What do you know about the history of Iran?' the old communist asks Fereshteh, 'Do you know who Mosaddeq was? What of the Constitutional Revolution?' She goes on to mention historical figures from contemporary and medieval Iran, figures who most likely would have been unknown to Fereshteh.[111] Leaders of progressive struggles in the 1950s

---

110 See footnote 7.
111 Tahmineh Milani, director, *Nimeh-ye Penhan*, 2001.

were to later complain about how 'Iranian leftist kids know more about Latin America and tiny leftist grouplets of the world than the history of their own country.'[112]

Thus, revolutionary internationalism could sometimes mean ignoring particular contextual realities. This is evident in Che's celebration of 'armed struggle', which he was to doggedly pursue, even in countries where local progressive forces did not see it as a particularly useful strategy. In an era of global radicalism, young revolutionary students in Tehran, Montevideo, Berlin, or Paris often came to think that to be 'Vietnamese' was to engage in open armed struggle, without much knowledge about the particular historical trajectories of their own society.

In this chapter, I have tried to write of the forgotten contributions that Iranians made to the Vietnam War and to advance two arguments. First, that the shah's attitude towards Vietnam and the manner of his participation in the war shows that he was not simply following orders from Washington and that he was ready to seek partners from the other side of the Iron Curtain as he engaged in the global Cold War. Second, that the Vietnam War was a central issue of identity to the Iranian opposition, both Islamist and Marxist. The tendency towards more global and transnational histories should hopefully result in fuller accounts that tell us what being global meant to various actors of the Cold War at all levels. But I hope to have shown why caution should be exercised in celebratory accounts of transnationalism. For an Iranian, to centre your imagination around Hanoi could mean losing sight of Tehran.

---

112 Quoted from an email to the author from Ali Parsa, 13 November 2016. Ali was recounting a memory from his father, Asghar Parsa, a pro-Mosaddeq member of parliament from the 1940s and 1950s who, as an Iranian diplomat in China at the time of the 1949 revolution with a personal letter from Zhou Enlai among his souvenirs, was no stranger to international Marxists. For Parsa's memoirs see Ali Asghar Parsa, *Farzand-e Khesal-e Khistan: Khaterati az Nehzat-e Melli*, 2009.

Bibliography

Primary Sources

Archival Material

Archiv für Forschung und Dokumentation Iran (AFDI).
Iranian Foreign Ministry Archives (IRFMA).
Lyndon B. Johnson Library, Austin, Texas.
National Archives and Records Administration (NARA).
Pre-1979 Revolution Iranian Political Pamphlet Collection, the
    University of Oklahoma (OU-IPPC).
WikiLeaks, Public Library of US Diplomacy.

Books and Pamphlets

'Alikhani, 'Alinaghi, ed. *Yaddashtha-ye 'Alam*, Volume 2, Bethseda,
    1993.
Larsen, Stanley R. and James Lawton Collins Jr,. *Allied Participation in
    Vietnam,* Washington D.C., 2005.
Rezayi, Reza. *Ghesmati az Defayiate Sazman-e Mojahedin-e Khalq-e
    Iran*
Soltanpur, Sayed. *Abbas Agha Kargar-e Iran Nasional*, 1979

Films

Hoveyda. Dir. Mostafa Showghi, 2017.
Nimeh-ye Penhan. Dir. Tahmine Milani, 2001.

Newspapers

Bakhtar-e Emruz
Hafteh
Keyhan
Negin
Peykar
Shahrvand

Secondary Sources

Alvandi, R. ed. *The Age of Aryamehr: Late Pahlavi Iran and Its Global Entanglements*, London, 2018.

Alvandi, R. *Nixon, Kissinger and the Shah: The United States and Iran In the Cold War,* New York, 2014.

Alvandi, R. and E. Gheorghe. 'The Shah's Petro-Diplomacy with Ceausescu: Iran and Romania in the era of Detente', *CWIHP*, Working Paper No. 74, 2014.

Chamberlin, P.T. *The Global Offensive: The United States, the Palestine Liberation Organization, and the Making of the Post-Cold War Order*, Oxford, 2012.

Chehabi, H.E. ed. *Distant Relations: Iran and Lebanon in the Last 500 Years.* London and New York, 2006.

Chehabi, H.E. 'South Africa and Iran in the Apartheid Era', *Journal of Southern African Studies* 42/4, 2016, 687–709.

Chehabi, H.E. 'The Cats That Did Not Meow: An Historian of Iran Discovers Thailand,' *Mizan Project*, 11 March 2020.

Chibber, V. 'The Return of Imperialism to Social Science', *European Journal of Sociology* 45/3, 2004, 427–441.

Chitsazian, M. 'Aya Iran dar Jang-e Vietnam Mosharekat Dasht?', *Institute for Iranian Contemporary Historical Studies*, n.d.

Conrad, S. *What is Global History?* Oxford, 2016.

Ebrahimkhani, H. *Tarikh-e Ravabet-e Iran va Viyetnam*, Tehran, 2007.

'Edward Said's Culture and Imperialism: A Symposium', *Social Text*, 10, Autumn 1994.

Fawcett, L. *Iran and the Cold War: The Azerbaijan Crisis of 1946*, Cambridge, 2009.

Fear, S. 'Saigon Goes Global: South Vietnam's Quest For International Legitimacy in the Age of Détente', *Diplomatic History* 42/3, 2018, 428–455.

Gallagher, J. and R. Robinson. 'The Imperialism of Free Trade', *The Economic History Review* 6/1, 1953, 1–15.

Green, N. 'Lost Voices from the Indian Ocean', *Los Angeles Review of Books*, 20 January 2017.

Hammer, E.J. 'The Bao Dai Experiment', *Pacific Affairs* 23/1, 1950, 46–58.

Jian, C. *Mao's China and The Cold War*, London, 2001.

Kashani-Sabet, F. *Frontier Fictions: Shaping the Iranian Nation, 1804–1946,* Princeton, 2000.

Keddie, N.R. and R. Matthee, eds. *Iran and the Surrounding World: Interactions in Culture and Cultural Politics,* Seattle, 2002.

Keller, R. *Mexico's Cold War: Cuba, the United States and the Legacy of Mexican Revolution,* Cambridge, 2015.

Kimball, J. *Nixon's Vietnam War,* Lawrence, USA, 1998.

Kimball, J. *The Vietnam War Files: Uncovering the Secret History of Nixon-Era Strategy,* Lawrence, USA, 2004.

Kuniholm, B. *The Origins of the Cold War in the Near East,* Princeton, 1980.

Langland, V. 'Transnational Connections of the Global Sixties as seen by a Historian of Brazil', in *Routledge Handbook of the Global Sixties,* ed. C. Jian et al, New York, 2018, 15–26.

Logevall, F. *Embers of War: The Fall of an Empire and the Making of America's Vietnam,* New York, 2013.

Milani, A. *Negahi be Shah,* Toronto, 2013.

McGlincey, S. 'Lyndon B. Johnson and Arms Credit Sales to Iran 1964–1968', *Middle East Journal* 67/2, Spring 2013, 229–247.

Mirsepassi, A. *The Quiet Revolution: The Downfall of the Pahlavi State,* Cambridge, 2018.

'Protocol Concerning the International Commission of Control and Supervision', *The American Journal of International Law* 67/2, 1973, 412–418.

Ramazani, R.K. *Iran's Foreign Policy, 1941–1973: A Study of Foreign Policy in Modernizing Nations.* Charlottesville, 1974.

Saikal, A. *The Rise and Fall of The Shah: Iran from Autocracy to Religious Rule,* Princeton, 2009.

Slobodian, Q. *Foreign Front: Third World Politics in Sixties West Germany,* Durham, USA, 2012.

Smith, R.B. *An International History of the Vietnam War,* New York, 1983.

Sorley, L. *A Better War: The Unexamined Victories and Final Tragedy of America's Last Years in Vietnam,* London, 1999.

Sternfeld, L. 'Iran's days in Egypt: Mosaddeq's visit to Cairo in 1951', *British Journal of Middle Eastern Studies* 43/1, 2016, 1–20.

Steele, R. *The Shah's Imperial Celebrations of 1971: Nationalism, Culture and Politics in Late Pahlavi Iran*, London, 2020.

Steele, R. 'The Keur Farah Pahlavi Project and Iranian–Senegalese Relations in the 1970s', *Iranian Studies* 54/1–2, 2021, 169–192.

Steele, R. 'Two Kings of Kings: Iran–Ethiopia Relations Under Mohammad Reza Pahlavi and Haile Selassie', *The International History Review* 43/6, 2021, 1375–1392.

Suri, J. 'The Cold War, Decolonization, and Global Social Awakenings: Historical Intersections', *Cold War History* 6/3, 2006, 353–363.

T. Nguyen, L.-H. *Hanoi's War: An International History of the War for Peace in Vietnam*, Chapel Hill, 2012.

Zhou, T. *Migration in the Time of Revolution: China, Indonesia and the Cold War*, Ithaca, 2019.

7

Iran and the Ogaden War, 1977–1978

Robert Steele

In the first half of the twentieth century, Iran's political and economic interests in Africa were limited. The majority of the continent was still under colonial rule, and Iran's security concerns were primarily local. With the decolonisation of Africa, which began in earnest in the late 1950s, and as the shah's international standing and Iran's economy grew, the shah came to view Africa as an area of the world in which Iran could pursue its interests. In the mid- to late 1960s and throughout the 1970s, Iran built ties with many African nations and began to insert itself into intra-African affairs. For example, in Central Africa, Iran gave economic aid to the government of Mobutu Sese Seko of Zaire (now the Democratic Republic of the Congo) and held negotiations with the government of Gabon about the purchase of Gabonese uranium.[1] In West Africa, Iran signed significant economic agreements with Senegal, including for the construction of an Iranian–Senegalese industrial complex and adjoining town, which would be named after Empress Farah.[2] In Southern Africa, Iran supplied the vast majority of South Africa's crude oil imports and by the late 1970s, the

1 Gabrielle Hecht, *Being Nuclear: Africans and the Global Uranium Trade*, 2012, 131–134.
2 Robert Steele, 'The Keur Farah Pahlavi Project and Iranian–Senegalese Relations in the 1970s', *Iranian Studies* 54/1–2, 2021, 169–192.

British even implored the shah to use his influence in the region to support UK–US-led proposals to help bring a resolution to the crisis in Rhodesia (Zimbabwe).[3]

Iran also developed strong security interests in Africa during this period, particularly in the areas bordering the Indian Ocean. Of particular concern to the shah was the Horn of Africa, where since the fall of his ally Emperor Haile Selassie in 1974, the Soviet Union had gained significant influence in Ethiopia. When war broke out between Ethiopia and Somalia in 1977, Iran provided support to Somalia to attempt to prevent further Soviet incursions. This conflict, the Ogaden War, began when the president of Somalia, Mohamed Siad Barre, convinced that he had the backing of the United States and taking advantage of the post-revolutionary political turmoil in Ethiopia, sent Somali troops to support the Western Somali Liberation Front in forcing the Ethiopians out of the Somali-populated Ogaden region. The Somali forces made quick gains and after just a few weeks, eighty-five per cent of the Ogaden was under Somali control.[4] In January 1978, the Ethiopians, with enormous support from the Soviet Union and thousands of Cuban troops, pushed back, and by March, the Somalis were forced to withdraw. Barre overestimated the extent to which the United States was willing to back him; the Carter administration had put forward a moral foreign policy agenda, which professed to prioritise human rights and democratic values, and was thus uneasy about backing an aggressive dictator. Moreover, Carter did not want to do anything drastic that might potentially raise tensions with the Soviet Union in the era of détente, so pushed for a peaceful resolution instead of increasing arms sales to Somalia.

Given US reticence, Barre looked elsewhere for support, and though for him the conflict was motivated by irredentism, he stressed to some potential allies the need for Islamic solidarity, and to others the dangerous implications of a Soviet victory. Barre found an ally in the shah. This

---

3 'The Implications of the Iranian Oil Situation for UK Policy Towards South Africa', undated document (1979), Foreign and Commonwealth Office (hereafter FCO) 8/3373, British National Archives, Kew. On Iran and Rhodesia, see FCO 36/2001 and FCO 36/2236.

4 Donna R. Jackson, 'The Ogaden War and the Demise of Détente', *The Annals of the American Academy of Political and Social Science* 632, 2010, 28.

chapter explores the reasons for, and the nature and implications of, Iran's involvement in the conflict, in order to understand how the shah conceptualised Iran's position not just in Africa, but the wider decolonised world in the late 1970s. The shah had shown himself willing and capable of supporting his regional allies militarily, as evidenced by his support of Sultan Qaboos of Oman in his war against the Dhofari rebels between 1972 and 1975.[5] But the nature of the conflict in the Horn of Africa was very different, and the shah's involvement demonstrates how far he was willing to go to support his allies and defend Iran's interests beyond its immediate sphere of influence. Although the shah did not give Siad Barre the same backing he gave to Sultan Qaboos, this was not because he did not want to, but rather because he was prevented from doing so by the United States. The Ogaden War is thus an example of not only the shah's ambitions in the Horn of Africa and the Indian Ocean, but also of his limitations in spite of the vast amounts of money he spent on Iran's military.

There is a significant body of literature on the Ogaden War, from the perspectives of both local and foreign participants, and much important work has been done to illuminate its regional and global dynamics.[6] The participation of regional actors in the conflict, in particular Egypt, Iran, and Saudi Arabia has been mentioned in the literature, but there have been no article-length analyses of the reasons why these states supported Somalia in the conflict, beyond the Cold War, and the ramifications of their involvement not just for the conflict itself but also their regional relationships. By examining in detail Iran's participation in the Ogaden War, and introducing

---

5 See James F. Goode, 'Assisting Our Brothers, Defending Ourselves: The Iranian Intervention in Oman, 1972–75', *Iranian Studies* 47/3, 2014, 441–462.
6 The most significant work on the Ethiopian perspective is Gebru Tareke, *The Ethiopian Revolution: War in the Horn of Africa*, 2009. On the United States, see Jeffrey Lefebvre, *Arms for the Horn: U.S. Security Policy in Ethiopia and Somalia, 1953–1991*, 1991; Donna R. Jackson, *Jimmy Carter and the Horn of Africa: Cold War Policy in Ethiopia and Somalia*, 2007; Louise Woodroofe, *Buried in the Sands of the Ogaden: The United States, the Horn of Africa, and the Demise of Détente*, 2013; and Nancy Mitchell, *Jimmy Carter in Africa: Race and the Cold War*, 2016. On the Soviet Union, see Robert G. Patman, *The Soviet Union in the Horn of Africa: The Diplomacy of Intervention and Disengagement*, 1990; and Radoslav A. Yordanov, *The Soviet Union and the Horn of Africa during the Cold War: Between Ideology and Pragmatism*, 2016.

new primary source material, this chapter, therefore, offers a unique per-spective, which both builds upon and contributes to existing scholarship on the conflict.

Iran's Security Interests in East Africa

The shah had developed a close relationship with Emperor Haile Selassie I of Ethiopia in the 1960s, which lasted until the latter's dethronement in 1974.[7] This relationship was almost entirely strategic, as both monarchs sought to find like-minded allies who could work together to balance the radicalism of the time. To Iran, the emergence of independent nations in Africa, and the departure of European colonial powers from the continent, presented opportunities to expand its interests, and given Addis Ababa's position as the de facto diplomatic capital of the continent, Ethiopia was seen as a stepping stone to the rest of Africa. But aside from these strategic concerns and the personal friendship between the shah and Haile Selas-sie, little more was done to advance this bilateral relationship during this period; trade relations remained modest and by the early 1970s, although the shah sought to expand his influence in East Africa, he was deterred from pursuing closer relations with Ethiopia 'in view of the Emperor's age and the country's backwardness and isolation'.[8]

The British withdrawal from the Persian Gulf in 1971 gave the shah unquestionable supremacy in the region, and once he had achieved this he began to articulate his global aspirations.[9] He spoke of his goal to create an economic and military union for the countries bordering the Indian Ocean, from Australia to India, Iran and South Africa. The security of the Indian Ocean should, the shah argued, be a concern for the countries of

---

7 On this relationship, see Robert Steele, 'Two Kings of Kings: Iran–Ethiopia Relations under the Shah and Haile Selassie', *The International History Review* 43/6, 2021, 1375–1392.

8 H.J. Arbuthnott to D.G. Allen, 5 October 1972, FCO 31/1126.

9 On Britain's withdrawal from the Persian Gulf and its impact on Iran, see Roham Alvandi, 'Muhammad Reza Pahlavi and the Bahrain Question, 1968–1970,' *British Journal of Middle Eastern Studies* 37/2, August 2010, 159–177; and Roham Alvandi, 'Nixon, Kissinger, and the Shah: The Origins of Iranian Primacy in the Persian Gulf', *Diplomatic History* 36/2, April 2012, 337–372.

the Indian Ocean, not the likes of the big powers, in particular the Soviet Union.[10] The shah's Indian Ocean policy was essentially an extension of his Persian Gulf policy in the late 1960s and early 1970s; a policy whose guiding principle was, as Ramazani writes, 'that great powers should keep out of the area'.[11] To pursue this Indian Ocean policy, the shah sought to develop ties with countries in East and Southern Africa and to increase Iran's military presence in the region. Accordingly, in 1972 the prime minister of Mauritius, Seewoosagur Ramgoolam, travelled to Iran to discuss the possibility of Iran building port and communication facilities on Mauritius.[12] Furthermore, as part of a naval agreement between Iran and South Africa, Iranian warships were able to put in at the naval base of Simon's Town in the Western Cape for repairs and maintenance, and from 1972, an Iranian navy representative was permanently based in South Africa.[13]

In this period, particularly after their ignominious expulsion from Egypt by Anwar Sadat in 1972, the Soviets also made inroads into East Africa, and offered their support to socialist regimes and militant leftist groups. In the context of his Indian Ocean policy, the shah viewed this increased Soviet presence in East Africa with trepidation. In a meeting with the US Secretary of Defense in July 1973, the shah said,

> They [the Soviets] moved into Egypt, almost got the Suez, and are now in Aden, Somalia (Djibouti) and the island of Socotra. We can not shut our eyes to the in-roads the Russians have made.[14]

This increase in Soviet activity in the region made the shah determined that 'Iran must take a more and more important role in the Indian Ocean'.[15]

---

10 R.K. Karanjia, *The Mind of a Monarch*, 1977, 234.

11 Rouhollah K. Ramazani, 'Iran's Search for Regional Cooperation', *Middle East Journal* 30/2, 1976, 180.

12 *Kayhan International*, 5 December 1972, 1.

13 Houchang Chehabi, 'South Africa and Iran in the Apartheid Era', *Journal of Southern African Studies* 42/4, 2016, 699.

14 Meeting between the Shah of Iran and the Secretary of Defense, Washington, 24 July 1973, *Foreign Relations of the United States* (hereafter *FRUS*), *1969–1976, vol. 27, Iran; Iraq, 1973–1976*, doc. 26.

15 Meeting between the Shah of Iran and the Secretary of Defense, Washington, 24 July 1973.

Prime Minister Hoveyda bidding farewell to the prime
minister of Mauritius, Seewoosagur Ramgoolam.

While Iran became more concerned with the Soviet expansion in East,
Southern, and Central Africa in the mid-1970s, greater congressional oversight made it increasingly difficult for the United States directly to arm
its allies on the continent. The weakness of the United States in Southern
Africa was exposed during the Angolan Civil War of 1975–1976. In the
conflict, the United States supported the Frente Nacional de Libertação
de Angola (FNLA) as a counter to the Soviet-backed Movimento Popular
de Libertação de Angola (MPLA). Washington viewed Soviet involvement in the conflict as a violation of détente, but scarred by its humiliating

withdrawal from Vietnam, was unwilling to provide the necessary support to the FNLA.[16] Then the Tunney Amendment of 20 December 1975 prohibited the United States from supporting covert military operations in Angola for the fiscal year, and the Clark Amendment, passed on 10 February 1976, made the ban unequivocal and permanent.[17] During a meeting on the situation in Angola and the possibilities of war spreading into Zaire, an exasperated Henry Kissinger said:

> I know that we are most moral – to a degree not rivaled by anyone in history, but to tell me that the U.S. would declare in a bill of lading that we were delivering arms to Zaire! Now really! What are we going to do when we really want to ship arms to Zaire? And this is something that could come up in six months or so. If we allow something like this to stop us then we are going to have a monumental problem. What can we tell Zaire – that we have these arms but can't deliver them? Now are you trying to tell me that we can't deliver arms?[18]

The answer to his question was that as far as arms deliveries were concerned, the administration was hamstrung. Kissinger blasted the Tunney Amendment as 'a national disgrace ... the worst American foreign policy disaster that I can remember'.[19]

Kissinger sent messages to Riyadh and Tehran, to convince his allies that

> we are not out of business, and that the Executive Branch is resolved to pursue the Angola matter vigorously and with full determination. We do not intend to sit idly by in the face of Soviet intervention.

Given the problems arising as a result of the Tunney Amendment,

---

16 Arthur J. Klinghoffer, 'US–Soviet Relations and Angola', *Harvard International Review* 8/3, January/February 1986, 16.
17 *The Washington Post*, 20 December 1975, 1; Mahmood Mamdani, *Good Muslim, Bad Muslim: America, the Cold War, and the Roots of Terror*, 2004, 82.
18 Memorandum for the Record, 12 March 1976, *FRUS, 1969–1976, vol. 28, Southern Africa*, doc. 182.
19 Cited in Mitchell, *Jimmy Carter in Africa*, 32.

Newspaper headline: 'God Save Africa!'

Kissinger urged the shah 'to make available funds to Zaire for additional equipment and arms which would help preserve the kind of military position for the non-communist forces which is essential if a negotiated settlement is to be achieved'.[20] The shah did not need a great deal of persuasion – Iran already had strategic interests in East and Southern Africa and to preserve its position, it was necessary to help its allies prevent the spread of Soviet influence.

Developments in Angola were viewed with some concern in Iran. The headline of an article in February 1974 in the semi-official daily, *Ettela'at*, which was known to convey the opinion of the state in its coverage, read: 'God Save Africa.'[21] It warned of the dangers facing Africa, of endless wars, and of a new kind of colonial interference bringing instability throughout the continent. It claimed that 'the ongoing war in Africa [specifically Angola] is greater than the war in Vietnam' and that 'Hitler's collaborators are seizing and mutilating the independence-seeking people of Africa.'[22] Articulating his concerns over the situation in Angola and Zaire, in a press conference during the visit of President Mobutu of Zaire, the

---

20 Henry Kissinger to Richard Helms, 20 December 1975, *FRUS, 1969–1976, vol. 28, Southern Africa*, doc. 159.

21 The publication of this article coincided with the state visits of the president of Zaire, Mobutu Sese Seko, and the president of Sudan, Jaafar Nimeiry.

22 *Ettela'at*, 9 Esfand 1352/28 February 1974, 5.

shah said to him 'we will provide any assistance that our African friends can ask of us and that is possible for us'.[23] This pledge of support was not merely lip service, and a US report from May 1977 suggests that Iran had indeed been providing military and economic aid to Zaire.[24] Moreover, this increasing Red encroachment in Africa coupled with US reticence prompted regional powers to work together to counter the Soviet threat.

The Safari Club

Given the temporary paralysis of the Executive Branch in the United States, Iran, Saudi Arabia, and Egypt assumed a greater role in the region.[25] But, although they were encouraged by the United States, it would be erroneous to view them merely as American proxies. They were state actors pursuing their own interests, which happened to align partially with the interests of Washington. For example, the director of the Saudi intelligence service, Kamal Adham, kept Kissinger abreast of the activities of Saudi Arabia and its allies in Angola. According to a report sent to Kissinger in December 1975, Egypt had sent a group of military advisors to Angola to assess the type of support needed, the results of which would be relayed to Iran and Saudi Arabia. The troika would then decide how much aid to send and how it would be delivered. Adham sent a message directly to the shah suggesting that he 'channel Iranian aid through South Africa, with which the Shah maintains good relations but with which neither Saudi Arabia nor Egypt has any contact'.[26] In response to the United States' offer to deliberate on the ways in which this aid might best be transferred, Adham

---

23 *Ettela 'at*, 5 Esfand 1352/24 February 1974, 13.

24 Briefing Paper, State Department, 'The Secretary's Meeting with the Shah of Iran', 13 May 1977, in Malcolm Byrne ed., *The Carter Administration and the "Arc of Crisis": Iran, Afghanistan and the Cold War in South West Asia, 1977–1981*. Wilson Center, Cold War International History Project Document Reader, https://www.wilsoncenter.org/publication/
the-carter-administration-and-the-arc-crisis-iran-afghanistan-and-the-cold-war-southern.

25 On the restoration of ties between Iran and Egypt, see Rouhollah K. Ramazani, 'Iran and the Arab–Israeli Conflict', *Middle East Journal* 32/4, 1978, 418.

26 US Embassy in Saudi Arabia to Kissinger, 21 December 1975, *FRUS, 1969–1976, vol. 28, Southern Africa*, doc. 162.

responded 'definitively that he would rather deal with the problem in direct coordination with Sadat and the Shah'.[27]

In September 1976, a covert intelligence alliance was set up by the heads of the secret services of Egypt, France, Iran, Morocco, and Saudi Arabia, called the Safari Club. It is often said that the idea for such an alliance was conceived by the director of the French *Service de Documentation Extérieure et de Contre-Espionnage,* Comte Claude Alexandre de Marenches, but as demonstrated Egypt, Iran and Saudi Arabia were already cooperating in Africa before this time.[28] Therefore, it appears as though the group represented the modest formalisation and expansion of intelligence ties that were already in operation. According to a document cited by the journalist Mohamed Heikal, an operational headquarters was set up in Cairo, which would 'evaluate what was going on in Africa, identify the danger spots, and make recommendations for dealing with them'.[29] In a recent article, Farid Boussaid has cautioned that despite the regular communications between members of the club, 'one needs to keep in mind that this alliance was relatively informal in nature and doubt exists in how much it has really functioned as a mechanism through which actions were coordinated.'[30] In practical terms the Safari Club was probably inconsequential, and in the two major conflicts in which its members were involved – the Shaba crises of 1977 and 1978 and the Ogaden War – it is difficult to detect sophisticated coordination.[31] However, the Safari Club is evidence that at this time its members recognised waning US influence in Africa, and the need to fill this vacuum to stop the spread of communism.

---

27 US Embassy in Saudi Arabia to Kissinger, 21 December 1975.

28 Rachel Bronson, *Thicker than Oil: America's Uneasy Partnership with Saudi Arabia,* 2006, 132.

29 Mohamed Heikal, *Iran: The Untold Story: An Insider's Account, from the Rise of the Shah to the Reign of the Ayatollah,* 1982, 113.

30 Farid Boussaid, 'Brothers in Arms: Morocco's Military Intervention in Support of Mobutu of Zaire During the 1977 and 1978 Shaba Crises', *The International History Review* 43/1, 2021, 195.

31 On the Shaba wars, see Piero Gleijeses, 'Truth or Credibility: Castro, Carter, and the Invasions of Shaba', *The International History Review* 18/1, 1996, 70–103; and Miles Larmer, 'Local Conflicts in a Transnational War: The Katangese Gendarmes and the Shaba Wars of 1977–78', *Cold War History* 13/1, 2013, 89–108; and Boussaid, 'Brothers in Arms'.

Events in Zaire in 1977 and the general Soviet penetration of Africa was viewed with alarm in Tehran. To illustrate this, every day in Farvardin 1356 (March–April 1977), articles appeared in Iran's main daily newspaper *Ettela 'at*, closely following developments in Zaire and reporting on the tour of the Chairman of the Presidium of the Supreme Soviet, Nikolai Podgorny, in Africa. The headline of one article read: 'Africa is becoming Red: What do the Soviets and Cuba want in Africa?', and the article warned that 'the Red danger severely threatens Black Africa.' It claimed that Podgorny's and Fidel Castro's tours of Africa, which occurred at around the same time, represented a 'carefully planned diplomatic attack', which ultimately sought to create Socialist regimes across the continent. It is no coincidence, it argued, that at the same time as these tours took place, Katangan Congolese soldiers in exile in Angola attacked Katanga in Zaire.[32] Other articles repeated concerns that Africa was the 'scene of a diplomatic attack from the Reds'[33] and warned that Zaire was 'becoming the new Vietnam'.[34] These articles provided justification for the intensification of Iran's involvement in Africa.

Iran and its allies had a reason to fear the Soviet threat, particularly in the Horn of Africa. Fidel Castro himself argued that the Horn of Africa presented an opportunity to inflict 'a severe defeat on the entire reactionary imperialist policy'.[35] He believed that Ethiopia had, as the historian Radoslav Yordanov observes, 'a powerful revolutionary potential to act as a counterweight to Egypt's defection', and that success in Ethiopia could also persuade a change of approach from Sadat, 'which would help to diminish the West's impact over the Middle East'.[36] Recognising the need

---

32 *Ettela 'at*, 9 Farvardin 1356/29 March 1977, 8. This point was made by the Moroccan ambassador to the United States, Abdelhadi Boutaleb, who said in a meeting with secretary of state, Cyrus Vance, that 'Morocco sees Katangan invasion of Zaire developing within framework built by African tours of Soviet President Podgorny and Cuban Premier Castro'. Telegram From the Department of State to the Embassy in Morocco, 17 April 1977, *FRUS, 1977–1980, vol. 17, Part 3, North Africa*, doc. 150.
33 *Ettela 'at*, 18 Farvardin 1356/7 April 1977, 8.
34 *Ettela 'at*, 7 Farvardin 1356/27 March 1977, 8.
35 Cited in Yordanov, *The Soviet Union and the Horn of Africa during the Cold War*, 164.
36 Yordanov, *The Soviet Union and the Horn of Africa during the Cold War*, 164.

to combat Soviet–Cuban encroachment in the Horn, in late May 1977 Iran's foreign minister, Abbas Ali Khal'atbari, was dispatched for his first visit to Sudan and Somalia.[37] In Mogadishu, Khal'atbari discussed increasing Iranian oil supplies to end Somali dependence on the Soviet Union.[38] This was part of a concerted effort on behalf of the Barre regime in Somalia and other regional powers concerned at increasing Soviet support for Mengistu's regime in Ethiopia, to reach out to one another and discuss ways in which they could cooperate to tackle Soviet expansionism. As Robert Patman has noted, in the first six months of 1977, there were around sixty visits between Somali government officials and 'conservative Arab states'.[39] By July 1977, the Saudis had sent at least $20 million worth of small arms to Somalia; some delivered directly aboard C-130s and some shipped through Egypt.[40] Saudi Arabia also offered Somalia $300–350 million in economic aid if it severed ties with the Soviets.[41] When war broke out in the Ogaden in July–August 1977, Barre felt assured that he would be able to call on his Islamic allies for support.

The Ogaden War: The Somali Offensive (July 1977 – January 1978)

Siad Barre had come to power following a military coup in 1969, and during the 1970s, the Soviets provided his regime with support both as a counterweight to the American backing of Ethiopia and to maintain a presence in the region after their ejection from Egypt in 1972. As a result of this Soviet support, Somalia's army grew from 4,000 men to 17,000; 3,600 Soviet advisors were sent to Somalia; 1,725 Somali soldiers were sent for training in the Soviet Union; two Soviet bases were established; and the Somali army began to foment unrest in Ethiopia.[42] Barre's brand of Somali

---

37 *Ettela'at*, 2 Khordad 1356/23 May 1977, 28.
38 Patman, *The Soviet Union in the Horn of Africa*, 211.
39 Patman, *The Soviet Union in the Horn of Africa*, 211.
40 Mitchell, *Jimmy Carter in Africa*, 272.
41 Patman, *The Soviet Union in the Horn of Africa*, 211.
42 Christopher Clapham, *The Horn of Africa: State Formation and Decay*, 2017, 57; David D. Laitin, 'The War in the Ogaden: Implications for Siyaad's Role in Somali History', *The Journal of Modern African Studies* 17/1, 1979, 99.

nationalism was predicated on a desire to unite Somali-populated areas in Kenya and Ethiopia, which included the Ogaden region. This region covers approximately 200,000 square kilometres, and though the majority of it is desert, it also contains two of the most populous cities in Ethiopia – Harar and Dire Dawa – and some of Ethiopia's richest agricultural land.[43] Thus, Barre's irredentism was motivated by economic interests perhaps as much as a desire to unite ethnic Somali populations.

Although Somalia had been supporting militant groups in the Ogaden, there were two reasons why Barre was encouraged to launch a full invasion in July 1977. First, this was an opportune moment. Ethiopia was politically and militarily weak; insurgents were making ground in several places and the armed forces had been purged of much of the top brass by the revolutionary Derg regime. Second, the Somali army, though numerically inferior, was far superior in terms of firepower as a result of the Soviet support it had received.[44] But there was also a feeling that as Ethiopia edged closer to the Soviet Union, bolstered by Soviet support its military would become more and more difficult to overcome. If Barre wanted to take the Ogaden, it was important to move quickly. In 1977, the Somalis still had the upper hand, and as Gebru Tareke writes, Ethiopia 'could not withstand a full-scale invasion by a well-equipped army. It was a moment not to be missed and they [Somalia] seized it with relish.'[45]

The war also had a Cold War dimension. The removal of Emperor Haile Selassie I in November 1974 led eventually to the collapse of the US–Ethiopia alliance in April 1977, as the Derg regime moved closer to the Soviet Union and the Carter administration became less tolerant of its human rights abuses and Marxist ideology.[46] A significant arms deal between the Soviets and Ethiopia in May 1977 convinced Mogadishu to reach out to Washington, and the Carter administration, aware of the strategic implications of a Soviet shift to Ethiopia, was open to talks. The United States thus agreed to supply defensive arms to Somalia and to encourage its allies to do the same. Even as this decision was being announced, however, Barre had already

---

43 Tareke, *The Ethiopian Revolution*, 184–186.
44 Tareke, *The Ethiopian Revolution*, 183.
45 Tareke, *The Ethiopian Revolution*, 184.
46 Lefebvre, *Arms for the Horn*, 149–172.

launched an attack on the Ogaden. As soon as the Carter administration found out, it cancelled the arms agreement, since Mogadishu had agreed that weapons could not be used to destabilise or attack its neighbours.[47]

The Carter administration was in a difficult position, for although it shifted towards Somalia, it also recognised that Ethiopia was the preeminent power in the Horn, so kept the door open to future rapprochement.[48] This dilemma led to indecisiveness, which at times exasperated America's allies in the region who wanted to intensify their support for Somalia and who were initially encouraged by the United States to do so, only to be instructed by Washington to pull back. For example, in June 1977, the Iranian foreign minister had informed the US ambassador in Tehran that Iran would shortly be sending a military mission to Somalia to assess its needs.[49] Iran had been encouraged to do so by US Secretary of State Cyrus Vance during his visit to Tehran in May, and had 'been led to believe' that the United States would also be sending a military mission.[50] The Somalis accepted the proposal for this Iranian mission on the proviso that it would bring with it a substantial supply of arms.[51] One month prior to the departure of the mission, on 6 July, Iran's vice-minister of war Hasan Tufanian sent a list to Washington of the arms they intended to send to Somalia and awaited approval.[52] Three days later, the US State Department submitted a series of issues they would like the Iranian mission to look into on the understanding that 'Somalis not rpt not be told that information to be obtained by Iranian team would be shared with us'.[53]

---

47 Lefebvre, *Arms for the Horn*, 176. The Barre regime claimed that the United States was fully aware of Somali operations in Ethiopia, and even encouraged them to 'liberate' the Ogaden. A message delivered to Barre from the Carter administration reportedly read, 'Whatever the Somalis do in Ogaden is their business. We would not take umbrage if they increased their guerrilla pressure there.' *Newsweek*, 3 October 1977, 19.
48 Mitchell, *Jimmy Carter in Africa*, 378.
49 Mitchell, *Jimmy Carter in Africa*, 273.
50 William Sullivan to Warren Christopher, 9 August 1977. WikiLeaks Cable: 1977TEHRAN07063_c.
51 Mitchell, *Jimmy Carter in Africa*, 294.
52 Sullivan to Secretary of State, 11 August 1977. WikiLeaks Cable: 1977STATE190575_c.
53 Cyrus Vance to US embassy in Tehran, 9 July 1977. WikiLeaks Cable: 1977STATE159686_c.

In the same letter, Cyrus Vance set out the US position vis-à-vis the transfer of American-made weapons by Iran. He wrote that the issue was still under 'intensive study', and that the United States was

bound by law to permit the transfer of U.S. origin arms only to a third country which we ourselves would sell or transfer similar equipment at that time. At the present time Somalia is not eligible to purchase US defensive articles under the arms export control act or to receive military assistance under the foreign assistance act of 1961. It has not yet been decided whether a determination by the secretary of state to permit such transfers will be given.[54]

Less than two weeks later, on 21 July, President Carter approved Tufanian's list.[55] Of course, the arms transfer would also have to be approved by Congress, but the US ambassador in Tehran, William Sullivan, argued that it 'would be natural, in these circumstances, for GOI [Government of Iran] to assume that appropriate clearance procedures were in train and that prior notification to Congress had been made at time of President's decision'.[56] Shortly after, on 9 August, two C-130 transport aircraft destined for Somalia were on standby at Mehrabad airport; one containing the five-man military mission and the other containing a shipment of US-made M-1 carbines. However, the aircraft containing the weapons was unable to take off, 'because of US block on transfer of arms', so the aircraft containing the military mission arrived in Mogadishu on 10 August empty-handed.[57]

Sullivan was promptly summoned to the Iranian Ministry of Foreign Affairs. There, the director of political affairs, Manuchehr 'Azima, told him that Iran was

totally confused by the US position and now found themselves in [an]

---

54 Cyrus Vance to US embassy in Tehran, 9 July 1977.
55 Sullivan to Secretary of State, 11 August 1977.
56 Sullivan to Secretary of State, 11 August 1977. WikiLeaks Cable: 1977STATE190575_c.
57 Sullivan to Secretary of State, 10 August 1977. WikiLeaks Cable: 1977TEHRAN07124_c.

extremely embarrassing position. As they had carefully explained to us earlier, the Somalis had insisted that the arms and the military mission would have to arrive in Somalia together.

Concerned that Somalia would, accuse Iran of 'bad faith', 'Azima 'urged that Washington, even though it might have to undertake further studies for [a] more extensive supply program, give immediate clearance for [the] current shipment'. No sooner had Sullivan returned to his office having been urged by 'Azima 'not to delay message seeking Washington clearance', he was 'set upon by my volatile little Somali colleague', who 'likewise urged immediate Washington action to release the rifles'.[58] In his dispatch to the state department, Sullivan requested that

> Since it was the US which got the Iranians involved [in] this whole exercise... I see no repeat no alternative to an immediate release permitting them to send this load of rifles to Somalia. It seems to me that such a small delivery will have miniscule significance to the military balance, whether in Ogaden or elsewhere. On the other hand, it could have a truly significant effect upon the political scales which are currently being weighted in Mogadiscio while our Washington deliberations continue.

The deputy secretary of state, Warren Christopher, responded that the United States could not legally permit the transfer of US-made weapons to Somalia, but that it was 'not rpt not discouraging transfer of non-US origin arms by third countries'.[59]

Sullivan responded by reminding Christopher that it was Secretary of State Cyrus Vance himself who had asked the shah to help in May. The Iranians were completely transparent, and a US objection could have been raised at any point since July; there was no reason why the administration should wait until the plane was loaded and ready to depart before

---

58 Sullivan to Secretary of State, 10 August 1977.
59 Christopher to Sullivan, 10 August 1977. WikiLeaks Cable:
1977STATE189617_c.

reconsidering their decision.[60] To add to Iran's – and Sullivan's – frustrations, the US military mission that was supposed to arrive in Somalia at around the same time as the Iranian mission had also been cancelled.[61] In response to US wavering, an exacerbated Sullivan wrote to Christopher that 'I am unable to articulate a US position because I have been unable to discern one from the signals I have received.'[62] Eventually, a solution was found, and on 14 August, the C-130 departed, loaded with two thousand German-designed G-3 rifles manufactured by the Ministry of War, along with two million rounds of ammunition.[63]

Lack of archival material from Iran makes it difficult to ascertain with certainty what Iran supplied, aside from the aforementioned German light arms. According to one newspaper, in the first months of the war, Iran had provided light arms, trucks, and hospital equipment.[64] Another claimed that in the first quarter of 1978, Iran provided over ten shipments of mortars, heavy artillery ammunition, and ground-to-air missiles, and as well as personnel.[65] The personnel were probably advisors. These weapons were not, for reasons already mentioned, the most recent technology produced in the United States, but 'obsolescent material' including American-produced M-48 tanks, which had reached Somalia via Oman.[66] Iran also provided 'financing for weapons bought on the free market'.[67] These apparently included German mortars acquired through Turkey, and some anti-tank weapons.[68]

Iran was slightly constrained in terms of what it was allowed to give to Barre, given that it would need US permission to use or supply US-made

60 Sullivan to Secretary of State, 11 August 1977. WikiLeaks Cable: 1977STATE190575_c.
61 Sullivan to Secretary of State, 9 August 1977, WikiLeaks Cable: 1977TEHRAN07063_c.
62 Sullivan to Secretary of State, 9 August 1977.
63 Sullivan to Department of State, 14 August 1977. Wikileaks Cable: 1977TEHRAN07186_c.
64 *The New York Times*, 1 January 1978, 1.
65 Amin Saikal, *The Rise and Fall of the Shah: Iran from Autocracy to Religious Rule*, 2009, 180.
66 Lefebvre, *Arms for the Horn*, 188.
67 *The Washington Post*, 3 March 1978.
68 Heikal, *Iran: The Untold Story*, 115.

weapons.[69] This did not stop Barre from asking. In September 1977, for example, the shah informed Ambassador Sullivan, 'in confidence' that a special emissary had recently been sent to Iran from Somalia to request 'aircraft and pilots from the Iranian Air Force to fly them'.[70] The US position was fairly consistent throughout the conflict with regard to the use of US weapons; they accepted, even encouraged, the supply of defensive equipment and economic assistance to Somalia, but they would '*not* serve in a coordinating role'.[71] The United States government made it clear to Iran, Saudi Arabia, and Egypt that any unauthorised use or transfer of American arms would be contrary to bilateral arms agreements and could have 'a potentially adverse impact on Congressional approval' of future sales.[72]

International Diplomacy

Notwithstanding the lack of materiel support from the United States, the Somalis made significant progress in the early stages of the war, penetrating deep into Ethiopian territory and seizing the cities of Delo, Elkere, Filtu, Jijiga, and Karamara. However, the Somali army failed to take Harar in a four-month battle lasting from September until January due to determined resistance from the defending Ethiopians. In November, Barre, weary of the growing ties between the Soviets and Ethiopia, and wanting to prove to the United States and other regional allies such as Saudi Arabia his anti-Soviet, pro-Western credentials, broke relations with the Soviet Union, expelled its military advisors, and abrogated the 1974 Treaty of Friendship.[73] During the lull in fighting in December and into January, the Soviets thus began a huge operation to bring equipment and military

---

69 Minutes of a National Security Council Meeting, 23 February 1978, *FRUS, 1977–1980, vol. 17, Horn of Africa, Part 1*, doc. 62.

70 The shah 'politely turned them down'. Sullivan to Secretary of State, 7 September 1977. WikiLeaks Cable: 1977TEHRAN07895_c.

71 Summary of Conclusions of a Special Coordination Committee Meeting, 16 March 1978, *FRUS, 1977–1980, vol. 17, Horn of Africa, Part 1*, doc. 75.

72 Presidential Directive/NSC-32, 24 February 1978, *FRUS, 1977–1980, vol. 17, Horn of Africa, Part 1*, doc. 64.

73 Guy Arnold, *Africa A Modern History: 1945–2015*, 2017, 494.

advisors to support the Ethiopian war effort. During this period as many as 225 Soviet transport planes travelled to Ethiopia – representing as much at fifteen percent of its transport fleet – with an estimated $1 billion worth of arms.[74] As Tareke has noted, this was similar in volume to the arms the Soviets delivered to the Arabs in 1973 and to the MPLA in 1975.[75]

Iran would be frustrated with American wavering for the second time during this period, when in December the State Department, concerned that the Soviets were 'on the verge of mounting major upgrading of their military materiel and personnel assistance to Ethiopia', urged Iran, Pakistan, and Turkey to refuse the Soviets permission to fly in their airspace.[76] Iran was eager to stop the planes from flying over, but at the same time was 'distressed and annoyed' with Washington for not relaying this request sooner, since it had already given permission for four Soviet planes destined for Ethiopia to enter its airspace.[77] Ambassador Sullivan was, in the words of historian Nancy Mitchell, 'apoplectic'.[78] Writing to the State Department, he said:

> By sheer gall and because countermeasures have been neglected, the Soviets have already managed to send a number of flights to Aden... If they [the Soviets] get away with this, they [America's regional allies, including Iran] will have a pretty low estimate of our resolve... [and] be contemptuous of the quality of our leadership on this issue.[79]

While the Soviet build-up in Ethiopia continued, Siad Barre intensified his efforts to solicit military support from his regional allies under the banner of 'Islamic solidarity'. During the short period from the end of December to the beginning of January, Barre visited Pakistan, Egypt, Sudan, Oman, Iraq, Syria, and Iran.[80] Siad Barre's trip to Iran took place

---

74 Arnold, *Africa A Modern History*, 497.
75 Tareke, *The Ethiopian Revolution*, 203.
76 Mitchell, *Jimmy Carter in Africa*, 352.
77 Sullivan to Secretary of State, 11 December 1977. WikiLeaks Cable: 1977TEHRAN10877_c.
78 Mitchell, *Jimmy Carter in Africa*, 352.
79 Sullivan to Secretary of State, 11 December 1977.
80 'Soviet Foreign Ministry and CPSU CC International Department Background

شاهنشاه: ایران وسومالی درمورد امنیت اقیانوس هند توافق دارند

انتقاد رئیس جمهوری سومالی از غرب

دیشب از طرف شاهنشاه آریامهر ضیافتی به شام بافتخار رئیس جمهوری
سومالی ترتیبیافت. والاحضرتشاهپور عبدالرضا پهلوی نیز حضور داشتند. در صفحات آخر و ٤

The shah and his half-brother, Prince 'Abdolreza Pahlavi,
with Siad Barre during his visit to Tehran.

in December. Accompanying him on the trip was a retinue of fifty high-level officials, and during the visit several meetings were held to deepen ties with Tehran and ensure the shah's continued support of Somalia in the conflict. This visit was particularly significant because President Carter was due to arrive in Tehran within days of Barre's departure, so this was an opportunity for Barre to urge the shah to put Somalia's case directly to the US president. During a banquet speech, the shah praised the 'friendly and fruitful' negotiations that had taken place. Framing Iran's interest in the Horn of Africa in the context of his Indian Ocean policy, the shah said, 'In

Report on the Somali–Ethiopian Conflict', 3 April 1978, TsKhSD [Russian Center for Preservation of Contemporary Documentation], f. 5, op. 75, d. 1175, ll. 13–23; translated by Mark Doctoroff. The Wilson Center, Cold War International History Project. http://digitalarchive.wilsoncenter.org/document/110975.

these negotiations, in particular, we agreed that the Indian Ocean should be a region of peace and security.'[81]

The intensification of Soviet support did not only cause concern for Barre, but the shah, too. He was anxious that the Ethiopian army, bolstered by Russian arms and Cuban manpower, could continue the offensive into Somalia, toppling the Barre regime and turning the whole of the Horn of Africa Red. During Carter's visit, the situation with Somalia was therefore at the top of the agenda. Describing the conflict in stark Cold War terms, the shah said that Barre 'sees his dispute with Ethiopia as a "Warsaw Pact problem" and part of a major Soviet drive'.[82] The shah assured the president that although he was keen to 'play a role' in bringing Ethiopia and Somalia together to discuss peace, 'Ethiopia should be reminded that if they are thinking of further encroaching on the internationally recognised borders of Somalia, it is not something that Iran can ignore.'[83] Carter, however, resisted subtle pressure from the shah to increase US support for Somalia, and rather in his New Year toast merely asked the shah to use his 'good influence' to encourage Ethiopia and Somalia to negotiate a peaceful resolution.[84]

In spite of the shah's insistence to Carter that he wanted to play a role in bringing a peaceful resolution to the conflict, Iranian newspapers focused on his statement that he would 'not remain indifferent to the invasion of Somalia'. This was not merely a message for the president of the United States, but for the Soviets, Cuba, and Ethiopia, too. And the message was received. Shortly after, the Ethiopian ambassador to Nigeria, Kesate Badema, called on the US ambassador to discuss the situation in the Horn. Badema stated that 'his government was alarmed by recent statements by the shah... [and] worried that President Carter's talks with the shah may have included discussions of possible transfer to Somalia of Iranian

81 Ettela'at, 8 Dey 1356/29 December 1977, 32.

82 President's Meeting with Shah, Department of State, 3 January 1978. WikiLeaks Cable: 1978STATE000576_d.

83 Ettela'at, 11 Dey 1356/1 January 1978, 4.

84 Jimmy Carter, Tehran, Iran Toasts of the President and the Shah at a State Dinner. Online by Gerhard Peters and John T. Woolley, The American Presidency Project https://www.presidency.ucsb.edu/node/242827; Jackson, Jimmy Carter and the Horn of Africa, 57 and 85.

شاهنشاه: ایران در مقابل تجاوز بهسومالی بی‌اعتنا نمی‌ماند

The shah in discussions with President Carter. The shah: 'Iran
will not remain indifferent to the invasion of Somalia.'

weapons originally provided by the U.S.'[85] Iran may not have been able to
use or supply US-made weapons, but the threat was taken seriously.

This pro-Somali lobbying from Iran was complicated somewhat by
Israel's support of Ethiopia in the conflict. Israel and Ethiopia had long
been allies; drawn together, in the words of Jeffrey Lefebvre, 'by a mutual
fear of Arab and Islamic encirclement'. While the likes of Iran and Saudi
Arabia had ceased to support Ethiopia as it edged towards the Soviet
Union after the fall of Haile Selassie, in the context of Israel's security
policy 'Addis Ababa's ideological orientation was of little importance'.[86]
In fact, during the Ogaden War, Israel provided Ethiopia with spare parts
for US-made weapons.[87] As Patman has noted, this 'led to the apparently
incredible situation whereby Tel Aviv briefly found itself on the same side
as the USSR, Cuba, Libya, and the PDRY [People's Democratic Republic
of Yemen]'.[88] Iran's support for Somalia in this conflict also strained its
relationship with one of its African allies – Kenya.

85 US embassy in Lagos to Secretary of State, 12 January 1978. WikiLeaks Cable:
1978LAGOS00472_d.
86 Jeffrey Lefebvre, 'Middle East Conflicts and Middle Level Power Intervention in
the Horn of Africa', The Middle East Journal 50/3, 1996, 395.
87 Lefebvre, Arms for the Horn, 186–189.
88 Patman, The Soviet Union in the Horn of Africa, 229.

Iran and Kenya

Iran and Kenya had established political relations in November 1971, exchanged ambassadors in December 1972, and subsequently Kenya became a major consumer of Iranian oil.[89] Iran also became one of Kenya's most important economic partners – by 1977 it was ranked second in imports (ten percent of the total) after Britain (twenty percent).[90] But despite these close economic ties, Nairobi became increasingly concerned about Iran's support for Barre, whose irredentism also threatened their Somali-inhabited north-east territories. On 10 January 1978, Kenya's foreign minister, Munyua Waiyaki, arranged a meeting with Iran's ambassador in Kenya, Ahmad Tavakoli, during which he raised concerns about the shah's statements during Carter's visit to Tehran. The local press gave prominent coverage to the meeting, particularly Waiyaki's perception that the shah's statements 'encouraged Somalia's territorial claims not only in the Ogaden but in Kenya as well'.[91]

In response, on 30 January 1978, the Iranian embassy in Nairobi issued a press release which stated that Iran's 'National Independent Policy, with regards to the events taking place in the Horn of Africa... has been misunderstood and even misinterpreted'. The statement articulated Iran's commitment to 'its traditional policy of solving international problems and disputes through peaceful means', but also reiterated the point that had been put to Carter, that 'Iran can not remain indifferent should Somalia be attacked and invaded within its internationally recognized borders.'[92] Despite Iran's claims that it had only provided medical aid to Somalia through its Red Lion and Sun Society, Waiyaki stated publicly that non-African powers like Iran had no right to interfere in African affairs.[93] In a private meeting in February, Ambassador Tavakoli told Waiyaki that 'Iran

---

89 Ahmad Bakhshi, 'Barresi-ye Tarikhi-ye Ravabet-e Khareji-ye Iran va Qareh-ye Afriqa', *Tarikh-e Ravabet-e Khareji* 35, 1387/2008, 59–60.

90 *Keyhan*, 29 Bahman 1356/18 February 1978, 2.

91 US embassy in Nairobi to Secretary of State, 11 January 1978. WikiLeaks Cable: 1978NAIROB00510_d.

92 Press Release, Imperial Embassy of Iran, Nairobi, 30 January 1978, FCO 31/2328.

93 The Red Lion and Sun Society (Anjoman-e Shir o Khorshid-e Sorkh-e Iran) was set up in the 1920s and was part of the International Red Cross and Red Crescent Movement.

felt that [the] Kenyan press was taking a communist line on the affairs of the Horn ... and that the Russian threat in Ethiopia ought to be regarded by the Kenyans much more seriously than their fears of Somalia'.[94] According to the British high commissioner, Stanley Fingland, 'Tavakoli implied that if he could not get more satisfaction there was a possibility that the Shah might decide to withdraw him for a period of months or more formally.'[95]

At a press conference on 18 February 1978, Iran's foreign minister, Abbas Ali Khal'atbari, announced that Iran was formally breaking relations with Kenya and recalling its ambassador. Pushing back against some of the claims put forward by Waiyaki, he said, 'It is as if the African foreign minister is unaware of the presence of non-Africans in the conflict, or he considers Cubans and others involved to be Africans.' Besides, he added, as 'one of the founding members of the United Nations who had always participated in international affairs and world peace... Iran cannot remain indifferent if a country's border is attacked.'[96] Iran's repeated insistence that it could not stand by while one country was attacked by another is remarkable considering its support for Somalia, which was the aggressor in the conflict.

The president of Kenya, Jomo Kenyatta, informed Tavakoli that 'he had been unaware of Dr Waiyaki's statements and that he wished the ambassador to know that he, Kenyatta, attached importance to Kenya's links with Iran.'[97] Fingland wrote that the Kenyans were 'puzzled by the suddenness of the Iranian decision', and although they wanted to maintain good relations with Tehran, did not think they owed an apology.[98] Tavakoli left Nairobi on 26 February, leaving Britain in charge of Iran's consular interests in Kenya, with the presence of an Iranian chargé d'affaires.[99] The British and Belgians made some attempts to mediate over the following weeks and encouraged Kenya to send a high-level mission to Tehran to negotiate directly with the Iranian government. These efforts failed

---

94 Stanley Fingland, 'Kenya–Iran Relations', 20 February 1978, FCO 31/2328.
95 Fingland, 'Kenya–Iran Relations', 20 February 1978.
96 *Keyhan*, 29 Bahman 1356/18 February 1978, 2.
97 Fingland report, 23 February 1978, FCO 31/2328.
98 Fingland report, 23 February 1978.
99 Fingland report, 28 February 1978, FCO 31/2328. The British continued to look after Iranian interests in Kenya until September 1980.

because Iran would only receive a mission if its purpose was to apologise, and although Kenya was willing to send a mission, it would not do so 'if this could be interpreted as a Kenyan gesture of apology'.[100]

It seems strange that such a seemingly trivial matter could result in the suspension of diplomatic relations, particularly between two countries that were such close economic allies, so what was the real reason for this diplomatic rift? Of course, it is entirely possible that the cause of the incident was that the shah considered criticism from Kenya as a personal slight. The shah had almost complete personal control over foreign policy, and on occasion political relationships could be affected by the shah's personal feeling towards the leader of a country. For example, as a result of President Pompidou declining an invitation to attend the 2500th anniversary celebrations at Persepolis in 1971, economic and political relations between Iran and France were strained for some time.[101] But is it conceivable that the shah was so thin-skinned that he would break diplomatic relations with a friendly country over comments made by its foreign minister? Another event perhaps sheds some light on this. A few months after the split, a representative of Iran's foreign ministry, Manuchehr Zelle, telephoned the British ambassador in Tehran, Anthony Parsons, to inform him that the shah had not received a response to his letter of condolence to the acting president of Kenya, Daniel Moi, following President Kenyatta's death. The Iranians were considering whether to send another message to congratulate Moi on his inauguration, but 'did not wish to do so if Moi's failure to acknowledge the first message was deliberate'. Parsons was asked by Zelle for the high commissioner's advice, 'without consulting the Kenyans'.[102] The fact that Iran raised such a 'tedious point', to use Parsons' expression, demonstrates that the shah perhaps did feel genuinely aggrieved by Kenya's response to its involvement in the Ethiopian–Somali conflict.

Personal feelings notwithstanding, the rift should also be seen in the broader context of the Ogaden War and Iran's policy in the Horn. Although

---

100 George Chalmers report, 12 July 1978, FCO 31/2328.
101 See Robert Steele, *The Shah's Imperial Celebrations of 1971: Nationalism, Culture and Politics in Late Pahlavi Iran*, 2020, 64.
102 Anthony Parsons report, 11 October 1978, FCO 31/2328.

Khal'atbari maintained that the attitude of Waiyaki had been the cause of the closure of Iran's embassy, foreign newspapers speculated that this action was taken to demonstrate that Iran had adopted a tough line and was willing to come to Somalia's defence if it were invaded by Ethiopia.[103] In other words, if Kenya's public criticism was not challenged, then this could undermine the seriousness of Iran's threat to intervene in the Horn. On 15 February, at nearly exactly the same time as Iran announced the closure of the embassy in Nairobi, an Egypt Air plane was intercepted in Kenyan air space by the Kenyan air force en route to Somalia and forced to land at Nairobi. It was found to contain a cargo of munitions, and according to the Kenyan government, this was the fourth Somali-bound Egyptian plane to enter its airspace in the past week.[104] In retaliation, Egypt seized two Kenyan aeroplanes in Cairo and arrested 22 crew members.[105] We know that Iran and Egypt were cooperating in the Ogaden, so it is surely no coincidence that these two diplomatic incidents occurred at the same time.

The shah's declarations during Carter's visit had also caught the attention of the Organisation of African Unity (hereafter OAU), which released a statement criticising Iran's role in the conflict:

> The recent statement of the government of Iran concerning the
> situation in the Horn of Africa is replete with very disturbing
> overtones. Iran had better address herself to the question of finding a
> peaceful solution to the crisis in the Horn of Africa and assist the OAU
> in this task.[106]

In 1968, during the shah's state visit to Ethiopia, the secretary general of the OAU had praised the shah for the role he 'plays in the great family of Asia and Africa'.[107] Ten years later, the tone was very different. Now, in its statement, the OAU declared that it 'has no room for any country

---

103 *Keyhan*, 30 Bahman 1356/19 February 1978, 6.
104 'Kenya Egyptian Plane Held', *AP Archive*, http://www.aparchive.com/
metadata/youtube/457d03e0f7aa4f0e3189a57e95d9b2f5.
105 *The New York Times*, 17 February 1978, 3.
106 OAU Press Release on Iran and the Horn of Africa, 20 January 1978.
WikiLeaks Cable: 1978ADDIS00310_d.
107 Steele, 'Two Kings of Kings', 8.

whose consuming passion is to extend her sphere of influence to Africa by playing the role of a mini-power'. In spite of Iranian attempts to downplay the statement as the opinion of just one OAU administrator, a report by the US embassy in Addis Ababa concluded that 'while [the] statement is somewhat one-sided, [the] embassy believes it probably reflects [the] views of most OAU members.'[108] From the 1960s, when Iran first reached out to independent Africa, the shah had insisted that Iran was committed to combatting 'the remnants of colonialism', but this image was becoming increasingly difficult to uphold and some African leaders came to perceive Iran as merely another imperial power.[109]

The Ethiopian Counteroffensive (January–March 1978)

In January 1978, the balance of the war shifted towards Ethiopia, as a result not only of Soviet support, but also the presence of the Cuban troops that had been airlifted in. By January there were 5,000 Cuban troops in the country. This reached as many as 18,000 by February, half of whom were transported directly from Angola.[110] The turning point of the war occurred on 22 January, when the Somalis launched their final attack on Harar. Armed with Soviet T-54 tanks and supported by Cuban ground troops and pilots flying jet fighter bombers, the Ethiopians routed the Somalis, killing as many as 3,000 and capturing tanks and weapons the Somalis left behind on the battlefield.[111] From this time, the Somalis were on the back foot, and over the following weeks, the Ethiopian counteroffensive forced them to abandon all of the towns and cities they had taken in the early months of the war.

The Americans had seriously underestimated the number of Cuban troops in Ethiopia; by as much as seventy percent.[112] By early February, when it became clear in Washington that the war had shifted in Ethiopia's

---

108 US embassy in Addis Ababa to Secretary of State, 8 February 1978. WikiLeaks Cable: 1978ADDIS00625_d.

109 Steele, 'Two Kings of Kings', 8.

110 Gebru Tareke, 'The Ethiopia–Somalia War of 1977 Revisited', *The International Journal of African Historical Studies* 33/3, 2000, 656.

111 Tareke, *The Ethiopian Revolution*, 205; Mitchell, *Jimmy Carter in Africa*, 374.

112 Mitchell, *Jimmy Carter in Africa*, 369.

favour, discussions took place over what to do if Ethiopia decided to continue its offensive into Somali territory. In a report by the director of the
Bureau of Intelligence and Research, Harold Henry Saunders, the capa-
bilities '(not the intentions)' of Egypt, Iran, Saudi Arabia, and Sudan to
provide assistance were evaluated. Saunders concluded that Iran was 'in a
far better position than any other state in the area to provide a wide range
of air support', would be able to provide technical and military advisors,
and could logistical problems of transportation be overcome, the introduction of 20,000 Iranian and Egyptian forces 'would give the Somalis clear
superiority over their opponents'.[113]

Later in February, during a National Security Council meeting, President Carter asked the CIA chief, Admiral Stansfield Turner, whether Iran
and Egypt were likely to do anything to stop an Ethiopian invasion of
Somalia. Turner told him they would not, but added that 'the Shah has
discussed what he would do in the Horn and has said he would send help
if the border was crossed.' The main problem for the United States was that
as things stood, they were on the side of the aggressor. 'The key, therefore,
is for us to get the Somalis out of the Ogaden', acting chairman of the
Joint Chiefs of Staff, General David Jones stated. 'Once they are out, then
we should support third country transfers.'[114] It is clear that although US
policy was to find a diplomatic solution to the situation in the Horn, should
this not be possible, they considered Iran to be key to preventing a Soviet–
Cuban-backed Ethiopian invasion of Somalia. General Jones argued that
'the participation of the Iranians would give the Somalis a good chance to
stop the invasion.'[115]

For the duration of the Ogaden War, from July 1977 until March 1978,
Iran had not only provided military aid, but had also supported Somalia
diplomatically. Indeed, as late as 6 March, a 'high official in the Shah's
Government' said that Iran 'cannot permit the Soviets to conquer all

113 Briefing Memorandum from the Director of the Bureau of Intelligence and
Research (Saunders) to Secretary of State Vance, 4 February 1978, *FRUS, 1977–
1980, vol. 17, Horn of Africa, Part 1*, doc. 53.
114 Minutes of a National Security Meeting, Washington, 23 February 1978, *FRUS,
1977–1980, vol. 17, Horn of Africa, Part 1*, doc. 62.
115 Minutes of National Security Meeting, Washington, 23 February 1978.

Africa' and was resolved to commit military forces to Somalia if necessary.[116] However, in spite of its public support, it is clear that in private the
shah's position was beginning to soften, perhaps as he realised that the
Carter administration would be unlikely to permit either the transfer of
American-made weapons, or their use by a third country, such as Iran, in
battle. In January, the shah had sent a message to Barre encouraging him
to undertake 'an offensive for peace', and these messages became more
urgent as the war dragged on.[117] At one point, the shah reportedly summoned the Somali ambassador in Tehran and said:

> I've had three messages from President Carter. You Somalis are
> threatening to upset the balance of world power. If you get out of the
> Ogaden we will see that you get all the aid you want, but it will be
> economic aid, not military. You must forget about the Ogaden.[118]

By early March 1978, it became clear that Ethiopia had won the arms
race, and Somali diplomats 'made known their disappointment with the
shah's promises, which they claim have produced little of either financial
or military value to their cause'.[119] On 9 March 1978, given the vast Soviet
and Cuban support for Ethiopia, and Siad Barre's inability to secure US
backing, Barre reluctantly informed Carter that he agreed to withdraw his
troops from the Ogaden region. In fact, as historian Donna Jackson notes,
'the "withdrawal" referred to by Siad was more like a rout.'[120]

Despite the failure of Iran, Saudi Arabia and Egypt, members of the so-
called Safari Club, to convince the United States to commit resources to the
conflict in the Horn, its efforts were not entirely in vain. As the US historical record shows, Washington was aware that these countries were primed
and ready to follow America's lead should it permit the use of third country
transfers, or decide to send forces itself. Whether or not the shah was sincere
when he repeatedly stated that Iran was ready to defend Somalia if it was

---

116 *The New York Times*, 7 March 1978, 16.
117 Sullivan to Secretary of State, 8 January 1978. WikiLeaks Cable:
1978TEHRAN00190_d.
118 Heikal, *Iran: The Untold Story*, 116.
119 *The Washington Post*, 3 March 1978.
120 Jackson, *Jimmy Carter and the Horn of Africa*, 100.

invaded by Ethiopia, the message was taken seriously in Washington and Iran's potential to come to Somalia's aid was discussed at the highest level. It is entirely plausible that even if Iran did not shape American policy in the Horn as the war developed, it did influence it. It is also possible that the shah's public declaration to support Somalia played a role in the decision of the Ethiopians – and the Soviets – not to cross the border into Somalia.

*

The withdrawal of the British from the Persian Gulf in 1971 allowed the shah attempt to assert Iranian hegemony of the Persian Gulf and subsequently attempt to establish a leading position in the entire Indian Ocean region. In this context, the shah was greatly concerned about the growing Soviet presence in the Horn of Africa, as reflected in articles published in Iran's semi-official dailies. Roham Alvandi has shown in his *Nixon, Kissinger, and the Shah* that in the late 1960s and early 1970s, the shah was able to manipulate the Nixon administration, in a sense, by exaggerating the Soviet threat in order to strengthen his case for increased US support.[121] But by the late 1970s, the situation had changed somewhat. No longer was the Soviet Union merely a faux threat exaggerated to elicit US support, but it posed a direct challenge to Iran's immediate and long-term strategy. Iran had no real historical links to Somalia, and only established political ties with the Barre regime in 1977 as a response to the heightened Soviet penetration of Ethiopia. As the Ogaden War developed, the shah provided materiel and diplomatic support to Somalia, precisely because he feared an Ethiopian victory would spell the collapse of Somalia and leave the Soviets unopposed in the Horn of Africa. This would have implications for the shah's Indian Ocean policy.

This chapter has argued that during the conflict, the shah influenced American policy to a degree, but he was also restrained by it. Iran did supply weapons to Somalia during the conflict, in collaboration with regional allies, most significantly Saudi Arabia and Egypt, but the shah was prevented by Washington from providing the type of support that

---

121 Roham Alvandi, *Nixon, Kissinger, and the Shah: The United States and Iran in the Cold War*, 2014.

could have slowed down the January counteroffensive. The support they did provide simply could not compete with the vast levels of support given to Ethiopia by the Soviet Union. To illustrate this disparity, between 1976 and 1980, Addis Ababa received as much as $2 billion worth of arms from the Soviet Union and the size of Ethiopia's army quadrupled from 65,000 to 250,000 soldiers. In the same period, Mogadishu imported $750 million worth of arms, and the size of Somalia's armed forces in 1980 was just 54,000 men.[122] The decision by Mogadishu in November 1977 to cut ties with the Soviet Union, and by extension the whole of the Socialist Bloc, without securing the support of the United States was, in Tareke's words 'a fateful decision, and one that would cost it dearly'.[123] From this time onwards, although other states, including Iran, helped to plug this gap, without real assistance from the United States this support would never have been able to match that of the Soviet Union.

Indeed, throughout the conflict there are indications that Iran was frustrated by the Carter administration's indecisiveness and failure to communicate its policy clearly.[124] Donna Jackson has argued that 'if events in the Horn of Africa had taken place ten or fifteen years previously, it seems unlikely that the American response to the usurpation of their influence by the Soviet Union would have been so calm.'[125] But the new administration was unwilling to get involved directly in the conflict, and rather than take sides, President Carter tried to play the role of peacemaker. He said, 'Those of us who have any influence at all must use it for this purpose … We want Somalia and Ethiopia to be friends again.'[126] To his credit, Carter maintained this stance, even under pressure from some of America's most powerful Middle Eastern and North African allies. The failure of these allies to secure US support prevented them from offering to Barre the type of assistance he needed to win the war. So, while Iran's support for Somalia in the Ogaden War demonstrates the aspirations of the shah to become a major power in the decolonised world in the 1970s, it also demonstrates the limitations of his independent global policy.

---

122 Lefebvre, *Arms for the Horn*, 202.
123 Tareke, *The Ethiopian Revolution*, 654.
124 Mitchell, *Jimmy Carter in Africa*, 295.
125 Jackson, *Jimmy Carter and the Horn of Africa*, 65.
126 *The New York Times*, 1 January 1978, 1.

Bibliography

Archival Material

The National Archives, London

Wilson Center, Cold War International History Project, https://www.
    wilsoncenter.org/program/cold-war-international-history-project

The American Presidency Project, https://www.presidency.ucsb.edu/

AP Archive, http://www.aparchive.com/

WikiLeaks Public Library of US Diplomacy, https://wikileaks.org/plusd/
    about/

Newspapers

Ettela'at
Kayhan International
Keyhan
Newsweek
The New York Times
Tehran Journal
The Washington Post

Published Sources

Alvandi R. 'Muhammad Reza Pahlavi and the Bahrain Question, 1968–
    1970,' *British Journal of Middle Eastern Studies* 37/2, August 2010,
    159–177.

Alvandi, R. *Nixon, Kissinger, and the Shah: The United States and Iran
    in the Cold War*, Oxford, 2014.

Alvandi, R. 'Nixon, Kissinger, and the Shah: The Origins of Iranian
    Primacy in the Persian Gulf', *Diplomatic History* 36/2, April 2012,
    337–372.

Arnold, G. *Africa A Modern History: 1945–2015*, London, 2017.

Bakhshi, A. 'Barresi-ye Tarikhi-ye Ravabet-e Khareji-ye Iran va
    Qareh-ye Afriqa', *Tarikh-e Ravabet-e Khareji* 35, 1387/2008, 32–75.

Belmonte, Monica L. ed., *FRUS, 1969–1976, vol. 27, Iran; Iraq, 1973–
    1976*, Washington, DC, 2012.

Boussaid, F. 'Brothers in Arms: Morocco's Military Intervention in Support of Mobutu of Zaire During the 1977 and 1978 Shaba Crises', *The International History* Review 43/1, 2021, 185–202.

Bronson, R. *Thicker than Oil: America's Uneasy Partnership with Saudi Arabia*, Oxford, 2006.

Burton, Myra F. ed., *FRUS, 1969–1976, vol. 28, Southern Africa*, Washington, DC, 2011.

Burton, Myra F. ed., *FRUS, 1977–1980, vol. 17, Part 3, North Africa*, Washington, DC, 2017.

Byrne, M., ed. *The Carter Administration and the "Arc of Crisis": Iran, Afghanistan and the Cold War in South West Asia, 1977–1981.* Wilson Center, Cold War International History Project, https://www.wilsoncenter.org/publication/the-carter-administration-and-the-arc-crisis-iran-afghanistan-and-the-cold-war-southern.

Clapham, C. *The Horn of Africa: State Formation and Decay*, Oxford, 2017.

Gleijeses, P. 'Truth or Credibility: Castro, Carter, and the Invasions of Shaba', *The International History Review* 18/1, 1996, 70–103.

Goode, J.F. 'Assisting Our Brothers, Defending Ourselves: The Iranian Intervention in Oman, 1972–75', *Iranian Studies* 47/3, 2014, 441–462.

Hecht, G. *Being Nuclear: Africans and the Global Uranium Trade*, Cambridge, USA, 2012.

Heikal, M. *Iran: The Untold Story: An Insider's Account, from the Rise of the Shah to the Reign of the Ayatollah*, New York, 1982.

Jackson, D.R. *Jimmy Carter and the Horn of Africa: Cold War Policy in Ethiopia and Somalia*, Jefferson, 2007.

Jackson, D.R. 'The Ogaden War and the Demise of Détente', *The Annals of the American Academy of Political and Social Science* 632, 2010, 26–40.

Karanjia, R.K. *The Mind of a Monarch*, London, 1977.

Klinghoffer, A.J. 'US–Soviet Relations and Angola', *Harvard International Review* 8/3, January/February 1986, 15–19.

Laitin, D.D. 'The War in the Ogaden: Implications for Siyaad's Role in Somali History', *The Journal of Modern African Studies* 17/1, 1979, 95–115.

Larmer, M. 'Local Conflicts in a Transnational War: The Katangese Gendarmes and the Shaba Wars of 1977–78', *Cold War History* 13/1, 2013, 89–108.

Lefebvre, J. *Arms for the Horn: U.S. Security Policy in Ethiopia and Somalia, 1953–1991*, Pittsburgh, 1991.

Lefebvre, J. 'Middle East Conflicts and Middle Level Power Intervention in the Horn of Africa', *The Middle East Journal* 50/3, 1996, 387–404.

Mamdani, M. *Good Muslim, Bad Muslim: America, the Cold War, and the Roots of Terror*, New York, 2004.

Mitchell, N. *Jimmy Carter in Africa: Race and the Cold War*, Stanford, 2016.

Patman, R.G. *The Soviet Union in the Horn of Africa: The Diplomacy of Intervention and Disengagement*, Cambridge, 2009.

Ramazani, R.K. 'Iran's Search for Regional Cooperation', *Middle East Journal* 30/2, 1976, 173–186.

Ramazani, R.K. 'Iran and the Arab–Israeli Conflict', *Middle East Journal* 32/4, 1978, 413–428.

Saikal, A. *The Rise and Fall of the Shah: Iran from Autocracy to Religious Rule*, Princeton, 2009.

Steele, R. 'Two Kings of Kings: Iran–Ethiopia Relations under the Shah and Haile Selassie', *The International History Review* 43/6, 2021, 1375–1392.

Steele, R. 'The Keur Farah Pahlavi Project and Iranian–Senegalese Relations in the 1970s', *Iranian Studies* 54/1–2, 2021, 169–192.

Steele, R. *The Shah's Imperial Celebrations of 1971: Nationalism, Culture and Politics in Late Pahlavi Iran*, London, 2020.

Tareke, G. 'The Ethiopia–Somalia War of 1977 Revisited', *The International Journal of African Historical Studies* 33/3, 2000, 635–667.

Tareke, G. *The Ethiopian Revolution: War in the Horn of Africa*, New Haven, 2009.

Woodroofe, L.P., *Buried in the Sands of the Ogaden: The United States, the Horn of Africa, and the Demise of Détente*, Kent, USA, 2013.

Woodroofe, L.P. ed. *FRUS, 1977–1980, vol. 17, Horn of Africa, Part 1*, Washington, DC, 2016.

Woodroofe, L.P. ed. *FRUS, 1977–1980, vol. 17, Part 2, Sub-Saharan Africa*, Washington, DC, 2018.

Yordanov, R.A. *The Soviet Union and the Horn of Africa during the Cold War: Between Ideology and Pragmatism*, Lanham, 2016.

8

Global Civil Rights in Iran: Race, Gender, and Poverty

Firoozeh Kashani-Sabet

'Humanity never tires of being hopeful.'

Mohammad Ali Islami Nodushan, 1968

In 1968, with much anticipation, the Human Rights Conference opened in Iran, from 22 April until 13 May.[1] One hundred and twenty-three nations, along with several UN agencies, sent representatives to Tehran as participants in the conference. In at least one instance, the event was called a 'jihad' aimed at eliminating racism and social injustices in both national and international settings. Although Geneva, Switzerland, had originally been mentioned as a possible host to open this convention marking the twentieth anniversary of the UN's Universal Declaration of Human Rights, issued in 1948, Tehran attained that honour.[2] The change in venue likely reflected the evolving composition of the United Nations, whose membership had expanded to include many non-Western states since its inception. Iran invoked its civilisational legacy in upholding the first charter of

---

1 International Conference on Human Rights: Concludes with Adoption of Proclamation of Teheran 1968, United Nations Office of Public Information, New York.
2 *Ettela'at*, 3 Ordibehesht 1347/23 April 1968, 7.

Stamps from Human Rights Conference

human rights, as articulated and preserved in the Cyrus Cylinder.[3] Using 'Telex' technology, reporters promptly broadcast the conference abroad, vastly expanding its reach beyond the Middle East.[4] Intended to address inequalities in gender, wealth, and race, the gathering brought to Tehran many luminaries, including Burmese diplomat, U Thant, the first non-Western Secretary General of the United Nations. As the shah delivered his opening remarks (in French), his speech was simultaneously translated into multiple languages and broadcast via radio and television to an international audience of millions.[5]

Missing from the conference were representatives from Communist China and East Germany[6] – an indication that the conference had become politicised despite the 'universal' recognition of human rights. Iranian dissidents, including 'ulama, critical of the regime, were also absent from these proceedings.[7] At the time of the conference, Iranian student groups

3 *Ettela'at*, 3 Ordibehesht 1347/23 April 1968, 7.
4 *Ettela'at*, 2 Ordibehesht 1347/22 April 1968.
5 *Ettela'at*, 2 Ordibehesht 1347/22 April 1968, 17.
6 *Ettela'at*, 3 Ordibehesht 1347/23 April 1968, 1.
7 For example, see the works of anti-Pahlavi religious figure, Ali Hojjati Kermani, who published several articles on Islam and race in the 1960s: Ali Hojjati Kermani, 'Islam va Tab'izat-e Nezhadi: Lakeh-e Nang bar Daman-e Tamaddon-e Konuni', *Dars-hayi az Maktab Islam*, 4th Year, No. 3, Ordibehesht 1341/Spring 1962, 38–43; idem., 'Islam va Tab'izat-e Nezhadi: Farziyeh-e Afsaneh-e Nezhadi Cheguneh beh Vojud Amad?' *Dars-hayi az Maktab-e Islam*, 4th Year, No. 6, Tir 1341 (Summer

abroad were networking to win the support of European leftists in their campaign against the shah, as this conference was not a place for them to air their grievances. In 1966, French philosopher Jean-Paul Sartre intervened by writing to support political prisoners sentenced to death in Iran.[8] Sartre had formed a committee in Paris, which had included Simone de Beauvoir, among others, to defend the rights of Iranian detainees, many communist or socialist in orientation.[9] Just months after the conference, in November 1968, Sartre's committee reported that several Iranian political prisoners had been tortured and deprived of due process.[10] These parallel and contradictory discourses challenged the authenticity of the Pahlavi state as host of the first Human Rights conference of the United Nations.

The Tehran conference invariably was compared with Bandung in Indonesia, organised and convened in 1955 by Sukarno (Koesno Sosrodihardjo) of Indonesia and Jawaharlal Nehru of India.[11] Both of those countries were emerging from colonialism and faced the complicated task of state-building. By contrast, Pahlavi Iran was being led by an autocratic figure that an Anglo-American sponsored coup had placed once again on the Iranian throne in 1953. Western-educated and firmly allied with America and the West in the Cold War, the shah's politics seemingly flouted the anti-imperialist ethos of the era.[12]

Iran's reporting of the Bandung conference indicated that some members of the United Nations had concerns that the gathering was an attempt to

---

1962), 35–37; idem., 'Manteq-e Tarafdaran-e Afsaneh-e Nezhadi', *Dars-hayi az Maktab Islam*, 4th Year, No. 12, Dey 1341 (Winter 1962/1963), 66–70, which talks about Nazi policies; and idem., *Dars-hayi az Maktab Islam*, 5th Year, No. 3, Azar 1342 (Novemer/ December 1963), which discusses among other matters race in America and references Harry Haywood's *Negro Liberation,* published in 1948.

8 Claudia Castiglioni. '"Anti-Imperialism of Fools"?: The European Intellectual Left and The Iranian Revolution', *The Age of Aryamehr: Late Pahlavi Iran and Its Global Entanglements*, ed. Roham Alvandi, 2018, 233.

9 'Jean-Paul Sartre constitue un comité pour la défense des prisonniers politiques iraniens', *Le Monde*, 22 March 1966, 6.

10 'Des détenus auraient été torturés récemment à Téhéran', *Le Monde*, 11 November 1968, 4.

11 For one such reference in a Persian newspaper, see *Ettela'at*, 5 Ordibehesht 1347/25 April 1968; and *Ettela'at*, 11 Ordibehesht 1347/1 May 1968, 6.

12 Gerard McCann, 'Where Was the *Afro* in Afro-Asian Solidarity? Africa's "Bandung Moment" in 1950s Asia', *Journal of World History* 30/1–2, 2019, 89–90.

create a separate bloc of countries or that it was giving communist China a virtual free rein in Asia. According to this report, however, the main source of opposition stemmed from the belief that the countries at Bandung were attempting to wrest power away from the West.[13] The participants reserved the right to shed light on racist practices in countries such as the United States and South Africa. In 1954, although the United States had passed the monumental Supreme Court decision, *Brown vs. the Board of Education*, which outlawed segregation in schools, 'the process of ending the Jim Crow laws in the American South was long and difficult'.[14] Countries such as South Africa and the United States thus adopted a defensive posture vis-à-vis the conference because of the prevalence of racial discrimination in their communities.

In his remarks Jalal 'Abdoh, the head of the Iranian delegation, remarked that communists had devised a 'new colonialism' (*este 'mar-e jadid*) through their ideology and militarism. 'Abdoh also referred to the situation in Palestine and requested that conference participants focus attention on it.[15]

Although Iran had a limited presence at the Bandung conference, its significance reverberated in the country in other ways. One of the notable attendees at Bandung was the American writer and activist Richard Wright. Born in Mississippi, Wright documented his difficult childhood, as well as the cruelty inflicted upon Black Americans, in his *oeuvres*. An observer at the conference, he reflected on the significance of the gathering: 'Only brown, black, and yellow men who had long been made agonizingly self-conscious, under the rigors of colonial rule, of their race and their religion could have felt the need for such a meeting.'[16] Upon Wright's death in 1960, an obituary of his appeared in an Iranian literary journal, *Sokhan*, which referenced his major works, including *Uncle Tom's Children* (*bacheh-haye Amu Tom*), available in 1938; *Native Boy* (*pesar-e*

---

13 National Library and Archives of Iran (hereafter NLAI), 296/018986, 'Konferans-e Bandung', Tir 1334/June-July 1955, 1–2.
14 This statement comes from the official website of the Office of the US Historian, US State Department: https://history.state.gov/milestones/1953-1960/bandung-conf.
15 NLAI, 296/018986, 'Konferans-e Bandung', Tir 1334/June-July 1955, 10.
16 Richard Wright and Gunnar Myrdal, *The Color Curtain: A Report on the Bandung Conference*, 1956, 14.

bumi), published in 1940; and his memoir, *Black Boy* (*pesarak-e siyah*), which appeared in 1945.[17]

A translated excerpt from his work, *Uncle Tom's Children*, comprising the first and third stories, appeared in an Iranian literary periodical in 1961. The work offered an intimate account of personal encounters with racism and slavery in America – subjects little known or scarcely explored in post-WWII Iran. As Wright's Iranian translator, Mahmud Kianoush and/ or the periodical's editors, explained, 'In these stories, one law is evident, and that is Blacks not having any rights. The Black must suffer, perform the most arduous tasks, receive the most insignificant rewards,' yet still become 'the prey of the hatred of the whites without giving them the smallest excuse'.[18] Iran's limited participation in Bandung thus should not be interpreted as a disengagement from Third World concerns or causes, which involved combating racism and other forms of discrimination. While the shah was wary of Nasser, and likely remembered Prime Minister Mosaddeq's warm embrace in Cairo in 1951, he did not represent the opinions of many Iranians of the era. Although the shah reprised similar themes in the 1968 Tehran conference, parallel discourses on race and inequality had prevailed in intellectual circles that quietly eschewed official Pahlavi

---

17 *Sokhan*, vol. 11/7–12 (November 1960–April 1961), 1115. For other relevant works, see: *Sokhan*, 'Jahan-e Danesh va Honar', 596, on Richard Wright. Also, A. Khwajeh Nuri, ed., *Mardan-e Khodsakhteh*, 2nd edition, 1976. The first edition was published in 1335/1956.

18 Richard Wright, translated by Mahmud Kianoush, 'Bacheh-haye Amu Tom' [*Uncle Tom's Children*], *Ketab-e Hafteh*, 23 Mehr 1340/15 October 1961, 10 and for a complete account, 9–91. The title hearkens back to Harriet Beecher Stowe's anti-slavery novel, *Uncle Tom's Cabin*, published in 1852. See my forthcoming essay for an analysis of this work regarding discussions of race in the Iranian context. The illustrations by Morteza Momayez deserve analysis as well. For another Wright excerpt and a brief biography, see Richard Wright, translated by Amir Hossain Jahanbegloo, 'Mardi keh beh Shikagow Raft', *Negin*, Bahman 1345/ February 1967, No. 21, 10–11 and 64–66. Jahanbegloo had also translated a story from Wright's *Eight Men*, 'Mardi keh Zir-e Zamin Zendegi Mikard' ['The Man who Lived Underground'] in 1335/1956. The story was part of an unpublished novel that has recently been released: Clifford Thompson, '"The Man Who Lived Underground" Review: Richard Wright's Lost Novel; The Work The Author Considered His Finest at Last Sees the Light of Day', *Wall Street Journal (Online)*, 23 April 2021.

politics. Some of these conversations became Islamist in orientation, while others such as the above discussion about Richard Wright maintained a non-religious tone.

Just five years before the human rights conference, on 5 June 1963 (15 Khordad 1342), Iran had experienced riots led by a religious figure, Ayatollah Ruhollah Khomeini. The clashes led to violence from both sides that the state police put down. The opposition was then subjected to surveillance and silenced with the eventual exile from Iran of Ayatollah Khomeini in 1964. To sceptics, Tehran was therefore an odd choice as the site for the first United Nations Conference on human rights – a concept that had gained in urgency after the totalitarian excesses of Nazi Germany.[19] Cynics rightly perceived these ironies as the shah stepped onto an international stage to advocate for human rights.

The conference was a mixed bag: on the one hand, an increasing number of nations participated in it as compared with the Bandung Conference of 1955.[20] On the other hand, most of the countries represented at the conference were dictatorships, like Iran itself. As some scholars have concluded, at Tehran 'even benign platitudes were dissent and division, and the substantive results of the conference far less obvious'.[21] The conference participants could not agree on much, and the Tehran daily newspaper *Ettela 'at* sardonically labelled the gathering the 'conference of indecision' (*bi tasmimi*).[22] At its conclusion, the Proclamation of Teheran (sic) reaffirmed the principle of international human rights and a commitment to upholding 'fundamental freedoms'.[23]

Like many countries of the non-aligned movement, Iran had endured imperial exploitation, but without becoming a formal colony of any foreign country. It had facilitated the Allied victory in the Second World War but

---

19 Ned Richardson-Little, *The Human Rights Dictatorship: Socialism, Global Solidarity and Revolution in East Germany*, 2020, Chapter 1.

20 Roland Burke, *Decolonization and the Evolution of International Human Rights*, 2010, 96.

21 Roland Burke, 'From Individual Rights to National Development: The First UN International Conference on Human Rights, Tehran, 1968', *Journal of World History* 19/3, 2008, 275.

22 *Ettela 'at*, 11 Ordibehesht 1347/1 May 1968, 6.

23 United Nations, *Final Act of the International Conference on Human Rights, Teheran, 22 April to 13 May 1968*, 1968.

had received little compensation for its sacrifices. Five years after the departure of foreign armies, in 1951, Dr Mohammad Mosaddeq led the fight for oil nationalisation. His removal from office and subsequent house arrest doomed the shah and the country. The shah suffered from a crisis of legitimacy after assuming the formidable task of following in the footsteps of Mosaddeq, the hero of Iran's oil nationalisation fight. While the shah had supported oil nationalisation, he had to defer to a seasoned politician who spearheaded the successful takeover and carried gravitas with the public. Unsure of his mandate, the shah left the country during the coup against Mosaddeq and returned a deeply compromised politician and an autocrat. Between 1953 and 1963, elections were held sporadically and at times post-poned or cancelled. Although the shah had put forward a platform of social reform known as the White Revolution, its results were mixed and did not bring about the broad redistribution of wealth and income that it promised. In fact, land reform was pursued unevenly in the north and south, turning many former landowners against the shah. The differences in the execution of land reform also enabled large 'agribusinesses' to develop.[24]

The conference remained silent on these domestic problems. However, it opened public debate in Iran on global human rights in ways not pre-viously experienced. Interpretations of the Tehran conference as lacking import call for further analysis, as do assessments of the shah, who was frequently compared with a panoply of other more popular world leaders of that generation, most of whom did not always display egalitarian politi-cal tendencies either. For instance, neither Sukarno nor Nehru would be remembered as democratic heads of state. Likewise, the domestic legacy of Gamal Abdel Nasser, the shah's nemesis, has been reassessed in light of his policies against the Muslim Brotherhood and others.[25] The measure of the

---

24 Mohammad Javad Amad, *Agriculture, Poverty and Reform in Iran (RLE Iran D)*, 2011, Chapter 5. Also, K.S. McLachlan, 'Land Reform in Iran', *The Cambridge History of Iran*, vol. 1, ed. W.B. Fisher, 1968, 684–714. For a fascinating analysis of recent findings, see Kevan Harris and Zep Kalb, 'Pen to the Tiller: Land Reform and Social Mobility Across the 1979 Iranian Revolution', *Journal of Agrarian Change* 19/3, 465–486.

25 Sara Salem, *Anticolonial Afterlives in Egypt: The Politics of Hegemony*, 2020, Chapter 2. Fawaz A. Gerges, *Making the Arab World: Nasser, Qutb, and the Clash That Shaped the Middle East*, 2018.

conference cannot simply be gauged by what it produced beyond the sessions, which admittedly would be difficult to quantify, but also by what it generated intellectually in Iran itself. For example, as a result of these conversations, the Ministry of Education in Iran vowed to incorporate human rights discourses into secondary school education. Subjects included the history of creation of the United Nations and the Universal Declaration of Human Rights.[26] The Iranian planners of the conference also requested that an Iranian translator be on hand to provide simultaneous Persian translations of foreign speeches (likely in French and/or English). In this way, Iran prepared to integrate and disseminate international human rights discourses in ways sanctioned by the state and that eschewed open attacks on the regime, which persisted as the most ironic legacy of the conference.[27]

In the aftermath of the conference, UN Human Rights prizes were awarded to several individuals, including posthumously Eleanor Roosevelt of the United States (d. 1962); Albert John Luthuli of South Africa (d. 1967); René Cassin of France (d. 1976); and Dr. Mehranguiz Manoutchehrian (d. 2000), lawyer and senator in Iran.[28] The recipients of these awards had played crucial roles in enabling human rights discourses and legislation through their activism. Notably, Eleanor Roosevelt had served as chairperson of the committee that drafted the Universal Declaration of Human Rights. The committee included the participation of other leading women such as Hansa Jivraj Mehta of India (d. 1995); Minerva Bernadino of the Dominican Republic (d. 1998); and Begum Shaista Suhrawardy Ikramullah of Pakistan (d. 2000), among others.[29]

Decolonisation (in Persian: *este 'mar zeda 'i* or *zedd-e este 'mari*) gained currency as a concept among the Iranian literati in the 1960s and 1970s.

---

26 NLAI, 297/48972, Vezarat-e Amuzesh va Parvaresh, 18 Ordibehesht 1348/8 May 1969.

27 NLAI, 297/48972, Vezarat-e Omur-e Kharejeh, 'Surat-e Jalaseh-e Sous-Commission-e Tahiyeh-e Barnameh-ye Marasem-e Sal-e Huquq-e Bashar', 10 Dey 1346/31 December 1967.

28 'United Nations Human Rights Prize': https://www.ohchr.org/en/about-us/what-we-do/un-human-rights-prize/previous-recipients.

29 United Nations, 'Women who Shaped the Universal Declaration': https://www.un.org/en/observances/human-rights-day/women-who-shaped-the-universal-declaration. Also, Rebecca Adami and Daniel Plesch, *Women and the UN: A New History of Women's International Human Rights*, 2021.

Iranian activists invoking different political ideologies focused on concepts such as 'Westernitis' (*gharbzadegi*) and the fight for political parity encompassed in critiques of imperialism and colonialism.[30] It is telling that such intellectuals (e.g., Jalal Al Ahmad and Simin Daneshvar), some of whom the United States had courted, played no overt role in the conference. This chapter expounds on the significance of this global movement by focusing on three themes that dominated the Human Rights Conference of 1968 in Tehran as a seminal moment for these social platforms: namely, race, gender, and economic inequality.

The conference has received the attention of diplomatic historians, who offer important and interesting insights about its international dimensions and state-to-state interactions. In addition, non-governmental organisations (hereafter NGOs) that had participated in the conference perceived the shortcomings of the UN as a venue for human rights activism.[31] NGOs were permitted to attend the conference as observers, not presenters. However, they were allowed to distribute written statements representing their positions. The NGOs remained critical of the Tehran conference for its failure to provide implementation policies. As Seán Macbride of the International Commission of Jurists observed, the 'discussions were constantly sidetracked into polemics'.[32] Still, Macbride concluded that despite the shortcomings of the conference, 'some useful work was done by it in regard to Women's Rights, Apartheid, Education and Economic and Social Rights'.[33]

Iran's experience as host nation has not been fully explored, particularly beyond the figures representing the elite.[34] Nor has the available literature

---

30 Hamid Dabashi, *Theology of Discontent*, 1993; Negin Nabavi, *Intellectual Trends in Twentieth-Century Iran: A Critical Survey*, 2003; Mehrzad Borujerdi, *Iranian Intellectuals and the West: The Tormented Triumph of Nativism*, 1996.
31 Samuel Moyn, *The Last Utopia: Human Rights in History*, 2010, 126.
32 Seán Macbride, 'Introduction: The Promise of Human Rights Year', *Journal of the International Commission of Jurists* 9/1, Part Two, June 1968, ii.
33 Macbride, 'Introduction: The Promise of Human Rights Year', iii.
34 Roland Burke, 'From Individual Rights to National Development: The First UN International Conference on Human Rights, Tehran, 1968, *Journal of World History* 19/3, September 2008, 275–296. Also, Roland Burke, *Decolonization and the Evolution of International Human Rights*, 2010. Andrew S. Thompson, 'Tehran 1968 and Reform of the UN Human Rights System', *Journal of Human Rights* 14/1, 2015,

sufficiently considered the significance of the moment for a Middle East that was shaken in the aftermath of the Six-Day War between Israel and its Arab neighbours, who expressed alarm over the Israeli occupation of territories acquired in 1967. Egyptian politician Sayyid Nufal, assistant secretary of the Arab League, attended the conference and gave voice to these concerns. In an interview with Iranian journalist Mostafa Ja'fari, Nufal had also reportedly stated that changing the name of the Persian Gulf to the Arabian Gulf was 'ludicrous' (*mozhek*), especially as he acknowledged Iran's support for its Arab neighbours in the United Nations.[35] State representatives tried to smooth over these tensions as the politics of decolonisation imbued the convention once it opened.[36]

Racial Inequality and Genocide

Political disagreements threatened to disrupt the unity of cause over the Palestinian refugee crisis as Arabs tried to maintain pressure on the international community to consider the far-reaching impact of the 1967 war. Attention shifted to parallel issues of social significance and humanitarian necessity, which sought to transcend politics – most notably, racism, hunger, poverty, and illiteracy. The actions and existence of the apartheid regime only magnified the divide between the poor and the greed of a minority ruling elite.[37] Iranian intellectuals had followed the travails of a young Nelson Mandela following his arrest in August 1962. At that time,

---

84–100; International Conference on Human Rights, Tehran, 1968. *External Affairs*, 20/6, 251; Sarah B. Snyder, 'The 1968 International Year for Human Rights: A Missed Opportunity in the United States', *Diplomatic History* 42/5, November 2018, 831–858; Robert Kolb, 'Human Rights Law and International Humanitarian Law Between 1945 and the Aftermath of the Teheran Conference of 1968', *Research Handbook on Human Rights and Humanitarian Law*, ed. Robert Kolb and Gloria Gaggioli, 2013, 35–52.
35 *Ettela'at,* 4 Ordibehesht 1347/24 April 1968, 1 and 4.
36 *Ettela'at,* 8 Ordibehesht 1347/28 April 1968. Also, *Ettela'at,* 3 Ordibehesht 1347/23 April 1968.
37 Diana Wylie, *Starving on a Full Stomach: Hunger and the Triumph of Cultural Racism in Modern South Africa*, 2001. For a long-term perspective, see Rhiannon Stephens, 'Poverty's Pasts: A Case for Longue Durée Studies', *The Journal of African History* 59/3, 2018, 399–409.

Mandela was facing two charges, one for inciting unrest by organizing a strike, and the second for travelling without valid documents. Mandela had left South Africa to attend the Pan African Freedom Movement conference. Months later, when he returned, he was apprehended and sentenced to five years in prison in November 1962.[38] In a piece titled, 'The Saga of a Black Man', (*hemaseh-e yek siyah*), excerpts from Mandela's statement in court were translated into Persian, notably this comment[39]: 'I want at once to make it clear that I am no racialist [*nizhadi*], and I detest racialism, because I regard it as a barbaric thing, whether it comes from a black man or from a white man. The terminology that I am going to employ will be compelled on me by the nature of the application I am making.'[40] The translation of Mandela's statement contributed to Iranian understanding of the intricacies of race relations outside of Iran. In this way, Iranians could begin to fathom Mandela's fight against racism and the struggles of Black South Africans through his unique vantage point. The subject of racism in South Africa found expression in another Persian article on the history of Western imperialism there and the development of South Africa's apartheid practices, which extended well beyond residential and economic matters to other spheres such as sports, cinemas, theatres, and restaurants.[41]

The focus on global racial struggles defined the early sessions of the conference. Two countries, the United States and South Africa, were confronting intensified domestic unrest as their Black communities demanded political and economic enfranchisement. Roy Wilkins, as representative of the United States, delivered a speech in which he referenced the shah's White Revolution, which had brought reforms in literacy, land reform, and women's rights, among measures in other domains. America seemed pleased with the reception of Wilkins's speech, which acknowledged the

---

38 Philip Bonner, 'The Antinomies of Nelson Mandela', in Rita Barnard, ed., *The Cambridge Companion to Nelson Mandela*, 2014, 44.

39 'Hemaseh-e Yek Siyah', *Ketab-e Hafteh*, 9, 1341/1962, 182.

40 To access Mandela's court statement online, refer to this site: https://www.un.org/en/events/mandeladay/court_statement_1962.shtml.

41 Hushang Moqtader, 'Tab'izat-e Nezhadi dar Ifriqa-e Jonubi', *Khirad va Kushesh*, No. 2, Tir 1348 (April 1969), 132–143.

Roy Wilkins, US Representative at the Human Rights Conference

social struggles in the United States without adopting a belligerent tone.[42] As Wilkins recalled, 'The black man soon found that the promises of constitution and law, as in so many other countries, were illusory.' In 1947, President Harry Truman's Civil Rights Commission had contained the then revolutionary sentence, 'Racial segregation must be eliminated from American life.' Wilkins affirmed the activism of Dr Martin Luther King, as well as the murder of his young colleague, Medgar Evers (d. 1963) – first field officer of the NAACP in Mississippi – as crucial events that 'destroyed apathy' toward racial discrimination.[43] Yet he remained hopeful that progress and freedom could be achieved and realised for Black Americans: 'Americans have discovered that poverty – often the end product of discrimination – cripples men .... There is not the slightest doubt in my mind about my country's glittering future for all Americans – black men and white, Indians, Protestants, Catholics, Jews, nonbelievers.'[44] To appeal to his Iranian audience, Wilkins also drew a comparison between the fundamental teachings of the prophet, Zoroaster, and the ethos of the

42 Snyder, 'The 1968 International Year for Human Rights', 15–17.
43 United States Mission to the United Nations, *Press Releases*, 'Statement by Mr. Roy Wilkins, Chairman of the United States Delegation at the International Conference on Human Rights, Teheran, Iran, April 24, 1968', 1968.
44 United States. President of the United States, *To Deepen Our Commitment: Interim Report*, 1968, 26.

Universal Declaration of Human Rights, adopted by the United Nations General Assembly in 1948. As Wilkins averred,

> The Universal Declaration points the way for ordered liberty. It encompasses two of the abiding principles of the great Iranian teacher, Zoroaster.[45]

The conference, coming hard on the heels of the tragic assassination of Dr Martin Luther King on 4 April 1968 in Memphis, Tennessee, served as a sobering reminder of the labours that lay ahead in realising the ideals of racial equality and universal enfranchisement. At the suggestion of Uganda's representative, the first session of the conference observed a minute of silence in honour of Dr King.[46] 'My country's flags are still at half-mast mourning the assassination of my friend', Wilkins lamented. It was meaningful to link Dr King's demise with the ideals of Tehran's international gathering, which shone a necessary light on racial inequality worldwide. Many Iranians likely only had a passing and inadequate knowledge of the intense struggles that African Americans had historically faced. For Wilkins, Iran's role as host of the conference gave global significance to Dr King's struggles: 'His life had purpose and his death will have meaning if we adopt all three of Zoroaster's principles which I now leave with you: "Good thoughts, good words, good deeds."'[47] Wilkins's speech was summed up and featured in the daily Persian newspaper *Ettela 'at*, which took to heart his conclusion that the only way to prevent racial clashes in the United States was to prevent Black political exclusion.[48]

For his engagement with racial issues, as well as his dignified stance, Wilkins received positive feedback from other American leaders. Durwood A. Busse, who had directed the Alborz Foundation, wrote to Wilkins that he 'appreciated your thoughtful presentation at the Iran-America Society'. Busse seemed to value Wilkins's deliberate tone in 'interpreting the racial

---

45 History Vault, Public relations for NAACP, Folder: 009057-002-0388, AmEmbassy Athens for VOA KOHL, Tehran, 23 April 1968.
46 *Final Act*, 1–2.
47 History Vault, Public relations for NAACP, Folder: 009057-002-0388, AmEmbassy Athens for VOA KOHL, Tehran, 23 April 1968.
48 *Ettela 'at*, 5 Ordibehesht 1347/25 April 1968, 6

problems which continue to face the USA, while also pointing out the forward strides which have been made during the past 20 years'.[49] For Wilkins's position was undoubtedly a precarious and sensitive one. On the one hand, he represented the long-disenfranchised community of Black Americans, and on the other, he stood as the diplomatic representative of his country, at a time when the United States was reckoning with its history of racial discrimination and its unpopular war in Vietnam. Given this complicated international picture, US Ambassador Armin H. Meyer and David H. Popper, head of the US delegation to the Iran Human Rights Conference, similarly expressed their gratitude for Wilkins's role in Tehran.[50]

America's social struggles reverberated in other ways. For Wilkins was not the only speaker to reference Dr King. Abdul Rahman Pazhwak, Afghanistan's representative, who had served in the UN, also highlighted the international significance of Dr King's leadership and asserted that the activist's contributions to humanity would never be forgotten.[51] Most likely endeavouring to please his Iranian hosts, Pazhwak then appropriately referenced the well-known couplet by Saadi, 'Human beings are members of one body/In creation they are of one mould', to emphasise this point. The famous couplet asserted the unity of all humanity, whose survival depended on every member of its community.[52]

The presence of Wilkins as US representative to the Tehran Human Rights Conference had enormous significance beyond its symbolic value of a Black diplomat engaging a host nation in race relations. Many Iranians of the era had proved naïve, if not downright ignorant and uncaring, about the abuses of global slavery, segregation, and apartheid as it then raged in the United States, South Africa, and elsewhere.[53] The conference broached conversations in Iran about civil and human rights in a global

---

49 Durwood A. Busse, Commission Representative in Iran, to Roy Wilkins, 29 April 1968.

50 Armin H. Meyer, US Ambassador, to Roy Wilkins, Executive Director, NAACP, 15 May 1968. Also, David H. Popper, Head of the US Delegation to the Human Rights Conference to Roy Wilkins, Executive Director, NAACP, 11 May 1968.

51 *Ettela'at*, 4 Ordibehesht 1347/24 April 1968, 6.

52 *Ettela'at*, 4 Ordibehesht 1347/24 April 1968, 6.

53 Firoozeh Kashani-Sabet, 'The Anti-Aryan Moment: Decolonization, Diplomacy, and Race in Late Pahlavi Iran', *International Journal of Middle East Studies* 53/4, November 2021, 691–702; and idem, *Heroes to Hostages*, Chapters 10 and 12.

context. As one writer found, the conference enabled the pursuit of anti-racist initiatives and laws intended to protect many of the world's dispossessed and included recognition for the dignity of 'displaced persons' (*avaregan*) as important steps toward equality and freedom.[54] The struggles of countries such as Angola and Mozambique to achieve equality also made headlines, as the representative of the Organisation of African Unity provided compelling statistics and documentation about South Africa's harsh treatment of its Black community.[55] Differences of opinion and indecision characterised the conference sessions. Tanzania's representative complained about the absence of Chinese participation and opposed the ways in which Cold War politics had seeped into the conference, though Ukraine also had independent representatives there.[56] Algeria's emissary Muhammad Yazid, while thanking the audience for its support over the assassination attempt against Colonel Houari Boumédiène, delivered an extemporaneous speech in which he insisted that human rights cannot be granted, but ought to be seized. He lamented the killing of Patrice Lumumba in Congo, Ernesto 'Che' Guevara in Bolivia, and Dr Martin Luther King in the United States as personal sacrifices of prominent figures in the fight for human rights.[57]

Among Iranian intellectuals, the conference inspired a spate of short articles. Following the gathering, Zahra Shahriar Naghavi commemorated the launch of Human Rights Day in December 1948 and penned a short piece on its relevance. Naghavi, who was one of the attendees at the 1968 conference, applauded the efforts of the United Nations to eliminate advantages based on 'colour and race' (*rang va nasl*). She emphasised the importance of protecting the rights of victims of war, so endemic to the Middle East. Wars, she argued, whether domestic or international, eroded the liberties of those caught in the crossfire. Naghavi stressed the need for medical and technological cooperation for the advancement of human rights. A few years later, another writer investigated the implications of the international human rights discourse in other facets of Iranian legal life

---

54 'Darbareh-e Huquq-e Bashar', *Nashriyeh-e Huquq-e Emruz*, No. 23, 31 Ordibehesht 1347/21 May 1968, 6–7.
55 *Ettela'at*, 5 Ordibehesht 1347/25 April 1968, 6.
56 *Ettela'at*, 4 Ordibehesht 1347/24 April 1968, 6.
57 *Ettela'at*, 4 Ordibehesht 1347/24 April 1968, 15.

and in the protection of civil liberties such as: the right to choose a nationality; marriage; seeking refugee status; freedoms of religion, expression, and thought; and the right to peaceful protest, among others – all subjects reinforced at the Tehran gathering.[58] Yet few overt criticisms emerged over Iran's failures to uphold some of these ideals. Instead, the conference and the domestic discourse on human rights focused on global crises, from South Africa to Vietnam, as well as gender rights and poverty.

Tehran buzzed with curiosity about the meaning of human rights. From the Minister of Justice Manuchehr Parto to other political representatives, speeches circulated broadly about the meaning of human rights. These topics had likely not excited such broad public interest since the Constitutional Revolution of 1906, when conversations about individual liberties had dominated public discourse as Iran convened its first parliament and drafted its constitution.[59] How fitting and symbolic, then, that the auditorium housing the assembly was none other than the east wing of the Majles (parliament) building.[60] But the political landscape in 1968 was vastly different from the one that had given birth to the country's first constitution. By then, Iran had become an entrenched monarchy that paid only lip-service to the much-vaunted parliament it had founded more than half a century earlier. Iranian parliamentarians acknowledged the Human Rights Conference as a milestone for their country, but one with historical precedence as they remembered the legacy of Cyrus the Great. The debates at the conference focused on the global landscape that necessitated social change, not the domestic one, which appeared, on its surface, racially and socially integrated. Thus, Majles representatives offered a whimsical picture of unity and tolerance in late Pahlavi Iran – a country, they argued, that had granted equal rights under the law to its citizens regardless of ethnicity, gender, race, or religious persuasion.[61] In reality, many

---

58 Saideh Farasiyun, 'Huquq-e Bashar va Jahan-e Emruz', *Nashriyeh Kanun* 168, Azar 1352/December 1973, 33.

59 Firoozeh Kashani-Sabet, 'Hallmarks of Humanism: Hygiene and Love of Homeland in Qajar Iran', *American Historical Review* 105/4, October 2000, 1171–1203.

60 *Ettela'at*, 3 Ordibehesht 1347/23 April 1968, 10.

61 Mashruh-e Mozakerat-e Majles, 22nd Majles, Session 55, 5 Ordibehest 1347/25 April 1968.

inequities existed in ways that a mere recognition of Iran's laws could not document. The Majles lacked the participation of dissidents and members of Afro-Iranian communities, though the Baluch had small representation. Still, reference was made to the racial struggles elsewhere, as in Rhodesia, where 'a rapacious minority' (*yek aqaliyat-e motejavez*) was killing its majority citizens based on race and colour.[62]

Majles representatives no doubt perceived the obligatory pressure to honour the shah's sister, Princess Ashraf Pahlavi, in their grandiose pronouncements. Implicit in these debates was a consideration of whether the monarchy as an antiquated mode of governance could effectively maintain the reins of the power while at the same alleviating blatant manifestations of inequality such as poverty and political inclusion. Despite embracing socially relevant causes, the shah persistently faced a crisis of legitimacy throughout his rule that made it difficult for him to trust or to rely on the institutions of governance. Although these foundations existed for the purpose of bringing legitimacy to the political process, the shah did not manage the political factions effectively or find a way to share power productively. After the coup, the elections were frequently tainted with cries of corruption and at times suspended. Though imperfect, Iran's constitution and parliament could have enabled the process of correcting electoral irregularities and addressing inequalities that had been overlooked by the original constitutionalists. By invoking these possibilities, some Majles deputies tried to look past the limitations of their country's political process during the conference, including monarchical overreach.

For the Iranian state and literary public, this gathering proved a monumental event despite achieving few concrete measures to eradicate world hunger, racism, or gender inequality. The conference provided a global and domestic forum for the appraisal of human rights abuses. The majority of Iranians, in a country with a population of over 20 million at that time, had most probably not travelled to global hubs of racial tension such as the United States, South Africa, Rhodesia, or Haiti.[63] Outside of the capital, few had likely interacted with individuals or communities of African or

---

62 Ibid.
63 Estimate of Iran's population by decade: https://www.worlddata.info/asia/iran/populationgrowth.php.

East Asian descent. As a consequence, the conference and its coverage in the press contributed significantly to the public's engagement with global social crises on the subjects of gender inequalities, food scarcity, and racial discrimination. Scholars have investigated different aspects of the human rights discourse in Iran, but the research landscape, to date, has not highlighted the interaction of these three key social challenges and their impact in Iran.[64]

The conference was notable for bringing face-to-face individuals who hailed from countries offering different experiences of decolonisation, from the coloniser to the de-coloniser. For example, following the speech of British diplomat Frank Roberts, in which he noted that those who were hungry could not be considered free, Ghana's representative delivered a speech about the horrors of apartheid in South Africa and then requested that the conference take actionable decisions (*tasmimat-e ejra'i*) against it. The most 'heated moment' came from the representative of Tanzania, also about apartheid in South Africa, and the excesses of this systemic racial discrimination. He lambasted the representatives of those countries who either tacitly or actively supported this injustice, warning that such gatherings lacked significance if they were not simultaneously accompanied by demonstrable social change and anti-discriminatory policies.[65] In a similar vein, Jamaica's representative focused on racial inequalities in Rhodesia and Portugal.

---

64 Here, my work departs from the scholarship of several scholars whose excellent research investigates other aspects of the politics of human rights in late Pahlavi Iran: Golnar Nikpour, 'Claiming Human Rights: Iranian Political Prisoners and the Making of a Transnational Movement, 1963–1979', *Humanity: An International Journal of Human Rights, Humanitarianism, and Development* 9/3, 2018, 363–388; Reza Afshari, *Human Rights in Iran: The Abuse of Cultural Relativism*, 2011; Roham Alvandi, 'The Age of Aryamehr: Late Pahlavi Iran and its Global Entanglements', Lecture at the University of Pennsylvania, Middle East Center, 12 November 2018. This lecture was followed by another related talk on 11 February 2019, also at Penn, entitled: 'Human Rights and the Global Origins of the Iranian Revolution.' Elements of these talks appeared in print in Alvandi, 'Introduction', *The Age of Aryamehr*, ed. Roham Alvandi, 2018, 1–34.
65 *Ettela'at*, 8 Ordibehesht 1347/28 April 1968.

Non-State Discourses on Human Rights

The debate on human rights went beyond formal state-to-state discourses as Iran's liberals embraced the occasion to reflect on its legacy. Literary scholar Mohammad Ali Islami Nodushan provided philosophical reflections on the historical meaning and significance of human rights. He argued that its import transcended any contemporary historical moment, as demonstrated in several religious and literary texts.[66] He regarded America's Declaration of Independence, which drew on Enlightenment principles espousing the separation of religion and state, as 'the first document about human rights'.[67] At the same time, Nodushan acknowledged that America's and Europe's theoretical adoption of human rights had not eliminated racism (*tab 'iz nezhadi*) or social disparities in their communities.[68] The tenets of human rights became empty platitudes, he maintained, in part because so-called democratic countries paid only lip-service to them and did not investigate the root causes of despair.[69] For Nodushan, food insecurity and economic disparities above all required redress and ranked as the primary condition of human suffering and therefore of human rights. As he wrote, 'more than half of the people in the world are hungry', and in his view both international and domestic conditions had created this deplorable reality. Other social obstacles such as illiteracy, including among people of the same race, undermined the global realisation of human rights. Governments and citizens both had the obligation to uphold and pursue these ideals.[70] Fazl Allah Safa of Iran's Education Ministry (*Vezarat-e Amuzesh va Parvaresh*), took a different approach. He ruminated on ideas calling for the equality of all human beings, yet he bemoaned humanity's inability to realise equality despite technological innovations, especially in an era of atomic energy and space exploration.[71] These principled pronouncements eschewed the controversies that swirled

---

66 Mohammad Ali Islami Nodushan, 'Yadi az huquq-e bashar', *Yaghma* 2, Ordibehesht 1347/April 1968, 58.
67 Nodushan, 'Yadi az huquq-e bashar', 59.
68 Nodushan, 'Yadi az huquq-e bashar', 59.
69 Nodushan, 'Yadi az huquq-e bashar', 61–62.
70 Nodushan, 'Yadi az huquq-e bashar', 64.
71 Fazl Allah Safa, 'Sokhani chand piramun-e konferans-e huquq-e bashar', *Ta'lim va Tarbiyat* 199–200, 1347/1968, 9–13.

around the shah and his clampdown on domestic dissent in the aftermath of the 1953 coup.[72]

The 1960s – a decade of tumult around the world – witnessed the fallout of another significant gathering: the 1967 International Tribunal on War Crimes convened in Stockholm, Sweden and Roskilde, Denmark by British mathematician and philosopher Bertrand Russell to assess America's intervention in Vietnam. The Tribunal had attracted the likes of Jean-Paul Sartre and Simone de Beauvoir, staunch antiwar activists and leading philosophers. Sartre had a prominent role as the Tribunal's Executive President. Tribunal members had travelled abroad to Southeast Asia to gather evidence of war crimes. The Tribunal concluded its second session in December 1967 and found the United States guilty of war crimes for its killing of civilian populations.[73] Although the Tribunal lacked formal legal status, and functioned more as a non-governmental entity, it shone a bright light on America's military excesses during the Vietnam conflict. Antiwar activist and Tribunal member Carl Oglesby, who described the scenes at the Tribunal as 'circuses,' supported demonstrations against the war, including in October 1967 outside the Pentagon.[74] Other protest marches followed in London and elsewhere.[75] However, some criticised the Tribunal for its one-sided investigation of war crimes, without a similar scrutiny paid to the excesses of Communist factions.[76] More recently, the Tribunal's distinct 'anti-Americanism' has been highlighted, including the 'anti-American' rhetoric of human rights politics in the 1970s, which Iranian revolutionaries also embraced.[77] American antiwar activists were invited to participate. They included Kwame Ture – originally from Trinidad and more famously

---

72 'Shah of Iran Keeps Tight Lid on Opponents' Activity', *The Christian Science Monitor*, 1 December 1971.

73 Guenter Lewy, *America in Vietnam*, 1978, 311–312.

74 Carl Oglesby, *Ravens in the Storm: A Personal History of the 1960s Antiwar Movement*, 2008, 128–131 and 136–137.

75 Thomas Alan Schwartz, *Lyndon Johnson and Europe: In the Shadow of Vietnam*, 2003, 187.

76 Howard Brick and Christopher Phelps, *Radicals in America: The US Left since the Second World War*, 2015, 141.

77 Umberto Tulli, 'Wielding the Human Rights Weapon against the American Empire: The Second Russell Tribunal and Human Rights in Transatlantic Relations', *Journal of Transatlantic Studies* 19, 2021, 215–237.

known by the name, Stokely Carmichael – who had chaired the Student Nonviolent Coordinating Committee and was a member of the Black Panthers; Carl Oglesby, head of Students for a Democratic Society (SDS); and the poet James Baldwin.[78]

The Tribunal had garnered considerable international attention. It adopted a position on war crimes and attempted to determine whether US actions in Vietnam and Laos constituted genocide. The United States tried to counteract the impact of the Tribunal by using diplomacy and relying on state-to-state interactions to protect its positions. These resulted in France denying visas to some Tribunal members.[79] US efforts to muddy the work of the Tribunal paid off somewhat when a number of notable African leaders – Kenneth Kaunda of Zambia, Léopold Sédar Senghor of Senegal, Julius Nyerere of Tanzania, and Haile Selassie of Ethiopia – withdrew their support at the start of the Tribunal's first session. Nonetheless, by the end of the year, in December 1967, the Tribunal ultimately found the United States guilty of war crimes and genocide.[80] The Tehran Human Rights Conference came just months after these controversial international developments. In Tehran, too, discussion of the Vietnam War was unavoidable, but the conference did not adopt measures to censure the United States for its actions in Southeast Asia.

The Russell Tribunal had not escaped the attention of Iranian intellectuals. In the summer of 1968, after the Human Rights Conference had concluded, the progressive journal, *Jahan-e No*, explored human rights through the lens of genocide (*qatl-e 'am*), or mass murder. In two fascinating pieces, Iranian writers familiarised Iranian audiences with both the Tribunal and the concept of genocide, a term coined by Raphael Lemkin in 1944. In his writings Lemkin, a Polish lawyer and refugee, had stressed the necessity of preventing genocide – defined as the 'extermination of nations and ethnic groups as carried out by the invaders'. In particular,

---

78 Umberto Tulli, 'Wielding the Human Rights Weapon against the American Empire', *Journal of Transatlantic Studies* 19, 2021, 219–220. Also, Luke J. Stewart, 'Too Loud to Rise Above the Silence: The United States vs. the International War Crimes Tribunal, 1966–1967', *The Sixties* 11/1, 2018, 26–27.
79 Stewart, 'Too Loud to Rise Above the Silence', 26–27.
80 Stewart, 'Too Loud to Rise Above the Silence', 18 and 31.

Lemkin decried the mass killing of Jews in the Holocaust.[81] At the time of the Tribunal, Carl Oglesby and Richard Shaull had co-authored a work, *Containment and Change*, which argued against American imperialism. Iranian translator Abdol-Hossein Al Rasul had referenced this text in his rendition of Oglesby's views on the subject.[82] The most substantive essay, however, featured Mostafa Rahimi's translation of Sartre's 'Genocide', which he rendered into Persian as *koshtar 'am*, or mass killing.[83] In a faithful translation of the essay, Mostafa Rahimi rendered into Persian an important passage about why the mass killing of Jews was genocide. As Sartre explained:

> Hitler had openly proclaimed his deliberate intention of exterminating the Jews: he used genocide as a *political means* and did not disguise the fact. The Jew had to be put to death wherever he came from, not because he had been caught preparing to fight, or because he was taking part in resistance movements, but simply *because he was Jewish*.[84]

Regarded as an opponent of Zionism and an advocate of Palestinian rights,[85] Rahimi nonetheless accepted that the indiscriminate and unjust mass killing of Jews had taken place during the Second World War, and through his translation promulgated awareness of these atrocities. Rahimi would later be remembered for penning a letter to Ayatollah Khomeini expressing his opposition to the creation of an Islamic Republic.[86] These parallel discourses on human rights revealed the tensions that existed in Iranian intellectual circles, which erupted in 1979.

---

81 Raphael Lemkin, *Axis Rule in Occupied Europe; Laws of Occupation, Analysis of Government, Proposals for Redress*, 1944, Preface xi.
82 Abdol-Hossein Al Rasul, trans., Charles Oglesby, 'Introduction to Genocide', *Jahan-e No*, 86–87.
83 Mostafa Rahimi, trans., 'Koshtar-e Am.' Jean-Paul Sartre, 'Genocide', *New Left Review*, March–April 1968, 13–25.
84 Sartre, 'Genocide,' 13.
85 Heshmat Hekmat, 'Mostafa Rahimi va Avvalin Nameh beh Ayatollah Khomeini', *BBC Persian*, 15 January 2012. Available online: https://www.bbc.com/persian/iran/2012/01/120115_mustafa_rahimi_letter_khomeini_islamic_revolution_islamic_republic.
86 Hekmat, 'Mostafa Rahimi va Avvalin Nameh'.

In June 1968 the shah received an honorary degree from Harvard University.[87] During his commencement address, the monarch proposed the creation of the Universal Welfare Legion – an international organisation like the Peace Corps. Fazl Allah Safa later referenced this speech in one of his articles. He argued that Iranian instructors needed to teach and discuss the shah's speech, which embraced human rights, to their students.[88] The Legion, to be composed of an international volunteer corps drawn from multiple nations and inclusive of different creeds, genders, and races, was intended to combat economic and social inequalities in an effort to advance human rights.[89] The irony and contradictions became intertwined yet inescapable as the Iranian state and its opposition adopted at times similar language to address the global themes of decolonisation and human rights.

Without resolving these tensions, the conference gave voice to other themes of universal import: gender and poverty. Perhaps the most fundamental takeaway from the human rights discourse was not its delivery of a blueprint for eliminating discrimination or world poverty, but rather its pursuit of unified and persistent calls for humanitarian interventions on these fronts.

The Second Sex

The Tehran Human Rights Conference had on its agenda the subject of gender discrimination, a cause that recalled the activism of Eleanor Roosevelt decades earlier. To embrace the theme of gender empowerment, Iran's Organisation for Women (*sazman-e zanan),* which superseded the Society for Women (*kanun-e banovan*), planned a publicity campaign for eliminating discrimination against women by printing handouts and posters

---

87 Roy Mottahedeh, *The Mantle of the Prophet: Religion and Politics in Iran,* 2000, 334. Also, James A. Bill, *The Eagle and the Lion: The Tragedy of American–Iranian Relations,* 1988, 169; Matthew K. Shannon, *Losing Hearts and Minds: American–Iranian Relations and International Education during the Cold War,* 2017, 85. For related discussions, see Afshin Matin-Asgari, *Iranian Student Opposition to the Shah,* 2002.
88 'Shah Urges Legion to Fight Poverty', *The Atlanta Constitution,* 14 June 1968.
89 Fazl Allah Safa, 'Piramun-e Notq-e Tarikhiye Shahanshah dar Daneshgah-e Harvard, Tashkil-e Lezhion-e Khedmatgozaran-e Bashar', *Amuzesh va Parvaresh,* (Ta'lim va Tarbiyat), Mehr–Aban 1347/Autumn 1968, 5–9.

for distribution in girls' schools.[90] Regarding gender, the conference built on other international gatherings that had featured women's rights, including the eighteenth session of the UN Commission on the Status of Women held in Tehran in March 1965. The stress on gender equality, not only in granting women voting rights, but also in providing economic opportunities and social liberties, ranked high among the demands made. Manuchehr Ganji, Iran's representative at the conference, maintained that more attention needed to be paid to the situation of women.

Iranian women responded to the global wave of feminism by participating in literacy and health campaigns, including policies aimed at controlling population growth. Just five years prior to the conference Iranian women had finally gained the right to vote. The decision to grant women suffrage came as part of the shah's White Revolution, or a social contract between the monarch and the people (*enqelab-e shah va mardom*). Conservative religious thinkers and some members of the ʿulama opposed measures that gave women visibility in the public sphere.[91] One religious thinker, Zayn al-ʿAbedin Qorbani, specifically addressed the various articles of the Universal Declaration of Human Rights regarding marriage, which held:

> Men and women of full age, without any limitation due to race,
> nationality or religion, have the right to marry and to found a family.
> They are entitled to equal rights as to marriage, during marriage and at
> its dissolution.[92]

While Qorbani recognised the Declaration's position that marriage should remain licit, with no restriction on race or nationality, he argued that Muslims, and specifically Muslim women, should not marry outside the faith. He also supported parental involvement in this process which, he argued, attempted to acknowledge some choice for young women in this

---

90 NLAI, 297/8409, Edareh-e Ettelaʿat va Matbuʿat-e Vezarat-e Amuzesh va Parvaresh, No. 794, 2 Ordibehesht 1347/21 April 1968.
91 Firoozeh Kashani-Sabet, *Conceiving Citizens: Women and the Politics of Motherhood in Iran*, 2011.
92 Universal Declaration of Human Rights: https://www.un.org/en/about-us/universal-declaration-of-human-rights.

personal matter.[93] Qorbani took on another crucial assertion in the Declaration – the recognition that women and men are 'entitled to equal rights as to marriage, during marriage and at its dissolution'. He highlighted Islam's recognition of gender equality in faith and prayer. He explained that divorce, while permissible, did not give women the same rights as men. On the matter of polygamy, Qorbani wondered whether in a society where the number of women exceeded the number of men, it made sense to restrict a man's marriage to only one woman at a time, thereby depriving other women of such companionship.[94] While modernist thinkers challenged such specious reasoning put forth by religious conservatives, the attention that Qorbani paid to the implications of universal human rights on Islam's positions regarding personal rights exposed the serious disagreements over these ideas – one that neither the conference nor Iranian society would effectively resolve.

The conference predictably lacked the active involvement of religiously conservative figures like Qorbani, who viewed such conversations suspiciously as further evidence of Westernitis and the erosion of Islam and cultural authenticity in Pahlavi Iran. The staging of the conference concealed these destabilising divides. Instead, the royal family and Iran's elite, some of whom upheld religious rituals publicly, embodied these values without addressing any contradictions in religious teachings. The queen, Farah Pahlavi, along with the shah's sister, Ashraf Pahlavi, defined some of the ideals of modern Iranian womanhood, which included an embrace of a secular lifestyle. During the conference the wife of Amir Abbas Hoveyda, Layla, played a visible role as well. The Hoveydas hosted the guests for an evening over 'Ash' and other Iranian delicacies. Coverage of the evening showed that participants wore traditional outfits representing their nations and conversed in regional languages (and only as an exception in French and English) in a conspicuous celebration of diversity and in

---

93 Zayn al-'Abedin Qorbani, 'Nazari beh E'lamiyeh-e Huquq-e Bashar – Tashkil-e Khanevadeh', *Nashriyeh-e Dars-hayi az Maktab-e Islam*, Dey 1343 (December 1964–January 1965), Sixth Year, No. 3, 18–21.
94 Zayn al-'Abedin Qorbani, 'Nazari beh E'lamiyeh-e Huquq Bashar (23): Chera Yek Mard Mitavanad Chand Zan Begirad', Dars-hayi az Maktab Islam, Mordad 1344 (Summer 1965), Sixth Year, No. 10, 28–32. For comparison, see the views of Morteza Motahhari, *Nezam-e Huquq-e Zan dar Islam*, 1389/2010.

a commemoration of the common humanity intended to unify the participants and as a recognition of cultural pluralism. However, not all pictured
participants were identified in the press. In addition, the low participation of international women in the conference was perceptible. Among
the notable women activists, Helena Benitez of the Philippines stood out,
along with Joko Robinson of Jamaica, who remarked that the women in
her country never had to combat the veil – a religious symbol whose political meanings oscillated in Iran amid feminist and Islamist discourses of
the late twentieth century. Robinson noted that Jamaican women opted
not to pursue careers in politics, but rather chose to become engaged in
social work and charitable activities.[95] Turkia Ould Daddah, Mauritania's
representative and member of the Commission on the Status of Women,
was interviewed and pressed the need to eliminate ignorance, disease,
and hunger to realise human rights. She noted further that women in her
country enjoyed equal rights as they could vote and enrol in universities
alongside the men.[96] However, she did not acknowledge that women in
Mauritania suffered serious discrimination in the form of genital mutilation, child marriage, and polygamy.[97]

Feminist thought – ideologies that promoted gender equality between
women and men – had entered the political discourse in Iran through international literature, global activism, and politics. On its founding in 1946,
the United Nations had created a Commission on the Status of Women,
bringing gender discrimination to the fore. In 1949, French writer Simone
de Beauvoir published her scathing feminist critique, *Le Deuxième Sexe*
('The Second Sex'). Although de Beauvoir's work appears not to have
been translated into Persian until later, its impact reverberated in Iranian
intellectual circles in other ways.[98] At the same time Iranian women politicians participated in international conferences that focused attention on
women's rights and circumstances. In 1971, Senator Mehranguiz Manoutchehrian attended a convention for women legal professionals in

---

95 *Ettela'at*, 8 Ordibehesht 1347/28 April 1968.
96 *Ettela'at*, 8 Ordibehesht 1347/28 April 1968, 15.
97 Fran P. Hosken, *The Hosken Report: Genital and Sexual Mutilation of Females*,
1979, 48.
98 Mehdi Kay Nia, 'Avamel-e Ravaniye Talaq', *Huquq: Nashriyeh-e Mahnameh-e
Qazayi*, Azar 1348, 50–51.

Santiago, Chile, a conference that had taken place in Tehran two years earlier.[99] Several years later, in June 1975, Princess Ashraf voiced support for Iranian women through her participation in the International Women's Year Conference in Mexico City. A polarising figure, Ashraf could not effectively represent the concerns and perspectives of rural, minority, religious or indigent women in Iran. Nonetheless, the gathering intended to promote political and educational opportunities for women worldwide. As Helvi Sipilä, secretary general of the conference, maintained, governments 'have not recognized the connection between women's problems and such things as food production, population and the environment'.[100]

Gender issues dominated headlines as the Islamic Revolution unfurled. In 1979, de Beauvoir faced controversy as she condemned the forced re-veiling of Iranian women. That year, in an academic gathering on the Middle East, Edward Said found de Beauvoir 'vain' and her plan to go to Tehran with Kate Millett to protest against the chador to be 'patronising and silly'.[101] Whatever the impact of de Beauvoir, who remained on the radar of Iranian leftists, feminism continued to face a mixed reception in Tehran. The meaning of veiling, too, would undergo hermeneutic differences.

The Hidden Hungry

Global economic disparities worsened the plight of the world's hidden hungry. In Iran's political bodies – the Senate and the Parliament – delegates debated these economic inequalities, which one deputy labelled

---

99 Mehranguiz Manoutchehrian, 'Kholaseh az Gozaresh-e Shanzdahomin Majma'e 'Omumi-ye Ettehadiyeh-e Bayn al-melali-ye Zanan-e Hoquqdanan, 14 ta 23 Novembre 1971, Santiago, Chile', *Kanun-e Vokala*, No. 118, Payiz 1350 (Autumn 1971), 59–67.

100 Judy Klemesrud, 'International Women's Year World Conference Opening in Mexico', *New York Times*, 19 June 1975.

101 Edward Said, 'My Encounter with Sartre', *London Review of Books* 22/11, 1 June 2000. Available online: https://www.lrb.co.uk/the-paper/v22/n11/edward-said/diary. For more on de Beauvoir and Said, see Janet Afary and Kevin Anderson, *Foucault and the Iranian Revolution: Gender and the Seductions of Islamism*, 116–117.

a new manifestation of 'slavery' (*bardegi*).[102] As with other themes, the response to hunger elicited different narratives. Iran experienced population growth in the decade leading up to the conference, with the majority of its population still living in unsettled communities. In addition, rural areas did not have sufficient access to piped water or electricity, and in some places, there were more households than housing units at the time.[103] These statistics reflected significant social differences in rural and urban communities and made it challenging to address food insecurity. While numbers confirmed some of these economic problems, they did not tell the whole story.

In 1965, a Shia scholar named Ahmad Mohassel Yazdi reflected on the ways to combat poverty in global communities, including in Iran. He lamented the pangs of hunger that destitute children experienced and wondered where their salvation might come from. Poverty, Yazdi observed, not only robbed the indigent of material comforts, but also of emotional stability. However, he noted that Islam and the Prophet Muhammad had provided a general concept and framework for reducing poverty and inequality in society, which needed to be embraced to bring about social justice. Recognising that new technologies and economic policies would likely relieve some aspects contributing to widespread poverty, Yazdi nonetheless acknowledged that no city or country had effectively combatted poverty and its concomitant problems and that in many countries the poor constituted a majority.[104]

The Pahlavi record on this issue, as with others, remained chequered. The shah had often spoken of his mission to mitigate the problems of poverty facing the world, exemplified in his Harvard University address. But in the late Pahlavi period, many Iranians suffered from poverty and in some places lacked easy access to potable water.[105] In 1961, a survey conducted by the Ministry of Labour and Social Services found that many

---

102 Parliamentary Sessions, 22nd Session, No. 55, 5 Ordibehesht 1347/25 April 1968.
103 Djamshid Momeni, trans, *National Census of Population and Housing, November 1966*, Markaz-e Amar-e Iran, 1969.
104 Ahmad Mohassel Yazdi, 'Rah-e Mobarezeh ba Faqr', *Ma'arif-e Ja'afari*, No. 4, Farvardin 1344/April 1965, 112–118.
105 Harrison E. Salisbury 'Village Mirrors Distress of Iran: Disease, Poverty And Poor Soil Plague Peasants', *The New York Times*, 24 November 1961.

The Hoveydas Hosting an Evening During the Conference

'unskilled workers, children and women particularly are lucky if they get the minimum wage. With the cost of living going up an average of 67 points per year for the past 14 years ... there is little need to wonder if there is much poverty.'[106] In addition, it was observed that the 'master-servant attitude generally prevails in public and private enterprise'.[107] Class disparities and barriers to upward mobility exacerbated poverty among the needy. The uneven economic development that Iran pursued exacerbated some of these inequities, even after the implementation of land reform.[108] The importance of confronting food insecurity and simultaneously of

---

106 '1961 Annual Labor Report for Iran', History Vault, 009237_009_0574.
107 '1961 Annual Labor Report for Iran', History Vault, 009237_009_0574.
108 Homa Katouzian, *The Agrarian Question in Iran*, 1981.

enabling 'food sovereignty', as recent scholars have termed it – that is 'the right of communities, peoples and states to independently determine their own food and agricultural policies'[109] – emphasised anew the struggles that colonised societies faced in realising human rights in their societies. In 1975, agriculture accounted for only around nine per cent of Iran's GDP, making it apparent that Iran would remain an importer of food. Agricultural production also suffered from the dearth of arable land and limited irrigation. Adding to these challenges was the low rate of literacy, estimated at approximately thirty-seven per cent in 1977, and some doubted the government's 'inflated' literacy statistics.[110] Food preservation lacked efficiency, and poor urban and rural families could not afford all their nutritional needs – a situation that resulted in diet deficiencies.[111]

Along with limited access to food and potable water, indigent populations lacked access to adequate housing. Ironically, the new Majles building that was inaugurated in time to welcome the conference participants had required substantial funding (30 million tomans), which was a significant expenditure at the time.[112] In 1964, Iran had instituted a Ministry of Urban Development and Housing to centralise urban planning and to establish housing regulations and guidelines. The Ministry provided incentives to the private sector for building government housing and worked with banking agencies to manage mortgage-financing. The Ministry had auxiliary committees to manage cooperatives and rural housing needs and worked with the Planning and Budget Organization (*sazman-e barnameh va budjeh-e keshvar*), founded in 1948, to consider and enable economic development. Iran pursued partnerships with various countries, including the United States, to develop housing projects.[113]

In 1973, it was estimated that Iran faced a serious housing shortage,

---

109 Tina Beuchelt and Detlef Virchow, 'Food Sovereignty or the Human Right to Adequate Food: Which Concept Serves Better as International Development Policy for Global Hunger and Poverty Reduction?' *Agriculture and Human Values* 29, 2012, 259–273.

110 Harvey Henry Smith and Richard F. Nyrop, *Iran: A Country Study*, 1978, xviii and 10. For background on these series of books, refer to this website: https://www.loc.gov/collections/country-studies/about-this-collection/.

111 Smith and Nyrop, *Iran: A Country Study*, 82.

112 *Ettela'at*, 3 Ordibehesht 1347/23 April 1967, 10.

113 *Housing and Urban Development in Iran*, 1976, 2–4.

leaving more than a million people with inadequate housing. Certain factors, including population growth and insufficient home construction during the Third and Fourth Development Plans, contributed to this short-fall.[114] A joint US-Iran Working Group on Housing was formed, which brought members of the US Department of Housing Development to Iran in 1975. Iran sought US expertise and assistance in 'high-density, low-rise housing', along with 'earthquake engineering'. Iran's Fifth Development Plan had 'more than doubled' the investment goal for housing.[115] The Working Group outlined a set of priorities to deal with the housing short-fall in Tehran caused by the rapid growth of the capital. Plans included urban development in several provincial cities. In Tehran itself, plans were considered for the creation of 'at least two major developments within the metropolitan area'.[116] Iran's government considered tax exemptions for foreign firms eager to engage in housing construction and also provided some subsidized housing for the lowest income groups.[117] None of these measures, however, adequately or quickly resolved the problem of housing and poverty in Tehran and other parts of the country.

In 1976, the British ambassador to Iran, Anthony Parsons, notably remarked on the country's 'uneven' distribution of wealth and income. The Iranian state had invested in social insurance, with approximately 1.2 million workers estimated as having such coverage, which extended to some dependents. Parsons observed that the 'construction of low-cost housing, a critical problem in Tehran and other rapidly growing centres, lags badly behind'.[118] At the same time, some of the shah's student critics in London, who had organised themselves as the Committee Against Repression in Iran (hereafter CARI),[119] published a scathing pamphlet entitled 'Iran: The Shah's Empire of Repression', which focused attention on the country's dire social problems just as the shah was proclaiming his

---

114 Smith and Nyrop, *Iran: A Country Study*, 84.
115 *Housing and Urban Development in Iran*, 4.
116 *Housing and Urban Development in Iran*, 4.
117 *Housing and Urban Development in Iran*, 5.
118 FCO 8/2998, 'Iran's Progress Towards a Welfare State', Her Majesty's Ambassador at Tehran to the Secretary of State for Foreign and Commonwealth Affairs, 21 October 1976, 8.
119 Ervand Abrahamian, *Iran Between Two Revolutions*, 1982, 499.

civilisational mission (*tamaddon-e bozorg*). The group faulted the shah for his poorly implemented land reform programme, which, in their words, had put the country's agriculture 'in ruins'. In turn, the inattention to agriculture, they contended, had forced Iran to become an importer of food products instead of an exporter.[120] In addition, workers' wages could not adequately keep up with the cost of living, particularly given that wages varied regionally. Desperate for any accommodation, the poor, according to them, lived in 'shanty towns of huts made from cardboard boxes and oil cans'.[121] CARI's focus on the shortcomings of the shah's social platform alarmed certain Western audiences. Although private British correspondence found the CARI pamphlet to be 'a very uneven production' and to contain 'grotesque exaggerations',[122] these 'exaggerations' apparently mattered little as strident criticism of the shah gained traction in European leftist circles.[123]

Others considered Iran's problems of poverty and housing as well. An American source found that the housing problems in Iran, while serious, were less 'acute' than in other comparable countries. Shanty towns existed in Tehran, Abadan, and Ahvaz, as well as in other cities, and their population was estimated at approximately 30,000 in the 1970s (as compared to the vast populations of squatters in Latin America, for example).[124] Shanty-town residents dwelt 'in makeshift huts using tin sheets, scrap wood, or whatever other materials might lie at hand'.[125] Mud huts no longer sufficed to alleviate the dearth of housing, and Iran sought to increase capacity in prefabricated units.[126] Urban construction focused on high-rise apartment buildings that accommodated multiple families and whose construction

---

120 FCO 8/2998, 'Iran: The Shah's Empire of Repression', Section 2.
121 FCO 8/2998, 'Iran: The Shah's Empire of Repression', Section 2.
122 FCO 8/2998, 'CARI Pamphlet on Iran'.
123 Castiglioni, 'Anti-Imperialism of Fools'.
124 Howard Handelman, 'The Political Mobilization of Urban Squatter Settlements: Santiago's Recent Experience and Its Implications for Urban Research', *Latin American Research Review* 10/2, Summer, 1975, 35–72.
125 Smith and Nyrop, *Iran: A Country Study*, 85.
126 Smith and Nyrop, *Iran: A Country Study*, 85.

Community on the outskirts of Tehran, built originally to
host participants in the 1974 Pan-Asian Games.

proved cost-effective.[127] In 1971, a Belgian firm began surveying areas
on the outskirts of Tehran for the construction of high-rise apartments.[128]

The government's investment in high-profile events such as the 1974
Asian Games gave the impression that the state cared less about the plight
of the poor at a time that it invested heavily in and hosted such conspicuous international gatherings. By contrast, the slums of Tehran stood out
as glaring failures of the shah's policies, especially as the revolution
broke out. Inhabitants of shanty towns who had faced callous evictions
in 1977–1978 participated in the cataclysm that brought down the Pahlavi
regime.[129] But, ironically, contemporary challenges have made poverty,
affordable housing, and food insecurity persistent issues in the Islamic
Republic as well.[130]

---

127 Smith and Nyrop, *Iran: A Country Study*, 85–86.
128 *Kayhan*, 23 Khordad 1350/13 June 1971, 15.
129 Farhad Kazemi, 'Urban Migrants and the Revolution', *Iranian Studies* 13/1–4,
1980, 264–265. Also, for a report from one of the revolutionary groups, see
Sazman-e Cherikhayeh Fada'iye Khalq-e Iran, *Gozareshati Az Mobarezat-e
Daliraneh-e Mardom-e Kharej az Mahdudeh* (Mordad 1357/Summer 1978).
130 Maziyar Ghiabi, 'The "Virtual Poor" in Iran: Dangerous Classes and Homeless

*

Iran, and its sovereign, maintained a complicated relationship with human rights, race and decolonisation. The success of Iran's engagement with the discourses of decolonisation cannot be measured only with a list of concrete actions undertaken in the aftermath of the Tehran Human Rights Conference. Rather, its success, I argue, can be gauged from the fact that it stimulated public engagement with subjects that were highly topical and urgent throughout the world at the time. Despite Iran's own history of slavery, and silence around it, Iranians nonetheless showed affinity for the colonial history that had badly oppressed Black citizens in different communities, particularly in Angola, Congo, South Africa, and the United States. At the same time Iran expanded its diplomatic ties and trade networks with a range of non-Western countries in Asia and Africa during those decades.[131]

Decolonisation, as others have argued, comprised many actors and encompassed a multitude of objectives.[132] Above all, however, it pointed to the urgent need to address humanitarian disasters that encompassed race relations, poverty, and gender, but also political disenfranchisement, illiteracy, and dictatorship. From an intellectual perspective, it harked back to the philosophical debates about *insaniyat* and *adamiyat* that had first launched Iran on the path of liberal reform in the early twentieth century.

By 1968, however, the world was a very different place. The horrors and humanitarian disasters of the Second World War brought under scrutiny totalitarian regimes that had committed large-scale genocides in the form of the Holocaust perpetrated against the Jews and the mass murder of Slavs

---

Life in Capitalist Times', *Crime, Poverty and Survival in the Middle East and North Africa: The 'Dangerous Classes' since 1800*, ed. Stephanie Cronin, 2020; Manata Hashemi, *Coming of Age in Iran: Poverty and the Struggle for Dignity*, 2020. Also, Rose Weilman, *Feeding Iran: Shi`i Families and the Making of the Islamic Republic*, 2021.

131 Shireen T. Hunter, *Iran and the World: Continuity in a Revolutionary Decade*, 1990. Also, Kashani-Sabet, *Heroes to Hostages*, Chapters 10 and 12.

132 Cyrus Schayegh and Yoav Di Capua, 'Why Decolonization?' *International Journal of Middle East Studies* 52, 2020, 137–145.

and Roma people.[133] In Iran, too, scores of people died or became victims of European imperialism. At the same time they endured hoarding, epidemics, and famine when the country lived through occupation for five long years, from 1941 to 1946.[134] Finally, the war unleashed a global refugee crisis, particularly for Palestinian Arabs in 1948, after the creation of the State of Israel – its Jewish citizens themselves victims of long-standing anti-Semitism.[135] In 1951, the Refugee Convention and its 1967 Protocol outlined the conditions that created refugee status and that necessitated the protection of refugee rights.[136] Yet the region, and indeed much of the world – then as now – grappled inadequately with refugee crises of varying aetiologies.

Scholarly consensus suggests that the Tehran conference achieved little of value. South Africa remained in the grips of apartheid for decades afterwards. Poverty, inadequate educational opportunities, and gender inequities persisted in Western and non-Western countries alike. Iran itself also dealt with these discrepancies despite its bloody revolution of 1979, which had promised to empower the weak, or *mostaz 'af.* On a global scale, decolonisation – a crusade initiated to wrest power away from colonisers, usually European or American, and restore it to indigenous communities – did not engender easy transfers of power or enable sufficient domestic social progress. The inspiring themes that galvanised the conference participants produced intangible results and left many decolonisation movements only partially fulfilled. Nonetheless, the pursuit of these ideals brought necessary awareness, prompted dialogue, and refined social programmes intended to realise humanitarian objectives. The majority of Iranians, an audience regarded as largely illiterate in the 1960s (estimated at around seventeen per cent for women and thirty-nine per cent for men),[137]

---

133 Daniel J. Goldhagen, *Hitler's Willing Executioners: Ordinary Germans and the Holocaust*, 1997.
134 See Chapter 1 of this volume.
135 Benny Morris, *Righteous Victims: A History of the Zionist–Arab Conflict, 1881–2001*, 2001. Also, Ilan Pappe, *The Ethnic Cleansing of Palestine*, 2007; Michael R. Fishbasch, *Records of Dispossession: Palestinian Refugee Property and the Arab–Israeli Conflict*, 2003; and Rashid Khalidi, *The Hundred Years' War on Palestine: A History of Settler Colonialism and Resistance, 1917–2017*, 2020.
136 The Refugee Convention, 1951: https://www.unhcr.org/4ca34be29.pdf.
137 'Educational Attainment in Iran', https://www.mei.edu/publications/educational-attainment-iran.

understood inherently that poverty and inequality necessitated social action. This simple and fundamental humanitarian realisation – if not the sophisticated language of human rights – reverberated among Iranians of various classes. Policymakers spoke eloquently, if at times pompously, about the value of human rights but, in the end, many failed to make sufficient reforms to combat social disparities. For their part, Iranian intellectuals, sometimes quick to criticise but slow to offer solutions, perceived these glaring social challenges and did not hesitate to bring these deficiencies and injustices to light. Whatever their differences, both groups – like the framers of Iran's first constitution – never ceased to remain hopeful and believed that humanity deserved their steadfast defence. This conviction endured as the indelible legacy of Tehran's human rights conference.

Bibliography

Abrahamian, E. *Iran Between Two Revolutions*, Princeton, 1982.

Adami, R., and Plesch, D. *Women and the UN: A New History of Women's International Human Rights*, London, Routledge, 2021.

Afary, J., and Anderson, K.B. *Foucault and the Iranian Revolution: Gender and the Seductions of Islamism*, Chicago, 2005.

Afshari, R. *Human Rights in Iran: The Abuse of Cultural Relativism*, Philadelphia, 2011.

Alvandi, R. 'Introduction', *The Age of Aryamehr: Late Pahlavi Iran and its Global Entanglements,* ed. R. Alvandi, London, 2018.

Alvandi, R., ed. *The Age of Aryamehr: Late Pahlavi Iran and its Global Entanglements*, London, 2018.

Bagley, F.R.C. 'The Iranian City in an Era of Change and Development', *Bulletin (British Society for Middle Eastern Studies)* 3/2, 1976, 100–109.

Bill, J.A. *The Eagle and the Lion: The Tragedy of American-Iranian Relations*, New Haven, 1988.

Bonner, P. 'The Antinomies of Nelson Mandela', in Rita Barnard, ed., *The Cambridge Companion to Nelson Mandela*, New York, 2014.

Boroujerdi, M. *Iranian Intellectuals and the West: The Tormented Triumph of Nativism*, Syracuse, USA, 1996.

Brick, H. and Phelps, C. *Radicals in America: The US Left since the Second World War*, Cambridge, 2015.

Burke, R. *Decolonization and the Evolution of International Human Rights*, Philadelphia, 2010.

Burke, R. 'From Individual Rights to National Development: The First UN International Conference on Human Rights, Tehran, 1968', *Journal of World History* 19/3, September 2008, 275–296.

Castiglioni, C. '"Anti-Imperialism of Fools"?: The European Intellectual Left and The Iranian Revolution', *The Age of Aryamehr: Late Pahlavi Iran and Its Global Entanglements*, ed. R. Alvandi, London, 2018, 220–259.

Dabashi, H. *Theology of Discontent*, New York, 1993.

Gerges, F.A. *Making the Arab World: Nasser, Qutb, and the Clash That Shaped the Middle East*, Princeton, 2018.

Ghiabi, M. 'The "Virtual Poor" in Iran: Dangerous Classes and Homeless Life in Capitalist Times', *Crime, Poverty and Survival in the Middle East and North Africa: The 'Dangerous Classes' since 1800*, ed. S. Cronin, London, 2020.

Harris, K. and Kalb, Z. 'Pen to the Tiller: Land Reform and Social Mobility Across the 1979 Iranian Revolution', *Journal of Agrarian Change* 19/3, 2019, 465–486.

Hashemi, M. *Coming of Age in Iran: Poverty and the Struggle for Dignity*, New York, 2020.

Housing and Urban Development in Iran, Washington, DC, 1976.

Hunter, S.T. *Iran and the World: Continuity in a Revolutionary Decade*, Bloomington, 1990.

International Conference on Human Rights, Tehran. *External Affairs*, 20/6, 1968, 251.

Kashani-Sabet, F. *Conceiving Citizens: Women and the Politics of Motherhood in Iran*, New York, 2011.

Kashani-Sabet, F. 'Hallmarks of Humanism: Hygiene and Love of Homeland in Qajar Iran', *American Historical Review*, October 2000, 1171–1203.

Kashani-Sabet, F. *Heroes to Hostages: America and Iran, 1800–1988*. Cambridge, 2023.

Katouzian, H. *The Agrarian Question in Iran*, Geneva, 1981.

Kay Nia, M. 'Avamel-e Ravaniye Talaq', *Huquq: Nashriyeh-e Mahnameh-e Qazayi*, Azar 1348, 50–51.

Kazemi, F. 'Urban Migrants and the Revolution', *Iranian Studies* 13/1–4, 1980, 257–277.

Kolb, R. *Human Rights Law and International Humanitarian Law Between 1945 and the Aftermath of the Teheran Conference of 1968*. Northampton, USA, 2013.

Lemkin, R. *Axis Rule in Occupied Europe; Laws of Occupation, Analysis of Government, Proposals for Redress*, 1944.

Macbride, S. 'Introduction: The Promise of Human Rights Year', *Journal of the International Commission of Jurists* 9/1, Part Two, June 1968.

Matin-Asgari, A. *Iranian Student Opposition to the Shah*, Costa Mesa, USA, 2002.

McCann, G. 'Where Was the *Afro* in Afro-Asian Solidarity? Africa's "Bandung Moment" in 1950s Asia', *Journal of World History* 30/1–2, 2019, 89–124.

Momeni, D. Trans. *National Census of Population and Housing, November 1966*, by Markaz-e Amar-e Iran, Austin, 1969.

Motahhari, M. *Nezam-e Huquq-e Zan dar Islam*. Tehran, 1389/2010.

Mottahedeh, R. *The Mantle of the Prophet: Religion and Politics in Iran*, Oxford, 2009.

Moyn, S. *The Last Utopia: Human Rights in History*, Cambridge, USA, 2010.

Nabavi, N. *Intellectual Trends in Twentieth-Century Iran: A Critical Survey*, Gainesville, 2003.

Nikpour, G. 'Claiming Human Rights: Iranian Political Prisoners and the Making of a Transnational Movement, 1963–1979', *Humanity: An International Journal of Human Rights, Humanitarianism, and Development*, 9/3, 2018, 363–388.

Nodushan, M.A.I. 'Yadi az huquq-e bashar', *Yaghma* 2, Ordibehesht 1347/April 1968.

Oglesby, C. *Ravens In the Storm: A Personal History of the 1960s Antiwar Movement*, New York, 2008.

Qorbani, Z. al-'Abedin. 'Nazari beh E'lamiyeh-e Huquq Bashar –
Tashkil-e Khanevadeh', *Nashriyeh-e Dars-hayi az Maktab-e Islam*,
Dey 1343 (Dec. 1964–Jan. 1965), Sixth Year, No. 3, 18–21.

Qorbani, Z. al-'Abedin. 'Nazari beh E'lamiyeh-e Huquq Bashar (23):
Chera Yek Mard Mitavanad Chand Zan Begirad', *Dars-hayi az
Maktab Islam*, Mordad 1344 (Summer 1965), 6th Year, No. 10, 28–32.

Richardson-Little, N. *The Human Rights Dictatorship: Socialism, Global
Solidarity and Revolution In East Germany*, Cambridge, 2020.

Said, E. 'My Encounter with Sartre', *London Review of Books* 22/11, 1
June 2000.

Salem, S. *Colonial Afterlives in Egypt: The Politics of Hegemony*,
Cambridge, 2020.

Sartre, J.-P. 'Genocide', *New Left Review*, March – April 1968, 13–25.

Schayegh, C. and Di Capua, Y. 'Why Decolonization?', *International
Journal of Middle East Studies* 52, 2020, 137–145.

Schwartz, T.A. *Lyndon Johnson and Europe: In the Shadow of Vietnam*,
Cambridge, USA, 2003.

Shannon, M.K. *Losing Hearts and Minds*: *American-Iranian Relations
and International Education during the Cold War*, Ithaca, 2017.

Smith, H.H. and Nyrop, R.F. *Iran: A Country Study*, Washington, DC,
1978.

Snyder, S.B. 'The 1968 International Year for Human Rights: A Missed
Opportunity in the United States', *Diplomatic History* 42/5, November
2018, 831–858.

Stewart, L.J. 'Too loud to rise above the silence: The United States vs.
the International War Crimes Tribunal, 1966–1967', *The Sixties* 11/1,
2018, 17–45.

Thompson, A.S. 'Tehran 1968 and Reform of the UN Human Rights
System', *Journal of Human Rights* 14/1, 2015, 84–100.

Thompson, C. '"The Man Who Lived Underground" Review: Richard
Wright's Lost Novel; The Work The Author Considered His Finest at
Last Sees the Light of Day', *Wall Street Journal (Online)*. 23 April
2021.

To Deepen Our Commitment: Interim Report, Washington, DC, 1968.

Tulli, U. 'Wielding the Human Rights Weapon against the American
Empire: The Second Russell Tribunal and Human Rights in

Transatlantic Relations', *Journal of Transatlantic Studies* 19, 2021, 215–237.

Wright, R. and Myrdal, G. *The Color Curtain: A Report On the Bandung Conference*, Cleveland, USA, 1956.

Yazdi, A.M. 'Rah-e Mobarezeh ba Faqr', *Ma'arif-e Ja'afari,* No. 4, Farvardin 1344/April 1965, 112–118.

9

Red Star Over Iran: Maoism and the Shah's Regime

William Figueroa

'We never use the term "Maoist". Later, people opposed to us called us Maoists, but we never used it.'[1] Mohsen Rezvani, the former student leader of *Sazman-e Enqelabi-ye Hezb-e Tudeh*, the Revolutionary Organisation of the Tudeh Party (hereafter ROTPI), prefers the term 'Marxism-Leninism-Mao Zedong Thought' to describe their party's orientation, following the nomenclature of the Chinese Communist Party (CCP). This was not coincidental, as the ROTPI was formed out of direct contacts between the CCP and activists within the Confederation of Iranian Students/National Union (hereafter CISNU). These student agitators travelled to China for the first time in 1963 and returned several times over the next two decades. Rezvani remains a self-proclaimed follower of Mao Zedong Thought to this day, a testament to the personal impact of these trips.

The popularity of Maoist politics among Iranian students was related to the decline of the traditional Iranian Left post-1953, the reconstitution of the Iranian opposition and the student movement from 1960 to 1963, the shift to violent anti-shah politics after 1963, and the growing rift between China and the Soviet Union that developed over the same period. It was reinforced by a global environment in which internationalism and Maoism

---

1 Mohsen Rezvani, interview with the author, 14 April 2018.

were increasingly in vogue among student radicals in the United States and Europe, as well as Third World revolutionaries. This was part of a broader rejection of the dominant Marxist currents endorsed by the Soviet Union, which emphasised a peaceful transition to socialism, in favour of China's more militant rhetoric. In this environment, students, activists, and revolutionaries around the world were attracted to the dynamic and uncompromising slogans of Maoism.

Beginning in 1965, the ROTPI began circulating Persian translations of Maoist texts and officially endorsed *Andisheh-ye Mau Tse Dun* ('Mao Zedong Thought').[2] Former members of the youth organisation of the Tudeh Party, the main Communist organisation in Iran and one of the country's most prominent political parties, the ROTPI argued that Tudeh leadership was overly enamoured with the Soviet Union, out of touch, and to blame for the disastrous coup of 1953 that drove the party into exile.[3] ROTPI members travelled to China for military and political training, played an active role in Chinese propaganda, and represented the internationalist trends that characterised the CISNU in the late 1960s. By 1969, the two major Iranian student organisations in the West, the CISNU and the ISA-US (Iranian Students Association in the United States) had Maoist majorities in their leadership.[4] According to Noureddin Kianouri, by 1969 the ROTPI had 'carried away a significant portion of the party's supporters in the West, perhaps 90 percent'.[5]

This Maoist high tide was not to last. By 1971, many Iranian leftists began to turn against China as a revolutionary model, partly because Beijing had begun openly supporting the Iranian government. Furthermore, the ROTPI was unable to establish a presence in Iran, nor was it able to engage in *mobarez-e mosalahaneh* ('armed struggle'). Other groups with different understandings of Marxism, often mediated by Islam, had come to the fore and successfully engaged in attacks on the shah's

---

2 The peculiar formula is a literal translation of the preferred Chinese term for Maoism: Máo Zédōng sīxiǎng.

3 Maziar Behrooz, 'Tudeh Factionalism and the 1953 Coup in Iran', *International Journal of Middle Eastern Studies* 33/3, 2002, 369–370.

4 Afshin Matin-Asgari, *Iranian Student Opposition to the Shah*, 2002, 98, 106.

5 Noureddin Kianouri quoted in Maziar Behrooz, *Rebels with a Cause: The Failure of the Iranian Left*, 2000, 20.

government, overshadowing their efforts. Although some Iranian guerrilla organisations continued to endorse aspects of Maoist theory or practice, they were all eventually crushed by government reprisals.[6] Others continued to operate overseas, as an ephemeral online presence, or merge with the US Communist movement, but they never again gained any leading influence.[7]

Scholarly attitudes towards Iranian Maoism have thus been characterised by a narrative of failure. This narrative is typical of studies of the Iranian Left. One can easily detect this disenchantment from the titles of such studies, from Maziar Behrooz's classic *Rebels with a Cause: The Failure of the Iranian Left* to Ali Mirsepassi's chapter, 'The Tragedy of the Iranian Left'.[8] Matin-Asgari's brief account of Iranian Maoism concludes that although the ROTPI influenced the Left, the organisation ultimately suffered from a lack of direction and theoretical incoherence that led to serious strategic blunders, and that this influence was not significant.[9] Whether failure or tragedy, the lines of inquiry into the Maoist movement have been limited to concern with its ultimate failure to take power or have a major impact on the Iranian revolution.

While well known to scholars of the Iranian Left, Iranian Maoism remains unknown outside the discipline. Within the small body of literature on Sino-Iranian relations, the direct connection between the ROTPI and the CCP is mentioned only in passing and often downplayed.[10] More recent works begin with Sino-Iranian rapprochement in the 1970s and make no mention of the episode.[11] It is also mostly absent from the histori-

---

6 Torab Haqshenas, 'Communism in Persia after 1953', *Encyclopædia Iranica*, 2001. Available online: https://iranicaonline.org/articles/communism-iii.

7 See the website of the Communist Party of IranMarxist-Leninist-Maoist (CPI-MLM): http://cpimlm.com/aboutusf.php?Id=1.

8 Ali Mirsepassi, *Intellectual Discourse and the Politics of Modernization*, 2000, 159–177.

9 Afshin Matin-Asgari, 'Iranian Maoism: Searching for a Third World Revolutionary Model', *MERIP* 44/270, 2014.

10 In addition to Matin-Asgari, 'Iranian Maoism', see Emadi Hafizullah, 'China's Ideological Influence and Trade Relations with Iran, 1960–1990', *Internationales Asienforum* 29/1, 1995.

11 John Garver. *China and Iran: Ancient Partners in a Post-Imperial World*, 2004; and Shirzad Azad, *Iran and China: A New Approach to Their Bilateral Relations*, 2017.

ography of China's foreign policy during the Cold War.[12] The literature in Persian and Chinese follows similar patterns, either ignoring the episode or emphasising its failures and missteps.[13]

Recently, some historians have begun to explore Maoism as a global phenomenon, focused on its reception in the West and in places like Peru, Indonesia, and India.[14] Julia Lovell's *Maoism: A Global History* is the most recent and comprehensive, and successfully demonstrates the global influence of Maoism as a constituent component of anti-colonial and anti-capitalist discourse. However, both Lovell's *Global Maoism* and Alexander Cook's *Mao's Little Red Book* lack any mention of Maoism in the Middle East. This omission essentially comes down to sources and linguistic limitations but demonstrates the lack of attention to Iranian Maoism even in the literature of global Maoism.

This chapter makes use of new and underutilised sources in Persian and Chinese to address this gap in the scholarship. Official Chinese newspapers like *People's Daily* provide a treasure-trove of information about the ROTPI in China and are juxtaposed with publications by Iranian opposition groups. It also draws on Hamid Shokat's series of interviews with former ROTPI members and those carried out by the author. Other sources include materials from the International Institute of Social History in Amsterdam, the Hoover Institution at Stanford University, and online archives like Nashriyeh Digital Iranian History archive at the University of Manchester and the Archive of Iranian Opposition Documents at iran-archive.com. All of these are drawn from partial collections and limited by what is accessible to researchers.

The ROTPI was not the only Iranian organization to make use of Maoist rhetoric. There were rival organisations like *Sazman-e Marksist-Leninist*

---

12 See John Garver, *China's Quest: A History of the Foreign Relations of the People's Republic of China*, 2016.
13 For some examples in Persian, see Mahmood Naderi, *Ma'uizm dar Iran*, 1397/2019; and Vali Allah Hami, *Ravabet-e Iran va Chin*, 1390/2011. For Chinese, see Yang Xingli, *Xian dai Zhongguo yu Yilang guan xi*, 2013; and Lin Zongxian, *Zhong gong yu Yilang guan xi zhi yan jiu*, 2014.
14 Alexander C. Cook, ed. *Mao's Little Red Book: A Global History*, 2014; Julia Lovell, *Maoism: A Global History*, 2019; and Quinn Slobodian, 'The Meanings of Western Maoism in the Global 1960s', *The Routledge Handbook of the Global Sixties: Between Protest and Nation-Building*, ed. Chen Jian et al, 2020.

Tufan ('the Marxist-Leninist Storm Organisation') and splinter group *Kadr-ha* ('Cadres'), as well as later militant Maoist organisations like *Sarb-edaran* (literally, 'those-with-heads-on-gallows') and Kurdish groups like *Komala* ('Society', short for 'Society of Revolutionary Toilers of Kurdistan'). Maoism was also studied by Marxist and Muslim militant organisations, including the *Fada'iyan-e Khalq* ('The People's Self-sacrificers') and the *Mojahedin-e Khalq* ('The People's Holy Warriors'), although they were not Maoist and rejected many key Maoist principles. This is not a full history of Iranian Maoism, but an examination of the only Iranian Maoist organisation that had direct ties to China. It will put the story of the ROTPI in conversation with recent works of Chinese and Iranian history and explore its impact on the Iranian opposition. What value did Iranian students in exile see in Maoism, and what did they take from their experiences in China? Why did China cultivate this relationship, and what were its limitations? What was the long-term impact on the Iranian opposition, and can we see the history of Iranian Maoism as something more than a failure?

Historical Background of the Iranian Maoist Movement

After its establishment in 1941, the Tudeh soon party emerged as the most influential Communist organisation in Iran. It was the only political party with significant influence among workers in critical industries and boasted a large following of intellectuals and university students.[15] The Tudeh suffered a serious blow to its credibility in 1945–1946, however, when it backed Soviet-sponsored separatist movements in Kurdistan and Azerbaijan and supported Moscow's demands for an oil concession.[16] In 1947, prominent party member Khalil Maleki broke away from the Tudeh, arguing that the leadership saw everything through the prism of the US-Soviet conflict and refused to analyse the local situation accurately.[17] Maleki later wrote that the party should have learned from the example of China and resisted Soviet pressure.[18]

---

15 Ervand Abrahamian, *A History of Modern Iran*, 2008, 107–113.
16 Abrahamian, *Modern Iran*, 111.
17 Yadullah Shahibzadeh, *Marxism and Left-Wing Politics in Europe and Iran*, 2019, 112.
18 Khalil Maleki, *Nehzat-e melli va edalat-e ejtemayi*, 1998, 57.

The main factor in the decline of the Tudeh was not internal opposition, however, but government oppression. Ali Rahnema describes how in the period after the British- and US-sponsored 1953 coup against Prime Minister Mohammad Mosaddeq, the Iranian state used violence and oppression against all competing centres of political power.[19] Government and military officials were purged, including teaching faculty at universities. Press censorship was instituted and hundreds of communists and pro-Mosaddeq protesters were arrested, beaten, or tortured in the months and years that followed. Nearly all the Tudeh leadership was executed, jailed, or driven into exile. Although the Tudeh remained culturally and intellectually influential among the Iranian Left, it could no longer function as an effective opposition party. From 1953 to 1960, open opposition in the country was largely non-existent.[20]

In the absence of meaningful political activity at home, Iranian students in Europe and North America began to organise themselves. By the late 1950s, there were new leftist, Muslim, and nationalist student networks growing in Britain, France, West Germany, and the United States, although they remained nominally apolitical. These were united under the CISNU, which brought together the major Iranian student groups in the United States and Europe, in April 1960. Based in Europe, the Confederation had the endorsement of the leading US- and Tehran-based student organisations and could claim to represent all Iranian students. The period of 1960 to 1963 saw a brief resurgence of domestic opposition, but violence once again broke out in June 1963.[21] This time, the cause was the shah's proposed White Revolution, a series of reforms that covered popular opposition demands like land distribution, women's enfranchisement, literacy, and resource nationalisation.[22] Although the ideas of the White Revolution were popular with the Iranian public, it faced opposition from liberals and leftists who were opposed to the shah's dictatorial power, and religious

---

19 Ali Rahnema. *The Rise of Modern Despotism in Iran: The Shah, the Opposition, and the US, 1953–1968*, 2021, 33–45, 63–66.

20 Matin-Asgari, *Student Opposition*, 26–29.

21 Abbas Amanat, *A History of Modern Iran*, 2017, 592–598.

22 Amanat, *Modern Iran*, 562; Ervand Abrahamian, *Iran Between Two Revolutions*, 1982, 419–446; and Nikki Keddie, *Modern Iran: Roots and Results of Revolution*, 2006, 140–146.

conservatives who objected to women's suffrage and changes in the traditional judicial system. In response to the protests, the government arrested Ayatollah Khomeini, then a prominent cleric critical of the reforms, which set off a fresh wave of protests and repression. As a result, after 1963, the centre of student opposition shifted from Iran to Europe and the United States.[23]

Two related developments were simultaneously unfolding on the international scene: the Sino–Soviet split and the rise of militant student activism in the West.[24] China and the Soviet Union had maintained a close alliance since 1949, but this partnership began to fray in the late 1950s. Ideological disagreements arose over what Moscow saw as Mao's reckless economic policy and bellicose stance towards the West, while Mao took issue with the Soviets' air of superiority and Khrushchev's policy of 'peaceful coexistence' with imperialism. Starting in 1959, Mao actively pursued an ideological clash, criticising the Soviets for moving away from the original principles of Marxism by preaching peace with capitalist countries, which they called 'Soviet revisionism'.[25] He linked these ideological disputes to his domestic enemies and used the opportunity to push a radical alternative to Soviet policy internationally. Where the Soviet Union advocated caution and economic development, the Chinese advocated armed struggle, anti-imperialism, and independent nationalism. China was increasingly associated with its vocal support for revolutionary struggles around the world and its advocacy for a militant approach to politics. Over time, this strategy became more about countering Soviet influence than supporting revolutionary movements.

As part of this strategy, the CCP actively recruited students who would endorse their agenda in the Sino–Soviet split. To this end, they translated Maoist materials and information about the Chinese position into a wide array of languages and distributed them globally. These efforts made the 'Little Red Book' one of the most printed books of the 1960s and

---

23 Matin-Asgari, *Student Opposition*, 62–77.
24 See Lorenz Lüthi. *The Sino–Soviet Split: Cold War in the Communist World*, 2008; and Jeremy Friedman. *Shadow Cold War: The Sino–Soviet Competition for the Third World*, 2015.
25 Lüthi, *Sino–Soviet Split*, 116.

1970s, with official editions in three dozen languages.[26] By the mid-1960s, Maoism was popular among student groups and Third World radicals from Berkeley to Beijing.[27] This attraction reflected the international trend toward student radicalism and the rise of New Left politics on campuses around the world, which culminated in a series of international protests in 1968.[28] The Iranian student movement played a significant role in this process and was directly impacted by the resurgence of popular Marxist and Maoist politics on US and European campuses.[29] Against this backdrop, Iranian Maoism would emerge as a cascading current within the student movement.

China and the Iranian Student Movement

The ROTPI originated in the British student movement at the University of Manchester. Activist students had been organised there since the late 1950s after successfully ousting the conservative leadership of the embassy-affiliated Society of Iranian Students in England.[30] Among them were Tudeh activists Parviz Nikkhah and Mohsen Rezvani, who were active in the European student movement and opposed the current Tudeh leadership. Their early opposition centred on strategic rather than ideological issues; the question of Chinese politics did not exist yet. Instead, they criticised the Central Committee for being content with remaining in exile. The Committee had also reflected on its own shortcomings at the Fourth Plenum in 1957 for failing to recognise the revolutionary nature of the oil nationalisation movement.[31] They blamed their 'state of paralysis' on a 'lack of internal democracy' and 'low level of theoretical knowledge of the leadership', among other things. These 'self-criticisms' were a key factor in convincing the younger generation to turn elsewhere. Rezvani would

---

26 Cook, *Little Red Book,* xiii.
27 See Lovell, *Global Maoism.*
28 See Jeremy Suri, *The Global Revolutions of 1968,* 2006.
29 Matthew K. Shannon, *Losing Hearts and Minds: American–Iranian Relations and International Education during the Cold War,* 2017, 82–83.
30 Matin-Asgari, *Student Opposition,* 30.
31 Behrooz, 'Tudeh Factionalism', 369–370.

later reflect that, at the time, though they opposed them ideologically, 'we didn't have a good weapon' to attack the Central Committee directly.[32]

The formation of the ROTPI as a Maoist faction was instigated by contact between Parviz Nikkhah and the Chinese Student Association in Bucharest, who approached the Iranians about hosting a youth delega-tion. This encounter led to an invitation to meet with CCP officials via the Chinese embassy in London.[33] At the time, there were no direct flights to Beijing, so Rezvani and a number of other students took a roundabout route from London to Paris to Rangoon, the capital city of Burma (present-day Myanmar). Rezvani recalls with some humour that when they arrived, they were surprised to be greeted by a stylish limousine and motorcycle escort. At the hotel, located in a large and richly decorated building, their hosts gave an enthusiastic welcome to their 'guests from Tehran' and a lavish meal. Rezvani marvelled that the CCP would extend such hospital-ity even to visiting students.

The next day, they boarded a flight alongside a disgruntled delegation from Albania, who complained bitterly to them about poor treatment and being packed tightly into a low-quality hotel. They were shocked and more than a little insulted, as Albania was at that time the only Western country allied with the Chinese in the Sino–Soviet split and was an important ally. An apologetic Chinese ambassador to Burma explained that the two del-egations had accidentally been switched; their hosts had confused the del-egates from the Iranian capital Tehran with the delegates from Tirana, the capital of Albania.[34] In fact, the CCP did not consider the Iranian students to be of particular importance but invited them as a part of a larger strategy of engaging with dissident student groups to gain support for its ideologi-cal war against the Soviets.

After a night at a peasant commune, the delegation flew to Beijing and met with representatives of the Communist Youth League. They learned that in addition to meeting with Nikkhah, the Chinese had also been in contact with other Iranian activists like Fereydun Keshavarz, a former

---

32 Rezvani, author interview.
33 Rezvani, author interview.
34 Hamid Shokat, *Negahi az darun be jonbesh-e chap-e Iran: Goftegu ba Mohsen Rezvani*, 1384/2005, 66–67.

Tudeh party leader who had broken away in 1958. China had been actively pursuing ties with Iranian dissidents to circumvent its lack of diplomacy with Iran. They also met with representatives from the Central Committee, who told them that the CCP once had a relationship with the Tudeh, but they had left when Khrushchev ordered the withdrawal of all Soviet experts from China.[35] The situation had left the Persian section of the CCP's international radio programme, Radio Peking, unable to broadcast.[36]

The students requested ideological and military training from their hosts, and in return offered to send delegates to replace the Tudeh experts at Radio Peking. In addition to ideological and military training, the Chinese also agreed to provide modest financial support. Cash was received at the Chinese embassy in London and collected by Rezvani directly.[37] Rezvani confirms the Chinese paid for flights, accommodation, and salaries for Radio Peking staff, as well as travel expenses.[38] A trip might cost upwards of $14,000, so the financial support was considerable, but relatively inexpensive. In addition to Rezvani, members like Kurosh Lashayi and Iraj Kashkuli were sent for military and ideological training, while others, like Mehdi Khanbaba Tehrani, worked at Radio Peking. The CCP repeatedly expressed that they were only willing to pay for individual expenses, however, as their experience with the Soviet Union had shown that unrestricted support could lead to unhealthy dependencies.[39] The more likely reason is that they were not genuinely supportive of armed revolution in Iran.

Despite its vocal support for violent revolution, China declined to provide either material support for armed struggle and resisted the ROTPI's pleas for a more relevant and opposition-based approach to Radio Peking's Persian service. Although there was an ongoing Kurdish separatist movement in Iran during the 1960s, one which was peasant-based and actively supported by the ROTPI, the CCP refused to comment.[40] This stood in

---

35 Shokat, *Rezvani*, 68; and Hamid Shokat, *Negahi az darun be jonbesh-e chap-e Iran: Goftegu ba Kurosh Lashayi*, 1383/2004, 51.
36 Shokat, *Rezvani*, 70.
37 Shokat, *Lashayi*, 85–86.
38 Shokat, *Rezvani*, 123–124.
39 Shokat, *Rezvani*, 123–124.
40 Hamid Shokat, *Negahi az darun be jonbesh-e chap-e Iran: Goftegu ba Mehdi Khanbaba Tehrani*, 1380/2000, 164.

contrast to their support for similar movements in Palestine and the Gulf. While willing to endorse the Iranian revolutionaries up to a point, Beijing was careful not to do anything that might harm a future partnership with the shah. This stands in contrast to its material support for Palestinian revolutionaries and the People's Front for the Liberation of the Arab Gulf (PFLOAG), which consisted primarily of Soviet-made small arms.[41] China, despite its public support for armed struggle, was more interested in reducing Soviet influence than funding revolutionary violence.

The Chinese made it clear they were primarily interested in the Iranian radicals as a strategic asset for their propaganda war with the Soviet Union. Repeatedly impressed upon the Iranian delegation were the CCP's grievances against the Soviet Union. The Chinese were anxious for the Iranians to adopt their view. Kashkuli recalls how this was the only way the Chinese tried to influence them directly:

> They were sensitive only to the global situation and focused on criticising Soviet politics. From the point of view of the Chinese, [the Soviets] had revised the fundamentals of Marxism-Leninism and violated its revolutionary principles.[42]

Happy to oblige, the ROTPI would go on to condemn the Soviet Union in its official publications and encourage the growing anti-Soviet attitude in the CISNU.[43] They similarly sought ideological support for their break with the Tudeh Central Committee and the prestige of affiliation with China's revolutionary agenda.

Whatever their intentions, the Chinese were clear that the Iranians should not just blindly copy the Chinese model and stressed that the Chinese experience was relevant only to China. The purpose of ideological educa-tion was to teach the method of adapting Marxist thought to the specific

---

41 Lillian Craig Harris, 'China's Relationship with the PLO', *Journal of Palestine Studies* 7/1, Autumn 1977; and Abdel Razzaq Takriti, *Monsoon Revolution: Republicans, Sultans, and Empires in Oman, 1965–1976*, 2013, 104.
42 Hamid Shokat, *Negahi az darun be jonbesh-e chap-e Iran: Goftegu ba Iraj Kashkuli*, 1386/2007, 38.
43 Matin-Asgari, *Student Opposition*, 108.

circumstances of Iran.[44] Rezvani recalls having this impressed upon him by none other than Chairman Mao. When meeting with the ROTPI delegates and other foreign visitors on a subsequent trip, Mao asked Rezvani what he was doing in China via a translator:

> I replied: 'I am here to study your thought and the experiences of China.' *'Bu hao!'* (No good!) he said. I can still hear it in my ears.[45]

Mao urged Rezvani to adapt Marxism to the Iranian situation and said that when the Chinese returned from the Soviet Union, they made many mistakes, and it was only after they stopped trying to copy the Soviet models that they achieved success – good advice that Rezvani and his fellow revolutionaries all but ignored.

The Revolutionary Organisation of the Tudeh Party

The Iranian delegation returned to Europe to lay the groundwork for a return to Iran. In April 1964, they met with Mehdi Khanbaba Tehrani and other like-minded students for an unofficial 'preparatory conference' held in Munich.[46] There, they laid out their critique of the Tudeh party as a revisionist organisation with an anti-revolutionary agenda and linked the Tudeh's inactivity to Khrushchev's policy of peaceful coexistence. Rezvani offered to use his contacts with the Chinese in the service of this splinter organisation, which remained underground for its first year. At this point, it was still unclear whether the organisation was going to be separate from the Tudeh party or a faction within it, but all agreed it was necessary to engage in an ideological struggle with the Tudeh leadership and relocate the organisation to Iran.[47]

In December 1965, the ROTPI was brought into official existence in Tirana, Albania. Initially, they focused their activities on exploring the experiences of other countries in search of a model for revolution in

---

44 Matin-Asgari, *Student Opposition*, 69.
45 Rezvani, author interview.
46 Shokat, *Lashayi*, 48.
47 Matin-Asgari, *Student Opposition*, 81–82.

Iran. Rezvani was sent to Algeria to meet Fereydun Keshavarz through his Chinese contacts.[48] In 1966, he and Kashkuli were also sent to Cuba, although they found the Cubans to be overly militaristic.[49] The search ended with a full endorsement of the Chinese approach. Early ROTPI activities also included the dissemination of pamphlets on Mao's theory of world revolution and translations of the works of Lenin and Mao. The organisation began to publish a newspaper called *Tudeh* ('Masses') that endorsed a Maoist reading of Iranian society. It argued that the shah's reforms had been ineffective, that Iran was still a 'semi-feudal, semi-colonial' country, and that revolution would begin among the peasants.[50]

Returning to Iran was the main obsession of the ROTPI activists, and the decision to do so would have profound consequences for the organisation. Work toward this goal began while the ROTPI was not yet officially established. After returning from China, Parviz Nikkhah had already been back to Iran to survey the political situation.[51] In April 1965, an assassination attempt was carried out against the shah. Although the attempt failed and the perpetrator had only tenuous connections to the Nikkhah Group organising within Iran, the Iranian security service, SAVAK, used this incident as an excuse to arrest the entire cell and charge them with subversive activities 'probably inspired from China'.[52] Led by the ROTPI faction, the CISNU responded to the arrest of the Nikkhah Group with a massive publicity campaign against the shah and a series of heated letters exchanged between the British and Iranian parliaments concerning the fate of the students.[53] This resulted in the commutation of Nikkhah's sentence from death to life imprisonment. The episode was an important moment in the history of the CISNU, which provided the organisation with its first significant victory in a direct confrontation with the shah's government,

---

48 Shokat, *Rezvani*, 71.
49 Shokat, *Rezvani*, 71.
50 *Pish besu-ye vahdat-e osuli-ye marksist-leninistha,* 1969, 39.
51 Shokat, *Lashayi*, 46–50.
52 'Report of Mr. Louis Blom-Cooper to Amnesty International', Iran, Nov 1965, 4, Justice in Iran (Amnesty International) file, Laurence Elwell-Sutton papers, University of St Andrews.
53 'British Committee for the Defence of Political Prisoners in Iran', Justice in Iran (Amnesty International) file, Laurence Elwell-Sutton papers, University of St Andrews.

and the shah with his first setback at the hands of a Maoist-oriented student groups.[54]

The ROTPI in China

In 1965, Kashkuli, Lashayi and several others were sent to Beijing for military and ideological training.[55] The curriculum included the Chinese revolution, Mao's theories on guerrilla warfare, and practical military lessons. Lessons were taught in Chinese with interpretation provided by two translators from Nanjing University. When they were not attending classes, students were housed in comfortable villas for foreign guests on the outskirts of Beijing, away from residential areas. The compounds were fenced and guarded so contact with the local Chinese or even other student groups was prevented. However, the group would occasionally sneak out or catch glimpses of other delegations and noted the presence of many Africans and Europeans in an analogous situation. The Iranians even took their meals separately from the Chinese, who ate meagre portions of cabbage and rice that were unappetising by Iranian standards.

Lashayi and Kashkuli also encountered the Chinese obsession with adaptability. Kashkuli noted that '[t]he remarkable thing was the Chinese professors always said the same thing before the lessons: Comrades, this is the experience of the Chinese revolution and should not be copied...You must identify the special conditions in your country and align Marxism with the Iranian situation.'[56] In a letter to Rezvani, Kashkuli writes that the teacher encouraged them to 'try to match the issues with the specific circumstances...and conditions in Iran.'[57] Kashkuli and Lashayi had the opportunity to do so when they returned from China later that year and were sent to Iran to contact the ongoing Qashqai revolt. Their efforts were unsuccessful, and a year later they narrowly escaped with their lives when the movement was crushed by government forces. Kashkuli's later attempts to foment Maoist rebellion in Iranian Kurdistan also failed to

---

54 Matin-Asgari, *Student Opposition*, 86–89.
55 Shokat, *Kashkuli* 35–40; and Shokat, *Lashayi*, 50–57.
56 Shokat, *Kashkuli*, 37.
57 Shokat, *Kashkuli*, 341.

act as the single spark that set off a prairie fire of peasant revolution.[58] As Peyman Vahabzadeh points out, this incident demonstrated the ROTPI's 'illusions about the realities of rural Iran' and the applicability of Maoist theory to Iran, though it did not deter the organisation from its chosen path.[59]

ROTPI activists were also sent to China to assist with its Radio Peking service. Radio Peking was the CCP's official Cold War radio propaganda operation, comparable to Radio Free Europe or Radio Moscow, albeit with a smaller audience.[60] It had commenced broadcasting in Persian on 15 October 1957 with the help of Tudeh experts, but the production of new programmes became impossible once they departed. By 1963, Radio Peking was not broadcasting in Persian at all.[61] Although the Persian component of Chinese radio broadcasts had a demonstrably miniscule audience, the CCP remained committed to broadcasting in a variety of languages.[62] It was important that China appeared to be engaged in global activism, and wide-ranging linguistic programmes were part of that image. Tehrani wanted to turn the whole station into a platform for anti-shah propaganda. However, the Chinese programmers insisted on more mundane broadcasts about agricultural statistics and the Chinese view on world affairs. Tehrani's requests were met with a flat refusal, although never an explanation. He was told that this was the policy of 'higher-up' comrades.[63] Without any real leverage against the CCP, Tehrani was forced to accept the situation without demur.

The ROTPI and the Cultural Revolution

In 1966, Mao launched the Cultural Revolution (1966–1976) to reassert

---

58 Shokat, *Tehrani*, 164.

59 Peyman Vahabzadeh, *A Rebel's Journey: Mostafa Sho'aiyan and Revolutionary Theory in Iran*, 2019, 21.

60 See Cagdas Üngör, 'Reaching the Distant Comrade: Chinese Communist Propaganda Abroad (1949–1976)', Ph. D. thesis, State University of New York at Binghamton, 2009.

61 Üngör, 'Distant Comrade', 311.

62 Üngör, 'Distant Comrade', 294.

63 Shokat, *Tehrani*, 116.

control over the party and push back against his opponents. He did this through the mass mobilisation of his supporters, especially students. His appeals targeted the CCP itself, and students were encouraged to 'bombard the headquarters' and rebel against any party member or authority figure who opposed Mao.[64] Eventually, this devolved into witch hunts to root out those with 'bourgeois' habits or mentalities but was more often used to target personal and political enemies. The resulting period became known for its ideological excesses, striking propaganda campaigns, and societal chaos.

Cultural Revolution propaganda began to portraying Mao as the sage-like leader of a global revolutionary movement, and the ROTPI was deployed as proof.[65] In October 1966, *People's Daily* published a letter from an anonymous Iranian chemistry student praising Mao's revolutionary ideology: 'Learning chemistry can't save my nation, [but] reading the works of Mao Zedong can.'[66] A 1967 article titled 'People of the World all Love to Read Mao's Book' told of an Iranian in Beijing who spoke enthusiastically about his meeting with Mao.[67] Other articles highlighted the 'serious study' of Mao Zedong Thought by Iranian students and trumpeted the ROTPI's publication of Maoist texts in Persian.[68] On 21 July 1967, *People's Daily* featured a conversation that ostensibly occurred between Tehrani and Chinese writer Jin Jingmai, author of *The Song of Ouyang Hai*, a popular novel promoting socialist martyrdom. Tehrani is said to have praised the vigour of a group of youthful swimmers, calling them 'Ouyang Hai-style youth! You should sing their praises.' He attributed this spirit to the education of Chairman Mao and reportedly shouted, 'Long Live Mao Zedong!'[69] On several other occasions, Tehrani was quoted in the Chinese press by his codename used in ROTPI correspondences, Laming Tongzhi (Comrade Ramin).[70] At a 1967 conference for African and Asian Writers in

---

64 Mao Zedong, 'Pào dǎ sīlìng bù', *People's Daily*, 5 August 1967.
65 See Barbara Mittler, *A Continuous Revolution: Making Sense of Cultural Revolution Culture*, 2016.
66 'Dú Máo zhǔxí de shū cái nénggòu jiùguó', *People's Daily*, 15 October 1966.
67 'Shìjiè rénmín dōu ài dú Máo zhǔxí de shū', *People's Daily*, 13 January 1967.
68 'Yīlǎng gémìng zhě fābiǎo wénzhāng', *People's Daily*, 26 October 1967.
69 'Zài Máo zhǔxí kāipì de hánglù shàng', *People's Daily*, 21 July 1967.
70 Shokat, *Rezvani*, 302.

Beijing, he told reporters 'the path of violent revolution is the only way for the liberation of the Iranian people. Only the raging fires of a People's War can burn away the decaying chains of slavery.'[71] The press also publicised meetings between delegates at the conference, including 'Ramin', with prominent officials like Zhou Enlai, Lin Biao, Kang Sheng, Chen Boda, and Mao Zedong.[72]

Whether or not these articles represent genuine conversations and convictions, they are indicative of the way in which the ROTPI's presence in China was mobilised in domestic propaganda. While Iran was not the centre of any specific campaign, the presence of Iranian and other international revolutionaries in China could be mobilised in the press to demonstrate the universal appeal of Mao Zedong's ideas. China was depicted as an active proponent of world revolution and potential leader of the global socialist movement.

As the Cultural Revolution intensified, its rhetoric had a major impact on the ROTPI. Some of its members, such as Majid Zarbaksh and Ali Shams, were greatly affected by the time they spent in China during the Cultural Revolution. Shams became particularly known for 'waving around his little red book' and leading self-criticism sessions, where some members broke down in tears for alleged bourgeois crimes.[73] In China, Kashkuli recalled how during this period, Mao's Little Red Book, officially titled *Quotations from Chairman Mao Zedong*, were read before and after every meal. Persian translations of *Quotations* were produced and distributed, which the ROTPI hailed as 'a concrete manifestation of internationalist assistance to our people' and urged Iranian revolutionaries to 'learn to apply these theories'.[74] A telegram sent by the ROTPI to the CCP on the 21st anniversary of the founding of the People's Republic of China in October 1970, reflected this understanding of the Cultural Revolution as a positive experience:

The Great Chinese Proletarian Cultural Revolution initiated and

---

71 'Yīlǎng dàibiǎo lā míng de fǎ yán', *People's Daily*, 2 July 1967.
72 'Máo zhǔxí línbiāo tóngzhì jiējiàn gèguó zuòjiā hé péngyǒu', *People's Daily*, 9 June 1967.
73 Shokat, *Rezvani*, 49–151; and Shokat, *Lashayi*, 81.
74 'Yīlǎng gémìng zhě fābiǎo wénzhāng', *People's Daily*, 26 October 1968.

led by Chairman Mao Zedong is a great historical event...Never let
China change its colour...The existence of a mighty Red China with
advanced levels of industry, science, and technology...are a great
inspiration to the people of the world.[75]

Lashayi said of this time that, when it came to Maoist dogma, 'we
became more Catholic than the Pope'.[76]

The ROTPI had looked to Maoism as a model for making revolution,
but for some, it now meant an intellectual and spiritual renewal attained by
purging oneself of bourgeois thoughts and actions. In an article quoted in
People's Daily, an unnamed Iranian Revolutionary wrote that:

> By reforming our world outlook, we can better understand Marxism,
> Leninism, and Mao Zedong Thought...we can change the objective
> world, that is, society. In other words, if we want to have a revolution,
> we must first have correct thinking.

The author claimed that the ROTPI had studied the works of Mao
and 'made great changes' in their personal and political lives.[77] This new
approach was off-putting for the leadership, who found the self-criticism
sessions overly dramatic (and were often the targets of accusations of bourgeois thought). Rezvani perceived this as a challenge to the leadership.[78]

Other members like Tehrani were disillusioned by what they saw in
China, including the purge of officials at the Radio Peking bureau where
he worked, and came to question the wisdom of following the Chinese
line.[79] By 1969, these underlying internal tensions spilled into the open
when some members, including Tehrani, left to form the splinter group
Kadr-ha ('Cadres') and *Tufan* ('Storm'), which had been created in 1965
as a rival Maoist party, stepped up its polemical attacks on the ROTPI.
While Maoist parties and sympathisers maintained a strong presence in
the CISNU, especially in the United States, the ROTPI itself was isolated

---

75 'Yīlǎng gémìng zhě diànhè wǒ guóqìng', *People's Daily*, 4 October 1970.
76 Shokat, *Lashayi*, 56.
77 'Yīlǎng gémìng zhě fābiǎo wénzhāng', *People's Daily*, 29 May 1968.
78 Shokat, *Rezvani*, 149–151.
79 Shokat, *Tehrani*, 223–224, 232, 278.

'The Collected Works of Mao Zedong, Vol 1', Persian
edition. Published in Beijing, 1969.

and under attack by both nationalist and smaller Maoist factions by the
1970s.[80]

ROTPI activists responded to the challenge of the Cadres and the Tufan
by doubling down on their convictions. They began a new publication
called *Red Star* (*Setareh-ye Sorkh)* in 1970, which openly trumpeted its
Maoist convictions.[81] At the same time, the shah had steadily been improving ties with China, which led to the establishment of official diplomatic
relations in 1971.[82] Despite Mao's warning, the ROTPI maintained a
narrow view of Maoist politics and continued to interpret events in Iran
through the lens of the Chinese experience, which blinded them to changing realities on the ground and proved unpopular over time. They maintained that Iran was a 'semi-feudal' country rather than one transitioning
to a capitalist economy, and championed a rural, peasant-based revolution.
This was despite having received reports to the contrary from members in
Iran as early as 1962, like Nikkhah, who argued that conditions were not
good for rural revolution and that the peasants were not enthusiastic about
a Maoist-style People's Republic.

---

80 Matin-Asgari, *Student Opposition*, 138–140.
81 *Haft sal setareh-ye sorkh (1349–1356)*, 1356/1977.
82 For details on how this process occurred and the impact on the CCP's official
relationship with the ROTPI, see William Figueroa, 'China and the Iranian
Revolution: New Perspectives on Sino–Iranian Relations, 1965–1979', *Asian Affairs*
53, 2022.

An issue of *Setareh-ye Sorkh*. Above the title: 'Forward under
the banner of Marxism-Leninism-Mao Zedong Thought'.

Criticised for its ideological rigidity and suffering from splits, confusion,
and the general disarray that characterised global Maoist politics in the
mid-1970s, the ROTPI was in decline.[83] While it did not endorse China's
pro-Tehran policy, it also did not criticise China outright. Furthermore,
its attempts to set up bases in Iran had failed, and several of its members
had been involved in highly public defections; for example, Nikkhah and
Lashayi had recanted their views and were now involved in creating a
pro-shah Maoist-style political party in Iran.[84] This contributed to a steady
decline in the popularity of Maoist factions. Throughout the early 1970s,
the National Front factions led a campaign against their ROTPI rivals in a
bid to gain greater control over the student union. Eventually, the Maoist
factions split from the CISNU and from each other, bringing an end to the
era of unified student activism.[85]

The Impact of Iranian Maoism

Although the Iranian Maoist movement only lasted a decade, it left an
unmistakable imprint on the tactics, rhetoric, and ideology of the Iranian
opposition. First, under the leadership of Maoist student groups, the
CISNU engaged in some of its most radical opposition to the shah. Though
initially cautious, attitudes quickly changed after violence broke out at

83 Matin-Asgari, *Student Opposition*, 145.
84 Matin-Asgari, *Both Eastern and Western*, 235; and Shokat, *Lasha'i*, 86.
85 Matin-Asgari, *Student Opposition*, 146–147.

Tehran University in June 1963. In January 1964, the CISNU adopted a resolution that stated that 'the shah speaks the language of bullets, one must speak to him in his own language'.[86] It is important to recognise that it was domestic developments that sent shockwaves throughout the community abroad and enhanced the appeal of Maoist politics, not the other way around. Other non-Maoist radical currents, like the Fada'iyan and the Mojahedin, were moving towards armed struggle and rejected key tenets of Maoism even as they engaged with its literature. Maoism did not radicalise Iranian students through its universal appeal or rhetorical power but did play a key part in their journey towards radical politics.

By 1965, the ROTPI had officially split from the Tudeh. As a minority faction in the CISNU, it was at the forefront of the new wave of radical, militant politics that was electrifying student movements around the world.[87] By 1968, it had joined the global student movement and participated in numerous anti-colonial, anti-war, and anti-shah activities. The Confederation was declared an 'anti-imperialist, democratic, and popular' organisation and members elected increasingly radical leaders. By 1969, Maoists had come to dominate the organisation and all five members of its secretariat were from Maoist factions.[88] The ISAUS experienced a similar evolution and took a pro-Chinese stance by 1969. By 1971, the CISNU had openly declared that the Soviet Union was pursuing an 'anti-people' foreign policy. The Confederation experienced incredible growth during this period; from 1969 to 1971 alone, its annual budget grew from 12,000 German marks per year to over 135,000 marks from 2,000 official members.[89]

The radicalisation of the student movement directly contributed to the CISNU's support of guerrilla organisations within Iran. This support amplified the impact of the guerrilla movement by making it an international issue and galvanising the opposition both inside and outside Iran through highly visible expressions of solidarity.[90] Ironically, it was partly

---

86 Matin-Asgari, *Student Opposition,* 67.
87 Matin-Asgari, *Student Opposition*, 98, 104–106.
88 Stephanie Cronin, *Social Histories of Iran: Modernism and Marginality in the Middle East*, 2021, 39.
89 Matin-Asgari, *Student Opposition,* 126.
90 Cronin, *Social Histories,* 44.

the rise of non-Maoist armed struggle in Iran that contributed to the demise of Maoist sympathies within the CISNU. When the guerrilla movement against the shah was launched with the Siahkal incident of 8 February 1971, the Maoist factions within the student movement were at the peak of their influence, and as students found an alternative to Chinese-sponsored radicalism, their enthusiasm for Maoist politics would soon wane.

This loss of influence did not translate to a less radical stance within the Confederation, and the politics that the ROTPI helped institutionalise remained. From 1972 to 1975, the CISNU engaged in numerous campaigns to support students arrested in connection with violent anti-shah activities. Through hunger strikes, newspaper articles, and public demonstrations, their involvement brought unwelcome attention to the shah's blatant use of political violence and led to a campaign against Iran for human rights violations from international organisations like Amnesty International. By 1974, they openly called for the overthrow of the shah, and Western media had become increasingly hostile towards his repressive policies.[91] The shah's government responded to the militant attacks and CISNU activities with increased repression, and many historians argue this combination of international pressure abroad and lack of political freedoms at home contributed to his eventual downfall.[92]

The guerrilla movement was also affected by Maoist politics. Emerging from the same intellectual, social, and political milieu as the student movement, both Islamic and Marxist guerrillas engaged with Maoism as part of an eclectic engagement with multiple Third World revolutionary trends. They read Maoist texts, among other strands of thought, in their search for a model of militant revolution. As Matin-Asgari notes:

> Guerrilla theorists, whether Muslim or Marxist, argued that armed action was the only viable option left...Their literature was also attentive to and even preoccupied with contemporary revolutionary theory and practice in Latin America, Algeria, Palestine, China, and Vietnam.[93]

---

91 Matin-Asgari, *Student Opposition,* 134–140.
92 Abrahamian, *Modern Iran*, 152.
93 Matin-Asgari, *Both Eastern and Western*, 216–217.

The two most prominent militant organisations were the Fada'iyan, and the Mojahedin, both of which grew out of clandestine groups that studied the works of Mao, Régis Debray, Che Guevara, and Liu Shaoqi.[94] While Maoism was not uniquely influential among this mix, it was part of a larger engagement with 'Third World' militant movements that reflected a turn towards internationalism and radical politics in the wake of brutal repression.

The Mojahedin incorporated Maoist texts and slogans into their early materials and ideological orientation. This has led some earlier scholars to erroneously see Maoism as their 'original' ideology and argue that the movement only adopted an Islamic orientation later.[95] Abrahamian argues instead that the organisation was always Muslim, and that a major split occurred in 1975, when some members left to form the 'Marxist Mojahedin' and explicitly endorsed Maoist theory. They were particularly influenced by Mao's essay 'On Contradictions', which they adopted as their primary 'handbook' on revolution.[96] In other words, while they did not explicitly endorse Maoism, Maoist texts formed an important part of their understanding of revolution.

Ultimately, Maoism was rejected by the guerrilla movement. Bijan Jazani, one of the most prominent Fada'iyan thinkers, derided the Iranian Maoist movement for its attempts to 'have a hand in events from afar and whose knowledge of the country is about the same as their knowledge of Burma and Nepal'.[97] He also criticised China's engagement with the Iranian state, which he charged was a way to 'deceive progressive forces at home' and 'relieve itself of possible political and propaganda pressures which might otherwise be brought'.[98] This assessment came to be shared by many in the student movement after China and Iran re-established relations in 1971 and was a major factor in the demise of Iranian Maoism. Ironically, it can be said that the Iranian guerrillas followed the advice Mao gave Rezvani far more closely than any Maoist – rather than dogmatically

94 Haqshenas, 'Communism in Persia'.
95 Ervand Abrahamian. *The Iranian Mojahedin*, 1989, 2.
96 Abrahamian, *The Iranian Mojahedin*, 156, 163.
97 Bizhan Jazani, 'Land Reform in Modern Iran' in *Capitalism and Revolution in Iran*, 1980, 72, 116.
98 Jazani, 'Land Reform', 94.

following the example of China or any other country, they sought to adapt Marxism to the Iranian context. Jazani and other guerrilla theorists had direct experience with repression in Iran and the changes brought about by the shah's reforms, which 'convinced them of the necessity of armed struggle without simply duplicating the existing models'.[99]

Iranian Maoism and the Shah's Regime

The popularity of radical organisations did not go unnoticed by their opponents and rivals. Religious conservatives like Khomeini began using phrases like *mostazafin* ('the oppressed') in his sermons and railed against imperialism and social inequality. This 'project of plagiarizing from the left, to buttress right-wing hegemony' impacted the language of the Islamic Revolution as well, such as the 1980 *Enqelab-e Farhangi* (Cultural Revolution).[100] The shah engaged in a similar project of co-opting popular leftist ideas to put them in the service of dictatorship. The 1963 White Revolution was draped in the language of popular reform, and opponents like Jalal Al-e Ahmad complained bitterly that 'the shah had stolen these ideas from thinkers like Maleki' and was using them to justify his own position.[101] Many of these reforms were successful in modernising Iran's economic, educational, and legal system, but often in ways that concentrated power and wealth into private hands. Furthermore, the changes to traditional society and lack of political reforms only heightened opposition to the shah from all sections of Iranian society. Still, the government perceived the venture as a success, and often claimed the White Revolution prevented a Red Revolution from taking place.

The shah was portrayed as the guiding force behind these reforms, the leader of the so-called 'Shah-People Revolution', a rhetorical flourish that was already beginning to resemble the language of Maoism and the New Left. Over time, the state became more involved in the production of an intellectual culture explicitly cultivated to counter the opposition, such as

---

99 See Peyman Vahabzadeh, *A Guerrilla Odyssey: Modernization, Secularism, Democracy, and Fadai Period of National Liberation in Iran, 1971–1979*, 2010, 14.
100 Matin-Asgari, *Both Eastern and Western*, 223.
101 Jalal Al-e Ahmad, *Dar khedmat va khianat-e roshanfekran*, 1977, 336–337.

the creation of the High Council of Culture and the Arts, which employed former Marxists and Maoists in prominent positions.[102] Central to these new propaganda efforts was the abandonment of cultural and moral Westernisation in favour of a rhetoric of cultural and spiritual renewal that drew on ancient Iranian history. This reinvigorated culture, the shah argued, was superior to both liberalism and socialism and would ultimately be accepted by the entire world. Zhand Shakibi describes this as an 'attempt…to make a discursive shift in Iran's position vis-à-vis the West, from student of the West to its mentor.'[103] In one article that laid out the Party's philosophy, the authors proclaimed:

> It is no coincidence that the peak of Iranian glory coincides with the rise of powerful and enlightened emperors. History shows that such emperors were committed to the people and occupied the role of commander while being active in the life and livelihood of society, so that whenever this role of commander has diminished for some reason, the growth of society and national prosperity has stagnated.[104]

Rastakhiz publications made it clear that the shah felt that it was imperative to 'introduce to the world the Aryan path of salvation'.[105]

According to Asadollah 'Alam, one of the most influential members of the shah's court in the 1970s, it was the shah's direct 'order and wish that we raise a hand against the Communists and use their language to crush them'.[106] As a result, the Rastakhiz Party adopted both the rhetoric and organisational principles of communist parties and even counted among its members ex-communists, and especially ex-Maoists. Former members of the ROTPI like Parviz Nikkhah, Firuz Fuladi, and Kurosh Lashayi occupied key positions, with Lashayi directly involved in formulating

---

102 Matin-Asgari, *Both Eastern and Western*, 193.
103 Zhand Shakibi, *Pahlavi Iran and the Politics of Occidentalism: The Shah and the Rastakhiz Party*, 2018, 135–136.
104 *Andisheh-ha-ye Rastakhiz*, Aban 1355/November 1976. Accessed at Nashriyah: Digital Iranian History Collection.
105 *Rastakhiz*, 28 Khordad 1355/18 June 1976.
106 Assadollah 'Alam, *Yaddasht-ha-ye 'Alam*, ed. A. Alikhani, 1393/2014, vol. 6, 285–286.

the shah's 'neither Eastern, nor Western' foreign policy.[107] He also spent over a thousand hours with 'Alam's close ally and ex-Tudeh organiser Mohammad Baheri attempting to harmonise state discourse with Marxist terminology at the shah's request. He proposed the idea of 'divine dialectics' whereby social changes instigated by the sovereign were viewed as divinely ordained, to distinguish from Marxist dialectics.[108] As noted, this pattern of defections was one of the factors that damaged the prestige of the Maoist movement abroad.

The propaganda and rhetoric of the shah's 'revolutionary' regime came to portray the shah as a sage-king whose revolutionary ideology would lead Iran and the world to spiritual renewal. As part of the shah's policy to crush the communists with their own words, this approach paralleled Maoist propaganda, which depicted Maoism as an anti-imperial, anti-Western philosophy that would eventually be embraced by all, and Mao as the 'Great Helmsman'. Like the White Revolution before it and the Cultural Revolution in China, it was meant to strengthen the shah's grip on power and remake society in his image, with himself at the helm. In the end, however, this ill-conceived venture did little to achieve its goals. Although the Rastakhiz Party was the sole legal political party in Iran from 1975 to 1978, its lack of popular support caused it to merely reinforce the perception that Iran was a totalitarian state.

Beyond a Narrative of Failure

Iranian Maoism has long been relegated to the margins of the historiography of the Iranian Left. Its influence on the rhetoric and tactics of the state and the opposition have been overlooked because it was on the losing side of history many times over – destroyed and derided by the Islamic Republic, and blamed by the rest of the opposition for its blunders and for fracturing the Left. Whatever truth there may be to these criticisms, this study insists that there is value in a deeper and more holistic interrogation of marginalised historical experiences. Viewed from this perspective, Iranian Maoism is more than a failure, but rather was a lively and meaningful

---

107 Matin-Asgari, *Both Eastern and Western*, 235.
108 Matin-Asgari, *Both Eastern and Western*, 235; and Shakibi, *Pahlavi Iran*, 231.

social movement which touched the lives of a generation of young Iranian activists, changed how they viewed Iran's place in the global community, mediated their transition to a new kind of politics, and was itself replaced as the international and domestic environment shifted.

The brief popularity of Maoism was spurred by the collapse of the traditional Iranian opposition groups in the wake of government repression, which led to a search for a new way forward among leftists and liberals. In contrast to the dominant Soviet theory of peaceful coexistence, China endorsed armed struggle against capitalism and supported contemporary militant movements. Against this backdrop, a small group of Iranian students in Europe established a limited partnership with the CCP to pursue their own revolutionary goals and gather supporters. Wielding Mao Zedong Thought as a weapon to critique the central committee of the Tudeh Party, and later their own members, the ROTPI and other Maoist factions became an important force in the early student movement.

China provided military training but did little else to support the ROTPI agenda, and eventually established official relations with the shah in 1971. This demonstrates a clear preference for the stability, enhanced international prestige, and strategic advantages that positive relations with the Iranian state could provide over the ideological imperatives of encouraging armed revolution. The ROTPI cadres found in China a useful set of rhetorical tools to criticise the inertia of the Tudeh and gain influence among the increasingly radical Iranian student population. Their relationship with the Chinese government, while limited, was significant in that it provided the CCP with effective internal propaganda at a low political and financial cost.

This episode also may have convinced the shah of the danger of Chinese ideological influence and contributed to his decision to open lines of communication with the People's Republic of China. Immediately following the attempt on his life by what he understood to be an Iranian Maoist radical, the shah began sounding the alarm about Chinese ideological infiltration in private conversations with US officials and public interviews, but secretly and simultaneously began softening his stance towards China as early as 1966. Combined with his adoption of Maoist-style rhetoric and the strategic deployment of ex-Maoists throughout his propaganda networks, it seems likely that his goal was to defang what he saw as the dangerous potential of Maoist ideology to influence Iranian youth.[109]

The events covered in this study are truly transnational, in the sense that they are not located in any one country and cannot be understood without reference to multiple overlapping social and political contexts. The insights that can be gained from such a study help to de-provincial-ise Iranian history and move us towards an understanding of where Iran belongs in a truly global history of the twentieth century. It also provides a crucial example of South-South interactions and explores the formation of political identities from an inter-Asian, rather than East-West perspective. Most studies of Iran's international or transnational relations have focused on Iran's ties with the West. Studies like this one allow us to re-examine the almost hegemonic discourse of 'Iran and the West' in much of the lit-erature and instead consider Iran's Asian identity. This trend of looking at Iran in an Asian context is already well-developed in the historiography of ancient, medieval, and early modern Iran, but we can now begin to extend this trend into the study of the twentieth century as well.

Bibliography

Abrahamian, E. *A History of Modern Iran*, Cambridge, 2008.

Abrahamian, E. *Iran Between Two Revolutions*, Princeton, 1982.

Abrahamian, E. *The Iranian Mojahedin*, New Haven, 1989.

'Alam, A. *Yaddasht-ha-ye 'Alam*, ed. A. Alikhani, 7 volumes, Tehran, 1393/2014.

Al-e Ahmad, J. *Dar khedmat va khianat-e roshanfekran*, Tehran, 1977.

Amanat, A. *Iran: A Modern History*, New Haven, 2017.

Amnesty International, 'British Committee for the Defence of Political Prisoners in Iran', Justice in Iran (Amnesty International) file, Laurence Elwell-Sutton papers, University of St Andrews.

Amnesty International, 'Report of Mr. Louis Blom-Cooper to Amnesty International', Iran, Nov 1965, Justice in Iran (Amnesty International) file, Laurence Elwell-Sutton papers, University of St Andrews.

---

109 See Figueroa, 'China and the Iranian Revolution', 113–116.

Azad, S. *Iran and China: A New Approach to Their Bilateral Relations*, Lanham, 2017.

Mittler, B. *A Continuous Revolution: Making Sense of Cultural Revolution Culture*. Harvard East Asian Monographs, 2016.

Behrooz, M. *Rebels with a Cause: The Failure of the Iranian Left*, London, 2000.

Behrooz, M. 'Tudeh Factionalism and the 1953 Coup in Iran', *International Journal of Middle East Studies* 33/3, 2002, 363–382.

Cook, A., ed. *Mao's Little Red Book: A Global History*, Cambridge, 2014.

Cronin, S. *In Social Histories of Iran: Modernism and Marginality in the Middle East*, Cambridge, 2021.

Craig Harris, L. 'China's Relationship with the PLO', *Journal of Palestine Studies* 7/1, Autumn, 1977, 123–154.

Figueroa, W. 'China and the Iranian Revolution: New Perspectives on Sino-Iranian Relations, 1965–1979', *Asian Affairs* 53, 2022, 106–123.

Friedman, J. *Shadow Cold War: The Sino–Soviet Competition for the Third World*, Chapel Hill, 2015.

Garver, J. *China and Iran: Ancient Partners in a Post-Imperial World*, Seattle, 2004.

Garver, J. *China's Quest: A History of the Foreign Relations of the People's Republic of China*, New York, 2016.

Hadi-zadah, M. *Chin va ertebatat-e Irani-Islami*, Isfahan, 1391/2012.

Hafizullah, E. 'China's Ideological Influence and Trade Relations with Iran, 1960–1990', *Internationales Asienforum* 29/1, 1995, 143–154.

Haqsenas, T. 'Communism in Persia after 1953', *Encyclopædia Iranica*, 2011. Available online: https://iranicaonline.org/articles/communism-iii.

Jazani, B. *Capitalism and Revolution in Iran*, London, 1980.

Keddie, N. *Modern Iran: Roots and Results of Revolution*, New Haven, 2006.

Lovell, J. *Maoism: A Global History*, London, 2019.

Lüthi, L. *The Sino–Soviet Split: Cold War in the Communist World*. Princeton, 2008.

Maleki, K., *Nehzat-e melli va edalat-e ejtemayi*, Tehran, 1998.

Matin-Asgari, A. *Both Eastern and Western: An Intellectual History of Iranian Modernity,* Cambridge, 2018.

Matin-Asgari, A. 'Iranian Maoism: Searching for a Third World Revolutionary Model', *MERIP* 270, Spring 2014.

Matin-Asgari, A. *Iranian Student Opposition to the Shah*, Costa Mesa, USA, 2002.

Mirsepassi, A. *Intellectual Discourse and the Politics of Modernization: Negotiating Modernity in Iran*, Cambridge, 2000.

Naderi, M. *Maoism dar Iran* (Maoism in Iran), Tehran, 1397/2019.

Rahnema, A. *The Rise of Modern Despotism in Iran: The Shah, the Opposition, and the US, 1953–1968*, London, 2021.

Revolutionary Organization of the Tudeh Party of Iran Abroad, *Pish besu-ye vahdat-e osuli-ye marksist-leninistha* (Towards the Unification of Marxist-Leninist Principles), 1969.

Revolutionary Organization of the Tudeh Party of Iran Abroad, *Haft sal setareh-ye sorkh (1349–1356)*, Rome, 1356/1977.

Shahibzadeh, Y. *Marxism and Left-Wing Politics in Europe and Iran*, Oslo, 2019.

Shannon, M. *Losing Hearts and Minds: American-Iranian Relations and International Education during the Cold War*. Ithaca, 2017.

Shokat, H. *Negahi az darun be jonbesh-e chap-e Iran: Goftegu ba Mehdi Khanbaba Tehrani,* Cologne, 1380/2000.

Shokat, H. *Negahi az darun be jonbesh-e chap-e Iran: Goftegu ba Kurosh Lashayi,* Cologne, 1383/2004.

Shokat, H. *Negahi az darun be jonbesh-e chap-e Iran: Goftegu ba Mohsen Rezvani,* Cologne, 1384/2005.

Shokat, H. *Negahi az darun be jonbesh-e chap-e Iran: Goftegu ba Iraj Kashkuli,* Cologne, 1386/2007.

Slobodian, Q. 'The Meanings of Western Maoism in the Global 1960s', *The Routledge Handbook of the Global Sixties: Between Protest and Nation-Building*, ed. Chen Jian et al, Abingdon, 2018, 67–78.

Suri, J. *Global Revolutions of 1968,* New York, 2006.

Takriti, A.R. *Monsoon Revolution: Republicans, Sultans, and Empires in Oman, 1965–1976*, Oxford, 2013.

Üngör, C. 'Reaching the Distant Comrade: Chinese Communist Propaganda Abroad (1949–1976)' Ph. D. thesis, State University of New York at Binghamton, 2009.

Vahabzadeh, P. *A Guerrilla Odyssey: Modernization, Secularism, Democracy, and Fadai Period of National Liberation in Iran, 1971–1979*, Syracuse, USA, 2010.

Vahabzadeh, P. *A Rebel's Journey: Mostafa Sho'aiyan and Revolutionary Theory in Iran*, London, 2019.

Vali Allah, H. *Ravabet-e Iran va Chin: qabl va ba'd az enqelab-e eslami*, Tehran, 1390/2011.

Xingli, Y. *Xian dai Zhongguo yu Yilang guan xi*, Beijing, 2013.

Zhand, S. *Pahlavi Iran and the Politics of Occidentalism: The Shah and the Rastakhiz Party*, London, 2018.

Zongxian, L. *Zhong gong yu Yilang guan xi zhi yan jiu –1979 Nian Zhi 2008 Nian*, Taipei, 2014.

10

Radical Voices from within the Metropolis: Decolonisation and the Iranian Left in Europe, 1957–1967

Leonard Willy Michael

Since the early twentieth century, the issue of colonialism (*este 'mar*) and the struggle for national liberation (*mobarezeh-ye azadibakhsh-e melli*) were crucial elements in the political identity of Iran's various Leftist groups and organisations. After the forced abdication of Reza Shah in 1941, it was particularly the Tudeh Party of Iran (*Hezb-e Tudeh-ye Iran*) as well as individuals and factions which split from it such as the grouping around Khalil Maleki, Anvar Khame'i, and Jalal Al-e Ahmad which came to contribute crucially to the way segments of Iranian society would look at global decolonisation. However, with the coup d'état of 19 August 1953 and the ensuing repression of the opposition to Mohammad Reza Shah, in particular the Tudeh, the space for anti-colonial activism inside the country dramatically contracted. Following the crackdown on the re-emerging opposition in the early 1960s, the centre of the opposition's activity finally shifted abroad. While the general public as well as moderate intellectuals were able to continue their engagement with global decolonisation within the limits set by the Pahlavi regime, organisations of the radical Left were forced to develop and disseminate their ideas on anti-colonial resistance from abroad. It was particularly among the community of Iranian university students and graduates based in Western Europe that these groups gained a foothold. Some scholars, most notably Afshin Matin-Asgari,[1] have underscored the significance of this community for the political history of modern Iran. Together with their compatriots at universities in North America and Iran, Iranian students in Europe managed to constitute 'the most active and persistent force of opposition to the shah's regime during the two decades prior to the 1978–79 Revolution',[2] which was mostly due to their activities within the framework of the Confederation of Iranian Students/National Union (hereafter CISNU), which had been created through a merger of three already-existing Iranian student organisations from Iran, Europe, and North America in 1962.[3]

Inspired by Matin-Asgari's emphasis on Europe as one of the central spaces for the political activism of Iranians in the 1960s and 1970s, this chapter will explore how Iranian radical Leftists who were based in Europe engaged with national liberation struggles around the world in the ten years following the independence of Ghana, which liberated itself from colonial oppression as the first state of Sub-Sahara Africa in 1957. With almost fifty territories becoming independent from European colonial empires, this decade arguably was the most dense and heated period of decolonisation and anti-colonial resistance after the Second World War.

Yet instead of looking at the CISNU, this chapter will focus on the publications of political organisations of the Iranian radical Left in Europe which constituted political actors distinct from the Confederation even though their members and sympathisers would often take up significant roles inside it. This approach is motivated by two observations concerning the nature of CISNU. Firstly, several of the events which were key in making the period under study a crucial phase in the history of global decolonisation occurred prior to the emergence of CISNU as a political organisation.[4] Secondly, the Confederation's character as a politically

---

1 Afshin Matin-Asgari, *Iranian Student Opposition to the Shah*, 2002.

2 Matin-Agari, *Student Opposition*, 1.

3 Matin-Agari, *Student Opposition*, 26.

4 As mentioned above, the CISNU was founded only in 1962. Its predecessor in Europe, the Confederation of Iranian Students in Europe, had been established in 1960 already but had initially been envisaged to primarily serve as a corporate rather than a political body. Matin-Agari, *Student Opposition*, 35–36.

inclusive body which was constituted not only by Leftist currents but also by nationalist groupings complicates the analytical isolation of the radical Leftist discourse on anti-colonial resistance from the total CISNU output. The line of inquiry taken up by this chapter not only allows us to cover the period prior to the Confederation's establishment but also opens a new perspective on the activities of representatives of the Iranian radical Left and their interactions with each other. For while the followers of these groups often were enthusiastic members of the CISNU, they were also active outside its organisational framework.

By drawing on the publications of three major Leftist organisations, namely the Tudeh Party, the League of Iranian Socialists in Europe (*Jame'eh-ye Sosiyalist-ha-ye Irani dar Orupa*; hereafter the Socialists) and the Revolutionary Organisation of the Tudeh Party of Iran (*Sazman-e Enqelabi-ye Hezb-e Tudeh-ye Iran*; hereafter ROTPI),[5] this study explores how these activists, who were based in the metropoles of Europe's dissolving colonial empires, looked at the proponents of national liberation around the world and how their perspectives changed over the years.[6] The chapter will argue that the various cases of anti-colonial resistance constituted both sources of inspiration and focal points of competition for anti-imperialist theories. The analytical engagement with decolonisation gave these radicals an opportunity to clarify their positions, confirm their theories, and attack the approaches of their respective political rivals.

---

5 The selection of periodicals analysed in this study is not claimed to be exhaustive. Rather, it attempts to represent the three major currents within the Iranian Left during the period under study, namely the pro-Soviet Marxist-Leninists (the Tudeh), the pro-Chinese Maoists (ROTPI), and the radical proponents of non-alignment (the Socialists). The Leftist sub-currents inside the nationalist National Front Abroad (*Jebheh-ye melli-ye Iraniyan-e moqim-e kharejeh*), which found expression in publications like *Bakhtar-e Emruz* or, later, *Iran-e Azad* for example, have not been considered.

6 In actuality, none of the organisations which are studied in this paper used the term 'decolonisation' (*este'marzadayi*). Instead, they conceived of the proponents of decolonisation as 'national liberation movements' (*jonbesh-ha-ye azadibakhsh-e melli*). Moreover, they hardly referred to the regions negatively affected by colonialism as the 'Third World' but, explicitly, as 'Africa, Asia, and Latin America'. Nonetheless, this paper occasionally makes use of the term 'decolonisation' and 'Third World' in order to connect its content and findings to the overall theme of this volume.

In the absence of other means of communication or spaces in which these groups could openly operate, print publications were the most important and often only way for them to present their analyses. Because of the scarcity of sources concerning the production of these periodicals, the exact extent to which they were circulated among the community of Iranian students in Europe is difficult to assess. At best, one can make educated guesses; the number of copies per issue may have varied from a few hundred in the case of the publications of the Socialists, whose resources were very limited,[7] to a few thousand in the case of the Tudeh, which benefitted from the support of its brother parties.[8] Yet these rough estimates still tell us little about the actual size of the readership of each periodical, which was probably larger since a single copy may have been read by more than one person.

The coverage of national liberation movements in countries such as Algeria, Congo, and Vietnam by the media outlets of these groups strikingly reflected the general trend within the Iranian Left. While the main representative of the pro-Soviet, Marxist-Leninist Left, the Tudeh, was increasingly unable to engage productively with the crisis which decolonisation all over the world had to face in the second half of the decade, the emerging radical groups which sympathised with Maoist and other non-Soviet ideological traits could embrace even the atrocities of the Vietnam War and present the conflict as an opportunity to achieve a world without colonial oppression and thus opened a new path to political activists.

For each of the three groups under study, decolonisation or, as they framed it, national liberation was not simply achieved through formal independence. The process included achieving not only full political sovereignty but also economic self-determination. The anti-colonial interest of the Iranian radicals in the developments in decolonising countries did therefore not cease with the flags of the colonisers being brought down but persisted far beyond the respective independence days.

The broad definition of colonialism, which was underlying this interest

---

7 Nasser Pakdaman, interview by Hamid Ahmadi (Research Association for Iranian Oral History, hereafter RAIOH), 5 January 2013, and Amir Pishdad, interview by Hamid Ahmadi (RAIOH), 10 September 2009.

8 Abteilung Finanzverwaltung und Parteibetriebe (Central Committee of the East German Communist Party, hereafter ZK SED), Aktennotiz, 2 July 1958, BArch DY 30/97100, fol. 212.

but was only very rarely made explicit by any of these groups, often over-lapped with the concepts of imperialism and neo-colonialism. Frequently, these different terms and theoretical frameworks were used without much rigour nor a clear-cut line drawn between them. Rather than pieces of scholarly enquiry, the analyses authored by individuals affiliated to the three groups under study have to be seen as means of political commu-nication which aimed to mobilise their readers for a certain cause. In this context, terms like 'imperialism', 'colonialism', and 'national liberation' often served as buzzwords which were meant to simplify complex political developments and make them easily understandable for the organisations' respective target groups. Hence, excluding certain texts relating to events in the decolonising world from this chapter because they do not explicitly mention 'colonialism' would be overly narrow and complicate the com-prehensive understanding of how the three groups engaged with the global process which we frame as decolonisation. Therefore, the texts that have been selected for the following analysis relate not only to struggles for formal independence but also to a number of other political conflicts which took place in spaces that were seen as having been shaped by colonialism but were not anti-colonial in the literal meaning of the term, such as the Iraqi Revolution (1958) or the Vietnam War (1955–1975).

Breaking the Silence, 1957–1960

When Ghana became independent from the United Kingdom on 6 March 1957, there was no organisation of the Iranian radical Left based in Europe whose organ could have reported on the event, let alone analysed it. The Iranian community in Western Europe was still relatively small, and the limited activity of political groups that had emerged during the premier-ship of Mohammad Mosaddeq such as the Tudeh-affiliated Organisation of Iranian Students in Germany (*Sazman-e Daneshjuyan-e Irani-ye Moqim-e Alman*) had been suppressed by the long arm of the consolidating regime of Mohammad Reza Shah by the mid-1950s.[9]

It was the exiled Tudeh Party that was first to fill this vacuum. In the wake

9 Hamid Shokat, *Jonbesh-e Daneshjuyi: Konfederasiyun-e Jahani-ye Mohasselin va Daneshjuyan-e Irani (Ettehadieh-ye Melli)*, 2010, 50, 55–56.

of the fierce persecution of its members and the dismantling of its organisational structures after the coup of 1953, the party leadership, along with
rank-and-file members, had been forced to leave Iran and received asylum
in the countries of the Eastern Bloc.[10] In the summer following the independence of Ghana, the central committee of the party as well as selected
cadres gathered in Moscow for the fourth plenum of the party, which was
the first official meeting of the Tudeh in exile. There, the participants not
only addressed past shortcomings of the party leadership but also sought to
formulate a strategy for the re-organisation of the Tudeh outside of Iran.[11]

In this strategy, the struggle against colonialism took up a central role:
within the framework of an 'anti-colonial united front (*jebheh-ye vahed-e
zedd-e este'mari*)', all 'national' forces should be united to overthrow the
regime of Mohammad Reza Shah and achieve full independence for Iran. By
'national' forces, the attendants of the plenum had first and foremost meant
the followers of the then-dissolved National Front of former Prime Minister
Mosaddeq, which, in their eyes, represented Iran's 'national bourgeoisie'.[12]
In Marxist-Leninist theory, the most prominent characteristic of this social
stratum was its economic and, thus, political independence from foreign
capital. For most of Mosaddeq's premiership, the Tudeh's executive committee inside Iran had refused to cooperate with him and his government. It
was the political opposition to this major actor of the years between 1951 and
1953 which was among the most criticised issues at the plenum in Moscow.[13]
In response to these criticisms and in line with the positive assessment of the
role of the national bourgeoisie in struggles for national liberation by Soviet
theoreticians following the twentieth congress of the Communist Party of the
Soviet Union (hereafter CPSU) in 1956,[14] the Tudeh leadership reconsidered

---

10 On the early practice of asylum-seeking by Tudehi refugees, see Iraj Eskandari's
memoirs. Babak Amirkhosravi and Fereydun Azarnur, eds. *Khaterat-e Siyasi-ye Iraj
Eskandari,* 1366/1987, vol. III, 7–10.
11 Central Committee of the Tudeh Party of Iran (hereafter CC TPI), 'Information
über das erweiterte ZK-Plenum der Toudeh-Partei des Iran', 10 December 1957,
BArch DY 30/97100, fols. 133–136.
12 'Pelenom-e vasi'-e (chaharom) Hezb-e Tudeh-ye Iran (1336)', *Asnad-e
Tarikhi-ye Jonbesh-e Kargari/Sosiyaldemukrasi va Komunisti-ye Iran*, ed. Cosroe
Chaqueri, 1369/1990, vol. I, 364.
13 'Pelenom-e vasi'', 359–360.
14 'The 20th Congress of the CPSU and the Problems of Studying the

its analyses and concluded at the plenum that it should have supported Mosaddeq's government, and put an alliance with the former constituents of the National Front at the top of the party's agenda.[15]

That the Tudeh explicitly called this strategy to overthrow the post-coup government of Iran 'anti-colonial', clearly implies that the party saw the country as part of the colonised world even though it was formally independent and had never been officially colonised. Later analyses by members of the party's executive committee confirm this impression. Providing the theoretical base for the party's slogan in an article published in 1960, Secretary Iraj Eskandari explicitly regarded Iranian society as 'semi-colonial' (*nimeh mosta'mereh*).[16] Three years later, central committee member Nur al-Din Kianuri followed this assessment and used the same term to describe 'the unlimited control of our country's political and economic life by imperialist capital'. After Mosaddeq's politics of nationalisation had temporarily contained this influence, the post-coup regime, by re-organising the Iranian oil industry and integrating the country into the Baghdad Pact, enabled 'the capital of the imperialist monopolies' to return in full force.[17] In the view of these Tudeh authors, the new government and Mohammad Reza Shah himself were only agents of colonialism, seemingly ruling an ostensibly independent country.

The first step in creating the envisaged 'anti-colonial united front' to mobilise the Iranian masses against this semi-colonial oppression and overthrow its domestic agents was the resumption of the Tudeh's publication activity, to which the plenum assigned the executive committee of the party.[18] In February 1958, after three years of silence,[19] the first exile periodical of the Tudeh, *Sobh-e Omid* ('Dawn of Hope'), was produced in

---

Contemporary East', *The Third World in Soviet Perspective: Studies by Soviet Writers on the Developing Areas*, ed. Thomas P. Thornton, 1964, 82–83.

15 'Pelenom-e vasi'', 359–360.

16 Iraj Eskandari, 'Mabani-ye 'elmi-ye sho'ar-e jebheh-ye vahed-e niru-ha-ye melli va demukratik beh-masabeh-ye khatt-e mashi-ye asasi-ye Hezb-e Tudeh-ye Iran', *Donya* 1/2, 1339/1960, 5.

17 Nur al-Din Kianuri, 'Eslahat-e arzi dar Iran', *Donya* 4/1, 1342/1963, 10.

18 Kianuri, 'Eslahat', 394–395.

19 The last issue of the central organ of the Tudeh inside Iran, *Mardom*, appeared in December 1955. 'Mobarezeh edameh darad', *Mardom*, 10 Farvardin 1339/30 March 1960].

the East German city of Leipzig, to where the executive committee had been relocated in the winter of 1957/58. Its production was funded by the Tudeh's hosting brother party, the Socialist Unity Party of Germany (*Sozialistische Einheitspartei Deutschlands* SED aka the East German Communist Party).[20]

Sobh-e Omid was the manifestation of the Tudeh's united front strategy. No explicit mention was made with regard to the affiliation of the newspaper or the Tudeh Party itself. While it was pro-Soviet and anti-American in tone, it tried not to alienate potential allies among the 'national' forces and, first and foremost, focused on criticisms against the shah's government. Although pieces on domestic developments received most of the space of the newspaper's two pages, questions of anti-colonialism were at times addressed as well. The very first issue of the bi-weekly included a report on the 'Afro-Asian Peoples' Solidarity Conference', which had taken place in Cairo in December 1957 and January 1958. In this short piece, the author, who used the pen name B. Saman, made explicit what the decision of the fourth plenum had only implied. Criticising the absence of official Iranian representation[21] at the conference, Saman wrote that

> We have to realise that the fate of Iran is not separate from the fate of the African and Asian nations. The national interests of Iran require that we maintain as many as possible brotherly relations to these nations.[22]

To the authors who contributed to *Sobh-e Omid* and later Tudeh publications, this connection between Iran and other countries of the 'Third World', meant not only that they had to support each other but also that the Iranians could learn from the experiences of other formerly colonised or

---

20 Aktennotiz, BArch DY 30/97100, fol. 212.
21 The prominent Tudeh member and student activist Babak Amirkhosravi was among the few Iranians who attended the conference in other capacities than as official representatives of their country. As a member of the secretariat of the Prague-based International Union of Students, he had been assigned to attend the gathering. Babak Amirkhosravi, *Zendeginameh-ye Siyasi*, 2020, 201–202.
22 'Konferans-e hambastegi-ye mellat-ha-ye Asiya va Efriqa', *Sobh-e Omid*, 17 Bahman 1336/6 February 1958.

still-decolonising nations. In *Sobh-e Omid*, this became especially apparent in the coverage of the Iraqi Revolution of July 1958. The authors not only considered the violent overthrow of the country's pro-British monarchy a great victory over colonialism, describing the killing of prime minister Nuri Sa'id as 'a symbol for ending the era of this impure bootlicker of colonialism' (*ramzi ast az beh-payan residan-e dowran-e tarikhi-ye in 'atabeh-busan-e palid-e est'mar*). They also took it as an inspiring role model for their own country's national liberation movement, praising the new 'anti-imperialist republican regime' of the new prime minister 'Abd al-Karim Qasim and applauding its allegiance to 'the politics of Bandung [i.e., non-alignment]' as well as its exit from the US- and British-sponsored Baghdad Pact. Comparing Iraq's pre-coup government to the contemporary situation in Iran, they stated that 'the pain is the same, thus the therapy must be the same too'.[23] The Tudeh analysts looked at Iraq not only as a role model for revolutionary change in their own country, but also as proof that such a transformation could be possible at all. Their analyses of the coup, where they first and foremost stressed the unity of all of Iraq's national forces as well as their support by the Soviet Union and other colonised countries as an essential reason for its success,[24] were clearly written as recipes for similar operations in Iran and reflected what the party regarded as crucial requirements to overthrow the shah's regime and decolonise their country.

The Iranian Left in Europe and the Heyday of Decolonisation, 1960–1965

With the considerable expansion of the Tudeh's propaganda apparatus in 1960, global decolonisation received significantly more attention. The start of the publication of the bi-weekly central organ, *Mardom* ('The People'),[25]

---

23 'Dorud beh khalq-e delavar-e 'Eraq', *Sobh-e Omid*, 31 Tir 1337/22 July 1958.
24 'Dorud beh khalq-e delavar-e 'Eraq', and 'Raz-e piruzi-ye mardom-e 'Eraq', *Sobh-e Omid*, 21 Mordad 1337/12 August 1958.
25 In the spring of 1965, the Tudeh decided to publish *Mardom* as a monthly under the title *Mahnameh-ye Mardom*. According to the editorial of the first issue of the *Mahnameh*, this change was due to the difficulties arising from the news character of the content of *Mardom* as a biweekly. Under the conditions of exile and persecution,

and the quarterly theoretical journal, *Donya* ('The World'), came at an auspicious moment: in 1960 alone, eighteen territories on the African continent became independent from the French, Belgian, and British Colonial Empires. The articles published in *Mardom* that year overwhelmingly covered the colonial wars in Algeria and Congo. In their analyses of these developments, the authors used an approach similar to the one present in *Sobh-e Omid*; reports on the colonial struggle in other places around the world were often taken as opportunities to remind the readers of the situation in Iran. These reminders were often simplistic in describing a given situation. For example, in an article on Moïse Tshombé, who was the president of Congo's renegade province Katanga at the time and had been involved in the assassination of the country's prime minister, Patrice Lumumba, the author equated the way he had come to power with the coup of 19 August 1953 and, thus, Tshombé with Mohammad Reza Shah, glossing over the significant differences between the coup of 1953 and developments in Congo.[26] Rather than in the supposedly superstructural differences, the Marxist-Leninist authors of the Tudeh were interested in the structural commonalities of the two autocrats, namely their reliance on foreign 'imperialist' powers in sustaining their rule. Moreover, by equating the developments in Congo to those in Iran, thereby making them easier to understand for their Iranian readers, they could use their analysis of developments in Central Africa as a means for mobilising their followers in Iran.

Besides the usual attacks on the United States as the actual perpetrator behind French, Belgian, or British oppression,[27] the tone of the articles in *Mardom* sometimes also reflected the style of East German propaganda to which the authors were exposed on a daily basis. This is particularly obvious in an article on the war in Algeria, in which the author explicitly

---

the central organ could not be distributed as quickly as necessary. The news had become irrelevant once the readers received them. Rather than on news, the new version of *Mardom* would now focus on 'the analysis of the most principal issues concerning Iran, the world, the party, and the movement'. 'Beh monasebat-e aghaz-e doureh-ye sheshom-e *Mardom*: bist-o-chahar sal dar sangar-e mobarezeh', *Mahnameh-ye Mardom*, Farvardin 1344/April 1965.

26 'Mobarezeh-ye mardom-e asir-e Kongu dar rah-e esteqlal va azadi', *Mardom*, 12 Bahman 1339/1 February 1961.

27 See for example 'Efriqa dar rah-e azadi va esteqlal', *Mardom*, 10 Ordibehesht 1339/30 April 1960.

mentions the high percentage of former members of the German SA and SS in the French Foreign Legion and their connection to the West German Chancellor Konrad Adenauer,[28] mirroring the East German denunciation of the Federal Republic of Germany as a fascist successor state to the national socialist Reich.[29]

Yet the Tudeh's propaganda branch not only engaged with such acute developments, it also set out to elaborate on the theory which drove its analysis of forms of colonial oppression and the struggle against them. For example, the future post-revolutionary editor-in-chief of *Mardom*, Manuchehr Behzadi, using his pen name Anusheh, explained the term 'neo-colonialism' to party sympathisers and members in an article which was published in *Donya* in early 1961. Based on the Leninist theory of imperialism as outlined in Lenin's *Imperialism–The Highest Stage of Capitalism*,[30] he argued that the strength of the Soviet-led Socialist Camp, which had emerged after the Second World War, made it more difficult for the imperialist powers to defend their colonial possessions, which, as important suppliers of raw materials and markets for the sale of industrial goods, were among the main pillars of their power. Thus, pressurised by socialism, the imperialist governments had come to employ more covert instruments in order to make sure that their interests and, more importantly, those of the industrial monopolies of their countries would be met even after the supposed independence of their colonies. This, first and foremost, included the support of the imperialists' allies inside the colonised or neo-colonised countries at the economic, military, and political level: these allies were members of the 'comprador' bourgeoisie, which, in contrast to its national counterpart, depended on extensive trade relations with the colonial metropolis, and the feudal landowners, who relied on imperialist

---

28 'Ashk va khun dar al-Jazireh va Kongu', *Mardom*, 11 Dey 1339/1 January 1961.
29 See for example 'Geheimbund Bonn-Algerien: Schmutziges Spiel im schmutzigen Krieg', *Berliner Zeitung*, 10 February 1960. While there were indeed almost 20,000 German soldiers involved in the war as members of the French Foreign Legion, the West German government actually tried to actively contain French efforts to recruit Germans for its armed forces. Klaus-Jürgen Müller, 'Die Bundesrepublik Deutschland und der Algerienkrieg', *Vierteljahreshefte für Zeitgeschichte* 38/4, 1990, 611–612.
30 V.I. Lenin, *Imperialism–The Highest Stage of Capitalism*, 2015.

support to safeguard their possessions. In Behzadi's eyes, these two distinct groups had to be the main targets of domestic anti-colonial action. He stressed that ousting them would require not only the unity of all national forces but also their reliance on Soviet support. While the domestic working-class led by its vanguard, the local Communist Party, should cooperate with the national bourgeoisie to overthrow these dependent elites, Soviet support should guarantee that the imperialist powers would not directly intervene from outside.[31]

This theory of neo-colonialism and resistance against it would remain the main conceptual foundation of the party's analysis of global decolonisation for years to come. From the mid-1960s onwards, it replaced the concept of semi-coloniality in contemporary analyses, which was becoming increasingly untenable for the pro-Soviet Tudeh following the Sino-Soviet split.[32] Like its conceptual predecessor, the theoretical framework of neo-colonialism equipped Tudeh theorists with a tool which proved useful in two respects. Firstly, it allowed them to continue criticising the economic and political influence of 'imperialist', i.e., Western state and non-state, actors in the countries of Africa, Asia, and Latin America even after they had achieved formal independence. Secondly, it provided them with an ideal justification to consider Iran, although it had never been officially colonised, as part of the colonised world and, thus, to connect the Tudeh's own struggle against the shah's regime to the conflicts which took place in formerly colonised countries or territories that were still in the process of achieving independence.

Behzadi, however, did not mention an aspect which probably was one of the issues most disputed among the party leadership and cadres in the early 1960s: the question of whether violence should be adopted to confront and eliminate colonial oppression. This issue was openly discussed

---

31 Anusheh [Manuchehr Behzadi], 'Darbareh-ye shiveh-ha-ye esteʿmar-e novin ya neʾukoloniyalism', *Donya* 2/4, 1339/1961.
32 Although having been used by Lenin as well, 'semi-colonial' was mainly associated with the writings of Mao Zedong, who had made extensive use of the term. Nonetheless, the Tudeh did not completely break with this concept after the Sino-Soviet Split. In articles on events and developments that had taken place prior to the split, 'semi-colonial' continued to be used by the party's authors. In analyses of contemporary developments, it was replaced by 'dependent' (*vabasteh*).

at the ninth plenum of the party's central committee in the East German city of Erfurt in September 1961, which assigned the executive committee to explore the prospects of armed struggle and to implement appropriate measures for its preparation.[33] While the deep crisis of the party leadership following the exposure of SAVAK informants inside the exile community in East Germany,[34] and probably also Soviet intervention soon stopped this process,[35] the interest of a considerable number of Tudeh members in this question continued to resonate in the Tudeh publications which engaged with anti-colonial movements around the world. In the perhaps most striking way, this is apparent in a report on the conquest of the city of Goa by Indian troops, which was published in *Mardom* in January 1962. The analysis considered the failure of previous attempts to solve the case of Goa at the diplomatic level as evidence that liberation from colonial oppression can hardly be achieved through negotiations. The author, who used the pen name M. Mani, argued that 'the experience of the anti-colonial struggles of all suppressed nations [...] shows with every step that the chain of colonialism can only be torn apart through organised and uncompromising struggle'.[36] A very similar attitude can be found in an article on the Algerian War of Independence which appeared a few months later. There, the author mentioned 'the application of all forms of struggle' among the three most essential lessons that could be learnt from Algeria's national liberation movement.[37]

Soon thereafter, these articles, which implicitly defended armed struggle as a legitimate means to achieve national independence, increasingly gave way to pieces which sought to emphasise the positive impact of the Soviet doctrine of peaceful coexistence on the activities of national liberation movements in Asia, Africa, and Latin America while mostly remaining

---

33 CC TPI, Information über 9. Plenum an Walter Ulbricht, 11 October 1961, BArch NY 4182/1292, fol. 13.

34 CC TPI, Information über die Arbeit des 10. Plenums, 17 May 1962, BArch NY 4182/1292, fols. 15–21.

35 Amirkhosravi, *Zendeginameh*, 288–289.

36 'Ba este'mar faqat ba mobarezeh bayad ruberu shod', *Mardom,* 11 Dey 1340/1 January 1962.

37 'Dars-e al-Jazireh pas az dars-e Kuba', *Mardom,* 15 Farvardin 1341/4 April 1962.

silent about the role of violence in their struggles. In theory, peaceful coexistence, which had become the determining principle of Soviet foreign policy at the twentieth congress of the CPSU in 1956, meant that a world war between the capitalist and the socialist world was no longer necessary in order to guarantee the victory of the latter over the former. In contrast to the polemics against it, the theory targeted the relationship between the Soviet Union and the US, and not the conflict between the colonised and their colonisers. As Roger Markwick has pointed out, the central committee of the CPSU, in fact, explicitly denied that peaceful coexistence would rule out violent resistance of national liberation movements to (neo-)colonial oppression.[38]

This was openly acknowledged by the Tudeh leadership.[39] However, at least since the Irano-Soviet rapprochement of September 1962,[40] if not since the aforementioned ninth plenum of the Tudeh the previous year, it was clear that the Soviet Union would not apply this exception to Iran and the Pahlavi regime but, instead, would prioritise its foreign policy objectives – i.e., strengthening Irano-Soviet relations – over the aims of the Tudeh. Hence, for the Tudeh, which relied on Soviet support and protection, any efforts to bring about an armed uprising against Iran's current government were off-limits. In this regard, the Soviet *raison d'état* outweighed the commandments of orthodox Marxism-Leninism.

That said, the propaganda branch of the Tudeh faced a dilemma. Since the very start of its activities in exile, it had published analyses which sought to situate Iran and the party's struggle within the context of the events that had taken place in the colonised and decolonising world and to learn from the national liberation movements in other countries. Now, with the achievement of Irano-Soviet détente, any advertisement of armed methods to achieve national liberation had become undesired, while the struggle for national sovereignty and emancipation continued to be at

---

38 Roger Markwick, 'Peaceful coexistence, détente and Third World struggles: the Soviet view from Lenin to Brezhnev', *Australian Journal of International Affairs* 44/2, 1990, 174–175, 183–184.
39 Iraj Eskandari, 'Hezb-e ma va mas'aleh-ye behbud-e monasebat-e dowlat-e Iran va Ettehad-e Jamahir-e Showravi', *Donya* 4/4, 1964, 19.
40 Roham Alvandi, 'The shah's détente with Khrushchev: Iran's 1962 missile base pledge to the Soviet Union', *Cold War History* 14/3, 2014, 440–443.

the top of the Tudeh's agenda. Thus, writing about anti-colonial move-ments which were resorting to violence to achieve their goals became complicated. In an exemplary way, this tension becomes apparent in an article by M. Nuri published in *Mardom* in May 1963. In this piece, the author sought to elaborate on how the doctrine of peaceful coexistence would impact global decolonisation and the activities of its proponents. Yet instead of providing an analysis of what this principle would mean for the practice of anti-colonial struggle, Nuri only vaguely explained that the proponents of 'various forms of [national liberation] struggle' would benefit from the efforts of the increasingly strong 'Socialist Camp' for world peace. World peace, as Nuri argued somewhat tautologically, would thwart the aggressive and exploitative plans of imperialism and its clients, and thus enable the nations suffering under colonial oppression to free themselves.[41]

This incomplete and unconvincing explanation did not remain unchal-lenged. Already in the spring of 1961, the League of Iranian Socialists in Europe had published the first issue of its organ, *Niru* (Force), and thus – at least to some extent – had broken the monopoly of the Tudeh on left-wing Persian-language publications in Europe.[42] The League of Socialists itself had been founded in late summer 1960 in Tehran. Regarding themselves as intellectual inheritors of Khalil Maleki's *Third Force* organisation,[43] in their manifesto, the founders elevated non-alignment to the central prin-ciple of their new organisation, explicitly and repeatedly denouncing the Tudeh Party as a Soviet client organisation in Iran, which had played a central role in the defeat of Iran's national movement in 1953.[44] Concern-ing decolonisation, they wrote:

> The League accepts the principles of the politics of independence from
> both world blocs and enthusiastically looks at the heroic struggles
> of the nations of Asia, Africa, and Latin America for the liberation

---

41 'Roshd-e jonbesh-e azadibakhsh-e melli dar sharayet-e hamzisti-ye
mosalematamiz', *Mardom*, 15 Khordad 1342/5 June 1963.
42 *Niru*, Ordibehesht 1340/May 1961.
43 Manuchehr Safa, ed. *Bayyaniyeh-ye Jame'eh-ye Sosiyalist-ha-ye Nehzat-e
Melli-ye Iran*, 1339/1960, 5.
44 Safa, ed. *Bayyaniyeh*, 4, 12–13.

from the pressures of the remnants of Western imperialism and the resistance against the influence of the Eastern Bloc.[45]

A central role in furthering the aims of the League was attributed to sympathisers who lived abroad, first and foremost to those among the growing community of university students in Western Europe.[46]

Prior to 1961, several of these Socialist students and graduates had been involved in publishing. Articles by prominent figures of the Socialist movement such as Hasan Malek, Maleki's half-brother, had already appeared in supposedly unpolitical corporate student periodicals like *Nameh-ye Parsi*.[47] At the third conference of the League of Socialists in Europe, which was formally independent from the one in Iran, the British branch of the organisation was then assigned to publish its newspaper, the aforementioned *Niru*, as the Socialists' central organ. Yet one year later already, *Niru* ceased to fulfil this function without having significantly covered the issue of global decolonisation.[48] It was only in 1964 that a group around the Paris-based students Amir Pishdad and Nasser Pakdaman came to produce the monthly, *Sosiyalism*, as a more continuous and more sophisticated organ of the organisation.[49]

In line with the fierce criticisms of the Tudeh Party by the foundation manifesto of the Socialist League, *Sosiyalism* very critically engaged with the anti-colonial strategy of the orthodox Marxist-Leninist party before they even published their own analyses of and statements regarding global decolonisation. In the second issue already, the Socialist author A. Kusha fundamentally denied the Tudeh the legitimacy to act as the proponent of a 'united front against colonialism'. Rather than an enemy of colonialism, they portrayed the Tudeh as acting as a colonial agent in favour of Soviet interest in Iran. In the eyes of Kusha, this had been shown by the

---

45 Safa, ed. *Bayyaniyeh*, 30.
46 Safa, ed. *Bayyaniyeh*, 15.
47 Afshin Matin-Asgari, 'A History of the Iranian Student Movement Abroad: The Confederation of Iranian Students/National Union (1960–1975)', Ph.D. thesis, University of California 1993, 81–83.
48 'Ancheh ke dar-bareh-ye Niru bayad bedanid…', *Niru*, Tir 1341/July 1962.
49 Homa Katouzian, *Khalil Maleki: The Human Face of Iranian Socialism*, 2018, 204.

Tudeh's support for the Irano-Soviet rapprochement; the Tudeh leadership, he asserted, could not 'form a united front against colonialism with Iran's national and progressive forces' while they were '[making] friends with colonialism and its lackeys in Iran upon the directive of their directors in Moscow'. According to the author, the Tudeh, which had not reformed its relationship to the USSR, effectively remained a pressure group for Soviet interest in Iran even if that made it necessary to neglect the needs of the Iranian nation. Kusha therefore called upon the base of the Tudeh Party to abandon their leadership and to join 'Iran's national movement and Socialist united front'.[50]

These attacks against the League's political rivals, which at the same time were statements of the organisation's own principles, continued in *Sosiyalism*'s articles on the development of decolonisation outside Iran. A piece on the Zanzibar Revolution of 1964, for instance, served as an opportunity to directly criticise the Soviet doctrine of peaceful coexistence. The author considered the violent overthrow of Sultan Jamshid ibn ʿAbdallah al-Saʿid as 'another piece of evidence to judge those who, under the pretext of "peaceful coexistence", consider the struggle of the nations of Asia, Africa and Latin America as dangerous'.[51] In the previous issue, a study of the Cuban Revolution on the occasion of the sixth anniversary of its victory over the regime of former President Fulgencio Batista had emphasised the overarching importance of self-reliance for a revolutionary movement and downplayed the significance of Soviet and Chinese support for its ultimate success. By considering the 'reliance on the imperishable power of the people', the qualities of the movement's leadership, and the 'local and national backing [of the revolution]' rather than the position of the two Socialist powers as the determining factors behind the ousting of the *ancien régime*, the author repudiated the positions of not only the pro-Soviet Marxist-Leninists but also the pro-Chinese Maoists, who constituted a quickly growing current within the Iranian Left towards the mid-1960s.[52]

---

50 'Jebheh-ye vahed-e zedd-e esteʿmar va zendeh bad dusti-ye Iran va Showravi', *Mahnameh-ye Sosiyalism*, Bahman 1342/February 1964.
51 'Dorahi pas az enqelab', *Mahnameh-ye Sosiyalism*, Farvardin 1343/April 1964.
52 'Sheshomin salgard-e enqelab-e Kuba', *Mahnameh-ye Sosiyalism*, Esfand 1342/March 1964.

Yet despite the open enmity between these groups, the League's engagement with national liberation movements paralleled that of the Tudeh in
many ways. Just like the pro-Soviet party, the Socialists did not only look
at the movements representing global decolonisation with the eyes of
internationalists but also regarded them as a source of inspiration and role
models which could be used to underline and strengthen their Iran-centred
visions. For example, the aforementioned article on Cuba concluded that
the revolution had been 'an experiment that is precious and gives hope to
all revolutionary movements around the globe.' Just like Tudehi authors
before them, the author stressed the importance of the Cuban example
particularly for Iran's national liberation movement by writing: 'It is the
duty of Iran's socialist and progressive forces to learn a lesson from the
immeasurable treasure of this revolution and to benefit from it, and to thus
bring closer the day of the victory of the Iranian people over despotism,
reaction and colonialism.'[53] The theory underlying the Socialists' analyses,
moreover, resembled to a large extent the theory of neo-colonialism as outlined by Behzadi in *Donya*. While the concept of the USSR as the foremost
sponsor and protector of national liberation movements, unsurprisingly, is
completely absent from *Sosiyalism*, the use of the differentiation between
old and new colonialism, the understanding of economic dependence, the
idea of corrupt pro-imperialist local elites as well as the anti-US-American
rhetoric strongly remind the reader of the analyses published in *Mardom*
or *Donya*.[54]

'Winners' and 'Losers' of the Crisis of Decolonisation, 1965–1967

Both the Tudeh and the Socialists also shared a deep concern regarding the
crisis that the global decolonisation movement was facing during the mid-
1960s. The wave of independences at the beginning of the decade had been
swiftly followed by waves of post-colonial coups and wars. The frustrat-
ing experience of witnessing how several post-independence governments

---

53 'Sheshomin salgard', *Mahnameh-ye Sosiyalism*, Esfand 1342/March 1964.
54 'Kudeta-ye al-Jazayer', *Mahnameh-ye Sosiyalism*, Tir 1344/July 1965 and
'Jame'eh-ye tabaqati va eqtesad-e vabasteh', *Mahnameh-ye Sosiyalism*, Farvardin
1346/April 1967.

came under attack and were often overthrown made it more difficult for the two organisations to present global decolonisation as a fully successful process and to offer neat recipes for the types of transformations that could occur in Iran, too. The focus of the authors therefore shifted from the search for lessons that could be learnt and applied in Iran to expressions for solidarity and appeals which called upon Iranians to support the threatened national liberation movements. For example, in late 1964, *Sosiyalism* 'utterly condemned' the 'military intervention of American and Belgian imperialism' in the context of the Simba Rebellion in Congo, and declared that the Congolese nation could be certain of the Socialists' material and ideal assistance 'on its way to independence and independence for its homeland',[55] which was closely resembled by a statement issued by the Tudeh in *Mardom*.[56] Similarly, the reactions of the organs of both organisations to the coup of Houari Boumedienne in Algeria in June 1965 were in unison over their concern about the fate of the country's meritorious national liberation movement.[57]

Yet among all these crises, it was the developments in Vietnam which first and foremost drew the attention of the authors of both *Sosiyalism* and *Mardom*. The crisis, the outbreak, and the intensification of the war in this Southeast Asian country did not only trigger expressions of solidarity and statements that denounced the crimes committed by US forces[58] but also served as another projection screen for the two periodicals to clarify the political standpoints of their respective organisations with regards to Iran. The Socialists harshly criticised the USSR's initially cautious position in the conflict and, thus, the one of the Tudeh by equating peaceful coexistence with the 'capitulation' of the Soviet Union to imperialism.[59] In contrast to the Tudeh, whose authors called upon Iranians to engage in protests for peace and solidarity campaigns within the existing legal

---

55 'Faje'eh-ye Kongu', *Mahnameh-ye Sosiyalism*, Azar 1343/December 1964.
56 'Terazhedi-ye Kongu', *Mardom*, 15 Azar 1343/6 December 1964.
57 'Al-Jazireh beh koja miravad', *Mahnameh-ye Mardom*, Mordad 1344/August 1965 and 'Kudeta-ye al-Jazireh', *Mahnameh-ye Sosiyalism*, Tir 1344/July 1965.
58 'Shah beh yari-ye dezhkhiman-e Viyetnam mishetabad', *Mardom*, 15 Tir 1343/6 July 1964 and 'Jenayat-e Amrika dar Viyetnam', *Mahnameh-ye Sosiyalism*, Bahman 1345/February 1967.
59 'Jang dar Viyetnam', *Mahnameh-ye Sosiyalism*, Farvardin 1344/April 1965.

framework,[60] the Socialists' authors, who did not refrain from repeatedly comparing the US forces in Vietnam to Hitler's armies during the Second World War,[61] explicitly advocated the outright overthrow of the Iranian monarchy, arguing that

> the government of Iran has taken every opportunity to support the American attack on Vietnam [...]. Consequently, those in our country who are revolutionary and progressive can effectively assist the Vietnamese people in only one way: by overthrowing the regime that has not only enslaved our people but also helped the Yankee conspirators enslave the Vietnamese people.[62]

While there were fundamental differences between these two approaches to address the Vietnam War, both groups agreed on the necessity to end this devastating conflict. Like the Socialists,[63] the Tudeh pointed to the risks that the war itself would pose to the Iranian population. With a surprisingly sacral tone, the party leadership called on the readers of *Mardom* to join a 'holy struggle to extinguish the flame of the Vietnam War' (*jehad-e moqaddas bara-ye khamush sakhtan-e na'ereh-ye jang-e Viyetnam*), which could easily spread to Iran.[64]

With the intensification of the war in Vietnam, however, this pacifist view became increasingly unpopular among the Iranian Left, from which a new organisation could greatly benefit. Already in 1964, the overwhelming majority of the student cadres and sympathisers of the Tudeh Party in

---

60 'Bar khalq-e qahreman-e Viyetnam keh ba moqavemat-e binazir dar-barabar-e amperiyalism-e motajavez-e Amrika az azadi-ye khodesh defa' mikonad', *Mahnameh-ye Mardom*, Shahrivar 1345/September 1966.

61 'Amperiyalism-e yanki dar Viyetnam', *Mahnameh-ye Sosiyalism*, Ordibehesht 1346/May 1967 and 'Jenayat-e Amrika', *Mahnameh-ye Sosiyalism*, Bahman 1345/February 1967.

62 'Amperiyalism-e yanki', *Mahnameh-ye Sosiyalism*, Ordibehesht 1346/May 1967.

63 'Amperiyalism-e yanki', *Mahnameh-ye Sosiyalism*, Ordibehesht 1346/May 1967.

64 'Bar khalq-e qahreman-e Viyetnam', *Mahnameh-ye Mardom*, Shahrivar 1345/September 1966.

Western Europe,[65] who had been deeply frustrated by their party's more passive stance on armed struggle and the perceived inertia of its leadership, had split and founded a new political group, the Revolutionary Organisation of the Tudeh Party of Iran (ROTPI).[66] Under the influence of the defeat of 1953, when the Tudeh had not attempted to use its networks inside the Iranian army to ward off the coup, and inspired by the successes of the armed national liberation movements of Cuba and Algeria, the founders of ROTPI considered violence the only means capable of not only overthrowing Mohammad Reza Shah's regime in Iran but also bringing imperialism to an end.[67] They asserted in one of their early internal publications:

> State power cannot be taken out of the hands of the united classes of [domestic] reaction and [foreign] imperialism through peaceful means. [...] the general method of the revolution cannot be anything else than the use of force and armed struggle [...].[68]

This conviction would decisively inform their theoretical engagement with decolonisation at a global level.

Yet it was only after a period of internal consolidation that ROTPI's analyses of colonialism and anti-colonial resistance became publicly available. At the outset, both its internal organisation and ideological orientation were tentative and subject to considerable internal debate. At the so-called 'Preparatory Conference', which took place as the founding meeting of ROTPI in Munich in the spring of 1964, the attendants agreed to create ROTPI only as a 'minimal organisation' (*sazman-e hadd-e aqalli*) which would support and coordinate the armed operations of its

---

65 According to estimates, ninety percent of the organisation of the Tudeh in Western Europe split away from the central committee. Mu'assasehye tahqiqati va entesharati-ye didgah, ed. *Khaterat-e Nur al-Din Kianuri*, 1371/1992, 440.

66 Hamid Shokat, ed. *Negahi az Darun beh Jonbesh-e Chap-e Iran: Goftogu ba Mehdi Khanbaba Tehrani*, 1368/1989, 131.

67 Hamid Shokat, ed. *Negahi az Darun beh Jonbesh-e Chap-e Iran: Goftogu ba Kurosh Lashayi*, 1382/2003, 33–38.

68 'Sanad-e shomareh-ye seh: enqelab-e Iran va vazayef-e mobarram-e komunist-ha [Esfand 1344]', *Negahi az Darun beh Jonbesh-e Chap-e Iran: Goftogu ba Kurosh Lashayi*, ed. Hamid Shokat, 1382/2003, 377.

members in Iran.[69] Contrary to the impression evoked by the group's labelling as 'Maoist', and its decision to send some of its members to China for military training, this small organisation did not constitute a distinctively Maoist group from early on. As Matin-Asgari has rightly pointed out, its orientation initially was an 'eclectic' mix of Maoist and Castroite traits. The organisation's emphasis on armed struggle as the only means to bring about revolutionary transformation and its harsh criticisms of the Tudeh's leadership were the only elements on which there was a broad consensus.[70] During the early years of ROTPI's existence, moreover, even the position on the Tudeh as a political organisation was unclear. While one internal faction aimed to establish a fundamentally new organisation, the other one emphasised the meritorious revolutionary traditions of the Tudeh and denounced merely the party's leadership in East European exile.[71] Against this background, it is not surprising that it only was at ROTPI's second congress in 1965 that the organisation decided to publish a central organ. Even then, in the eyes of several participants, this ran contrary to ROTPI's design as a 'minimal organisation'.[72] Notwithstanding the opposition, the first issue of *Tudeh* ('The Masses'), ROTPI's central organ, appeared in April 1966.[73]

From early on, *Tudeh*, which, in contrast to the publications of ROTPI's mother organisation, continued to explicitly consider Iran in its contemporary state as 'semi-colonial',[74] paid attention to national liberation movements around the world and managed to demonstrate that armed struggle was a suitable strategy at times when the proponents of global decolonisation were under attack. At a point where the Iranian Maoists' political rivals were not able anymore to take violent conflicts as a confirmation of their own strategies, ROTPI still did so by presenting lessons which could

---

69 Hamid Shokat, ed. *Negahi az Darun beh Jonbesh-e Chap-e Iran: Goftogu ba Mohsen Rezvani*, 1384/2005, 63–72.

70 It was only in 1967 that ROTPI emerged as an exclusively Maoist group. Matin-Asgari, 'Student Movement', 264, 324.

71 Matin-Asgari, 'Student Movement', 324.

72 Shokat, ed. *Lashayi*, 40–41 and Shokat, ed. *Rezvani*, 111.

73 *Tudeh*, Farvardin 1345/April 1966.

74 ROTPI Executive Committee, 'Dakheli: tarh[-e barnameh]', August 1968, 5.

be learnt not only from the war in Vietnam[75] but also from other atrocities such as the coup of Suharto in 1965 and the ensuing mass killings in
Indonesia.[76]

It was the case of the Vietnam War which particularly inspired the
Iranian Maoists. The conflict provided them with a projection screen
which they could use to outline their revolutionary plans for Iran's future
and attack the analyses of their political rivals. Unlike the Socialists and
the Tudeh, ROTPI embraced the escalating war in Vietnam and the neighbouring countries as an opportunity to start a world war on imperialism
and colonial oppression. In its view, the war showed that 'it is only armed
struggle and the People's War[77] [and not the Soviet doctrine of peaceful
coexistence] by which the people will be able to end imperialist intervention and domination, to free themselves and to secure their national
independence'.[78] The resistance of the Vietnamese, moreover, demonstrated 'how a people – however small and weak it may be – can resist
the attack of the largest of the world's powers by having a correct political
line, a revolutionary leadership and adequate organisations [...].' To the
authors of *Tudeh*, Vietnam was 'a good and clear example of the nature,
form and way of a revolution against American imperialism', but not the
only case. They were convinced that 'there are and there will emerge other
Vietnams', which would play the decisive role in the defeat of imperialism. The system of colonial oppression had to be defeated in the decolonising world, where they considered it to be in its weakest position.[79]

Yet merely having the certainty of more Vietnams emerging was not
enough for the ROTPI authors. In the spirit of the later published 'Message
to the Tricontinental' by Ernesto 'Che' Guevara,[80] the Iranian Maoists were

---

75 'Konferans-e seh qareh'i', *Tudeh*, Farvardin 1345/April 1966.
76 'Tajarebi az kudeta-ye fashisti-ye Andunezi', *Tudeh*, Azar 1345/December 1966.
77 The author hereby meant the concept of the People's War as outlined in Mao
Zedong's *On the Protracted War*, 1954.
78 'Qat'nameh-ye dovomin konferans-e sazman dar-bareh-ye Viyetnam', *Tudeh*,
Farvardin 1345/April 1966.
79 'Amperiyalism-e Amrika cheguneh mitavan nabud kard', *Tudeh*, Tir 1345/July
1366.
80 In this pamphlet, which was published in 1967, Guevara wrote: 'How close we
could look into a bright future should two, three or many Vietnams flourish
throughout the world with their share of deaths and their immense tragedies, their

determined to create them. In the first issue of *Tudeh* already, they had therefore declared:

> The flames of the [Vietnamese] war for national liberation are about to burn the roots of imperialism in Asia, Africa, and Latin America. By starting a revolutionary war in our homeland, we can poke the fire and accelerate the extinction of the system of slavery.[81]

This was not only diametrically opposed to the Tudeh Party's appeal that a few months later would call the Iranian nation to extinguish the flame of the Vietnam War but also much more radical than the Socialists' position, who had merely called for an unspecified overthrow of the shah's regime to support the war efforts of the Vietnamese people.

ROTPI's analytical engagement with armed national liberation movements not only in Vietnam but also in Thailand,[82] Bolivia, Venezuela, and Colombia[83] opened a new and radical path to revolutionary change and anti-colonial transformation to the Iranian Left. The frustration of the Iranian students in Europe about the deadlock in which Iran's entire opposition had been caught since the repression of overt political activities in the summer of 1963 as well as their links to the emerging New Left of Western Europe constituted a fertile environment for the spread of Maoism and other approaches that saw violence as a necessary means to achieve

---

everyday heroism and their repeated blows against imperialism, impelled to disperse its forces under the sudden attack and the increasing hatred of all peoples of the world.' That this was understood as a call to arms by his contemporaries becomes apparent in the title of the German translation of the text for example. Instead of merely translating the original title, the translators and prominent political activists Rudi Dutschke and Gaston Salvatore published the treatise under the striking title 'Let's create two, three, many Vietnams.' Ernesto 'Che' Guevara, 'Message to the Tricontinental', accessed 26 April 2021, https://www.marxists.org/archive/guevara/1967/04/16.htm and Ernesto 'Che' Guevara, 'Schaffen wir zwei drei, viele Vietnam', trans. Rudi Dutschke and Gaston Salvatore, accessed 3 August 2021, http://www.infopartisan.net/archive/1967/266738.html.

81 'Konferans-e seh qareh'i', *Tudeh*, Farvardin 1345/April 1966.
82 'Jang-e khalq-e Tayland sho'lehvar mishavad', *Tudeh*, Esfand 1345/March 1967.
83 ''Ala-gharm-e khiyanat-e reviziyunist-ha: niruha-ye mosallah-e azadibakhsh piruz mishavad', *Tudeh*, Farvardin 1346/April 1967.

decolonisation.[84] Even before 1969, when all members of the CISNU secretariat came from one of the Maoist factions,[85] the Maoists' hegemony
within the student opposition to the shah's regime had become obvious.

This practical and theoretical hegemony was reflected by the composition of the group of Iranian activists who organised the protest against
Mohammad Reza Shah at the occasion of his state visit to West Berlin on
2 June 1967.[86] The demonstration, during which the student Benno Ohnesorg was shot dead by a West Berlin police officer, marked a watershed
moment in the history of the German student movement and played a decisive role in its radicalisation. While the event itself was only of secondary
importance to the Iranian student opposition, it constituted an ideal opportunity for the participating Iranian activists to outline their convictions
and political positions in front of a large non-Iranian audience. Rather
than followers of the Socialists, the Tudeh, or the National Front, it was a
group around the Berlin-based ROTPI sympathiser and CISNU secretary
Bahman Nirumand[87] who organised the protests on that day and managed
to mobilise German activists to join them.[88]

In West Germany, Nirumand was not unknown. In his extremely influential book *Persien: Modell eines Entwicklungslandes* ('Persia: A Model of
a Developing Nation'),[89] over a hundred thousand copies of which would
eventually be printed and sold, he had not only introduced his perspective
on the difficult political and socio-economic situation in his home country
to a large German readership but had also enthusiastically engaged with
global decolonisation. As Quinn Slobodian assumes, Nirumand's great

---

84 Matin-Asgari, 'Student Movement', 292–293.
85 The secretariat of the organisation which was elected for one year in 1969 was
solely composed of members of the Maoist factions within the CISNU. Matin-
Asgari, 'Student Movement', 342–343.
86 Mohammad Reza Shah's trip to West Berlin was part of his state visit to the
Federal Republic of Germany. He was touring the country from 27 May 1967 to 4
June 1967 and had to face protests by Iranian and German students in several other
cities as well. Eckard Michels, *Schahbesuch 1967: Fanal für die
Studentenbewegung*, 2017, 117–119, 148–167.
87 Matin-Asgari, 'Student Movement', 298, 331.
88 Michels, *Schahbesuch 1967*, 135–138, 171–173.
89 Bahman Nirumand, *Persien, Modell eines Entwicklungslandes oder die Diktatur
der Freien Welt*, 1967.

success is likely to have been based on exactly this 'outline of a global context that linked the struggles in Iran, Vietnam, and the rest of the Third World'.[90] On the eve of the protests of 2 June, Nirumand held a speech during a teach-in at the lecture theatre of the Freie Universität Berlin in which he reiterated this emphasis on the global interconnectedness of anti-imperial struggles. In front of approximately 2,000 German and Iranian students, he not only denounced the dictatorship in Iran but also demanded solidarity with national liberation movements around the world.[91] At least in West Germany, which was the epicentre of the Iranian student movement abroad at the time, a ROTPI sympathiser had emerged as the face of the Iranian anti-imperialist opposition to the shah.

In contrast, the Tudeh, which had opened the Persian-language discourse on decolonisation in Europe ten years earlier, remained silent. For a variety of reasons, the party leadership refrained from any active involvement in the events on and prior to 2 June. Not only the marginalisation of the Tudeh within the Iranian student movement but also the Soviet interest in maintaining good relations with the regime in Tehran as well as the anti-Soviet orientation of the overwhelming majority of both Iranian and German student activists in the West made any significant engagement of the orthodox Marxists-Leninists virtually impossible. Thus, although the leadership of this foremost representative of the Iranian orthodox Marxist-Leninist Left was based only few hours by train away from Berlin in Leipzig, no organised involvement of Tudeh members or sympathisers has been found.[92] Only after the event, *Mardom* published a poem eulogising Ohnesorg and an article by Manuchehr Behzadi, who praised the 'just and democratic demands' of the Iranian students who had participated in the protests in Berlin.[93]

The struggle against colonial oppression in Asia, Africa, and Latin

---

90 Quinn Slobodian, *Foreign Front: Third World Politics in Sixties West Germany*, 2012, 108.

91 Slobodian, *Foreign Front*, 104, 108–110 and Bahman Nirumand, *Weit enfernt von dem Ort, an dem ich sein sollte*, 2011, 124.

92 However, it is very likely that members and sympathisers of the party participated in the protests, either individually or as members of CISNU.

93 'Safari keh bara-ye shah va mohafel-e hakemeh-ye Alman-e Gharbi resva'i beh bar avard', *Mahnameh-ye Mardom*, Khordad 1346/June 1967.

America was of great interest to the Iranian Leftist activists who lived in Europe as students, graduates, or exiles. Considering their opposition to the regime of Mohammad Reza Shah as part of a struggle for national liberation as well, they felt closely connected to the numerous movements which actually achieved this liberation for themselves or were fiercely fighting for it. From the outset of its publication activities in 1958, the exiled Tudeh Party catered to this interest by extensively covering the development of global decolonisation. In the first years of their propaganda efforts abroad, they used the successes of various national liberation movements, particularly on the African continent, as proof for their orthodox Marxist-Leninist theories and visions for Iran as well as inspiring messages that could mobilise sympathisers. To the League of Socialists, which came to challenge the Tudeh's media monopoly in Europe as the first Leftist organisation by the early 1960s, the engagement with anti-colonial resistance additionally offered an opportunity to attack the Soviet doctrine of peaceful coexistence or criticise pro-Soviet and pro-Chinese Leftists by underscoring the importance of non-alignment to any revolutionary liberation movement.

To both organisations, the crisis of global decolonisation that came with the post-colonial wars in Congo and Vietnam and the post-colonial coups in Algeria and Indonesia constituted a serious challenge. The deceleration of a process which had been dramatic in speed during the late 1950s and early 1960s, complicated a productive propagandistic engagement with the emerging violent and often long-lasting conflicts between colonisers and the colonised. From the perspective of the Tudeh and the Socialists, it thus became increasingly difficult to present global decolonisation as an entirely successful process and to offer neat recipes for the decolonising transformation of Iran itself. In the central organs of the two rival organisations, consequently, the proponents of national liberation saw a transformation from role models for the struggle in Iran into recipients of Iranian solidarity and support.

ROTPI, in contrast, regarded this crisis as an opportunity. Based on the conviction that only a world-wide conflict could bring imperialist domination to an end, the authors of this newly established organisation, which took up a staunchly Maoist position after an initial period of internal reflection and consolidation, embraced the colonial and anti-imperial wars as opportunities. Considering the start and continuation of an armed conflict as a success in itself, they managed to present 'lessons' that could be learnt from events which were seen as defeats by others. By presenting even the cruelties of war as an opportunity, ROTPI's revolutionary messages offered a new sense of agency to the otherwise frustrated Iranian Left and thus side-lined political rivals like the Tudeh, which had officially rejected armed struggle as a means suitable to achieve revolutionary change in Iran.

Bibliography

Archival Material

Bundesarchiv, BArch (German Federal Archive)
DY 30/97100 Sozialistische Einheitspartei Deutschlands: Beziehungen
    der SED mit der Volkspartei Iran (Tudeh-Partei)
NY 4182/1292 Nachlass Walter Ulbricht: Beziehungen SED und
    Volkspartei Irans

Newspapers

Berliner Zeitung
Mahnameh-ye Mardom
Mahnameh-ye Sosiyalism
Mardom
Niru
Sobh-e Omid
Tudeh

Other Primary Sources

Executive Committee of the Revolutionary Organisation of the Tudeh
    Party of Iran. 'Dakheli: Tarh[-e Barnameh]', August 1968.
'Pelenom-e vasi'-e (chaharom) Hezb-e Tudeh-ye Iran [1336]', *Asnad-e
    Tarikhi-ye Jonbesh-e Kargari/Sosiyaldemukrasi va Komunisti-ye Iran*,
    ed. Cosroe Chaqueri, Cambridge, USA, 1369/1990, vol. I, 355–400.
'The 20th congress of the CPSU and the problems of studying the
    contemporary East', *The Third World in Soviet Perspective: Studies by*

Soviet Writers on the Developing Areas, ed. T.P. Thornton, Princeton, 1964, 78–87.

Amirkhosravi, B., and F. Azarnur, eds. *Khaterat-e Siyasi-ye Iraj Eskandari*, n.p., 1366/1987.

Amirkhosravi, B. *Zendeginameh-ye Siyasi*, Spanga, 2020.

Anusheh, M. [Manuchehr Behzadi]. 'Darbareh-ye shiveh-ha-ye este'mar-e novin ya ne'ukoloniyalism', *Donya* 2/4, 1339/1961, 45–61.

Eskandari, I. 'Mabani-ye 'elmi-ye sho'ar-e jebheh-ye vahed-e niru-ha-ye melli va demukratik beh-masabeh-ye khatt-e mashi-ye asasi-ye Hezb-e Tudeh-ye Iran', *Donya* 1/2, 1339/1960, 1–15.

Eskandari, I. 'Hezb-e ma va mas'aleh-ye behbud-e monasebat-e dowlat-e Iran va Ettehad-e Jamahir-e Showravi', *Donya* 4/4, 1342/1963, 3–31.

Forutan, Q. *Yademani az Gozashteh*, n.p., 1993.

Guevara, E. 'Message to the Tricontinental', accessed 26 April 2021. https://www.marxists.org/archive/guevara/1967/04/16.htm.

Guevara, E. 'Schaffen wir zwei drei, viele Vietnam', trans. Rudi Dutschke and Gaston Salvatore, accessed 3 August 2021, http://www.infopartisan.net/archive/1967/266738.html.

Kianuri, N. 'Eslahat-e arzi dar Iran', *Donya* 4/1, 1342/1963, 9–28.

Lenin, V.I. *Imperialism–The Highest Stage of Capitalism*, London, 2015.

Mao, Z. *On the Protracted War*, Beijing, 1954.

Mu'assasehye tahqiqati va entesharati-ye didgah, ed. *Khaterat-e Nur al-Din Kianuri*, Tehran, 1371/1992.

Nirumand, B. *Weit enfernt von dem Ort, an dem ich sein sollte*, Reinbek, 2011.

Nirumand, B. *Persien, Modell eines Entwicklungslandes oder die Diktatur der Freien Welt*, Reinbek, 1967.

Pakdaman, N. Interview by Hamid Ahmadi (Research Association for Iranian Oral History), *Video Oral History Collection*, 5 January 2013.

Pishdad, A. Interview by Hamid Ahmadi (Research Association for Iranian Oral History), *Video Oral History Collection*, 10 September 2009.

Safa, M., ed. *Bayyaniyeh-ye Jame'eh-ye Sosiyalist-ha-ye Nehzat-e Melli-ye Iran*, Tehran, 1339/1960.

Shokat, H., ed. *Negahi az Darun beh Jonbesh-e Chap-e Iran: Goftogu ba Mehdi Khanbaba Tehrani*, Saarbrücken, 1368/1989.

Shokat, H., ed. *Negahi az Darun be Jonbesh-e Chap-e Iran: Goftogu ba Mohsen Rezvani*, n.p., 1384/2005.

Shokat, H., ed. *Negahi az Darun beh Jonbesh-e Chap-e Iran: Goftogu ba Kurosh Lashayi*, Tehran, 1386/2007.

Secondary Literature

Alvandi, R. 'The shah's détente with Khrushchev: Iran's 1962 missile base pledge to the Soviet Union', *Cold War History* 14/3, 2014, 423–444.

Katouzian, H. *Khalil Maleki: The Human Face of Iranian Socialism*, London, 2018.

Markwick, R. 'Peaceful coexistence, détente and Third World struggles: The Soviet view from Lenin to Brezhnev', *Australian Journal of International Affairs* 44/2, 1990, 171–194.

Matin-Asgari, A., 'A History of the Iranian Student Movement Abroad: The Confederation of Iranian Students/National Union (1960–1975)', Ph.D. thesis, University of California, 1993.

Matin-Asgari, A. *Iranian Student Opposition to the Shah*, Costa Mesa, USA, 2002.

Michels, E. *Schahbesuch 1967: Fanal für die Studentenbewegung*, Berlin, 2017.

Müller, K. 'Die Bundesrepublik Deutschland und der Algerienkrieg', *Vierteljahreshefte für Zeitgeschichte* 38/4, 1990, 609–641.

Shokat, H. *Jonbesh-e Daneshjuyi Konfederasiyun-e Jahani-ye Mohasselin va Daneshjuyan-e Irani (Ettehadieh-ye Melli)*, Los Angeles, 2010.

Slobodian, Q. *Foreign Front: Third World Politics in Sixties West Germany*, Durham, USA, 2012.

11

Fighting for an Islamic Liberation Theology: Iranian Intellectuals and Global Decolonisation

Javier Gil Guerrero

In recent years, as part of projects such as the 'Global Cold War', 'Global Sixties', or the 'Global South', close attention has been paid to the interactions between Iran and other countries beyond the well-studied cases of the United States or the Soviet Union. Yet when viewed in relation to other conflicts of the Global South, the genealogy of the ideological discourse that fanned the flames of the Iranian Revolution is worthy of renewed scrutiny.

The Iranian Revolution was not an entirely nativist event, untainted by foreign ideas and can best be understood if one considers the complex beliefs and ideas, both local and imported, of the Iranian dissidence. Yet one then needs to ask if those ideas were universal, or if the ideology behind the Iranian Revolution could only have taken root on Iranian soil. Moreover, was the Iranian revolutionary discourse of use for other dissident movements in other regions? Was it a discourse that could survive in different cultural and religious contexts on other continents? Also, up to what point was the Iranian revolutionary discourse unique, or part of larger trends taking place in the Global South?

The historian Arif Dirlik has written that one must use a 'double vision' while studying the Cold War era, looking at political events in terms of both their local and international dynamics.[1] In this chapter, I will investigate how Ali Shariati, Jalal Al-e-Ahmad, Ahmad Fardid, and other Iranian intellectuals tried to frame the Iranian resistance movement against the Pahlavi monarchy within the framework of the different decolonisation movements taking place around the world in the 1960s and 1970s. Although the Pahlavi state was not a colony of Western powers during that period, it was perceived and portrayed as such by opposition intellectuals. Among the themes explored and denounced by them was the cultural imperialism of the West, which they considered as more pervasive and devious than political and economic imperialism. Going beyond the exploitation of Iran's natural resources, it endangered the country's spiritual and cultural heritage.

This was a tendency present already in many countries of the postcolonial Global South. As Asef Bayat has noted, intellectuals and leaders like Ali Shariati, Ahmad Fardid, Frantz Fanon, Aimé Césaire, Kwame Nkrumah, Julius Nyerere, Jomo Kenyatta, and Ahmed Ben Bella 'embarked upon "alternative" politico-economic projects which were based upon a declared refutation of capitalism and emphasis on national and indigenous resources, values, and traditions'.[2] The result was a series of deviations (depending on the cultural milieu of the thinker in question) from orthodox Marxism that came as a result of combining Marx's teachings with one's social and religious heritage.

In the case of Shariati, combatting the reality of imperialism required an ideological rearmament of Iran through the development of a thought that mixed Shia Islam with Marxism. His proposal mirrored the Liberation Theology movement developed by some Catholic priests and theologians in Latin America in the late 1960s and 1970s during their fight against right-wing dictatorships on the continent. With this new interpretation, some Iranian intellectuals sought to position Iran within the global struggle against colonialism and to develop a theory of resistance that, albeit

---

1 Arif Dirlik, 'The Third World in 1968', *1968: The World Transformed*, eds. Carole Fink, Philipp Gassert, and Detlef Junker, 1998, 295–317.
2 Assef Bayat, 'Shari'ati and Marx: A Critique of an "Islamic" Critique of Marxism,' *Alif: Journal of Comparative Poetics* 10, 1990, 19–41.

anchored on a concern with cultural authenticity, could appeal and inspire movements beyond those in the country or the region. This resulted in an intense dialogue between the different traditions of Shia Islam with the new leftist ideologies and schools of thought taking root in Europe and beyond.

The intention of these intellectuals was nothing less than to broaden the horizons of the Iranian resistance to embrace new global movements and contribute, with a particular Iranian and Shia perspective, to the debates on colonialism and decolonisation taking place around the world. This sometimes led to a tension in the discourse between 'nativist' and 'cosmo-politan localist' tendencies.[3] Under this new intellectual approach, Iranian intellectuals sought to establish a brotherhood of the 'oppressed' and 'dis-possessed' not limited to national, sectarian, or religious loyalties. Yet that did not mean discarding tradition and religion, but developing an ideology firmly rooted in religion that would be open and accessible to oppressed peoples of different faiths. Coupling Marxism with religion brought new ideological and spiritual dimensions to the decolonisation struggle beyond the narrow approach of communism.

Towards Shariati

Samad Behrangi (1939–1968), Seyyed Fakhroddin Shadman (1907–1967), Ahmad Fardid (1910–1994) and Jalal Al-e Ahmad (1923–1969) were among the most important Iranian intellectuals to raise questions about modernity, imperialism, and Iranian identity – which in turn influenced the thought and writings of Ali Shariati (1933–1977).

The schoolteacher, essayist, translator, and folklorist Behrangi shared with Shariati a death mired in controversy. Unable to swim, he somehow ventured into the Aras River and drowned.[4] His death came at a moment when he was gaining notoriety due to his acerbic sociopolitical tracts. Behrangi abhorred the Iranian bourgeoise and its superficial infatuation with the West, the inequality of Iranian society, and the pervasive American influence. His antidote was revolutionary struggle.

---

3 Siavash Saffari, 'Ali Shariati and Cosmopolitan Localism', *Comparative Studies of South Asia, Africa and the Middle East* 39/2, August 2019, 282–295.
4 Michael C. Hillmann, 'Behrangi, Samad', *Encyclopaedia Iranica*, IV/1, 110–111.

Behrangi coined the term *Amrikazadegi* ('Americatoxication'), antici-
pating Fardid's *gharbzadagi* ('Westoxication').[5] Influenced by sociologist
Taqi Modarresi, he condemned the Westernised middle class as alienated,
immoral, and disconnected from the problems of common Iranians. He
paid particular attention to the education system, those working in it, and
the influence of the *farhangian*. He believed the Westernised upper classes
were infecting Iranian society with a materialist and individualist outlook.[6]
They were creating a cultural environment that, in Behrangi's view, was

> limited to the four walls of their home and embraces wife and children
> (if they have any) and their route restricted to the route from office and
> school to home. Their hobbies are for amusement and taking up time.
> Their free time is spent in idleness and diversion. [Their] energies are
> spent in satisfying the stomach and its appurtenances. The result of all
> this: superficial and conservative men are produced.[7]

Behrangi's criticism was not influenced by religion. Rather, it responded
to his secular and leftist mentality. In lieu of focusing on the West in
general, Behrangi narrowly directed his arrows at the United States. He
considered America's influence so pervasive that Iranians no longer cared
about their real problems – those rooted in their heritage, culture, and circumstances – but on foreign (American) ones instead.[8]

Shadman took a different approach to the question of Western hegemony. In his view Iran should act like Japan; that is, it should appropriate
Western power and knowledge to be able to stand up to the West and
survive. Failure to imitate the Japanese model would condemn Iran to the
fate of the impoverished African countries. Absorbing Western civilisation
was not an infatuation with the West, just the poisoned chalice Iran had
to drink to avoid being taken over by more developed countries. He also
did not propose blindly imitating the West or embracing its customs and

---

5 Brad Hanson, 'The "Westoxication" of Iran: Depictions and Reactions of
Behrangi, al-e Ahmad, and Shariati', *International Journal of Middle East Studies*
15/1, February 1983, 1–23.
6 Hanson, 'The "Westoxication" of Iran', 4.
7 Hanson, 'The "Westoxication" of Iran', 5.
8 Hanson, 'The "Westoxication" of Iran', 1–23.

mentality. Shadman loathed the frivolous urbanite Iranians – the *fokoli*, enchanted by the West (*farangi*). The *fokoli* took a naïve approach to Westernisation, forgetting that it was a means to undermine the independence, stability, and prosperity of Iran. Worse, they would end up interiorising the prejudices and egotism of Westerners.[9]

Acting as mediators and translators of Western culture and imperialism, the *fokoli* would constitute a fifth column within the society in an existential struggle for Iran. As Shadman once stated:

> We are among those great nations who have suffered major defeats
> yet survived. But Western civilization is altogether a different kind of
> foe equipped with a different kind of armour. In my opinion, however,
> the victory of Western civilization in Iran will be our last defeat, for
> there will be no more Iranian nation left to endure [another] loss from
> another enemy.[10]

In his book *Taskhir-e Tamaddon-e Farangi*, Shadman calls on Iranians to become self-reliant and proud of their heritage while avoiding a gullible attitude towards Western progress.[11] But he is not calling for obscurantism and isolation. Shadman was born into a clerical family but he had been educated at the Sorbonne and the London School of Economics. He, in fact, considered the traditionalist and hidebound ulema as a threat like that of the *fokoli*. Yet, he considered that Iranians were not under the spell of those ulema but under that of the *fokoli* and so was more concerned by the latter:

> The *fokoli* is the biggest enemy of Persian and therefore the obstacle
> in the way of true progress. He will never [be able to] lead us to
> European civilization, because the wretched man is himself lost
> in perplexity and darkness. [On the other hand,] expecting honest

9 Mehrzad Boroujerdi, *Iranian Intellectuals and the West: The Tormented Triumph of Nativism*, 1996, 55–58.
10 Ali Gheissari, *Iranian Intellectuals in the Twentieth Century*, 1998, 86.
11 Ali Gheissari, 'Shadman, Sayyed Fakhr-al-Din', in *Encyclopaedia Iranica*, online edition, 2000 (updated in 2010). https://www.iranicaonline.org/articles/shadman.

guidance from a Westerner stems from stupidity and lack of experience and is a symptom of not knowing the Westerner. Therefore, we must capture Western civilization without the mediation of either one: one is an ignorant wrongdoer and the other a wise ill-wisher.[12]

The solution to this dichotomy of the enemies within, between an obscurantist clergy and the frivolous *fokoli*, is a sort of modernist Islam. For Shadman, an Islam rightly understood was not a hindrance to Iran, but a source of strength and independence. Shadman's synthesis defends a measured appropriation of modernity without losing Iran's soul. We can see this approach in his proposal to bring together religious centres and universities in Iran, creating a system of education that would leave neither science nor religion aside and would guarantee a truly Iranian approach to modernity.

Ahmad Fardid dwelled further on the idea of *fokoli*. His concern was that under the Pahlavis, Iranians were becoming a society of zombies, of soulless consumers of ideological and material Western products.[13] Iranians were being force-fed a modernity that would make them break with their past and traditions and turn them into rootless Westernised ghosts. Fardid, like Shariati, studied at the Sorbonne and brought Heidegger's philosophy with him on his return to Iran. His critique of the West is firmly entrenched in the Heideggerian discourse. It was an irony that seemed to escape everyone that Fardid's (and Shariati's) opposition to the West was grounded in arguments borrowed from Western thinkers.[14]

Fardid's thinking was condensed in his popular neologism, *gharbzadegi*, which has been translated in many ways: 'plagued by the West', 'West-struckness', 'Westoxication', 'Occidentitis', 'Westamination', and even 'Euromania'.[15] Fardid was following Shadman's approach: the problem lay not with Western technology and science, but with the Western world-view (*Weltanschauung*) that accompanied those innovations. Neither an extremist reaction nor blind imitation; because the solution could not be a

---

12 Gheissari, *Iranian Intellectuals in the Twentieth Century*, 87.
13 Ali Mirsepassi, *Transnationalism in Iranian Political Thought: The Life and Times of Ahmad Fardid*, 2017, 149.
14 Ali M. Ansari, *The Politics of Nationalism in Modern Iran*, 2012, 188.
15 Gheissari, *Iranian Intellectuals*, 89.

flat rejection of modernity and Western thought nor an *uncritical* accept-
ance of those ideas.[16] Here, Fardid was in accord with Ehsan Naraqi, challenging the universal validity of Western civilization or even the idea of
universal solutions for political, social, and economic problems. 'In this
chaotic and disorderly world', declared Naraqi, 'the only thing which
could lead us to the shores of salvation is serious and sincere attention to
our own cultural life, national spirit, and historical heritage'.[17]

Fardid's thinking is not that of a nativist. Nor is that of Behrangi or
Shadman. They fought against a monopolization of the discourse by the
West and against the idea of the universality of that discourse. Theirs was
a proposal for a plurality of discourses in the world, and for the voices,
cultures, and systems of the Global South to be put on equal footing with
those of Europe. In the past, the West and the East were engaged in a
relation of cultural borrowing and exchange, but no longer. The East now
found itself in a position of servitude, and the dialogue of the past became
a monologue of the West. Thus, while their discourse was centred on Iran,
it could be replicated and reformulated in any other Third World country.
Their real enemy was the 'project' of European Enlightenment.

If Fardid coined the term *gharbzadegi*, it was Jalal Al-e Ahmad who
popularised it.[18] Ironically, it could be said that Ahmad contributed to
gharbzadegi by earning money as a translator of European literature.[19]
Against the accusations of incoherence and collaboration with the spread
of the *gharbzadegi* malady, Hamid Dabashi has defended Ahmad's translations as part of his effort to fight against Western encroachment.

> Translating European sources into Persian, a crucial cultural
> phenomenon that has so far remained completely unexamined, was
> perhaps the single most important mechanism for creating 'The
> West' as the most significant Other in the Muslim (Iranian) collective
> imagination. [...] these, and similar, translations contributed to the
> collective construction of the compelling image of 'The West' as the

---

16 Boroujerdi, *Iranian Intellectuals and the West*, 64.
17 Gheissari, *Iranian Intellectuals*, 93.
18 Jalal al-e Ahmad, *Occidentosis: A Plague from the West*, 1984.
19 Ali Mirsepassi, *Intellectual Discourse and the Politics of Modernization:
Negotiating Modernity in Iran*, 2004, 100.

most important generalized Other in the Iranian collective imagination. Importer of the most sensitive symbolic artefacts from 'The West', Al-e Ahmad's generation continued to measure elements of its own identity in terms of a constructed dominant myth: 'The West'.[20]

But this interpretation can hardly be reconciled with Ahmad's repeated statements on the dangers of importing Western social sciences, which would destroy, through *literature*, the historical identity of Iran and the common mythologies of Iranians.

Ahmad's concern with the West was mixed with an apprehension of industrialisation and technological innovations. In fact, he coined the term *mashinzadegi* or 'intoxication with the machine'.[21] *Gharbzadegi* and *mashinzadegi* were part of the same process, and the consequence of this plague was, in his own words, the loss of authenticity, beauty, poetry, and the spirit.[22] Because, in the hands of the West, civilisation had become a mere vehicle for 'consumption'.[23]

The only possible defence against this dual threat was to embrace the authentic culture of Islam; not an inoffensive and fossilized relic ready for museums and the history books, but an *authentic* Islam, that of Muhammad and the Twelve Imams. A religion that was pure and alive, dynamic, sustained by revolutionaries and martyrs. For in this struggle Iran could not opt to 'retreat into the abyss of traditional customs'.[24] An effective religious resistance against *gharbzadegi* could not be a reactionary one. In this sense, Ahmad was impressed by what he saw in Israel, since he advocated the kind of religious nationalism that he perceived in socialist Zionism.[25] Although he found the Israeli model of 'theo-politics unconstrained by norms or the international legal order' appealing, Ahmad's

---

20 Hamid Dabashi, *Theology of Discontent*, 2017, 58.
21 Ajay Singh Chaudhary, 'Religions of Doubt: Religion, Critique, and Modernity in Jalal Al-e Ahmad and Walter Benjamin', Ph.D thesis, Columbia University 2013, 106–107.
22 Mirsepassi, *Intellectual Discourse*, 106.
23 Hanson, 'The "Westoxication" of Iran', 1–23.
24 Hanson, 'The "Westoxication" of Iran', 1–23.
25 Bernard Avishai, 'Among the Believers: What Jalal Al-e Ahmad Thought Iranian Islamism Could Learn from Zionism', *Foreign Affairs* 93/2, March/April 2014, 115–124.

view of Zionism was nevertheless nuanced and fluid, and he would eventually condemn it as racist and part of the Western imperial machinations in the Middle East.[26]

Shariati's Islamic Liberation Theology

Using these premises as a platform, Shariati would propose the weaponisation of religion as a solution to the malaises diagnosed by Behrangi, Shadman, Fardid, Ahmad and other intellectuals (such as Ehsan Naraghi). The novelty of Shariati resides in his revolutionary conceptualisation of Shiism and its emancipatory potential. Shariati's analysis is similar to the ones mentioned, but he adds a new dimension that results in a reinterpretation of Shia Islam under Marxist principles. Here Shariati's rationale mirrors that of Catholic Liberation Theology.

Gustavo Gutiérrez, the author of a seminal book on this new approach to Christian theology, declared that all theology should be a 'critical reflection on Christian praxis in the light of the Word'.[27] What he meant was that theology could not remain aloof from the real circumstances of humanity. And given the state of affairs, Christianity should be grounded in 'a preferential option for the poor'. God's love is universal but not neutral. It is also not an ahistorical abstraction but is made manifest in history. And in a history understood as a struggle between social classes, with a large part of humanity exploited and oppressed, God is not on the side of the privileged few. Moreover, God does not limit Himself to show his affection to those who suffer, He also commands us to take part in a struggle to end an unjust status quo (and here Gutiérrez meant actually fight to end injustice, not merely to alleviate it with charity and acts of compassion).[28]

For Liberation Theology, faith, properly understood, means fighting

---

26 Eskandar Sadeghi-Boroujerdi and Yaacov Yadgar, 'Jalal's Angels of Deliverance and Destruction: Genealogies of Theo-politics, Sovereignty and Coloniality in Iran and Israel', *Modern Intellectual History* 18/1, 2019, 1–25.
27 Gustavo Gutiérrez, *A Theology of Liberation: History, Politics and Salvation*, 1973, 13.
28 Roberto S. Goizueta, 'Liberation Theology 1: Gustavo Gutiérrez,' *The Wiley Blackwell Companion to Political Theology*, eds. William T. Cavanaugh and Peter Manley Scott, 2018, 282.

against all evil in order to free mankind from sin, and this liberation is a spiritual liberation as well as a political liberation.[29] God does not want the faithful to be spectators in this struggle, but to become agents of change. Positive religion is not an abstract or detached exercise but a school of practice. Faith must remain engaged with the reality of the world and become the engine of historical transformation.[30]

Shariati fully agreed with this discourse that was taking shape in the context of the armed struggle in Latin America, although there were some differences. Gutiérrez made clear on several occasions that 'preferential option for the poor' did not mean 'exclusivity'. God's love was for everyone, even for tyrants. In Shariati's discourse we do not see that opening for the oppressors. In this sense, Shariati had a more Marxist outlook regarding the enemies of the exploited.

Like Gutiérrez, who had used passages of the Bible (like that of the Exodus) to portray the struggles of the Old Testament as akin to those of the communist guerrillas in the Cold War, Shariati used the basic concepts of Shia Islam and infused them with political, social, and economic readings.[31] *Tawhid* and *shirk* became symbols not just of monotheism and idolatry, but also of egalitarianism and rebellion against the idols of money, privilege, and monarchy.[32] The famous story of Cain and Abel (Qabil and Habil) is reinterpreted as a dialectic of the oppressed and the oppressors. Cain becomes a symbol of capitalism, imperialism, tyranny, of *estebdad* ('political despotism') and *estesmar* ('economic exploitation').[33] Imam Hoseyn and Yazid were also turned into archetypes of the leftist struggle against right-wing dictators and monarchs.[34] And so was Shariati's favourite personage from early Islam: Abu Dahr, who in Shariati's

---

29 Gutiérrez, *A Theology of Liberation*, 21–42.

30 Christopher Rowland, 'The Theology of Liberation,' *The Cambridge Companion to Liberation Theology*, ed. Christopher Rowland, 1999, 2–3.

31 Gustavo Gutiérrez, *Teología de la Liberación, Perspectivas*, 1975, 204.

32 Dustin J. Byrd, 'Ali Shariati and Critical Theory: From Black Affirmation to Red Negation,' *Shariati and the Future of Social Sciences: Religion, Revolution and the Role of the Intellectual*, eds. Dustin J. Byrd and Seyed Javad Miri, 2017, 117.

33 Kingshuk Chatterjee, *'Ali Shari'ati and the Shaping of Political Islam in Iran*, 2011, 89.

34 Assaf Moghadam, 'Mayhem, Myths, and Martyrdom: The Shi'a Conception of Jihad,' *Terrorism and Political Violence* 19/1, 2007, 125–143.

famous book was turned into an anachronistic champion of the oppressed who 'believed Islam to be the refuge of the helpless, the oppressed and the humiliated people and Uthman, the tool of capitalism, was the bastion to preserve the interests of the usurers, the wealthy and the aristocrats'.[35]

Shariati loved the binary approach to Islam and politics. In the role assigned to him by Shariati, Abu Dahr angrily complains that the 'capital, wealth, gold and silver which you have hoarded must be equally divided among all Muslims. Everyone must share in the others' benefits in the economic and ethical system of Islam, in all blessings of life.' The evil Caliph Uthman, on the other hand, 'saw Islam in ceremonies, external show and the pretence of piety and sanctity. He did not believe that religion should interfere with the poverty of the majority and the opulence of the minority.'[36]

In Shariati's writings, the Prophets and the companions of the Prophets are turned into symbols. They become allegories for his view of religion and politics; revolutionary martyrs who do not just die for Allah, but for equality, emancipation, and social justice.[37] In fact, for Shariati it is all one and the same. Shariati was calling for a revolutionary vanguard composed of 'enlightened souls', those who had apprehended the revolutionary pro-gramme of Islam. They had to assume the position of the 'committed and revolutionary leadership responsible for movement and growth of society on the basis of its worldview and ideology, for the realization of the divine destiny of man'. That struggle would be an armed struggle, as he point-edly called on his audience during a speech in 1972: 'Die! So that others may live.'[38]

It should come as no surprise that Shariati's daring rereading of Quranic passages and Shia traditions met with resistance. This came not just from the conservative clergy, but even from fellow progressive Islamic intel-lectuals who shared many of Shariati's political views. Fardid thought

35 Ali Shariati, *And Once Again Abu-Dhar*, retrieved from Shariati.com: http://www.shariati.com/english/abudhar/abudhar1.html.

36 Ali Shariati, *And Once Again Abu-Dhar*, retrieved from Shariati.com: http://www.shariati.com/english/abudhar/abudhar1.html.

37 Ali Rahmena, 'Ali Shariati', *Pioneers of Islamic Revival*, ed. Ali Rahmena, 1994, 213–214.

38 Charles Tripp, *Islam and the Moral Economy*, 2006, 162–163.

Shariati had gone too far in his eclecticism and too often interpreted passages of the Quran out of context. In Fardid's view, Shariati was attempting the impossible in trying to square Islamic tradition with Marxism and French existentialism. In the end, Shariati was transforming God into a human being.[39] In a similar fashion, Ayatollah Morteza Motahari felt that Shariati was advancing political and sociological arguments at the expense of theology and religion.[40]

In turn, Shariati spared no criticism in his attacks on the clergy. He condemned quietist Islam for being the handmaiden of tyrants and those preachers who had foregone their mission to awaken the masses and, instead, exercised *estehmar* (in Shariati's use of the term, 'religious alienation').[41] The ulema had deactivated religion, domesticated it, divested it of its 'progressive and this-worldly essence' in order to stifle its emancipatory potential. [42]

Apolitical Islam was a religion at the service of oppression.[43] True Islam belonged to the *mojahedin* ('Islamic fighter') not to the *mojtahed* ('Islamic jurist').[44] Shariati said on several occasions that he expected a lot from the clergy and that is why he was so hard on them.[45] Yet he felt that as long as the clergy remained aloof from the struggle for political and economic liberation, Islam had to be rescued from their hands.[46] On some occasions, Shariati's frustration with the clergy led him to embrace a Marxist critique of institutionalised religion.[47] Convinced that the faithful often adopted a passive attitude given the preponderance of the clergy, he came close to

---

39 Mirsepassi, *Transnationalism in Iranian Political Thought*, 293.
40 Ervand Abrahamian, 'Ali Shari'ati: Ideologue of the Iranian Revolution', *MERIP Reports* 102, January 1982, 24–28.
41 Chatterjee, *'Ali Shari'ati and the Shaping of Political Islam in Iran*, 93.
42 Behrooz Ghamari-Tabrizi, 'Contentious Public Religion: Two Conceptions of Islam in Revolutionary Iran', *International Sociology* 19/4, December 2004, 504–523.
43 Mirsepassi, *Political Islam, Iran, and the Enlightenment*, 25.
44 Ervand Abrahamian, *A History of Modern Iran*, 2008, 145.
45 Ali Shariati, *Construire l'identité révolutionnaire*, 2010, 8.
46 Abrahamian, *A History of Modern Iran*, 145–146.
47 Afshin Matin-Asgari, 'Marxism, Historiography and Historical Consciousness in Modern Iran: A Preliminary Study', *Iran in the 20th Century Historiography and Political Culture*, ed. Touraj Atabaki, 2009, 223.

advocating an anarchist approach to Islam.[48] Hence his aim was to popularize a 'de-clericalized Islamic theology' (*eslam menhay-e akhund*).[49]

In addition to being dubbed the 'Rousseau of the Iranian Revolution', Shariati has also been referred as the 'Iranian Luther'.[50] In his cursory reading of the Protestant Reformation, he came to admire it and backed the idea of a populist transformation of Shia Islam that would leave religious and political sovereignty in the hands of the masses.[51]

Yet Shariati was no Marxist. Like the Catholic priests who espoused Liberation Theology, he faulted Marx for disregarding the spiritual dimension in his otherwise acute analysis. Marx only understood 'half of the social reality'.[52] His economic reductionism failed to take into account a broader and richer dimension to the unjust realities it so well addresses.[53] Moreover, by keeping man at the centre of everything and forgetting the spiritual dimension of reality, Marxism is perpetuating many of the problems it wants to solve.[54] As Al-e Ahmad wrote in his introduction to André Gide's account of his trip to Moscow, the Soviet Union was nothing more than a 'deceitful mirage'.[55]

It is true that Shariati's thinking helped give form to some resistance movements like the People's Mujahedin of Iran (*Mojahedin-e-Khalq* or MEK), which eventually moved from a position of advocating an Islamic classless society to a more purist and Marxist-Leninist agenda, but neither

---

48 Shahrough Akhavi, 'Islam, Politics and Society in the Thought of Ayatullah Khomeini, Ayatullah Taliqani and Ali Shariati', *Middle Eastern Studies* 24/4, 1988, 404–431.

49 Siavash Saffari, *Beyond Shariati: Modernity, Cosmopolitanism, and Islam in Iranian Political Thought*, 2017, 82.

50 Sukidi, 'The Travelling Idea of Islamic Protestantism: A Study of Iranian Luthers', *Islam and Christian-Muslim Relations* 16/4, 2005, 401–412.

51 Akhavi, 'Islam, Politics and Society in the Thought of Ayatullah Khomeini', 404–431.

52 Esmaeil Zeiny, 'Spokesmen of Intellectual Decolonization: Shariati in Dialogue with Alatas', *Shariati and the Future of Social Sciences: Religion, Revolution and the Role of the Intellectual,* eds. Dustin J. Byrd and Seyed Javad Miri, 2017, 64–84.

53 Nilesh Sharan, 'La Teología de la Liberación en América Latina y en Irán: un verdadero proyecto transglobal y transmoderno', *Iberoamericana* XVIII/68, 2018, 97–118.

54 Nilesh Sharan, 'La Teología de la Liberación en América Latina', 97–118.

55 Dabashi, *Theology of Discontent*, 57.

Shariati's views nor those of most of his followers underwent such evolution.[56]

In fact, post-revolutionary Iran would quickly move to suppress Marxist organisations, while many on the Iranian left rushed to prove their religious credentials. As the ideologue behind the Tudeh Party, Ehsan Tabari, claimed:

> It is important to emphasise that in some countries religion serves as the ideological basis for class struggle, in some instances operating as the ideology of revolutionary forces… It is noteworthy in many respects that the ideological and organizing role which religion has time and time again played in revolutionary movements in the distant past has been manifested with a new orientation in the present-day conditions.[57]

Even so, one year after praising the socialist credentials of Shia Islam, Tabari was imprisoned and tortured. The leader of the Tudeh Party was only released after a humiliating public recantation and conversion to Islam. Accordingly, Ervand Abrahamian has criticised Khomeini as Janus-faced: 'revolutionary against the old regimes and conservative once the new order was set up'. According to Abrahamian, the revolutionary cloak was a mere ploy to gain the endorsement of the left.[58]

This is also what separates Liberation Theology from thinkers like Frantz Fanon, who argued that the Third World should give up its religious traditions in order to stand up effectively to Western imperialism. Shariati's message was the opposite: the peoples of the Third World could not fight imperialism unless they first regained their cultural and religious identities. Those were the most powerful weapons in their arsenal in their challenge to the West.[59] Khomeini could not agree more. The Ayatollah even sent a letter to Mikhail Gorbachev in the late 1980s, asking him to

---

56 Misagh Parsa, *States, Ideologies & Social Revolutions*, 2000, 99.
57 Ehsan Tabari, 'The Role of Religion in Our Revolution', *World Marxist Review* 25/12, 1982, 68–74.
58 Ervand Abrahamian, *Khomeinism: Essays on the Islamic Republic*, 1993, 37–39.
59 Ervand Abrahamian, 'Ali Shari'ati: Ideologue of the Iranian Revolution', 24–28.

study Islam and contemplate its anti-imperialist potential as a remedy to fill the ideological vacuum of a declining communist ideology.[60]

Global Nativism

Only in the past few years has the Iranian revolutionary discourse began to be studied within a broader transnational framework, with consideration of the different revolutionary or insurgent discourses of the 1960s and 1970s in other parts of the world.[61] Traditionally, Shariati's thinking has often been described as a *nativist* ideology that could be of no use in a non-Iranian context. Yet Shariati's stance was profoundly influenced by Western thought, and it closely mirrored that of the religious left in Latin America.

Shariati called for a 'return to the self' (*bazgasht beh khish*), but this was informed by his reading of foreign authors like Heidegger, Jean-Paul Sartre, Fanon and Roger Garaudy. His understanding of Shia Islam was also heavily influenced by his classes with Louis Massignon, George Gurvitch, and Jacques Berque.[62] Shariati confessed that he felt like a 'kindergartener' or 'a little elementary school pupil' before Massignon, and that his soul could no longer contain his affection for him.[63] His knowledge of Catholic Liberation Theology came from the journal *Esprit*, and the writings of Emmanuel Mounier.[64] Shariati's worldview was thus as much a product of his Western education as of his Shia and Iranian heritage. His stay in France was not like that of Khomeini's. Hamid Dabashi argues that in his 'critical and creative conversation' with a diverse range of global emancipatory discourses, Shariati abandoned 'nativism, regionalism, and tribalism' in favour of 'a globality of learning and action'.[65] By combining his strong Shia faith with socialism and 'Sartrian existentialism', Shariati

---

60 Jon B. Perdue, 'A Marriage of Radical Ideologies', *Iran's Strategic Penetration of Latin America*, eds. Joseph M. Humire and Ilan Berman, 2014, 12.

61 See Arang Keshavarzian, and Ali Mirsepassi, eds. *Global 1979: Geographies and Histories of the Iranian Revolution*, 2021.

62 Chatterjee, *'Ali Shari'ati and the Shaping of Political Islam in Iran'*, 77–78.

63 Brena Moore, *Kindred Spirits: Friendship and Resistance at the Edges of Modern Catholicism*, 2021, 109–110.

64 Boroujerdi, *Iranian intellectuals*, 109.

65 Hamid Dabashi, *Islamic Liberation Theology: Resisting the Empire*, 2008, 114.

navigated 'the topography of a liberation theology beyond any particular domain or denomination'.[66] Nevertheless, although he read attentively the articles on Catholic-Marxist dialogue in *Esprit*, Shariati always avoided quoting the thinkers behind this movement or making any explicit reference to Catholic Liberation Theology.

Thus, Shariati was adamant that there was nothing to learn from the West, and that the ideas of justice, freedom, equality, and fraternity were already present in the Quran. He even went so far as to suggest that the Western ideas of justice, freedom, equality, and fraternity had been taken from Islam, and that the concepts that the West had been so proudly lecturing to the world about during the last five hundred years were nothing more than a degraded conception of stolen notions. Here, Shariati's approach resembles that of other radical intellectuals of the Global South. In Tanzania, Julius Nyerere had already declared in 1962 that

> we, in Africa, have no more need of being 'converted' to socialism than we have of being 'taught' democracy. Both are rooted in our own past – in the traditional society which produced us. Modern African socialism can draw from its traditional heritage the recognition of 'society' as an extension of the basic family unit.[67]

The fact that Shariati's primary concern was the impact of the so-called Western imperial designs in Iran, Argentine semiotician Walter D. Mignolo argues, does not make his preoccupations any less 'universal'. Shariati's critique of the 'colonial matrix of power' from the vantage point of Iran lends itself to a project of 'cosmopolitan localism'.[68] This is something that is exemplified in Shariati's attitude towards nationalism, which he considered less pernicious than the 'false bonds' and 'fake common denominators' such as humanism and more effective in developing anticolonial fronts across the Global South.[69]

---

66 Hamid Dabashi, *Post-Orientalism: Knowledge and Power in Time of Terror*, 2009, 201.
67 Bayat, 'Shari'ati and Marx', 19–41.
68 Walter D. Mignolo, *The Darker Side of Western Modernity: Global Futures, Decolonial Options*, 2011, 287.
69 Chatterjee, *'Ali Shari'ati and the Shaping of Political Islam in Iran'*, 111.

Nationalism was tied to Shariati's obsession with authenticity. The West has turned the oppressed masses from around world away from 'what they are'. Instead of remaining true to their values, they have been modelled into creatures that please the West. They have become what the West 'built' of them and 'wanted' of them.[70]

> In the past, Romans, Iranians, Arabs, Chinese, Blacks, and others, each had their particular cultures and civilizations. But today, Europe, with its violent robotic civilization is slaughtering all other cultures and replacing them with its own civilization. So now everyone speaks the same way, and about the same things. Cities, buildings, attire, gender relations and everything else, everywhere in the world, have been homogenized and a singular global cultural and civilizational design has been imposed. We no longer have inwardly Eastern culture and outwardly Western culture.[71]

Authenticity, properly understood, becomes the cure for Western-imposed assimilation.

Here authenticity purports a modernity that coexists with cultural autonomy. The goal was to have an independent modernization based on one's culture and religion. Not a retreat to an idealized past nor an artificial modernization that merely copies Western modernisation and undermines a country's religious and cultural traditions.[72] As Siavash Saffari has argued, Shariati's frame of reference was Iran, but his analysis and ideas situate him within the broader spectrum of the Global South. The idea of 'a return to self' should not be understood as a reactionary and nativist outcry, but as 'a call for moving toward a new universal grounded in the particular'.[73]

---

70 Ali Shariati, *Fatemeh is Fatemeh*, retrieved from Shariati.com: http://www.shariati.com/english/fatemeh/fatemeh1.html.
71 Siavash Saffari, 'Ali Shariati and Cosmopolitan Localism', *Comparative Studies of South Asia, Africa and the Middle East* 39/2, August 2019, 282–295.
72 Esmaeil Zeiny, 'Spokesmen of Intellectual Decolonization: Shariati in Dialogue with Alatas', *Shariati and the Future of Social Sciences: Religion, Revolution and the Role of the Intellectual*, eds. Dustin J. Byrd and Seyed Javad Miri, 2017, 64–84.
73 Saffari, *Beyond Shariati*, 156–161.

This is the discourse that helped ignite one of the most important actions of the Iranian opposition abroad. Apart from the massive protests outside the White House during the shah's final visit to Washington in November 1977, nothing came close to the impact of the German students' protest of June 1967 against the visit of the shah. The demonstrations that resulted in the iconic death of the young student Benno Ohnesorg, shot by the West German police, were an impressive – albeit fleeting – sign of European solidarity with the Iranian opposition. In his speeches to meetings of student radicals, Iranian activist Bahman Nirumand constantly stressed the link between the Iranian struggle and other liberation struggles taking place elsewhere. For him, the Bantus in South Africa, the Vietcong in Vietnam, and the Iranian dissidents were one and the same. Yet he proposed nationalist-flavoured revolutions as long as globalisation remained a tool of cultural imperialism. Only after the success of these revolutions, would these countries transition 'into an international "solidarity of the poor peoples."'[74]

Hamid Dabashi has argued that the 'emancipatory and cosmopolitan' dimension of Shariati's thought has been 'incarcerated, normatively severed, and framed – held tightly in pigeonholes like "Iran", "the Middle East", or even "Islam"'.[75] This kind of labelling effectively robs Shariati and the Iranian Revolution of their rightful place in the global 1970s. According to Dabashi, although Shariati's *topos* was Iran and Shia Islam, one can easily extrapolate and use his discourse for other causes in different regions. Although grounded in a particular place and culture, his discourse was valid and could resonate in global struggles. Here, the common struggle of the Global South is understood as one of unity in diversity.

In this understanding of Shariati's legacy, although his 'rediscovery of local identity' undermined revolutionary Iran's potential in laying out a common vision with other countries and projected its predicament as part of a larger transnational struggle, his weaponization of religion has proved to be a very effective tool in the struggle against Western hegemony.[76]

---

74 Quinn Slobodian, *Foreign Front: Third World Politics in Sixties West Germany*, 2012, 108–109.
75 Dabashi, *Islamic Liberation Theology*, 114.
76 Raewyn Connell, *Southern Theory: The Global Dynamics of Knowledge in Social Science*, 2007, 134.

Perhaps this might help explain the proliferation of 'Liberation Theologies': although conceived by Catholic priests in Europe and Latin America, scholars now talk of many Liberation Theologies beyond the 'Islamic Liberation Theology' of Shariati: 'Black Theology of Liberation'[77], 'Feminist Liberation Theology'[78] and even a 'Palestinian Liberation Theology'.[79] This would confirm the idea that 'particular attachments', rather than separating and isolating one's discourse, constitute the 'point of entry into global solidarities and cosmopolitan belongings'.[80]

Although Shariati's thinking (and that of his predecessors) was very influential in the Iranian Revolution, one does not see many traces outside Iran or the Middle East. Even though his writings have been translated into French, Turkish, and English, the interest in his ideas, beyond the scholars who study him, remains negligible. We can clearly see the influence of prominent foreign authors on Shariati, but not the other way around. Even after the creation of the Islamic Republic, Shariati's thinking received scant attention by the otherwise meticulous agencies of the US government.[81] In the memoranda and reports of American diplomats, intelligence officers, and consultants, Shariati is barely mentioned. And this is not the result of carelessness: US archives are filled with thousands of documents dealing with the minutest detail relating to Iran.

However, a rare US document written shortly after the Iranian Revolution warns of the radical impact of his thought:

> Although the debate between Shariati and his opponents involves interpretation of history and religion, these are more than sterile

---

77 See James H. Cone, *A Black Theology of Liberation*, 2010.

78 There is a Feminist Liberation Theologians' Network (FLTN) created by U.S. and Canadian feminist scholars, ministers, and activists as well as a Feminist Theology journal devoted to the question.

79 See Christy Femila J, 'Palestinian Liberation Theology: Challenges to Christian-Muslim Relations,' *Gurukul Journal of Theological Studies* 22/1, January 2011, 20–31.

80 Saffari, 'Ali Shariati and Cosmopolitan Localism', 282–295.

81 See for example: State Department, memorandum, 'Academic views of Iran,' 10 October 1980. CIA Freedom of Information Act Electronic Reading Room (hereafter FOIA), CIA-RDP81B00401R000400130001-6.

academic exercises. Both sides are arguing political action, and at least some who follow Shariati are invoking his ideas to support terrorism.[82]

It is true that until it was too late, American diplomats and intelligence officers never assigned much importance to religion in Iran. They cynically regarded the use of Islam by the opposition as an unavoidable toll to pay if one wanted to connect with the masses.[83] But in relation to Latin America one finds dozens of government documents analysing Liberation Theology and its impact in the Hispanic world. One does not find a similar preoccupation in Washington with the question of Islamic Liberation Theology.[84] The Shia variant of Liberation Theology was not deemed a factor worthy of meaningful consideration beyond Iran. When the State Department hosted a seminar with several academic specialists on Iran in 1980, no one mentioned Shariati or adequately addressed the innovative Shia Islamic concepts that had fuelled the revolutionary flames. The mix of nationalism, Islam, and socialism escaped the scholars' attention.[85]

This is also the result of a largely pragmatic foreign policy of the Islamic Republic. In June 1982 Tehran hosted a much-publicised 'World Conference of Liberation Movements', and Khomeini often compared the struggle of Iran with that of the African and Latin American nations fighting against imperialism. 'Iran and these countries have suffered similar pains', his eventual successor as Supreme Leader, Ali Khamenei, frequently remarked. But this was mere rhetoric. Khamenei even went so far as to declare that Iran would 'accept as one of us any nation in the world which is suffering under the scourge of global arrogance', but Iranian ties with these 'resistant' countries were never that important.[86]

---

82 CIA National Foreign Assessment Center, research paper, 'Islam in Iran', March 1980. FOIA, CIA-RDP81600401 8000400110.

83 CIA National Foreign Assessment Center intelligence, memorandum, 'Iran: the Tudeh Party and the communist movement', 8 December 1978. FOIA, CIA-RDP80T00634A000500010030-8.

84 See for example: CIA Directorate of Intelligence, research paper, 'Liberation Theology: Religion, Reform, and Revolution', April 1986. FOIA, CIA-RDP97R00694R000600050001-9.

85 State Department, memorandum, 'Academic views of Iran', 10 October 1980. FOIA, CIA-RDP81B00401R000400130001-6.

86 Foreign Broadcast Information Service, analysis report, 'Current directions in

Tehran could invite the descendants of Che Guevara and, as Hajj Saed Qassemi did, tell them that Guevara was a true believer in God given the common goals of Islam and socialism.[87] But this was, like the joint committees created with Nicaragua and Cuba, mere 'window dressing'.[88] Propaganda gestures and lofty rhetoric were not followed by meaningful action. Words did not match deeds. In fact, Cuba and Nicaragua, like other 'resistant' countries in Latin America and Africa, much to Tehran's dismay, remained neutral in the Iran-Iraq war, refraining from any substantive action that could jeopardise their relations with Saddam Hussein's Iraq.

The reality of the war with Iraq and the international isolation of the regime severely limited the reach of Iran's foreign policy. But in the 1980s Iranian meddling in Latin America paled in comparison with that of Muammar Gaddafi's Libya.[89] Support for guerrillas was non-existent, and, although relations were fluid with regimes like Nicaragua, Iran preferred to cultivate ties with reactionary regimes such as Argentina, Chile, and Brazil (countries that could hardly be described as part of the 'resistance front'). There was no sponsorship of subversion in Latin America. The guerrillas and movements embracing Liberation Theology received no special attention from Iran,[90] and the Iranian regime limited the export of its revolutionary ideas to small Shia communities in places like Guyana and Colombia.[91]

Thus, while the similarities between the Catholic/Latin American and the Islamic/Iranian Liberation Theologies are irrefutable, this was never translated into any special connection between the two movements and regions. Whereas Shariati's thinking could be considered as one of 'cosmopolitan localism', the ideas behind the Iranian Revolution did not resonate much beyond the Middle East. While this ideology strongly influenced the

Iranian foreign policy', 11 April 1985. FOIA, IA-RDP87T00434R000200150042-4.
87 Perdue, 'A Marriage of Radical Ideologies', 12.
88 CIA Directorate of Intelligence, memorandum, 'Iranian goals and activities in Latin America', 18 December 1987. FOIA, CIA-RDP90T00114R000700820001-1.
89 CIA Directorate of Intelligence, memorandum, 'Iranian goals and activities in Latin America,' 18 December 1987. FOIA, CIA-RDP90T00114R000700820001-1.
90 CIA Directorate of Intelligence, research paper, 'Iran: the struggle to define and control foreign policy', May 1985. FOIA, CIA-RDP86T00587R000200190005-3.
91 CIA Directorate of Intelligence, memorandum, 'Iranian goals and activities in Latin America', 18 December 1987. FOIA, CIA-RDP90T00114R000700820001-1.

Revolution, the new regime that was created as a result was by no means ready to adapt that ideology to a global or transnational crusade.

Bibliography

Archives

Central Intelligence Agency's Freedom of Information Act Electronic Reading Room, (FOIA)/(CREST), https://www.cia.gov/readingroom/home.

Secondary Sources

Abrahamian, E. 'Ali Shari'ati: Ideologue of the Iranian Revolution,' *MERIP Reports* 102, January 1982, 24–28.

Abrahamian, E. *A History of Modern Iran*, Cambridge, 2008.

Abrahamian, E. *Khomeinism: Essays on the Islamic Republic*, Berkeley, 1993.

Ahmad, J. *Occidentosis: a plague from the West*, Berkeley, 1984.

Akhavi, S. 'Islam, politics and society in the thought of Ayatullah Khomeini, Ayatullah Taliqani and Ali Shariati'. *Middle Eastern Studies* 24/4, 1988, 404–431.

Ansari, A.M. *The Politics of Nationalism in Modern Iran*, Cambridge, 2012.

Atabaki, T., ed. *Iran in the 20th Century Historiography and Political Culture,* London, 2009.

Avishai, B. 'Among the Believers: What Jalal Al-e Ahmad Thought Iranian Islamism Could Learn from Zionism', *Foreign Affairs* 3/3, October/November 2014, 115–114.

Bayat, A. 'Shari'ati and Marx: A Critique of an "Islamic" Critique of Marxism', *Alif: Journal of Comparative Poetics* 10, 1990, 19–41.

Boroujerdi, M. *Iranian Intellectuals and the West: The Tormented Triumph of Nativism*, New York, 1996.

Byrd, D.J. and S.J. Miri, eds. *Shariati and the Future of Social Sciences: Religion, Revolution and the Role of the Intellectual*, Leiden, 2017.

Cavanaugh, W.T. and P.M. Scott, eds. *The Wiley Blackwell Companion to Political Theology*, Hoboken, 2018.

Chatterjee, K. *'Ali Shari'ati and the Shaping of Political Islam in Iran*, New York, 2011.

Cone, J.H. *A Black Theology of Liberation*, New York, 2010.

Connell, R. *Southern Theory: The Global Dynamics of Knowledge in Social Science*, Cambridge, 2007.

Dabashi, H. *Islamic Liberation Theology: Resisting the Empire*, New York, 2008.

Dabashi, H. *Post-Orientalism: Knowledge and Power in Time of Terror*, New Brunswick, USA, 2009.

Dabashi, H. *Theology of Discontent*, New York, 2017

Femila, J.C. 'Palestinian Liberation Theology: Challenges to Christian-Muslim Relations', *Gurukul Journal of Theological Studies* XXII/1, January 2011, 20–31.

Fink, C., P. Gassert, and D. Junker, eds. *1968: The World Transformed*, Washington, 1998.

Ghamari-Tabrizi, B. 'Contentious Public Religion: Two Conceptions of Islam in Revolutionary Iran', *International Sociology* 19/4, December 2004, 504–523.

Gheissari, A. 'Shadman, Sayyed Fakhr-al-Din', *Encyclopaedia Iranica*, 2000. https://www.iranicaonline.org/articles/shadman.

Gheissari, A. *Iranian Intellectuals in the Twentieth Century*, Austin, 1998.

Gutiérrez, G. *A Theology of Liberation: History, Politics, and Salvation*, Maryknoll, USA, 1973.

Gutiérrez, G. *Teología de la Liberación, Perspectivas*, Salamanca, 1975.

Hanson, B. 'The "Westoxication" of Iran: Depictions and Reactions of Behrangi, Al-e Ahmad, and Shariati', *International Journal of Middle East Studies* 15/1, February 1983, 1–23.

Hillmann, M.C. 'Behrangi, Samad', *Encyclopaedia Iranica* IV/1, 110–111.

Humire, J.M., and I. Berman, eds. *Iran's Strategic Penetration of Latin America*, New York, 2014.

Keshavarzian, A., and A. Mirsepassi, eds. *Global 1979: Geographies and Histories of the Iranian Revolution*, Cambridge, 2021.

Mignolo, W.D. *The Darker Side of Western Modernity: Global Futures, Decolonial Options*, Durham, USA, 2011.

Mirsepassi, A. *Intellectual Discourse and the Politics of Modernization: Negotiating Modernity in Iran*, Cambridge, 2004.

Mirsepassi, A. *Transnationalism in Iranian Political Thought: The Life and Times of Ahmad Fardid*, Cambridge, 2017.

Moghadam, A. 'Mayhem, Myths, and Martyrdom: The Shi'a Conception of Jihad', *Terrorism and Political Violence* 19/1, 2007, 125–143.

Moore, M. *Kindred Spirits: Friendship and Resistance at the Edges of Modern Catholicism*, Chicago, 2021.

Parsa, M. *States, Ideologies & Social Revolutions*, Cambridge, 2000.

Rahmena, Ali, ed. *Pioneers of Islamic Revival*, London, 1994.

Rowland, C., ed. *The Cambridge Companion to Liberation Theology*, Cambridge, 1999.

Sadeghi-Boroujerdi, E., and Y. Yadgar. 'Jalal's Angels of Deliverance and Destruction: Genealogies of Theo-politics, Sovereignty and Coloniality in Iran and Israel', *Modern Intellectual History* 18/1, 2019, 1–25.

Saffari, S. 'Ali Shariati and Cosmopolitan Localism', *Comparative Studies of South Asia, Africa and the Middle East* 39/2, August 2019, 282–295.

Saffari, S. *Beyond Shariati: Modernity, Cosmopolitanism, and Islam in Iranian Political Thought*, Cambridge, 2017.

Sharan, N. 'La Teología de la Liberación en América Latina y en Irán: un verdadero proyecto transglobal y transmoderno', *Iberoamericana* XVIII/68, 2018, 97–118.

Shariati, A. *Construire l'identité révolutionnaire*, Paris, 2010.

Shariati, A. *Fatemeh is Fatemeh*. Accessed July 20, 2021. http://www.shariati.com/english/fatemeh/fatemeh1.html.

Shariati, A. *And Once Again Abu-Dhar*. Accessed July 20, 2021. http://www.shariati.com/english/abudhar/abudhar1.html.

Singh Chaudhary, A. '*Religions of Doubt: Religion, Critique, and Modernity in Jalal Al-e Ahmad and Walter Benjamin*', Ph.D thesis, Columbia University, 2013.

Slobodian, Q. *Foreign Front: Third World Politics in Sixties West Germany*, Durham, USA, 2012.

Sukidi. 'The Traveling Idea of Islamic Protestantism: A Study of Iranian Luthers', *Islam and Christian-Muslim Relations* 16/4, 2005, 401–412.

Tabari, E. 'The Role of Religion in Our Revolution', *World Marxist Review* 25/12, 1982, 68–74.

Tripp, C. *Islam and the Moral Economy*, Cambridge, 2006.

12

The 'International Family': The Organisation of Iranian People's Fada'i (Majority) and the 'Anti-Imperial World' in the Age of National Liberation[1]

Carson Kahoe

On the afternoon of 19 August 1953 (28 Mordad 1332), tanks rolled through the streets of Tehran, heralding the coup that would depose Iran's prime minister, Mohammad Mosaddeq. Restoring Iran's shah to power, the coup was orchestrated by the British MI6 and the American CIA. It forever altered Iran's history, but its full impacts echoed far beyond the country's borders. At his peak, Mosaddeq was one of the most famous leaders in the world. His campaign to nationalise Iran's oil industry earned him the admiration of others who also sought to wrest control of their natural resources from imperialist powers.[2] In Egypt, where nationalists pursued a campaign to nationalise the Suez Canal, crowds of admirers thronged the streets to

---

1 The phrase 'international family' is drawn from Peyman Vahabzadeh, *A Guerrilla Odyssey: Modernization, Secularism, Democracy, and the Fadai Period of National Liberation in Iran, 1971–1979*, 2010, 247.
2 Roy Mottahedeh, *The Mantle of the Prophet: Religion and Politics in Iran*, 2009, 126.

see Mosaddeq on a 1951 visit, literally carrying his car down the street.[3] The coup itself – spurred by British and American fears that Mosaddeq's success in Iran would inspire similar revolts elsewhere, from Indonesia to Chile – is a testament to Mosaddeq's international influence.[4]

The oil nationalisation campaign and the subsequent 28 Mordad coup, as it is known in the Iranian calendar, stand as defining chapters of Iran's encounter with imperialism in the twentieth century, thrusting Iran into the spotlight of global anti-colonial struggle. Yet because Iran was never formally colonised, the country's role in this period of global unrest is often understated and misunderstood. Many Americans, particularly in academic fields like political science and critical terrorism studies, more readily associate the Iranian Revolution with global terrorism than with global decolonisation.[5] This conclusion results from a short-term understanding of Iran's history and its struggles against European imperialism in the nineteenth and twentieth centuries.

In truth, Iranians were deeply embedded in the global anti-colonial moment of the mid-twentieth century. The global nature of imperialism engendered a shared consciousness in those who fought against it. United in purpose with movements across Asia, Africa, and Latin America, many in Iran pursued common ideals of independence and spoke a common vocabulary of national liberation. Central to this international solidarity was the idea of anti-imperialism – opposition to a global system of empire. This idea became an organising concept in Iran and beyond, but terms like empire, imperialism, and anti-imperialism were highly variable and contingent over time, in different places, and even among various anti-imperial movements in the same place.

This chapter probes the definition of imperialism used by one Marxist Iranian militant organisation[6] – *Sazman-e Charik-ha-ye Fada'i-ye Khalq-e*

---

3 Ervand Abrahamian, *The Coup: 1953, the CIA, and the Roots of Modern U.S.-Iranian Relations*, 2013, 195, 229.
4 Abrahamian, *The Coup*, 88.
5 David C. Rapoport, 'The Four Waves of Modern Terrorism', *Transnational Terrorism*, ed. Steven M Chermak and Joshua D Freilich, 2016; Alvin Z. Rubinstein and Donald E. Smith, 'Anti-Americanism in the Third World', *The Annals of the American Academy of Political and Social Science* 497, 1988, 35–45.
6 Or rather, a collection of interrelated groups that all claimed *fada'iyan* in their

Iran ('Organisation of the Iranian People's Fada'i Guerrillas', OIPFG or Fada'iyan for short) – and evaluates that notion's role in shaping the group's ideas around domestic and international solidarity. In this moment of heightened global consciousness, how did this group define imperialism and anti-imperialism, and how did this understanding align its sense of solidarity with movements around the world? Deconstructing the OIPFG's answers to these questions will reveal which groups it saw as natural anti- imperial allies and which groups it regarded as imperialist.

Officially formed in 1971 as the People's Fada'i Guerrillas, the Fada'iyan never truly formed a single, unified organisation.[7] Successive waves of guerrillas, often with contrasting ideas, principles, and priorities, all claimed the term *fada'i* (roughly, 'self-sacrificer') and waged armed struggle against the shah's regime throughout the 1970s. After the Revolution, the Fada'i movement continued to fracture, producing some factions that pursued armed struggle and others that shifted toward traditional party politics in an effort to shape the new revolutionary state.

Because the Fada'i movement contained diverse and sometimes conflicting ideologies, there is no definitive Fada'i definition of imperialism. Therefore, this chapter will focus on one faction that dominated the movement's party politics in the period immediately following the Revolution. After a series of fractures starting in June 1980, this faction called itself the OIPF-M, adding 'Majority' to the name and dropping 'Guerrillas' in a self-conscious shift away from armed struggle.[8] Focusing on the group's weekly periodical – *Kar* ('Labour'), published in its first iteration from 1979 to 1982 – this chapter will analyse the Majority faction's discourse on imperialism, as well as its reporting on struggles against imperialism elsewhere in the world.[9] In doing so, it will illuminate the ways in which

---

title. At varying times and through several splits, groups of militants referred to themselves varyingly as the People's Fada'i Guerrillas (1971), the Organisation of the People's Fada'i Guerrillas (1974), the Organisation of the Iranian People's Fada'i Guerrillas (1975), and the Organisation of the Iranian People's Fada'iyan – Majority (1981) Vahabzadeh, *A Guerrilla Odyssey*, 36–37.

7 Vahabzadeh, *A Guerrilla Odyssey*, viii, 31–32.

8 Vahabzadeh, *A Guerrilla Odyssey*, 73; Val Moghadam, 'Socialism or Anti-Imperialism? The Left and Revolution in Iran', *New Left Review* 166, November-December 1987, 21.

9 In some regards, the movement's periodicals present contradictory ideas,

the group's definition of imperialism informed its conceptions of international solidarity.

Such an analysis provides depth to the literature on the international perspectives of the Fada'i movement and Iranian Left more broadly. Peyman Vahabzadeh's and Ali Rahnema's books on the Fada'iyan intricately detail the movement's history and ideological debates, but they provide no specific study of the Fada'iyan's evaluations of imperialism and global affairs.[10] Looking more broadly, Val Moghadam and Nozar Alaolmolki highlight the salience of Third Worldism to the Fada'i movement and the influence of Third World anti-colonial actors on the Iranian Left.[11] Moghadam also analyses the role that a binary worldview constructed around the ideas of imperialism and anti-imperialism played in shaping the OIPF-M's post-revolutionary domestic political policies.[12] However, neither author turns that understanding of imperialism outward to analyse the Fada'i movement's evaluation of its anticolonial contemporaries, focusing instead on the Iranian Left's factionalism.

This analysis intends to broaden the literature documenting Iranians' participation in anti-imperial struggles. Roy Mottahedeh notes the extent to which facets of pre-Revolutionary Iranian society viewed the country through a colonial frame, and Hamid Dabashi highlights the Third Worldist and anticolonial currents underpinning the Revolution.[13] While acknowledging the latter point, Mehrzad Boroujerdi claims that the Revolution's anti-imperial currents were incidental to the nativist analyses of intellectuals like Jalal Al-e Ahmad and Ali Shariati.[14] Rejecting this analysis,

---

reflecting the diversity of opinions within the movement itself. Still, taken together, this reporting broadly delineates the ways that Fada'iyan related ideas about imperialism to their politics and their understanding of the world.

10 Vahabzadeh, *A Guerrilla Odyssey*; Ali Rahnema, *Call to Arms: Iran's Marxist Revolutionaries: Formation and Evolution of the Fada'is, 1964–1976*, London, 2021.

11 Moghadam, 'Socialism or Anti-Imperialism?'; Nozar Alaolmolki, 'The New Iranian Left', *Middle East Journal* 41/2, 1987, 218–233.

12 Moghadam, 'Socialism or Anti-Imperialism?'

13 Mottahedeh, *The Mantle of the Prophet*; Hamid Dabashi, *Theology of Discontent: The Ideological Foundations of the Islamic Revolution in Iran*, 1993.

14 Mehrzad Boroujerdi, *Iranian Intellectuals and the West: The Tormented Triumph of Nativism*, 1996, 67–76, 111–15.

Eskandar Sadeghi-Boroujerdi argues that Al-e Ahmad's engagement with the period's anti-colonial thinkers makes his work more likely a critique of racial capitalism than a call for nativist chauvinism.[15] Shirin Deylami similarly rejects analyses of Al-e Ahmad as nativist, and Arash Davari makes a similar argument for Shariati, situating his work firmly within an anticolonial milieu.[16]

By analysing ideas of imperialism within the Fada'i movement, this chapter will provide another frame of reference for evaluating Iranians' participation in global anti-imperialism. At the same time, it will highlight the influence of anti-imperialist discourses in shaping the OIPF-M's concepts of solidarity with its contemporaries around the world. What the organisation's supporters would have read – and what they might have believed – about the period of global conflict through which they were living will explain why imperialism and anti-imperialism triggered political action among the Fada'i.

The Fada'iyan and a New Iranian Anti-Imperialism, to 1979

The political and intellectual landscape following the removal of Mosaddeq in 1953 fuelled a newfound antipathy towards the United States, which ultimately set the stage for the Fada'iyan's ascent. Alongside the defeat of the secular liberal nationalist National Front a decade later, the coup discredited liberal constitutionalism as a method for safeguarding Iran's independence from imperial intervention.[17] At the same time, two seminal public theoreticians, Jalal Al-e Ahmad and Ali Shariati, began to articulate a new oppositional vernacular that criticised the shah by combining a Marxist critique of Iranian society with a reimagined Iranian Shi'ism

---

15 Eskandar Sadeghi-Boroujerdi, 'Gharbzadegi, Colonial Capitalism and the Racial State in Iran', *Postcolonial Studies* 24/2, April 2021, 173–194.

16 Shirin S. Deylami, 'In the Face of the Machine: Westoxification, Cultural Globalization, and the Making of an Alternative Global Modernity', *Polity* 43/2, 2011, 242–263; Arash Davari, 'A Return to Which Self?: Ali Shari'ati and Frantz Fanon on the Political Ethics of Insurrectionary Violence', *Comparative Studies of South Asia, Africa and the Middle East* 34/1, January 2014, 86–105.

17 Evaleila Pesaran, 'Towards an Anti-Western Stance: The Economic Discourse of Iran's 1979 Revolution', *Iranian Studies* 41/5, December 2008, 694–696.

organised around resistance to oppression.[18] For the Fada'iyan, a Marxist group whose self-given title, *fada'i*, evoked religiously connoted self-sacrifice, this new oppositional framework set the stage for a rise to national prominence.

These developments dovetailed with the zeitgeist of the 'rebellious sixties', wherein the Fada'i movement found its roots. A repressed rebellion in 1963 pushed Iran's student movements underground, where many studied the period's great anti-colonial movements in China, Vietnam, Cuba, and Algeria. They read Frantz Fanon, Aimé Césaire, Che Guevara, and other theoreticians, participating fully in a Third Worldist sentiment inaugurated with the 1955 Bandung Conference.[19] Students and members of the National Front abroad in Europe grew increasingly radical, and it was there, drawing influence and support from many countries across the world, that the pursuit of armed struggle first appeared as a valid strategy.[20]

The same international atmosphere similarly influenced two small groups of students, one from Tehran and one from Mashhad, that would come together in Tehran's universities between 1963 and 1965. Committed to Marxism and inspired by revolutionary movements from Cuba to Vietnam, these groups merged in April 1971 to form the People's Fada'i Guerrillas after most of their founding members had been arrested.[21] Immediately preceding the merger, thirteen Fada'iyan gained national attention with an attack on a regional gendarmerie in the Caspian town of Siyahkal. Though quickly quashed, their brazen assault shattered the state's image

---

18 Ervand Abrahamian, *Iran Between Two Revolutions*, 1982; Nikki R. Keddie and Yann Richard, *Roots of Revolution: An Interpretive History of Modern Iran*, 1981; Margaret Kohn and Keally D. McBride, 'Westoxification/Detoxification: Anti-Imperialist Political Thought in Iran', *Political Theories of Decolonization: Postcolonialism and the Problem of Foundations*, ed. Keally D. McBride and Margaret Kohn, 2011, 40–43; Pesaran, 'Anti-Western Stance', 697–699; and Sadeghi-Boroujerdi, 'Gharbzadegi, Colonial Capitalism and the Racial State in Iran', 9–11.
19 Shariati, himself, engaged in the global 1960s as well, critiquing and translating Fanon's *The Wretched of the Earth* while he studied in France. Moghadam, 'Socialism or Anti-Imperialism?', 9; Abrahamian, *Iran Between Two Revolutions*, 464–466.
20 Vahabzadeh, *A Guerrilla Odyssey*, 5–6.
21 Vahabzadeh, *A Guerrilla Odyssey*, 21–31; and Moghadam, 'Socialism or Anti-Imperialism?', 10.

of invulnerability and prompted student demonstrations, making them a symbol of resistance.[22]

The operation marked the start of a guerrilla campaign that the Fada'iyan would wage throughout the 1970s. With arms smuggled from Palestine and Libya, the group launched attacks on targets whose symbolic significance highlighted both their ideology and the state's vulnerability, for example, assassinating a textile tycoon, university police, and SAVAK agents.[23] A wave of clashes with state forces in 1976 decimated the group, but the rising tide of revolution in 1978, along with the shah's release of political prisoners that spring, lifted the floundering Fada'iyan. By February 1979, they led the armed mass uprising that delivered the shah's government its death blow.[24] In 1979, the OIPFG was Iran's most popular leftist group, drawing half a million supporters in that year's May Day rally.[25]

The group's popularity notwithstanding, the Fada'iyan, hollowed by years of SAVAK suppression, struggled to transition from an underground guerrilla network to a mass political movement. After the Revolution, the group's simmering ideological divisions bloomed into a series of fractures. Following the November seizure of the US Embassy in Tehran, a majority of the group, convinced of Khomeini's anti-imperialist credentials, fatefully threw its weight behind him. By early June 1980, the minority split away to form its own minority group, retaining the name 'Organisation of Iranian People's Fada'i Guerrillas', while the majority faction soon thereafter identified itself as 'Organisation of Iranian People's Fada'i Guerrillas (Majority)'. By May Day 1981, the majority group dropped 'Guerrillas' and rechristened itself the OIPF-M.[26] The OIPF-M drew increasingly

---

22 Vahabzadeh, *A Guerrilla Odyssey*, 29, 210–211; and Rahnema, *Call to Arms*, 256–269.

23 Vahabzadeh, *A Guerrilla Odyssey*, 35–41, 100. One of the group's founders, Bijan Jazani, called this concept 'armed propaganda'. With the group's assassination of a SAVAK double agent that had infiltrated the Tudeh Party (Iran's traditional communist party), the group claimed the mantle of the 'new Communist movement', succeeding where the Tudeh had failed.

24 Vahabzadeh, *A Guerrilla Odyssey*, 38, 50–52; and Abrahamian, *Iran Between Two Revolutions*, 488–495.

25 Peyman Vahabzadeh, 'FADA'IAN-E ḴALQ', *Encyclopaedia Iranica*, 2015, https://www.iranicaonline.org/articles/fadaian-e-khalq.

26 Vahabzadeh, *A Guerrilla Odyssey*, 73.

close to Iran's traditional communist Tudeh party and praised the new Islamic Republic for its anti-imperialist rhetoric. Undeterred by Khomeini's increasing authoritarianism, the OIPF-M remained content until it was purged, along with all other leftist groups, in 1983 and 1988.[27]

The Imperial System and Iran

The OIPF-M's blind faith in Khomeini is rooted in its polarised, zero-sum understanding of imperialism. In broad strokes, this conceptualisation is visible in an early essay from one of the founding Fada'iyan. The 1967 essay, titled '*Masa'el-e Jonbesh-e Zedd-e Este'mari va Azadibakhsh-e Khalq-e Iran va 'Omdetarin Vazayef-e Kommunist-ha-ye Iran dar Sharayat-e Konuni*', ('Issues for the Iranian People's Anti-Colonial and Liberation Movement and the Most Profound Duties of Iran's Communists in the Current Moment'), defines America's imperial relationship with Iran.[28] Through a policy of 'obstruction of revolution' (*mavane'-ye enqelab*), the United States kept the shah in power, and in return for his 'extreme dependence on imperialism', the shah pursued a foreign policy of 'imperialist politics' on America's behalf. The United States cemented its grip on the country by buying the loyalty of Iran's 'comprador bourgeois elites' (*nokhbegan-e burzhvazi-ye kompradur*) who endorse this colonial relationship because, as the oligarchy, they profit from the exploitation of Iran's working class in the capitalist system. The essay terms this arrangement 'compradorism' (*kompradurism*) and declares it 'the societal foundation for neocolonialism', as feudalism was for the old imperialism.[29] A later Fada'i publication from 1976 called *Nabard-e Khalq* ('The People's Battle') would add that such 'native military regimes' (*rezhim-ha-ye nezami-ye mahali*) as the shah's form the

---

27 Vahabzadeh, *A Guerrilla Odyssey*, 66–76.

28 Rahnema, *Call to Arms*, 18.

29 Bijan Jazani, 'Masa'el-e Jonbesh-e Zedd-e Este'mari va Azadibakhsh-e Khalq-e Iran va 'Omdetarin Vazayef-e Kommunist-ha-ye Iran Dar Sharayat-e Konuni', Autumn 1967. Available online: https://iran-archive.com/sites/default/files/2021-08/bijan-jazani-masaele-jonbeshe-zedde-estemari.pdf.

Visually representing America's policy of 'obstruction of
revolution' (*mavane'-ye enqelab*). *Kar*, 1 July 1981.

backbone of the 'Nixon strategy' (*estratezhi-ye Niksun*) for safeguarding American interests.[30]

Taken together, this analysis indicates a broad alliance acting in defence of America's imperialist system. The OIPFG and OIPF-M's weekly paper *Kar*[31] enumerates that alliance, identifying three strata of actors that perpetuate US imperialism. First were the American imperialists themselves, the international institutions they piloted, and their European and Japanese counterparts who were fundamentally 'allied with one another in the pillage and exploitation of the working class', both abroad and at home.[32] Next were the reactionary regimes that acted as imperialism's regional policemen, including Iraq's 'fascist regime' and Pakistan's 'dictatorial military regime of Zia-ul-Haq', as well as Turkey, Jordan, Saudi Arabia, Egypt, and the southern Persian Gulf's Arab states.[33]

Finally, and most insidiously, there were the Iranian moderates, liberals, and capitalists whom *Kar* feared would reproduce the dependence and exploitation that marked the shah's regime. The paper argued that America wanted 'the victory of the National Front ... [and] the moderate religious faction' because they sought to compromise with the imperialists, resurrect the 'royal generals and oppressors' in the army, and reintegrate Iran into the capitalist order.[34] Such a government 'of the petty bourgeoisie' – of

---

30 'Jonbesh-e Mosalahaneh-ye Iran va Enqelab-e Mantaqeh', *Nabard-e Khalq*, June 1976, 136.
31 *Kar* was originally the OIPFG's publication; after 16 July 1980, its masthead specifically noted that it was the organ of the *aksariyyat* – the OIPF-M. The *aqaliyyat* (Minority) published its own *Kar* as well. For simplicity's sake, when this chapter refers to *Kar*, it means both the pre-fracture publication and the paper of the OIPF-M.
32 'Dadgah-e Laheh va Shurayeh Amniyat Muasesati Dar Khedmat-e Emperialism-e Amrika', *Kar*, 24 December 1979; 'Bani-Sadr, Dar Fekr Ettehad Ba Emperialism-e Orupa va Zhapon', *Kar*, 16 April 1980.
33 'E'lamiyeh-ye Ettehadiyeh-ye Zanan-e 'Araq: Hampeymani-ye Rezhim-e Fashisti-ye 'Araq Ba Erteja'e 'Arab va Hamahangi Ba Emperialism-e Amrika', *Kar*, 25 August 1981; and 'Rezhim-e Diktaturi-ye Nezami-ye Zia-'ul-Haq Doshman-e Khalq-ha-ye Pakestan va Mantaqeh va Nukar-e Sarsepordeh-ye Emperialism-e Amrika', *Kar*, 9 July 1980.
34 'Personel-e Enqelabi-ye Niruhaye Mosallah: Ba Emperialism-e Jenayatkar-e Amrika va Rezhim-e Fashisti-ye 'Araq Peykari Portavan Khahim Kard! Vali Forsat-e Sudju'i Beh Timsaran-e Shahanshahi va Sarkubgaran-e Artesh Nakhahim

'imperialism's servile and criminal capitalists' (*sarmayehdaran-e jenay-atkar va sarsepordeh-ye emperialism*) – could not protect the people's 'democratic rights and freedoms' because they shared 'the very same goals [as] American imperialism' and acted as its 'friends and spies'.[35] After documents taken from the US embassy showed meetings between Iran's foreign minister, Ebrahim Yazdi, and American officials, *Kar* denounced his 'unambiguous support for America' and demanded his removal. Mehdi Bazargan, the Provisional Government's prime minister, was similarly charged.[36] Later, when the Islamic Republic's first president, Abolhassan Bani Sadr, attempted to thaw relations with Europe, *Kar* criticised him for being 'united in thought with the imperialism of Europe and Japan'.[37]

In sum, the Fada'iyan broadly defined 'imperialism' to include entities connected to the United States, its allies, or capitalism. By this definition, 'imperialism' was an omnipotent, many-headed hydra, and anyone who accepted anything short of Iran's complete opposition to the major capitalist and imperialist powers merely invited the return of the beast. As a result, different actors with vastly different positions, motivations, and scales of power were all collapsed together as being united with imperialism. The

---

Dad!', *Kar*, 23 April 1980; 'Emperialism-e Amrika Cheh Hokumati Barayeh Iran Mikhahad?', *Kar*, 14 June 1979; and 'Barresi-ye Asnad Neshan Midahad: Ahdaf-e Ahzab va Mohafel-e Buržvazi Liberal Haman Ahdaf-e Emperialism-e Amrika Ast', *Kar*, 9 January 1980. Of course, Iran would need an army in a few months, when Saddam Hussein launched his invasion.

35 'Emperialism-e Amrika Cheh Hokumati Barayeh Iran Mikhahad?'; 'Sarmayehdaran-e Liberal Dustan va Jasusan-e Emperialism-e Amrika', *Kar*, 9 January 1980; and 'Barresi-ye Asnad Neshan Midahad: Ahdaf-e Ahzab va Mohafel-e Burzhvazi Liberal Haman Ahdaf-e Emperialism-e Amrika Ast.'

36 'Bazargan va Yazdi Az Raftan-e Shah Beh Amrika Hemayat Kardand; Ba Vojud-e Efsha'e Ravabat-e Hsaneh-ye Yazdi Ba Emperialism-e Amrika Toust-e Daneshjouyan-e Peirou-ye Khatt-e Emam Chera Yazdi Mamur Residegi Beh Shekayat-e Mardom Dar Sarasar-e Iran Mishavad?', *Kar*, 19 December 1979; and 'Aqa-ye Yazdi, Poshtibani-ye Sarih-e Shoma Az Amrika Mobarezat-e Zedde-Emperialisti-ye Mardom Ra Kahesh Nakhahad Dad', *Kar*, 31 May 1979.

37 'Bani-Sadr, Dar Fekr Ettehad Ba Emperialism-e Orupa va Zhapon'. The paper decried his attempts 'to breed in the masses this delusion that the imperialism of Germany, Japan, France, etc. is not united with American imperialism, but instead is its enemy and our friend'.

National Front appeared to be as dangerous to the Revolution as the American warships mustering in the Persian Gulf.

Such an impossibly broad definition distorted the group's risk analysis of the domestic Iranian political situation, leading to some tragic ironies. For one, by rejecting the liberal nationalist and moderate religious factions in the name of protecting the people's 'democratic rights and freedoms', the Fada'iyan condemned some of the only factions that were actually committed to building democratic institutions in Iran. For another, in his meetings with American officials, Yazdi was given intelligence warning of Saddam Hussein's upcoming invasion of Iran. Still, his association with the Americans rendered him an enemy of the people's Revolution.[38]

For the Fada'iyan, nearly everyone who was not one of these tools of American imperialism was part of the anti-imperial masses. Reporting on mass demonstrations, *Kar* praised the risen 'people', who outnumbered the bourgeois compradors. The paper reported marches commemorating Mosaddeq, defying 'American imperialism's aggression', and demonstrating solidarity with Palestine.[39] Emphasising the popular nature of these marches, the paper once boasted that 'hundreds of thousands of bodies' filled the streets.[40] Though these masses included a range of professionals, including doctors, nurses, and teachers, workers received *Kar*'s greatest attention.[41] Brickmakers in East Azerbaijan, 'militant oil workers' in Ahvaz and southern Iran, 'proletarian farmers' of Shushtar, the Turkman and Baloch proletariat, tailors from Tehran, factory workers,

---

38 'Bazargan va Yazdi az Raftan-e Shah Beh Amrika Hemayat Kardand', Kar, 19 December 1979.

39 'Mardom-e Mobarez-e Iran Ba Sherkat Dar Rahpeyma'i-ye Ruz-e Shanbeh Khatare-ye Qayam-e Zedde-Emperialisti Si-ye Tir Ra Gerami Midarand', *Kar*, 19 July 1979; 'Rahpeima'i 'aliyeh Emperialism-e Amrika', *Kar*, 24 May 1979; and 'Az Ahdaf-e Zedde-Emperialisti-Zedde-Sahiunisti Rahpeima'i-ye Ruz-e Qods Qate'aneh Hemayat Mikonim', *Kar*, 20 August 1979.

40 A plausible figure, given the Fada'iyan's popularity at the time. 'Dar Tazahorat-e 'azim-e Zedde-Emperialisti Chohar-e Azar Keh Beh De'ut-e Sazman-e Charikha-ye Fada'i-ye Khalq-e Iran Bargozar Shod', *Kar*, 26 November 1979.

41 'Nameh-ye Yek Mo'alem-e "Paksazi" Shodeh Beh "Kar": Chera Ma Ra Az Peikar Ba Emperialism va Solteh-ye Farhangi-ye An Mahrum Kardeh-id?', *Kar*, 22 July 1981; and 'Ettela'iyeh va Qat'nameh Pezeshkan va Parastaran va Kadr-e Darmani Bimarsetan-ha-ye Amuzeshi-ye Tehran', *Kar*, 3 September 1979.

unemployed masses: all were united in a popular front against imperialism and capitalism.[42]

So when these anti-imperialist masses stormed the streets carrying portraits of an old cleric from Qom, many Fada'iyan (particularly those who would form the OIPF-M in 1980) happily followed him as the Revolution's head.[43] At various times, *Kar* committed itself to following the Imam.[44] Following a bombing of the Islamic Republican Party's headquarters in Tehran, *Kar* mourned the blast's martyrs and implored all Iranians to 'join hands ... under the brave leadership of Imam Khomeini'.[45]

Their faith was rooted in neither a shared devotion to socialism nor a common vision for Iran's future. Instead, taken with the Ayatollah's incendiary anti-imperialist rhetoric, the OIPF-M assumed that mobilisation of the anti-imperialist masses naturally heralded the causes of social justice they sought.[46] The OIPF-M's support for Khomeini belies both the group's paternalistic view of the masses and the binary worldview that aligned all militant anti-imperialists as natural allies. For one, despite their belief that

42 'Dehqanan-e Zehemteksh-e Jelgun (Shushtar): Zamindar Nabud Ast, Dehqan Piruz Ast', *Kar*, 2 January 1980; 'Be Da'ut-e Setad-e Markazi-ye Shura-ha-ye Torkman Sahra va Kanun Farhangi Siasi-ye Khalq-e Torkman Zehmtekshan-e Torkaman, Baloch va Zaboli', *Kar*, 16 January 1980; and 'Sendika-ye Mostaqel-e Kargaran-e Khiat-e Tehran va Humeh', *Kar*, 16 January 1980; 'Tazahorat-e Zedde-Emperialisti-ye Kargaran-e Kurepezkhaneh-ha-ye Azarbaijan-e Sharqi', *Kar*, 19 December 1979; 'Khast-ha-ye Khalq-e Torkman', *Kar*, 22 March 1979; 'Ba Paksazi-ye Enqelabi-ye Karkhaneh-ha, Mobarzeh-ye Zedde-Emperialisti Ra Erteqa' Dahim', *Kar*, 24 December 1979; and 'Gozaresh-e Rahpeima'i-ye Zedde-Emperialisti-ye Bikaran', *Kar*, 24 December 1979; 'Naftgaran-e Mobarez Hafari va Mobarezat Peigir-e Anan (Qesmat-e Dovvum) 'aliye Sherkat-ha-ye Emperialisti Dar Jonub', *Kar*, 24 December 1979.
43 Vahabzadeh, *A Guerrilla Odyssey*, 47; and 'Sevvomin Salgard-e Enqelab-e Zedde-Emperialisti va Mardomi-ye Iran Beh Rahbari-ye Emam-e Khomeini Mobarak Bad', *Kar*, 3 February 1982.
44 'Sevvomin Salgard-e Enqelab-e Zedde-Emperialisti va Mardomi-ye Iran Beh Rahbari-ye Emam-e Khomeini Mobarak Bad'.
45 'Ettela'iyeh-ye Komiteh-ye Markazi-ye Sazman-e Fada'iyan-e Khalq-e Iran (Aksariyat) Darbareh-ye Faj'eh-ye Enfejar-e Daftar-e Markazi-ye Hezb-e Jomhuri-ye Eslami', *Kar*, 1 July 1981.
46 Afshin Matin-Asgari, 'The Left's Contribution to Social Justice in Iran: A Brief Historical Overview', *Iran's Struggles for Social Justice: Economics, Agency, Justice, Activism*, ed. Peyman Vahabzadeh, 2017, 265.

Themes of unity against 'imperialism' permeated *Kar*'s pages.
Above: The banner reads, 'Workers of the world unite', *Kar*, unknown date;
Right top: 'The armed mobilization of the masses is the guarantor of victory for
our people', *Kar*, 20 November 1980;
Right bottom: 'Only if the people unite / Will America and Iraq be
unable to do any wrong. Unite', *Kar*, 20 November 1980.

they acted on behalf of the masses, the Fada'iyan never built a meaning-ful working-class constituency.[47] As a result, they drew false conclusions about the actual beliefs and motivations of the masses.

In addition, the Fada'iyan seemed unable to read events beyond the con-fines of their ideology. When local workers went on strike, for instance, the Fada'iyan saw popular class revolution rather than a localised demand for improvement in material conditions.[48] This ideological projection is clear in one *Kar* headline reporting on 'the anti-imperialist march of the unem-ployed', who presumably would have been concerned with more immedi-ate matters than American imperialism.[49] Though many Iranians, including Jalal Al-e Ahmad, distrusted Marxism as an alien ideology, the Fada'iyan could not imagine that the masses would see them as anything but a van-guard because that is how they saw themselves.[50] This ideology compelled them to view the post-revolutionary landscape through the binary of a united camp of imperialists against a united camp of anti-imperialists. As members of the anti-imperial camp, they acted to advance their camp's presumably common goal. For the OIPF-M, that meant supporting the loudest anti-imperialist of them all: Khomeini.

A Global Binary

The ideological projection did not stop at Iran's borders. Internationally, the OIPF-M separated friend from foe based on the same imperial/anti-imperial binary. *Kar* called for a foreign policy 'consistent with the inter-ests of the revolution' to promote an 'alliance with the lines of progressive governments and powers in the region and the world'.[51] The paper bubbled with talk of a global 'resistance front' and 'subversion front' against impe-rialism and debated an 'anti-imperialist and anti-Zionist Islamic front'.[52]

---

47 Vahabzadeh, *A Guerrilla Odyssey*, 222.
48 Vahabzadeh, *A Guerrilla Odyssey*, 250.
49 'Gozaresh-e Rahpeima'i-ye Zedde-Emperialisti-ye Bikaran'.
50 Dabashi, *Theology of Discontent*, 78.
51 'Telegram-e Kargaran-e Foulad-e Ahvaz Beh Mardom-e Mobarez-e Irland', *Kar*, 20 May 1981.
52 'Jebhe-ye Barandazi Beh Sarkardegi-ye Emperialism-e Amrika Bar Tabl-e Jang Mikubad. Mottahed Shavim!', *Kar*, 30 September 1981; 'Qat'nameh-ye Konferans-e

It discussed OPEC's role in opposing imperialism and hoped the Economic Cooperation Council could ensure 'socialist cooperation ... "for each country and for the entirety of their societies."'[53] Calling for unity with 'the global camp of revolution', the paper proposed 'a union of all the anti-imperial forces' as 'a guarantor of the Revolution's victory'.[54] Only a 'global anti-imperial movement' – a 'union of all the proletariat' – would ensure the Revolution's 'victory against the aggression and machinations of American imperialism and its domestic allies'.[55]

Specific conflicts provided litmus tests to sort friend from foe. The US embassy seizure was one such test. Objections arose from the United States and 'other imperial governments' – Britain, France, Italy, West Germany, and the European Parliament – as well as from the local reactionary regimes – Turkey, Egypt, Oman, Saudi Arabia, Israel, and Pakistan. Meanwhile, the students who seized the embassy enjoyed support from 'the progressive forces of the world': Cuba, the USSR, North Korea (DPRK), Vietnam, the People's Democratic Republic of Yemen, Libya, the Popular Front for the Liberation of Palestine (PFLP), the African National Congress, the Union of the African People of Zambia, the People's Front for the Liberation of Eritrea, the Chilean Opposition, and the Chad Liberation Front. *Kar* equated the embassy seizure to Vietnam's own 'anti-American struggle' and urged Iranians to draw 'great internationalist lessons' from

---

Jebhe-ye Payedari: Estefadeh Az Tamam-e Emkanat Baraye Mobarzeh Ba Emperialism va Sehiounism', *Kar*, 30 September 1981; and 'Jebhe-ye Eslami-ye Zedde-Emperialisti Zedde-Sehiounisti Gam-e Mostbati Ast Mashrout Bar Inkeh...', *Kar*, 25 August 1981. Indeed, this language, Ahmadinejad's 'Axis of Resistance', and the Islamic Republic's 'Resistance Economy' in the face of American nuclear sanctions all draw from a similar vein.

53 'Ekhtetam-e Movafaqiyat Amiz-e Ajlas-e Shouraye Hamyari-ye Eqtesadi', *Kar*, 8 July 1981; and 'Naqsh-e OPEC Dar Mobarezeh 'aliyeh Emperialism!', *Kar*, 21 May 1981.

54 'Gostaresh-e Monasebat Ba Ardu-ye Jahani-ye Enqelab Dar Khedmat-e Enqelab', *Kar*, 14 October 1981; and 'Ettehad-e Tamam-e Niru-ha-ye Zedde-Emperialist Zamn-e Piruzi-ye Enqelab Ast', *Kar*, 23 September 1981.

55 'Barayeh Moqabeleh Ba Emperialism-e Amrika Ettehad Hameh-ye Zehemtekshan Yek Serverat Tarikhi Ast', *Kar*, 21 May 1980; 'Beh Monasebat-e Mo'arefi-ye Vazir-e Kharejeh-ye Jadid', *Kar*, 1 July 1980; and 'Gam-ha-ye Mosbat-e Dowlat Dar Siasat-e Khareji va Tut'eh-ha-ye Emperialism-e Amrika 'aliye Enqelab', *Kar*, 23 September 1981.

their progressive allies.[56] Iraq's invasion of Iran in 1980 worked similarly. '[T]he region's reactionary regimes' – Jordan, Egypt, Saudi Arabia, Oman, and the Gulf States – supported 'the reactionary Iraqi regime's war of aggression', while 'the global front of revolution' – the 'progressive Arab governments of Algeria, Libya, Democratic Yemen and Syria' – supported Iran. The USSR and DPRK played peacemaker, pursuing 'peace-seeking efforts'.[57]

More than a mere cheerleader, the global camp of revolution endured countless struggles, across space and time, which *Kar* viewed as extensions of Iran's. It equated the Iranians fighting Iraq to 'France's army of farmers' in the Napoleonic wars and the militants of the Paris commune. Their valour equalled 'the heroism of the Soviet people' against fascism and the 'legendary and age-long resistance' of the Vietnamese against France and America. The paper declared: 'The epic opposition of the masses of people of Khorramshahr, Abadan, Susangerd, Dezful, and our compatriots in other western cities will live in our memory as our equivalent of Dien Bien Phu, Leningrad, and Paris.'[58] For *Kar*, equating these disparate struggles revealed the universality of anti-imperialism; a blow anywhere advanced the 'people's' liberation everywhere.

The universality of anti-imperialism expressed here melded nicely with the Fada'iyan's socialist internationalism and with its global binary. It allowed them to apply the lessons learned by their international counterparts directly to their experience in Iran. Throughout Asia, they saw in new socialist states potential blueprints for Iran's future. Yet the persistent belief in a universal experience of imperialism (and anti-imperialism) runs counter to the prevailing anti-imperialist tradition in Iran. For his part, Jalal Al-e Ahmad viewed Marxism as a symptom of *gharbzadegi* in part for the tendency of socialist internationalism to erase national differences:

Would that mean that the means of production identifies the individual,

---

56 'Nazari Bar Safara'iha-ye Jahani: Dustan va Doushmanan-e Jonbesh-e Zedde-Emperialisti-Demokratik-e Khalq-ha-ye Iran va Jahan', *Kar*, 19 December 1979.
57 'Niru-ha-ye Terqikhah-e Jahan Az Defa'-e Qehremaneh-ye Khalq-e Ma Hemayat Mikonand!', *Kar*, 8 October 1980.
58 'Az Tajrobiyat-e Mobarezati-ye Khalq-ha-ye Jahan Dars Begirim', *Kar*, 20 November 1980.

that is, it is his Identification Card? ... But what about language? History? Religion? Customs?[59]

Similarly, Ali Shariati believed internationalism to be a Western lie designed to negate the cultural character of Eastern societies, accusing those intellectuals who advocated it as contributing to their own 'ethnocide'.[60]

Indeed, the OIPF-M's belief in the universal experience of imperialism sometimes papered over uncomfortable realities. In some cases, the group's identification with other conflicts represented deep and genuine connections between armed movements. In other cases, the equation of experiences under colonialism ran counter to historical realities. In any case, *Kar*'s coverage of foreign actors reveals the extent to which the members of this organisation understood their struggle as part of a larger global drama.

In Praise of Third World Communists

Around the world, the OIPF-M viewed itself as being in communion with, to borrow Peyman Vahabzadeh's phrase, an 'international family' of Marxist-Leninist groups.[61] This was particularly true of conflicts taking place in Iran's immediate geographic neighbourhood, in which the Fada'iyan often felt they had some sort of stake. *Kar* praised India's communists and expressed its 'revolutionary solidarity' with socialist Libya and Algeria.[62] In the People's Democratic Republic of Yemen, the Fada'iyan credited the new socialist state for the country's development of industry and agriculture, progress toward overcoming unemployment, and general 'conquest of backwardness' (*ghalabeh bar 'aqabmandegi-ha*).[63]

---

59 Dabashi, *Theology of Discontent*, 53, 62.
60 Mehrzad Boroujerdi, *Iranian Intellectuals and the West: The Tormented Triumph of Nativism*, 1996, 111–112.
61 Vahabzadeh, *A Guerrilla Odyssey*, 247.
62 'Hamkari-ha-ye Fani-ye Iran va Libi Hambastegi-ye Enqelabi 'aliyeh Emperialism', *Kar*, 27 January 1982; and 'Didar-e Ra'is Jomhur-e Aljazayer Az Ettehad-e Shouravi', *Kar*, 17 June 1981.
63 'Dastavard-ha-ye Enqelab va Sousialism: Jomhuri-ye Demokratik-e Khalq-e Yemen Dar Rah-e Ghalbe Bar 'aqabmandegi-ha va Pishravi Besuye Sousialism', *Kar*, 10 December 1980; and 'Beh Monasebat-e Aval-e Tir Mah Salruz-e Ta'asis-e Jomhuri-ye Demokratik-e Khalq-e Yemen', *Kar*, 17 June 1980.

But a few specific conflicts crystallised the Fada'iyan's conviction of universal anti-imperial struggle, one of the most notable being the conflict in Israel and Palestine. *Kar* argued that Israel's continued existence relied on the support of imperialist countries, and the paper regularly decried Zionism in the same breath as 'regional reaction' and 'global imperialism' in working 'against the aspiration of the Palestinian people'.[64] Like the shah's regime, Zionism menaced liberation movements beyond Israel's borders, and *Kar* denounced Israel's 'criminal aggression' against Lebanon and Syria in 1981.[65] Israel, like 'the Camp David conspiracy', ultimately served American imperialism.[66]

The OIPF-M took a similar interest in Afghanistan, but *Kar*'s coverage of the Soviet invasion highlights a tension between OIPF-M's strict dedication to Marxism-Leninism and concepts of anti-imperialism. The OIPF-M celebrated the Afghan communist party's 1978 rise to power and praised its efforts in 'eradicating illiteracy'.[67] As the country descended into civil war and Soviet invasion, *Kar* bemoaned the Afghan 'counter-revolutionaries', who were 'common enemies' of the Afghan and Iranian revolutions.[68] *Kar* took no issue with the Soviet invasion, siding with the country's communists over those who saw the Soviets as invading foreigners (or perhaps imperialists). However, it did not hesitate to criticise Tehran's antipathy to Afghanistan's communists, accusing Ali Khamenei (then a member of the Majles) and Foreign Minister Sadeq Qotbzadeh of sending 25 million rial

---

64 '42 Sal-e Qabl, Sehiunist-ha-ye Esra'ili Beh Komak-e Keshvar-ha-ye Emperialisti Sarzamin-e Felestine Ra Eshghal Kardand Amma Saranjam: Khalq Qahreman-e Felestin Ast Keh Piruz Khahad Shod', *Kar*, 21 May 1980; and 'Emperialism, Sehiunism, va Erteja'-e Mantaqeh Dar Barabar-e Arman-e Khalq-e Felestin', *Kar*, 26 July 1979.
65 'Esra'il Khoud Ra Amadeh Hamleh Beh Suriyeh Mikonad', *Kar*, June 10, 1981; and 'Tajavoz-e Jenayatkaraneh Sehiunism Dar Labnan Gush-ha-ye Az Tute'e-ha-ye Emperialism-e Amrika 'aliyeh Khalq-ha-ye Mantaqeh Ast', *Kar*, 10 June 1981.
66 'Tahajom-e Emperialisti Beh Labnan Halqe-ye Digari Az Tuz'eh-ye Camp Deivid', *Kar*, 20 May 1981.
67 'Afghanistan Dar Rah-e Mohv-e Bisavadi', *Kar*, 27 May 1981.
68 'Emperialism Dam Migostarad Hushyar Bashim! Enqelab-e Iran va Afghanistan Doushmanan-e Moshtaraki Darand', *Kar*, 25 November 1981; and 'Motabu'at-e Emperialisti Vaqihaneh Beh Ertebat-e Amrika Ba Zedde-Enqelabiyun-e Afghanistan E'teraf Mikonand', *Kar*, 29 July 1981.

Visually representing the dual threat of Zionism and
American imperialism. *Kar*, 24 February 1982.

to aid the same Afghan reactionaries as America and Pakistan.[69] In the following decade, the OIPF-M continued to praise the accomplishments of
Afghan communism, while the Islamic Republic provided substantial aid
to the forces fighting the Soviet-backed government.

Beyond Iran's immediate vicinity, the OIPFG praised communists
throughout Asia. By 'bolstering socialism' in the country, communist
Mongolia conquered 'centuries of backwardness', repeating a preoccupation with socialism's purported ability to advance Asian countries into
modernity.[70] The paper celebrated 'New Laos', described Korea's early
twentieth-century revolution against Japan as 'part of the global proletarian revolution', and praised 'New Cambodia' for 'revitalizing national

---

69 'Dar Mobareze-ye Mardom-e Khavarmianeh ʿaliyeh Emperialism-e Amrika,
Shouraye Enqalab Dar Kenar-e Kist?', *Kar*, 16 April 1979.
70 'Beh Monasebat-e Salruz-e Eʿlam-e Jomhuri-ye Khalq Dar Maghulestan (28
Novambr-e 1924 – 7 Azar-e 1313) Maghulestan Ghalabeh Bar ʿaqabmandegi-ye
Qorun Dar Moddat-e Kamtar Az Nim Qarn', *Kar*, 3 December 1980; and 'Jomhuri-ye
Khalq-e Maghulestan Dar Rah-e Tahkim-e Sousialism', *Kar*, 13 August 1980.

value, architecture, and societal progress'.[71] No Asian communist state received more attention or praise, however, than Vietnam, which combined socialism with direct action against US imperialism. *Kar* commemorated 'the complete freedom of Vietnam' as drawing the world closer 'to the breaking of America's global imperialism'.[72] Vietnam's glorious revolution provided 'the foundation for peace and socialism in Southeast Asia', and the paper praised Vietnam's policies to 'eradicate illiteracy'.[73]

China stands as a notable exception to this coverage, with the publications' changing perspectives tracking ideological trends taking place within the Fada'i movement over time. An edition of *Nabard-e Khalq* from 1974 praised 'Comrade Mao Zedong' as 'a great Marxist-Leninist' and related his experience to that of the Fada'iyan.[74] These proclamations make sense for a guerrilla movement that, following the Sino-Soviet split, drew more inspiration from Maoism's advocacy for armed struggle than it did from the Soviet concept of 'peaceful coexistence' with the United States.[75] However, as the OIPF-M grew closer to the pro-Soviet Tudeh following the Revolution, its coverage of China grew highly critical. By summer 1981, *Kar* condemned China's 'reactionary politics' and its 'alliance with imperialism and betrayal of revolution'.[76]

In Central and South America, *Kar* celebrated the Sandinistas, lionised Salvadorian revolutionaries who 'frightened imperialism', decried the

71 'Mardom-e La'os Miguyand: Zaman Hamanand-e Rud-e Mekong Beh 'aqab Baz Nakhahad Gasht; La'os Kohan Mota'aleq Be Gozashte Ast va Hargez Baz Nakhahad Gasht, La'os-e Novin Be Ayandeh Minegarad', *Kar*, 19 September 1980; 'Taqvim-e Enqelab-e Jahani: Enqelab-e Koreh: Joz'i Az Enqelab-e Jahani-ye Prouletaria', *Kar*, 10 September 1980; 'Enqelab-e La'os: Dastavard-ha va Cheshmandaz-ha', *Kar*, 25 February 1981; and 'Mosalmanan-e Kampuchia Khastar-e Hemayat-e Mosalmanan-e Jahan Az Jomhuri-ye Khalq-e Kampuchia Shodand', *Kar*, 20 May 1981.
72 'Beh Monasebat-e Panjomin Salgard-e Fath-e Saigon (Shahr-e Ho Chi Minh)', *Kar*, 30 April 1980.
73 'Shahr-e Ho Chi Minh Dar Rasta-ye Enqelab-e Sousialisti-ye Vietnam Beh Pish Miravad!', *Kar*, 4 February 1981; and 'Cheguneh Vietnam-e Enqelabi Bisavadi Ra Rishhekon Kard?', *Kar*, 4 February 1981.
74 'Andisheh-ye Mao Zedong va Enqelab-e Ma', *Nabard-e Khalq*, April 1974.
75 Rahnema, *Call to Arms*, 48, 67–70.
76 'Siasat-e Khareji-ye Chin: Peyvand Ba Emperialism va Khiyanat Beh Enqelab', *Kar*, 24 June 1981.

execution of Bolivian miners by its coup government, and warned of imperialism's plots to 'smash Jamaica's independence'.[77] As with Vietnam, the
biggest regional thorn in America's side – Cuba – received the most prominent coverage. Cuba appeared as a beacon for workers around the world.
Kar studied Cuba's revolution and dissected its improvements in Cuban
housing and literacy.[78] It also published Fidel Castro's speeches, quoting
his defiance against 'Reagan's threats'.[79] The paper's coverage of Chile
provides an interesting counterpoint to its coverage of China, reflecting the
heterogeneity of perspectives contributing to *Kar*. After the Revolution,
the majority faction that would form the OIPF-M renounced armed struggle, dropped its enthusiasm for revolutionary China, and abandoned its
previous critique of the Soviet Union's reformism. Yet a 1980 article cited
the CIA-sponsored coup that killed Salvador Allende – Chile's democrati-
cally elected communist president – as a 'negation of reformism, [and a]
vindication of revolution', reflecting the fact that much of *Kar* remained
influenced by a minority of Fada'iyan who still saw armed struggle as a
valid tactic.[80]

In Africa, there was no equivalent to Cuba or Vietnam, but there was
no shortage of anti-colonial struggles to celebrate. *Kar* cheered Ethiopia's 'orientation toward socialism', celebrated the 'brave struggle of the
people of Namibia', and declared Mozambique 'a country unbound from

77 'Beh Monasebat-e Salgard-e Enqelab-e Nicaragua', *Kar*, 22 July 1981;
'Tashkil-e Dowlat-e Mouqat-e Demokratik-e Enqalabi-ye Nicaragua', *Kar*, 28 June
1979; 'Lash-e Niruha-ye Vabasteh Beh Emperialism Barayeh Darham Shekastan-e
Esteqlal-e Jama'ika', *Kar*, 12 November 1980; 'Boulivi: Hezaran Ma'danchi Tust-e
Kudetagaran-e Boulivi E'dam Shodand', *Kar*, 13 August 1980; and 'Piruz-ha-ye
Enqelabiyun-e El Salvador Emperialism Ra Beh Vahshat Andakhteh Ast', *Kar*, 15
July 1991.
78 'Cheguneh Cuba-ye Sousialisti Bisavadi Ra Nabud Kard', *Kar*, 3 September
1980; and 'Moshkel-e Mosken Dar Cuba-ye Enqelabi Cheguneh Hal Shod?', *Kar*,
20 August 1980.
79 'Jang-e Mikrobi-ye Amrika 'aliyeh Kuba', *Kar*, 16 February 1982; 'Fidel Castro:
Cuba Az Tahdid-ha-ye Reagan Harasi Nadarad', *Kar*, 29 April 1981;
'Teraznameh-ye Enqelab-e Cuba: Castro Az Tajarob va Dastavord-ha-ye Enqelab-e
Cuba Sokhan Miguyad', *Kar*, 17 December 1980.
80 'Tajrobeh-ye Shili: Nafi-ye Reformism, Asebat-e Enqelab', *Kar*, 17 November
1980; and Vahabzadeh, *A Guerrilla Odyssey*, 69.

colonialism'.[81] Highlighting again the interconnected nature of these struggles, the paper declared that 'the victory of the people of Zimbabwe is a
victory for all the oppressed peoples of Africa and the world'.[82] Perhaps the
greatest attention was paid to South Africa, another imperial policeman.
As with Israel and the shah, 'South Africa's racists' enforced America's
'politics of aggression' in Africa through their 'assault against revolutionary Angola' and their 'racial discrimination and bondage' of Black South
Africans.[83]

This reporting raises interesting elements about the OIPF-M's worldview and the way these Fada'iyan related themselves to Third World revolutionaries. The preoccupation with 'backwardness' suggests a concern
with a similar backwardness in Iran, which *Kar* asserts can best be solved
by socialism. The celebration of revolutionary Latin American groups
reflects the initial interest in Latin American revolutionaries that first
inspired early Fada'iyan, as well as the organisation's internal tensions
later on. Additionally, the paper's sincere interest in African revolutionary
struggles reflects a sense of comradeship under common experiences of
exploitation. Yet the implication that colonial oppression of Africa was
equal to that of Iran sits uncomfortably with the persistence of anti-Black
racism in Iran, even as intellectuals and groups like the Fada'iyan came to
identify with their revolutionary counterparts on the continent.[84]

European Socialism

Instead of colonialism, capitalism and its opponents took centre stage

---

81 'Etioupi: Samtegiri Beh Suye Sousialism', *Kar*, 20 May 1981; 'Yazdah Sal-e
Peikar-e Delavaraneh-ye Mardom-e Namibia', *Kar*, 25 August 1981; and
'Mozambik, Keshvari Raha Shodeh Az Este'mar', *Kar*, 20 August 1980.
82 'Piruzi-ye Khalq-e Zimbabwe Piruzi-ye Hameh Khalq-ha-ye Setamdideh-ye
Afriqa va Jahan Ast', *Kar*, 13 March 1980.
83 'Tajavozat-e Nežadparastan-e Afriqa-ye Jonubi Dar Angoula', *Kar*, 12 August
1981; 'Tahajom-e Nežadparastan 'aliyeh Angola-ye Enqelabi Gushe-ha-i Az
Siyasat-e Tajavozkaraneh-ye Emperialism-e Amrika', *Kar*, 2 September 1981; and
'Soweto: Faryad-e Siyahan-e Afriqa-ye Jonubi', *Kar*, 11 June 1980.
84 Firoozeh Kashani-Sabet, 'Colorblind or Blinded by Color?: Race, Ethnicity, and
Identity in Iran', *Sites of Pluralism Community Politics in the Middle East*, ed. Firat
Oruc, 2019, 153–180.

in the Fada'iyan's coverage of America and Europe. *Kar* criticised the West's 'flimsy democracy' and, noting American racial violence, labelled '26 black youths' killed in Atlanta 'casualties of criminal imperialism'.[85] However, the paper only rarely mentioned race in its criticism of the West, perhaps reflecting a disinterest in racial dynamics of imperialism relative to economic. It focused instead on workers' movements, discussing strikes of US air-traffic controllers and miners, rallies of French metal-smelting workers, and protests in England against 'the foundations of the capitalist order'.[86] The paper reprinted an article by Secretary-General of the Communist Party of the USA, Gus Hall, who denounced America as 'the global leader of terrorism'.[87] Though these workers and communists were not exactly liberation movements, *Kar* positioned them comfortably in 'the global camp of revolution'.[88]

In addition to this coverage of contemporary workers' movements, *Kar* filled its pages with a fixation on radical European history, which it viewed as inspiration for anti-imperial struggle across the globe. A recurring column entitled 'A History of the World's Workers' Movement' traced the development of socialism in Europe from the 1848 revolutions in France and Germany to the First International and 'the world's first workers' government' in the Paris Commune, whose principles and guidelines were 'ageless'.[89] Karl Marx and Friedrich Engels received praise as 'teacher[s] of workers around the world'.[90] As a rule the group viewed socialism and anti-imperialism synonymously, and it praised Europe's communist states accordingly. *Kar* celebrated socialism in Bulgaria, Czechoslovakia, and East Germany as a bulwark against capitalism

85 'Mobarezeh-ye Daneshjuyan Dar Orupa va Amrika', *Kar*, 13 August 1980; and '26 Javan-e Siyahpust Qorbani-ye Emperialism-e Jenayatkar', *Kar*, 20 May 1981.
86 'Mouj-e Tazahorat-e Mardom-e Engelis Payeh-ha-ye Nezam-e Sarmayedari Ra Murod Hamleh Qarar Dadeh Ast', *Kar*, 15 July 1981.
87 'Emperialism-e Amrika, Rahbar-e Terorism-e Jahani', *Kar*, 2 September 1981.
88 'Rahpeima'i-ye 'azim-e Solh Dar Aleman-e Gharbi Bar-e Digar Sabet Kard Solh Khast Barhaq Ardu-ye Jahani-ye Enqelab Ast', *Kar*, 21 October 1981.
89 'Asul va Rahnemud-ha-ye Komun Javdah-e-And', *Kar*, 16 August 1979; 'Ijad-e Avalin Tashkilat-e Beinomelalli-ye Kargaran', *Kar*, 21 June 1979; and 'Enqelab-e 1848 Miladi-ye Faranseh', *Kar*, 31 May 1979.
90 'Beh Monasebat-e Heshtad-o-Panjomin Salmarg-e Frederik Engels: "Engels Amuzgar-e Kargaran-e Sarasar-e Jahan"', *Kar*, 30 July 1979.

and militarism, and Hungary earned points for its resistance movement against the Nazis.[91]

However, no communist state received such positive treatment as the Soviet Union. This position is slightly surprising given the early Fada'iyan's antipathy toward the USSR (and its nefarious role in Iran). Indeed, the pre-revolutionary essay, 'Issues for the Iranian People's Anti-Colonial and Liberation Movement', rejected the idea of cultivating ties with the Soviet Union, since its relationship with the shah's regime after 1961 constituted 'a contradiction with proletarian internationalism'.[92] At the start of guerrilla operations in 1971, early Fada'iyan gravitated toward revolutionary Maoism because of the USSR's 'peaceful coexistence' with the United States. Still, the group remained open to support wherever it could find it, including in the Soviet Union. For a time in 1976, members of the OIPFG met with Soviet agents in Europe to discuss support. However, the Soviets made their pro-vision of aid conditional on the Fada'iyan's publication of an article com-memorating the anniversary of the October Revolution, as well as their providing intelligence on Iranian politics, military, and society. The negoti-ating Fada'iyan refused, with one reportedly saying, 'We are not spies.'[93]

By 1979, that position had changed, reflecting *Kar*'s new antipa-thy toward China. Fada'iyan resumed talks with Soviet agents after the Revolution, and in 1979 Farrokh Negahdar, a Fada'i who would later push for the OIPF-M's merger with the pro-Soviet Tudeh, was elected to the Fada'iyan's central committee.[94] On 12 November that year, above a picture of Lenin, *Kar*'s front page announced that 'the Great October Revolution [was] tantamount to the start and prelude [*saraghaz*] to the proletarian revolutions around the world', ostensibly crediting the USSR

91 'Shanzdahomin-e Kongre-ye Hezb-e Komunist-e Chekoslovaki Ba Movafeqiyyat Beh Kar-e Khoud Payan Dad', *Kar*, 15 April 1981; 'Taqvim-e Enqelab-e Jahani, Beh Monasebat-e Salruz-e Enqelab-e Bolgharestan', *Kar*, 3 September 1980; 'Sousialism Dar Sarzamin-e Aleman: Darham Shekastan-e Dastgah-e Nezami-Bourukratik-e Kohan Shart-e Moqadamati-ye Piruzi-ye Har Enqelab-e Vaq'ean Khalqi Ast', *Kar*, 8 October 1980.
92 Jazani, 'Masa'el-e Jonbesh-e Zedd-e Este'mari va Azadibakhsh-e Khalq-e Iran va 'Omdetarin Vazayef-e Kommunist-ha-ye Iran Dar Sharayat-e Konuni', 13.
93 Rahnema, *Call to Arms*, 394–395; and Vahabzadeh, *A Guerrilla Odyssey*, 42–43.
94 Vahabzadeh, *A Guerrilla Odyssey*, 66–73.

Celebrating the 'Great October Revolution' on
Kar's front page, 12 November 1979.

as the source of Iran's anti-imperial revolution.[95] Contacts continued, and
by March 1981, three Fada'iyan members travelled secretly to Moscow as
honoured guests of the Soviet Union. From that year onward, the OIPF-M
grew very close to the Tudeh, consulting with the party on all major decisions and pushing for a merger by 1983. The Majority faction's contacts
with the Soviet Union paid off starting in April that year, when purges in
Iran led to the flight of as many as 1,600 Fada'iyan to the USSR.[96]

95 'Be Monasebat-e Shast-o-Dovvomin-e Salgard-e Enqelab-e Kabir-e Octobr',
Kar, 12 November 1979.
96 Vahabzadeh, *A Guerrilla Odyssey*, 74–75.

These facts explain in part *Kar*'s obsequious coverage of the Soviet Union following the Revolution. Aside from praising the October Revolution, the paper drew inspiration from the Soviet resistance to Nazi fascism.[97] It heralded the USSR as a beacon of progress for workers, celebrating Soviet unions, their eradication of unemployment, and the 'decrease of working hours' and 'increase in rights' for Soviet workers.[98] The USSR was a bastion of social and national progress, too, illustrating a cohesive multi-national state that reserved a large role for its women. Everything Soviet was fashionable – even the 1980 Moscow Olympics represented 'a victory of socialism over global imperialism'.[99]

In addition to crediting Soviet history for Iran's revolution, *Kar* canonised its leaders. The paper celebrated the hundredth birthday of 'comrade Stalin' and the 102nd birthday of Lenin, 'the great teacher of workers and proletariat around the world'.[100] Leonid Brezhnev was similarly praised. The paper relayed Brezhnev's message of support for the Iranian people and quoted his opinions on global affairs.[101] After the 1981 bombing of the Islamic Republican Party's headquarters, the paper relayed Brezhnev's 'message of condolence' to Khomeini.[102]

This worship of Soviet history, politics, and leaders corresponded to the OIPF-M's complete faith in the Soviet Union as a global leader of anti-imperialism. *Kar* took Brezhnev at his word when he declared, 'Our power

---

97 'Hamaseh-ye Moqavemat Dar Leningrad: Agahi, Ettehad, Sazmandehi', *Kar*, 20 November 1980; and 'Be Monasebat-e Shast-o-Dovvomin-e Salgard-e Enqelab-e Kabir-e Octobr: Enqelab-e Kabir-e Octobr Beh Manzaleh-ye Aghaz va Moqaddameh-ye Enqelabat-e Prouloteri-ye Sarasar-e Jahan', *Kar*, 12 November 1979.
98 'Naqsh-e ʿazim-e Zanan-e Shouravi Dar Sakhteman-e Sousialism', *Kar*, 28 January 1981; and 'Afzayesh-e Hoquq-e Kargaran va Karmandan-e Shouravi', *Kar*, 29 April 1981.
99 'Olympic-e Moscow, Piruzi-ye Sousialism Bar Emperialism-e Jahan', *Kar*, 6 August 1980.
100 'Beh Monasebat-e Yeksad-o-Dahomin Salruz-e Tavalod-e Lenin', *Kar*, 23 April 1980; and 'Beh Monasebat-e Yeksadomin-e Sal-e Tavalod-e Rafiq-e Estalin', *Kar*, 9 January 1980.
101 'Le'onid Brežnef: Magar Mitavan Dar Barabar-e Mahrumiyat va Mosa'eb-e Miliun-ha Felestini Cheshm Forubast', *Kar*, 27 May 1981.
102 'Payam-e Tasaliyat-e Le'onid Brežnef Beh Emam Khomeini', *Kar*, 1 July 1981.

is and will be in the service of peace.'[103] When the Soviet Army invaded Afghanistan, the paper blamed the conflict not on Soviet interference but on 'international reaction and global imperialism, led by America'.[104] As Afghan's mujahedin fought against the Soviets, *Kar* published messages from Soviet Muslim clergy and announced Soviet support for 'the liberation struggle of the world's Muslims'.[105]

Ireland: The Enemy of My Enemy

One notable exception to the Fada'iyan's focus on socialist conflicts was the passing attention it paid to the Troubles in Northern Ireland. Perhaps because of their shared enemy in the British Empire, perhaps because of Irish Republicans' own appropriation of an anti-imperial framework to justify their struggle, members of the Fada'iyan identified with the struggle of the 'militant people of Ireland' (*mardom-e mobarez-e Irland*).[106] As the Provisional Irish Republican Army (PIRA) gained international attention with its hunger strikes in British prisons in 1980 and 1981, the OIPF-M came to view Irish militants as comrades in anti-imperial struggle and a source of inspiration.

Kar's first article on Ireland focused on a 1979 strike of postal workers in the Republic of Ireland, celebrating the workers purely on a class basis. The following year, the paper began to employ the language of anti-imperialism in its reporting on Ireland, reflecting the language used among Irish Republicans themselves. *Kar* noted a 'colossal rally' protesting in support of PIRA members engaged in hunger strikes 'in the colonialist British prisons'. Demonstrators in Dublin 'burned the flag of British imperialism' and bemoaned the squalor forced upon 'Irish liberation and nationalist combatants' in 'prisons of British imperialism'.[107]

---

103 'Le'onid Brežnef: Qodrat-e Ma Dar Khedmat-e Solh Ast va Khahad Bud', *Kar*, 13 May 1981.
104 'E'lamiye Moshtarak-e Mosalmanan-e Shouravi va Afghanistan', *Kar*, 15 July 1981.
105 'Da'ut-e Rouhaniyun-e Shouravi Az Mosalmanan Sarasar-e Jahan', *Kar*, 29 July 1981.
106 'Telegram-e Kargaran-e Foulad-e Ahvaz Beh Mardom-e Mobarez-e Irland.'
107 'Irland: Tezahorat-e 'azim-e Mardom-e Irland Dar Defa' Az E'tesab-e Ghaza-ye Zendaniyan-e Siyasi', *Kar*, 26 November 1980.

Interest spiked with the hunger strike of Bobby Sands in 1981, which was reported all over the world.[108] According to *Kar*, the PIRA member was 'sentenced to fourteen years in prison for the crime of struggling in the path of Ireland's freedom'. As Sands neared death, *Kar* described a 'wave of agitation' sweeping the world in solidarity against British imperialism. The paper noted the support of Iran's Majles alongside expressions of solidarity from socialist countries.[109] For a time, *Kar* followed the Irish people's 'courageous struggle against decrepit English imperialism' (*peykar-e delavaraneh-ye khoud 'aliyeh emperialism-e fartut-e Engelis*). Later in May, it published a telegram from steel- and auto-workers' unions in Ahvaz announcing 'the common struggles of the peoples of Iran and Ireland against the imperialists'.[110] The telegram compared the Irish people's 'opposition of more than seven hundred years against the British government' to Iran's war 'against mercenary enemies like Iraq and against American imperialism'. It continues, 'we too in our corner of the world … will continue our fateful struggle in the footsteps of Bobby Sands with the sacrifice of everything for the independence and freedom of our compatriots.'

One month after Sands's death, the paper lost interest. After all, the only thing animating the connection between the Fada'iyan and the PIRA was its shared enemy. But interest remained for the broader Iranian public and particularly for the Islamic Republic. Like *Kar*, state media around the time of Sands's strike began to include Ireland among the list of anti-imperial movements enjoying the benevolent patronage of the Islamic Republic. Blaming British imperialism for his death, the Islamic Republic's leadership made great rhetorical use of Sands and the hunger strikers, comparing their sacrifice to Christ's and commissioning murals of the strikers on the streets of Tehran. Not long after, the state changed the name of the

---

108 Mansour Bonakdarian, 'Iranian Consecration of Irish Nationalist "Martyrs": The Islamic Republic of Iran and the 1981 Republican Prisoners' Hunger Strike in Northern Ireland', *Social History* 43/3, July 2018, 293–331.

109 'Dar Shast-o-Panjomin Ruz-e E'tesab-e Ghaza-ye Bobby Sands, Muj-e E'teraz va Mobarzeh 'aliye Emperialism-e Engelis, Irland-e Shomali va Sarasar-e Jahan Ra Fara Gerefteh Ast', *Kar*, 6 May 1981.

110 'Khalq-e Irland Beh Peykar-e Delavaraneh-yeh Khoud 'aliyeh Emperialism-e Fartut-e Engelis Edameh Midahad', *Kar*, 13 May 1981; and 'Telegram-e Kargaran-e Foulad-e Ahvaz Beh Mardom-e Mobarez-e Irland.'

street on which the British Embassy's entrance was located from 'Winston Churchill Street' to 'Bobby Sands Street'. Hardline factions of the Islamic Republic continue to invoke the memory of Sands and the hunger strike to rally hostility toward Britain.[111]

*

On the whole, the Fada'iyan's coverage of anti-imperial movements belies a vastly oversimplified conceptualisation of the relationship between the imperial core and those in Iran (and the rest of the world) who interacted with it. Domestically, this binary led the OIPFG to distrust liberal and moderate politicians in the Provisional Government as tools of imperialism and favour Khomeini instead. Internationally, the binary situated the shah's regime as completely and unambiguously dependent on American imperialism. This analysis falls within a New Left historiography of decolonisation that consistently underestimates the extent to which subordinate powers in neo-imperialism exercised a degree of independence. Undercutting the idea of the shah's overwhelming dependence on the United States required by the Fada'iyan's rigid binary, the shah maintained friendly relations with China and the Soviet Union, even purchasing small arms from the latter and making state visits to Moscow in the mid-1960s to remind the United States not to take his friendship for granted.[112]

More strikingly, despite the shah's close alignment with American interests, it is worth noting that he himself employed the discourses of decolonisation and anti-imperialism, albeit in a framework altogether divorced from the ideas put forth by the Fada'iyan. Internationally, he positioned Iran as a leader of, and source of inspiration for, other decolonising nations. Domestically, he wielded the language of imperialism and decolonisation as a bludgeon to discredit his critics, including the Fada'iyan. Following the attack at the gendarmerie at Siyahkal, the government-aligned newspaper Ettela'at published an article declaring the Fada'iyan's terrorism to

---

111 Bonakdarian, 'Iranian Consecration of Irish Nationalist "Martyrs",' 297–305, 328.
112 Rahnema, Call to Arms, 74; and Moghadam, 'Socialism or Anti-Imperialism?', 12.

be 'directly in the service of colonial interests' by sowing divisions which imperialists would exploit.[113]

The fact that the shah and Fada'iyan both could decry each other's 'imperialism' underscores the term's flexibility. In the decades leading to the Revolution, the Iranian state and a range of non-state actors, including the Fada'iyan (along with other dissident groups), earnestly attempted to define 'decolonisation' and champion their own 'anti-imperialism'. Operating from entirely different initial premises, both actors marshalled those definitions in the service of diametrically opposed agendas, and each impacted Iranian society in different ways as a result. This juxtaposition of the state and non-state definitions of imperialism is further complicated by the overlapping definitions employed by the Fada'iyan and Khomeini, each of which still led to radically different ends.

Perhaps the greatest flaw in the OIPF-M's understanding of Iranian and global decolonisation was its dogmatic adherence to Marxism-Leninism and the discourse of national liberation that flowed from it. Vahabzadeh notes that the Fada'iyan, like many of their Third World counterparts, saw adherence to Marxism-Leninism as an inflexible marker of identity. As just one consequence, they understood their mission to be mobilizing a homogenised, united *khalq* ('people') for their liberation from imperialism. Yet the Fada'iyan failed to recognise their own alienation from the very *khalq* they sought to represent. Their idea of 'the people' was a theoretical construct, more reflecting the group's understanding of what the working class *should* be than how Iran's masses really *were*.[114]

The group's reading of international conflicts served as an echo chamber, further blinding them to this disconnect and reinforcing their Manichean belief in 'people' versus 'oppressor' framework. In the age of decolonisation, the Fada'iyan saw everywhere stories that confirmed their binary understanding of the world. Marxism-Leninism, embodying the struggle of 'the people', consistently appeared as the sole tool by which peoples across Asia repelled empire and conquered the persistent issues that had plagued them: unemployment, illiteracy, women's role in politics,

---

113 Rahnema, *Call to Arms*, 87.
114 Vahabzadeh, *A Guerrilla Odyssey*, 247–252.

ethnic separatism,[115] and general 'backwardness'. Furthermore, a conviction of socialism's singular capacity to oppose imperialism underwrote the group's later full-throated dedication to the Soviet Union, abandoning a deeply-rooted Iranian suspicion of Russian intentions.

Critically, their conviction in and reporting on an international anti-imperial front reinforced their binary understanding of the anti-imperial front at home. Given their homogenised ideal of *khalq*, Khomeini's populism sanctified his image to the OIPF-M as the people's representative, legitimating him as a servant of the 'people' – on their side of the binary. The OIPF-M's inability to imagine an anti-imperialism outside the confines of their definition of Marxism-Leninism cost it dearly. *Kar* ceased its publication in February 1982, and by the paper's second period of publication two years later, the OIPF-M's leadership had mostly fled to the Soviet Union to escape arrest in Iran.[116]

This inflexible dedication to Marxism-Leninism conflicts with the group's idea of decolonisation as well. Despite the Fada'iyan's roots in Iranian Third Worldism, *Kar*'s exclusive focus on Marxism belied a persistent Euro-centric foundation for Iran's liberation. It rooted its own movement, and indeed all anti-imperial movements, in European socialism. In its own way, by failing to conceive of the world beyond the categories of labour and capital, and by seeking to conquer Iran's 'backwardness', it failed to imagine beyond Western categories of the world, vindicating Al-e Ahmad's critique of Marxists as *gharbzadeh*.[117] The group's failure to recognise the alienation of many Iranians from Marxism underscores its inability to see the 'masses' as anything other than a proletariat to be mobilised. Though well-versed in the political and economic dimensions of imperialism, the OIPF-M appeared illiterate in the type of cultural decolonisation theorised by thinkers like Al-e Ahmad and Shariati, whom they rarely, if ever, mentioned in *Kar*. Limited as they were by their particular discourse of national liberation, they could only see a world of imperialists and revolutionaries. They learned the hard way the dangers in such a reductive worldview.

---

115 After all, the paper was being published during an ethnic uprising in Iranian Kurdistan.

116 Vahabzadeh, 'FADA'IAN-E ḴALQ'.

117 Dabashi, *Theology of Discontent*, 53, 62.

Bibliography

Primary Sources

Jazani, B. 'Masa᾽el-e Jonbesh-e Zedd-e Este῾mari va Azadibakhsh-e
Khalq-e Iran va ῾Omdetarin Vazayef-e Kommunist-ha-ye Iran Dar
Sharayat-e Konuni', Iran, Autumn 1967. iran-archive.com.
Kar
Nabard-e Khalq

Secondary Sources

Abrahamian, E. *Iran Between Two Revolutions*, Princeton, 1982.
—. *The Coup: 1953, the CIA, and the Roots of Modern U.S.-Iranian
Relations*, New York, 2013.
Alaolmolki, N. 'The New Iranian Left', *Middle East Journal* 41/2,
Spring 1987, 218–233.
Bonakdarian, M. 'Iranian Consecration of Irish Nationalist "Martyrs":
The Islamic Republic of Iran and the 1981 Republican Prisoners'
Hunger Strike in Northern Ireland', *Social History* 43/3, July 2018,
293–331.
Boroujerdi, M. *Iranian Intellectuals and the West: The Tormented
Triumph of Nativism*, Syracuse, USA, 1996.
Dabashi, H. *Theology of Discontent: The Ideological Foundations of the
Islamic Revolution in Iran*, New York, 1993.
Davari, A. 'A Return to Which Self?: Ali Shari'ati and Frantz Fanon on
the Political Ethics of Insurrectionary Violence', *Comparative Studies
of South Asia, Africa and the Middle East* 34/1, January 2014, 86–105.
Deylami, S. 'In the Face of the Machine: Westoxification, Cultural
Globalization, and the Making of an Alternative Global Modernity',
Polity 43/2, 2011, 242–263.
Kashani-Sabet, F. 'Colorblind or Blinded by Color?: Race, Ethnicity, and
Identity in Iran', *Sites of Pluralism: Community Politics in the Middle
East*, ed. Firat Oruc, Oxford, 2019, 153–180.
Keddie, N. and Richard Y. *Roots of Revolution: An Interpretive History
of Modern Iran*, New Haven, 1981.

Kohn, M. and K.D. McBride. 'Westoxification/Detoxification: Anti-Imperialist Political Thought in Iran', *Political Theories of Decolonization: Postcolonialism and the Problem of Foundations*, ed. K.D. McBride and M. Kohn, New York, 2011.

Matin-Asgari, A. 'The Left's Contribution to Social Justice in Iran: A Brief Historical Overview', *Iran's Struggles for Social Justice: Economics, Agency, Justice, Activism*, ed. P. Vahabzadeh, New York, 2017.

Moghadam, V. 'Socialism or Anti-Imperialism? The Left and Revolution in Iran', *New Left Review* 166/1, November–December 1987, 5–28.

Mottahedeh, R. *The Mantle of the Prophet: Religion and Politics in Iran*, London, 2009.

Pesaran, E. 'Towards an Anti-Western Stance: The Economic Discourse of Iran's 1979 Revolution', *Iranian Studies* 41/5, December 2008, 693–718.

Rahnema, A. *Call to Arms: Iran's Marxist Revolutionaries: Formation and Evolution of the Fada'is, 1964–1976*, London, 2021.

Rapoport, D. 'The Four Waves of Modern Terrorism', *Transnational Terrorism*, ed. S.M. Chermak and J. Freilich, London, 2013.

Rubinstein, A. and Smith, D. 'Anti-Americanism in the Third World', *The Annals of the American Academy of Political and Social Science* 497, 1988, 35–45.

Sadeghi-Boroujerdi, E. 'Gharbzadegi, Colonial Capitalism and the Racial State in Iran', *Postcolonial Studies* 24/2, April 2021, 173–194.

Vahabzadeh, P. *A Guerrilla Odyssey: Modernization, Secularism, Democracy, and the Fadai Period of National Liberation in Iran, 1971–1979*, Syracuse, USA, 2010.

——. 'FADA'IAN-E ḴALQ – Encyclopaedia Iranica', *Encyclopaedia Iranica*, 2015.

Picture Sources

Chapter 1

Image 1: Ru Nevesht-e Asnad-e Marbut beh Vaqayeh-e 1320. Source: NLAI, 264/30251.

Image 2: *Aftab-e Taban*, No. 20, 8 Shahrivar 1321/30 August 1942, 1–2.

Image 3: *Iran-e Ma*, 'Siyasat-e Eqtesadi-ye Millspaugh', 2nd Year, No. (138)/282, 10 Azar 1323/1 December 1944, 1–2.

Image 4: *Baba Shamal*, First Year, No. 11, 2 Tir 1322/June 1943, 1.

Image 5: *Ashofteh* ('Bewildered'), 1 Shahrivar 1324/23 August 1945.

Image 6: *Baba Shamal*, 25 Mordad 1324/16 August 1945.

Image 7: *Mard-e Emruz*, No. 44, Single Issue (tak shomareh), Mordad 1324.

Image 8: *Ashofteh*, 15th Year, No. 8, 27 Ordibehesht 1324/17 May 1945.

Chapter 3

Image 1: Demonstration in Tehran in favour of oil nationalisation, 1951. Source: Iranian Petroleum Museum, Tehran.

Image 2: Women at protest in support of oil nationalisation, 2 July 1951. Source: BP Archive 78148_114.

Image 3: Mud huts in the shantytown of Kaghazabad, 1948. Source: BP Archive 78030_226.

Image 4: Troops deployed to put down strike in Abadan, April 1951. BP Archive Source: 78148_071.

Chapter 7

Image 1: Prime Minister Hoveyda bidding farewell to the prime minister of Mauritius, Seewoosagur Ramgoolam. *Tehran Journal*, 7 December 1972.

Image 2: 'God Save Africa', *Ettela'at*, 9 Esfand 1352/28 February 1974, 5.

Image 3: The shah and his half-brother, Prince 'Abdolreza Pahlavi, with Siad Barre during his visit to Tehran. *Ettela'at*, 8 Dey 1356/29 December 1977, 1.

Image 4: The shah in discussions with President Carter. The shah: 'Iran will not remain indifferent to the invasion of Somalia.' *Ettela'at*, 11 Dey 1356/1 January 1978, 1.

Chapter 8

Image 1: Stamps from Human Rights Conference.

Image 2: Roy Wilkins, US Representative at the Human Rights Conference. *Ettela'at*, 1 Ordibehesht 1347/21 April 1968, 1.

Image 3: The Hoveydas Hosting an Evening During the Conference. *Ettela'at*, 7 Ordibehesht 1347/27 April 1968, 20.

Image 4: Community on the outskirts of Tehran, built originally to host participants in the 1974 Pan-Asian Games. *Housing and Urban Development in Iran*. United States [Washington]: U.S. Dept. of Housing and Urban Development, 1976, 11.

Chapter 9

Image 1: 'The Collected Works of Mao Zedong, vol. 1', Persian edition. Published in Beijing, 1969.

Image 2: An issue of *Setareh-ye Sorkh*. Above the title: 'Forward under the banner of Marxism-Leninism-Mao Zedong Thought'.

Chapter 12

Image 1: A visual representation of America's policy of 'obstruction of revolution' (*mavane'-ye enqelab*). *Kar*, 1 July 1981.

Image 2: 'Workers of the world unite', *Kar*, unknown date.

Image 3: 'The armed mobilization of the masses is the guarantor of victory for our people', *Kar*, 20 November 1980.

Image 4: 'Only if the people unite /Will America and Iraq be unable to do wrong. Unite', *Kar*, 20 November 1980.

Image 5: A visual representation of the dual threat of Zionism and American imperialism. *Kar*, 24 February 1982.

Image 6: Celebrating the 'Great October Revolution' on the front page of *Kar*, 12 November 1979.

List of Contributors

Arash Azizi, Clemson University

Arash Azizi is a lecturer in History and Political Science at Clemson University. He holds a Ph.D in History and Middle Eastern Studies from New York University (NYU). He is the author of *Shadow Commander: Soleimani, the U.S., and Iran's Global Ambitions* (2020) and *What Iranians Want: Women, Life, Freedom* (2024), both published by One World Publications.

Thomas Bédrède, Université Sorbonne Nouvelle

Thomas Bédrède is a Ph.D student at the Sorbonne Nouvelle's Graduate School of European, International, and Area Studies (MAGIIE) and a member of the Centre for Research on European and International Affairs (ICEE). His doctoral research focuses on Iran and the Saadabad Pact. He holds an MA in History from the University of Nantes and, in late 2019, graduated with distinction from Université Sorbonne Nouvelle's two-year MPhil programme in Iranian Studies. Specialising in the international history of Iran during his studies, he wrote his MPhil thesis on Iran's foreign policy in the period from the outbreak of the Second World War up to the Anglo-Soviet invasion of Iran in August 1941.

Mattin Biglari, SOAS University of London

Mattin Biglari is a postdoctoral research fellow at SOAS, University of London. His research focuses on the social and environmental history of oil in Iran and the wider Middle East, also engaging with science and technology studies (STS), energy/environmental humanities, subaltern studies and critical political theory. He is the author of *Refining Knowledge: Labour, Expertise and Oil Nationalisation in Iran* (Edinburgh University Press, forthcoming 2024). He completed his Ph.D in 2020 at SOAS, University of London, winning the 2021 BRISMES Leigh Douglas Memorial Prize for the best UK-based Ph.D thesis in Middle East studies. He is also a member of the Oil Cultures of the Middle East and Latin America (OCMELA) research group and a co-founding member of the SOAS Walter Rodney Collective.

Fernando Camacho Padilla, Universidad Autónoma de Madrid

Fernando Camacho Padilla is Associate Professor in History at the Universidad Autónoma de Madrid (UAM). He received his BA in History at the University of Seville, and has a double Ph.D degree from UAM and Pontificia Universidad Católica de Chile (2013). He has held academic positions at Stockholm University, Uppsala University, Dalarna University and Södertörn University College (Sweden). Most of his research has focused on Chile-Sweden political connections (1964–1990) and Middle East–Latin America diplomatic and cultural relations. He has recently edited the book *Miradas de Irán. Historia y Cultura* (La Catarata, 2021), together with other scholars from his university.

William Figueroa, University of Groningen

William Figueroa is Assistant Professor of History and Theory of International Relations at the University of Groningen. He holds a Ph.D in History from the University of Pennsylvania and has held postdoctoral fellowships at the University of Pennsylvania's Middle East Center and the University of Cambridge's Centre for Geopolitics. His research covers historical and contemporary relations between China and the Middle East, with a focus on connections between China and Iran. More broadly, he is interested in the history of the Cold War, travelogues and cross-cultural encounters, and international relations in the Global South. His dissertation, 'China and the Iranian Left: Transnational Networks of Social, Cultural, and Ideological Exchange, 1905–1979', uses previously overlooked Persian and Chinese sources to explore connections between constitutionalists, nationalists, communists, and student activists in three revolutions, and was awarded the 2022 Mehrdad Mashayekhi Dissertation Prize from the Association of Iranian Studies.

Javier Gil Guerrero, Instituto Cultura y Sociedad, Universidad de Navarra

Javier Gil Guerrero is a professor at the Instituto Cultura y Sociedad, Universidad de Navarra specialising in US foreign policy in the Middle East and in Iranian contemporary history. He has previously taught at Francisco de Vitoria University in Madrid. Over the last few years, he has had several research and teaching posts at universities in the United States, Israel, Iran, and Lebanon. His articles have been published in journals such as the *British Journal of Middle Eastern Studies*, *Middle East Critique*, *Historia del Presente*, and the *Journal of Cold War Studies*. Gil Guerrero's first book, titled *The Carter Administration and the Fall of Iran's Pahlavi Dynasty*, was published by Palgrave Macmillan in 2016.

Carson Kahoe

Carson Kahoe is an independent researcher who holds a master's degree from Queen's University, Belfast and a bachelor's degree from the University of Pennsylvania. His dissertation at Queen's University compared the discourses of international solidarity and anti-imperialism employed by the Provisional Irish Republican Army and the Organization of Iranian People's Fada'iyan (Majority).

Firoozeh Kashani-Sabet, University of Pennsylvania

Firoozeh Kashani-Sabet is the Walter H. Annenberg Professor of History at the University of Pennsylvania, and was the director of its Middle East Center from 2006 to 2019. She is the author of several books, including *Frontier Fictions: Shaping the Iranian Nation* (1999), *Conceiving Citizens: Women and the Politics of Motherhood in Iran*, which received the Book Prize from the *Journal of Middle East Women's Studies* for outstanding scholarship in Middle East gender relations (2011), and *Heroes to Hostages: America and Iran, 1800–1988* (2023). She is also the author of a novel, *Martyrdom Street* (2010) and co-editor with Beth Wenger of *Gender in Judaism and Islam: Common Lives, Uncommon Heritage* (2014).

Leonard Willy Michael, University of St Andrews

Leonard Willy Michael is a historian of twentieth-century West Asia and Central Europe focusing on transnational and intellectual history. His Ph.D project, commenced at the University of St Andrews in 2019, is centred on the exile of the communist Tudeh Party of Iran in divided Germany from 1953 to 1979. He has prepared for the doctoral stage during his masters at the same institution, which he finished with a dissertation on the historiographical agenda of Bizhan Jazani, a major theoretician of the 1970s guerrilla movement of Iran. Previously, he studied Islamic Studies and Economics at the Universities of Bamberg, Marburg, and Tehran.

Pardis Minuchehr, University of California, Santa Barbara

Pardis Minuchehr is a visiting scholar at the University of California, Santa Barbara. She holds a Ph.D. from Columbia University in Comparative Literature and Middle Eastern Studies and has held academic positions at the University of Pennsylvania, George Washington University, the University of Virginia, and California State University Long Beach. She has published widely on Iranian language, literature and history.

Robert Steele, Institute of Iranian Studies, Austrian Academy of Sciences

Robert Steele is a postdoctoral researcher in the Institute of Iranian Studies at the Austrian Academy of Sciences. Previously, he was a postdoctoral fellow at the Department of Near Eastern Languages and Cultures at the University of California, Los Angeles, and he holds a Ph.D in Arab and Islamic Studies from the University of Exeter. He is the author of *The Shah's Imperial Celebrations of 1971: Nationalism, Culture and Politics in Late Pahlavi Iran* (2020). His second monograph, on Iran's relations with Africa in the late Pahlavi period, will be published by Cambridge University Press.